Acclaim for *Lift Up Thy Voice*

"In *Lift Up Thy Voice* Mark Perry has provided a panoramic sketch of the most turbulent period of American history. In reading this book we see moving before our very eyes how one family made the transition from slave owners to freedom fighters; from southerners to Yankees; from white to black. My students—black and white, undergrads and grads, female and male—will embrace this book . . . which, though crammed full of history and facts, reads like a Toni Morrison novel."
—Andrew Billingsley, University of South Carolina

"Perry offers the fascinating family history of the Grimkés and the quintessential American racial pathologies that most slaveholders would have denied but which the Grimkés faced head-on. . . . An absorbing look at America's seminal reform movement and the fascinating family that led the struggle."
—*Booklist*

"The historical background is deftly handled; while clarifying policies, people, organizations and ideas, Perry never loses sight of his primary subjects. The Grimkés' personal struggles and their public and published works hold the center to make this book eminently readable."
—*Publishers Weekly*

ABOUT THE AUTHOR

Mark Perry is the author of *Conceived in Liberty: Joshua Chamberlain, William Oates, and the American Civil War,* a main selection of the History Book Club now available from Penguin, and three other books. An award-winning writer, he has written on history, the Middle East conflict, and American foreign policy for numerous magazines and newspapers. He lives in Arlington, Virginia.

LIFT UP THY VOICE

The Grimké Family's Journey

from Slaveholders

to Civil Rights Leaders

MARK PERRY

Penguin Books

PENGUIN BOOKS

Published by the Penguin Group
Penguin Putnam Inc., 375 Hudson Street,
New York, New York 10014, U.S.A.
Penguin Books Ltd, 80 Strand, London WC2R 0RL, England
Penguin Books Australia Ltd, 250 Camberwell Road,
Camberwell, Victoria 3124, Australia
Penguin Books Canada Ltd, 10 Alcorn Avenue,
Toronto, Ontario, Canada M4V 3B2
Penguin Books India (P) Ltd, 11 Community Centre,
Panchsheel Park, New Delhi – 110 017, India
Penguin Books (N.Z.) Ltd, Cnr Rosedale and Airborne Roads,
Albany, Auckland, New Zealand
Penguin Books (South Africa) (Pty) Ltd, 24 Sturdee Avenue,
Rosebank, Johannesburg 2196, South Africa

Penguin Books Ltd, Registered Offices:
Harmondsworth, Middlesex, England

First published in the United States of America by Viking Penguin,
a member of Penguin Putnam Inc. 2001
Published in Penguin Books 2003

1 3 5 7 9 10 8 6 4 2

Grateful acknowledgment is made for permission to reprint texts from
the collections of the William L. Clements Library, University of Michigan,
and the Moorland-Spingarn Research Center, Howard University.

THE LIBRARY OF CONGRESS HAS CATALOGED THE HARDCOVER EDITION AS FOLLOWS:
Perry, Mark.
Lift up thy voice : the Grimké family's journey from
slaveholders to civil rights leaders / Mark Perry.
p.   cm.
Includes bibliographical references.
ISBN 0-670-03011-2 (hc.)
ISBN 0 14 20.0103 1 (pbk.)
1. Racially mixed people—United States—Biography.   2. Grimké family.
3. Abolitionists—United States—Biography.   4. Social reformers—United States—Biography.
I. Title.
E185.98.A1 P47 2001
973.5'092—dc21
[B]   2001017594

Printed in the United States of America
Set in Horley Oldstyle
Designed by Nancy Resnick

For my two sisters
Anne and Lois

Men cannot *imprison,* or *chain;* or *hang* the *soul.*

JOHN BROWN

CONTENTS

PART THREE: THE GRIMKÉ BROTHERS

CHRONOLOGY

1784   John Faucheraud Grimké marries Mary Smith in Charleston. He is descended from German and French Huguenot stock; she is from an English and Scottish family. Together they will have fourteen children, of whom eleven will survive into adulthood.

1792   Sarah Moore Grimké—sometimes called Sally by her family—is born, the sixth child and second daughter of John Grimké and Mary Smith Grimké. She is a precocious child.

1801   Henry Grimké, the ninth child of the family, is born.

1805   Angelina Emily Grimké is born, the thirteenth child of John Grimké and Mary Smith Grimké. She is closest to her sister Sarah, whom she calls Mother.

1817   Sarah Grimké converts to Presbyterianism; the next year her sister Angelina refuses confirmation in the Episcopal Church.

1819   Judge John Faucheraud Grimké dies at Long Branch, in New Jersey, after a long illness. He has been nursed, in his last months, by his daughter Sarah.

1820   The Missouri Compromise is passed.

1821   Sarah Grimké moves to Philadelphia and joins the Quaker community.

1822   Denmark Vesey's conspiracy is unearthed in Charleston.

1824   Charles Grandison Finney begins his ministry in upstate New York.

1829   David Walker issues his "Appeal" in Boston.

1831   Nat Turner's rebellion breaks out. In Boston, William Lloyd Garrison begins publishing *The Liberator*. Theodore Dwight Weld takes up his ministry in New York.

1833   Great Britain abolishes slavery; in the United States, the American Anti-Slavery Society is formed in Philadelphia.

1834   The Lane Seminary Debates are held in Cincinnati; Lane's seminarians call for "immediate emancipation."

1835   The "Abolition Summer" sees the beginning of widespread attacks on the abolitionist movement. Angelina Grimké writes to Garrison in support of the abolitionist cause.

1836   Angelina Grimké writes "An Appeal to the Christian Women of the South." Her sister Sarah writes "An Epistle to the Clergy of the Southern States."

1837   The abolitionist publisher Owen Lovejoy is murdered in Alton, Illinois. Angelina Grimké writes her "Letters to Catherine Beecher." Sarah Grimké publishes her own "Letters on the Equality of the Sexes."

1838   Angelina Grimké testifies before a special committee of the Massachusetts legislature. Angelina and Sarah Grimké deliver a series of six lectures on the rights of women. Angelina Grimké marries Theodore Dwight Weld in Boston.

1839   Weld and Grimké publish *Slavery as It Is*. Mary Smith Grimké dies in Charleston.

1843   Henry Grimké and Nancy Weston begin their relationship in South Carolina.

1848   The Seneca Falls Convention is held in upstate New York.

1849   Archibald Grimké, the first son of Henry Grimké and Nancy Weston, is born in South Carolina.

1850   Francis Grimké, the second son of Henry Grimké and Nancy Weston, is born in South Carolina. The Compromise of 1850 is authored in Washington, postponing a divisive break between North and South. The Fugitive Slave Act is passed by the U.S. Congress.

1852   Henry Grimké dies in South Carolina. *Uncle Tom's Cabin* is published. John Grimké, the third son of Henry Grimké and Nancy Weston, is born in Charleston, two months after his father's death.

1854   The Kansas-Nebraska Act is passed, fueling bitter feelings between the North and South. The Eagleswood School is opened in New Jersey by Theodore Dwight Weld, Angelina Grimké Weld, and Sarah Grimké.

1859   John Brown leads an attack on the federal arsenal at Harper's Ferry.

1861   The Civil War begins when Confederate forces open fire on Fort Sumter, in Charleston Harbor.

1863   Abraham Lincoln issues the Emancipation Proclamation. Both Archibald and Francis Grimké are in hiding in Charleston as Union forces close in on the city. Charlotte Forten travels to Port Royal, South Carolina, and begins her famous journal. Theodore Dwight Weld tours the West on behalf of the antislavery movement.

1865   Charleston is liberated. Robert E. Lee surrenders at Appomattox. The Welds and Sarah Grimké move to Hyde Park, Massachusetts.

1866   Archibald and Francis Grimké are admitted to Lincoln University, outside Philadelphia.

1868   Angelina Grimké Weld meets Archibald and Francis Grimké at Lincoln University.

1870   Angelina Weld and Sarah Grimké "vote" in a local election in Hyde Park.

1873   Sarah Moore Grimké dies in Hyde Park. Francis Grimké begins studies at Howard University.

1874   Archibald Grimké attends Harvard University.

1875   Francis Grimké leaves Howard to attend the Princeton Theological Seminary.

1877   Francis Grimké is named assistant pastor of the Fifteenth Street Presbyterian Church in Washington, D.C. A special commission awards Republican Rutherford B. Hayes the presidency—called "the Great Betrayal" by former abolitionists.

1879   Archibald Grimké marries Sarah Stanley. Angelina Grimké dies in Hyde Park. Francis Grimké marries Charlotte Forten.

1880   Angelina Weld Grimké, the daughter of Archibald and Sarah Stanley Grimké, is born.

1883   Sarah Stanley leaves Archibald Grimké, taking their daughter, Angelina, with her to Michigan.

1884   Archibald Grimké gives his "Madonna of the South" address.

1887   Angelina Weld Grimké returns to Boston to live with her father.

1891   Archibald Grimké publishes his biography of William Lloyd Garrison, to be followed a year later by his biography of Charles Sumner.

1894   Archibald Grimké is named consul in Santo Domingo.

1895   Theodore Dwight Weld dies in Boston. Booker T. Washington delivers his "Atlanta Exposition Address," otherwise known as the Atlanta Compromise. Nancy Weston Grimké dies in Washington, D.C.

1898   Archibald Grimké returns from the Dominican Republic. He joins the American Negro Academy and inaugurates the "great debate" with Booker T. Washington.

1903   William Monroe Trotter and Booker T. Washington confront each other during the "Boston Riot." Angelina Weld Grimké and her father argue bitterly about her life. W. E. B. Du Bois's *The Souls of Black Folk* is published.

1904   The Carnegie Hall Conference is held in New York, in an attempt to resolve the Grimké/Trotter–Booker T. Washington controversy.

1906   Archibald Grimké publishes "The Heart of the Race Problem," written two years earlier.

1907   Archibald and Francis Grimké break with William Monroe Trotter, and Archibald joins the Niagara Movement.

1909   Francis Grimké is named to the "Committee of Forty."

1910   The Committee of Forty establishes the National Association for the Advancement of Colored People, ending the division among the nation's black leaders.

1913   Archibald Grimké is appointed to head the Washington, D.C., chapter of the National Association for the Advancement of Colored People.

1914   Charlotte Forten Grimké dies in Washington, D.C.

1915   John Grimké, estranged from his brothers, dies in Florida.

1915   Angelina Weld Grimké writes *Rachel*, the first example of what would come to be called the Harlem Renaissance.

1919   Archibald Grimké is awarded the Spingarn Medal for outstanding leadership of the black community.

1930   Archibald Grimké dies in Washington, D.C.

1937   Francis Grimké dies in Washington, D.C.

1958   After years of self-imposed obscurity, Angelina Weld Grimké dies a recluse in New York City.

MAJOR CHARACTERS

CATHERINE BEECHER: The elder daughter of Lyman Beecher, and a well-known American educator, Catherine Beecher founded a seminary for female students in Hartford, Connecticut, and invited Angelina Grimké to teach there. An admirer of the Grimké sisters, she was also one of their earliest critics, arguing that women needed to stay in the domestic "sphere" and not involve themselves in politics. She was the author of *The American Woman's Home*, the bible of nineteenth-century female propriety and domesticity.

HENRY WARD BEECHER: After his father, Lyman, Henry Ward Beecher was the most noted minister of the nineteenth century. He supported John Brown, sending him rifles bought with donations given by his Brooklyn parishioners; the guns were known as Beecher's Bibles. In the 1870s, he would be forced to defend himself against scandalous charges that he had had an affair with the wife of Theodore Tilton.

LYMAN BEECHER: The Reverend Lyman Beecher was the most famous religious man in America in the nineteenth century, and the head of a family of respected educators, theologians, and writers. He left his congregation in Connecticut to head the Lane Seminary. During the Lane Debates, he took sides against Theodore Dwight Weld, whom he admired.

JAMES G. BIRNEY: A former Alabama slaveholder and close associate of the Tappan brothers, Birney became one of the most astute political thinkers in the antislavery movement. He ran for president on the ticket of the antislavery Liberty party.

LYDIA MARIA CHILD: Child was an abolitionist, suffragette, and Boston writer whose "Appeal in Favor of That Class of Americans Called Africans" represented a unique contribution to the early abolitionist cause. She introduced Angelina and Sarah Grimké to the Boston abolitionist community. In 1838, she bravely escorted Angelina to the Massachusetts State House, where the latter gave testimony on slavery before a special committee of the state legislature.

FREDERICK DOUGLASS: A writer and leader of the black community in the nineteenth century, and a good friend of William Lloyd Garrison's, Douglass caused enormous controversy in his waning years with his marriage to his white secretary, officiated over by Francis Grimké. He was the author of the hugely popular *Narrative of the Life of Frederick Douglass*. Although he was a friend of John Brown's, he refused to support Brown's raid on Harper's Ferry.

W. E. B. DU BOIS: An author, orator, and black leader, Du Bois was a founder of the Niagara Movement and a rival to Archibald Grimké for leadership of the black community. He authored *The Souls of Black Folk*, the first written critique of Booker T. Washington's "Atlanta Compromise." Controversial and outspoken, he enjoys a posthumous reputation as a black leader that has eclipsed the legacies of both Archibald and Francis Grimké.

CHARLES GRANDISON FINNEY: Finney was a New York revivalist and former lawyer whose 1830s message of salvation helped to provide the foundation for the abolitionist crusade.

T. THOMAS FORTUNE: Born a slave in Florida, Fortune founded and was editor of the *New York Age* and the *New York Freeman*. He began his career as a journalist by staking out an uncompromisingly militant position in favor of black rights, but later he would be known for his unstinting support of Booker T. Washington. Plagued by alcoholism and mental instability, he eventually distanced himself from Washington and recovered his reputation as a fine journalist.

WILLIAM LLOYD GARRISON: A steadfast abolitionist and true revolutionary, Garrison founded and edited the most prominent abolitionist newspaper of his time, *The Liberator*. He captured control of the American Anti-Slavery Society and rejected abolitionists who believed that political action provided the most practical program for eradicating slavery.

ANGELINA WELD GRIMKÉ: Named for her aunt Angelina Grimké (Weld), Angelina was the daughter of Archibald Grimké and Sarah Stanley Grimké. After a difficult childhood, she became a teacher in Washington, D.C., and continued to help her father throughout his career. Her poetry and essays are remembered now as the first examples of the Harlem Renaissance. A lesbian, she spent her later life living as a recluse in New York City.

ARCHIBALD GRIMKÉ: The first son of Henry Grimké and Nancy Weston Grimké, Archibald came north and earned a degree from Lincoln University before graduating with a law degree from Harvard University. Later consul in Santo Domingo, a biographer of William Lloyd Garrison and Charles Sumner, and one of Booker T. Washington's most outspoken critics, he also played a fundamental role in building the power of the National Association for the Advancement of Colored People.

CHARLOTTE FORTEN GRIMKÉ: The wife of Francis Grimké, Charlotte Forten was probably the most prominent black woman author of the nineteenth century. Her early journals are still studied for their precisely detailed firsthand accounts of black life on South Carolina's Sea Islands during and following the Civil War. Charlotte Forten was the daughter of Robert Bridges Forten and Mary Virginia Woods Forten, a prominent Philadelphia black couple. She was well known to the Boston abolitionist community and befriended Robert Gould Shaw, a white officer who would lose his life leading a black regiment in an attack on Battery Wagner, outside Charleston.

FRANCIS JAMES GRIMKÉ: The second son of Henry and Nancy Weston Grimké, Francis came north and earned a degree at Lincoln University. He then attended the Princeton Theological Seminary and became a pastor at the Fifteenth Street Presbyterian Church of Washington, D.C. After an interlude spent at a church in

Jacksonville, Florida, he returned to Washington, where he built a reputation as one of America's most influential black voices. With his brother Archibald, he questioned the leadership role of Booker T. Washington and was one of his most severe and well-known critics. Francis was a moralist who balanced a strong belief in black independence with sometimes controversial and radical views about how best the black community should respond to white racism. His sermons on these topics were widely circulated in the African American community.

HENRY GRIMKÉ: A brother of Sarah and Angelina Grimké, Henry Grimké bought the Cane Acre plantation in Beaufort in the 1840s after the death of his wife. His relationship with Nancy Weston led to the births of three sons, Archibald, Francis, and John. He died of typhoid fever in 1852, leaving his younger children and Nancy Weston to his son Montague Grimké.

JOHN GRIMKÉ: The third son of Henry Grimké, born after his father's death, John later broke with his family and moved to Florida. He rejected the life followed by his brothers and rarely corresponded with them. A deeply embittered man, he lived and worked as a laborer in the black community until his death.

JOHN FAUCHERAUD GRIMKÉ: A grandson of John Paul Grimké, Charleston's best-known silversmith, John Faucheraud Grimké received his law training in Great Britain, where he befriended Charles Pinckney and Benjamin Franklin. Returning to America, he served in the Continental Army, was with Washington and Lafayette at Yorktown, and then returned to Charleston, where he became a noted judge and political figure. He was the father of fourteen children, including Angelina, Henry, Sarah, and Thomas Grimké. He died in Long Branch, New Jersey, nursed by his favorite daughter, Sarah.

MARY SMITH GRIMKÉ: The wife of Judge John Grimké and mother of his children, "Polly" Grimké argued about slavery with her daughters Sarah and Angelina and attempted to convince them to abandon their lives as Quakers and abolitionists. An impatient and often intemperate woman, she was a staunch defender of the South and its slave system and never moderated her views.

NANCY WESTON GRIMKÉ: The mother of Archibald, Francis, and John Grimké, the "madonna of the South" was a devout woman with a strong belief in education. She was Henry Grimké's mistress at Cane Acre and his defender after his death. After the Civil War, she joined her two elder sons in the North.

SARAH MOORE GRIMKÉ: The second daughter of Judge John Grimké and Mary Smith Grimké, Sarah was a precocious child and a formidable and creative thinker. While her sister Angelina focused on presenting the abolitionist cause in public, Sarah—"Sally" to her siblings—mentored the movement through her writings. She never married, instead concentrating her energies on personal growth and religious activity. Her "Epistle to the Clergy of the Southern States" demolished Southern arguments that slavery was defended by Scripture. Sarah Grimké is widely regarded as the mother of the Woman Suffrage movement.

THOMAS GRIMKÉ: A brother of Sarah and Angelina, and a well-known Southern lawyer and intellectual, Thomas Grimké supported and served as a leader of the American Colonization Society and bravely opposed the nullification doctrines of John Calhoun.

HENRY CABOT LODGE: A Massachusetts legislator, the head of the famous Massachusetts Republican family, and a classmate of Archibald Grimké's at Harvard University, Lodge remained his lifelong friend and occasional political opponent.

CATHERINE MORRIS: The sister of Israel Morris, Catherine opened her Philadelphia home as a meeting place for prominent Quakers. She befriended Angelina and Sarah Grimké and remained their friend despite their split with the Philadelphia Quaker community after Angelina's 1838 letter to William Lloyd Garrison.

ISRAEL MORRIS: A Quaker leader and Philadelphia merchant, Israel Morris befriended Sarah Grimké and served as her sponsor at the Fourth and Arch Street Meeting. An intelligent and kind man, and the widowed father of eight, he proposed to Sarah, whom she loved and admired, but she rejected his suit.

LUCRETIA COFFIN MOTT: An outspoken abolitionist, a Quaker minister, and a leading suffragette, Mott was a close friend of the Grimké sisters'; she introduced them to the abolitionist movement and urged them on in their public careers. Sarah Grimké viewed Mott as the model of what a Quaker should be. Mott refused to be intimidated by the more staid and conservative wings of the Society of Friends. With her friend Elizabeth Cady Stanton, she helped to organize the Women's Rights Convention at Seneca Falls in 1848.

WENDELL PHILLIPS: A Massachusetts abolitionist, defender of William Lloyd Garrison, talented orator, and champion of Angelina and Sarah Grimké, Phillips later became a strong supporter of Archibald Grimké, and his intellectual mentor. He gave the funeral oration at the grave site of Angelina Grimké in 1879, saying that no one had made a greater contribution to the antislavery cause.

GERRIT SMITH: A wealthy businessman and agriculturist, Gerrit Smith was an adamant abolitionist and a formative voice in the American Anti-Slavery Society. He was a member of "the secret six," the committee of financiers that supported John Brown. As one of the strategists of the antislavery movement, he defended Angelina and Sarah Grimké's appearances before "mixed" audiences.

SARAH STANLEY: The daughter of a Michigan Episcopal minister, Sarah Stanley married Archibald Grimké but later left him to pursue her own career. She apparently reacted poorly to the pressures brought to bear on a white woman who married a black man. She sent their one daughter, Angelina Weld Grimké, back to her father at the age of seven because she was unable to care for her. She traveled and wrote extensively but was plagued by mental instability. She finally committed suicide in San Diego.

ARTHUR AND LEWIS TAPPAN: New York philanthropists, the Tappan brothers bankrolled almost all of the nineteenth century's most important reform movements, doing everything from providing homes for former prostitutes to underwriting the formation of temperance and abolitionist organizations. After losing control of the American Anti-Slavery Society to forces aligned with William Lloyd Garrison, they continued their campaign by forming their own antislavery concern and launching James G. Birney on his quest for the presidency.

WILLIAM MONROE TROTTER: Outspoken, articulate, and brilliant, William Monroe Trotter, after Booker T. Washington, W. E. B. Du Bois, and Archibald Grimké, was the best-known black leader of his time. As the publisher and editor of the *Boston Guardian*, he laid the groundwork for the rise of black militancy with his unyielding criticism of Washington's "Atlanta Compromise." He and the Grimké brothers spent their careers alternately supporting and criticizing one another.

BOOKER T. WASHINGTON: The founder and first president of the Tuskegee Institute and the author of *Up from Slavery*, Washington was the undisputed leader of the black community in the 1890s, despite opposition to his "Atlanta Compromise" speech of 1895. He and the Grimké brothers fought over leadership of the black community from 1898 until 1903, when W. E. B. Du Bois and the Niagara Movement eclipsed much of the Tuskegeean's power.

ANGELINA GRIMKÉ WELD: The thirteenth child of Judge John Grimké and Mary Smith, Angelina was the sister of Sarah, Henry, and Thomas Grimké. Her "Appeal to the Christian Women of the Southern States" had such influence and made such an impact that it now stands as one of the leading documents of the abolitionist movement. Her appearance before the Massachusetts state legislature in 1838 is remembered as a turning point in the movement. She married Theodore Dwight Weld, the movement's most creative spirit and organizer, and supported the education and early-adult years of her brother's sons Archibald and Francis.

THEODORE DWIGHT WELD: The son of a congregational minister, Weld was undoubtedly the most influential and talented political organizer of his time. He became Charles Grandison Finney's chief lieutenant, headed the Oneida Revival, led the Lane Debates, and wrote *Slavery as It Is*. He trained a generation of political activists and, through his political techniques, inaugurated tactics that would be used by four generations of American progressives.

LIFT UP
THY
VOICE

—

PROLOGUE

"...we defied the law of South Carolina"

John Grimké had never known a child so precocious. Nearly every evening, as he descended the stairway of his Charleston home to his study to ensure that the lamps were shuttered and secure, he would spy his twelve-year-old daughter, Sarah, furtively replacing his law books on their shelves—one at a time, neatly, and as quietly as she could. He admired her intelligence, but it bothered him that she pursued a life of books and learning. This was not what he wanted for her. Nor, he believed, was it what young ladies should do. Sometimes she could carry things too far. When he caught her with her brother's Latin text, he angrily grabbed it away and forbade her to open it again. She begged to be allowed to read it, saying that it would cost him nothing, as she could teach herself the language from the book, just as she had taught herself geography and mathematics and history. But John Grimké was firm. Geography, mathematics, and history were one thing; Latin was quite another.

John Grimké valued his daughter. When he needed someone with whom to discuss politics, or the arts, or literature, he turned to her, young though she was, and told her his thoughts and opinions on the world of Charleston, the South, and the nation. He couldn't help but admit she was intelligent. So gradually—grudgingly—he allowed her some minor indiscretions. He knew that her older brother Thomas shared his school lessons with her, that he gave her books, and that they spoke endlessly together of the wide world beyond their own small community. John Grimké also permitted his daughter to read his law books, but without letting on that he knew she was doing it. Appearances were important. Once, but only once, he let slip his own doubts about the customs he defended, telling his daughter that if she were a man, she would be the greatest lawyer in South Carolina.

There were some things, however, that John Grimké would *not* tolerate. One day when Sarah was barely eleven, her father had caught her reading to her young slave, a black girl of ten named Hetty. Hetty was Sarah's boon companion, her servant and playmate, and (outside of her brother Thomas) her favorite person. John Grimké discovered that his daughter had been tutoring Hetty, in violation of the family's traditions, Southern customs, and the strict slave codes of the state. He was horrified, not least because as one of the state's leading jurists, he had had a hand in authoring those codes, and he agreed with them. That Sarah's impropriety had been going on for some time was demonstrated by the fact that little Hetty knew the alphabet and was able to read simple children's books. For Grimké, such a practice was intolerable, and despite his broad-minded views and his own questions about slavery, he would not allow it—especially not from Sarah, a young girl whose place in life was ordained: someday, he imagined, she would be the wife of a plantation owner and the mistress of a large home of her own, with children, friends, a church, and slaves.

The punishment for Sarah's indiscretion was swift and certain. Hetty was harshly reprimanded, shaken, chased from Sarah's room, and nearly beaten. Sarah herself was lectured in the sternest tones, with John Grimké's angry voice making her sin known to her siblings. Her father's rage frightened Sarah, and though she never again read to Hetty, she vowed that she would do everything she could to teach slave children about the wonderful things she had learned from books. Years later, thinking back on the incident, she would feel pride in what she had done: "I took an almost malicious satisfaction in teaching my little waiting-maid at night, when she was supposed to be occupied in combing and brushing my locks. The light was put out, the keyhole screened, and flat on our stomachs before the fire, with the spelling-book under our eyes, we defied the law of South Carolina."

Hetty died several years later, in the midst of her own childhood, apparently carried off by some silent disease; the cause of her death remains unknown and, because she was a slave, uncataloged. After a moment's distress, as if the family had lost some moderately important piece of furniture, life among the rest of the Grimkés went on. But Sarah was inconsolable; after Hetty died, she refused to take another servant. She would remember the girl her whole life, writing of her in her diaries and letters. The two incidents, John Grimké's reprimand and Hetty's death, seem oddly linked in these passages, as if Sarah could only conclude that the denial of learning had led inextricably to Hetty's demise. It was perhaps from that moment that Sarah Grimké's obsessive abhorrence of slavery was implanted in her soul—like the memory of Hetty, never to be expunged.

Nor did Sarah's vow remain unfulfilled. Slowly, certainly, and with great self-assurance for a child of her years, she found ways around her father's rules. She taught slave children in a special Sunday school, reading to them from the Bible and encouraging them to peer over her shoulder at the words. Her father knew what she was doing, but he quietly and deliberately ignored her rebellion. He had doubts of his own about the laws that bound South Carolina together, doubts that were far graver than he could ever express. Slavery was a fact, to be sure, yet its existence not only bound blacks in servitude to whites, but also bound whites in fealty to a pernicious custom that infected and weakened their society. John Faucheraud Grimké knew this, understood this, and worried about his state and his family. But like many, many other men of his day—like almost all of them, in fact—he did nothing.

———

The people of the small world inhabited by Sarah Grimké had come to America by boat. Judge John Faucheraud Grimké's father's forebears were German merchant Protestants: fastidious, prudent, well spoken. The Faucherauds, Judge Grimké's mother's ancestors, were among South Carolina's leading families, and among its oldest. Having fled France in 1685 following the revocation of their rights as Protestants by the Edict of Nantes, they knew something of repression, and they carried the story of their past with them, making it a part of their family lore: they came to America, where they found freedom and hope. The Grimkés and Faucherauds had much in common, having both gained rights to large swaths of rich land ripe for the planting of cotton and sea rice. John Grimké owned two homes: a large and elegant house in central Charleston and an "up-country" plantation in the foothills of the Appalachians, called Belmont, where the family wintered. John Grimké added to the family holdings by buying large tracts of land in other South Carolina districts. His slaves raised livestock and grew cotton and vegetables. When the cotton crop came in, his overseers would bring the harvest to Charleston, rolling the huge bales through the streets to the waiting ships bound for England, where new textile mills were just beginning to fuel the Industrial Revolution.

There were other families as well—families that served the Grimkés. They, too, had come to America by boat. They inhabited meager rooms set aside for them in the Charleston home, or crowded shacks sited well away from the large, porticoed Belmont manse. Their ancestors had survived the crucible of the "Middle Passage," formed friendships and bonds beyond their chains, endured the whips of their purchasers and the loud, ringing cries of the slave auctioneers, and then, with their new owners, traveled to the fields of the South.

These new Americans would never forget what they saw in Charleston, a city like none they had ever seen. It was not the city that awed them, but the fact that human beings could be, and were, bought and sold there, like so much property. All black slaves were sold: men, women, the old, the young, the healthy and infirm, the intelligent and modest, those frightened and those vowing revenge. Every one of them coveted freedom. The Grimkés were full participants in slavery—in buying, selling, holding, punishing, feeding, and discarding slaves. Judge John Faucheraud Grimké's forebears, and the judge himself, gave their overseers strict instructions on "what" (they would not say "whom") to purchase, and for what purpose. These slaves built the Grimké family's wealth, just as they built that of nearly every other affluent Charleston family.

One such slave, Olaudah Equiano (who later took the name Gustavus Vassa), left a vivid account of the Middle Passage and of a slave pen into which he was herded.

> On a signal given, such as the beat of a drum, the buyers rush at once into the yard where the slaves are confined, and make choice of that parcel they like best. The noise and clamour with which this is attended, and the eagerness visible in the countenances of the buyers, serve not a little to increase the

apprehensions of the terrified Africans, who may well be supposed to consider them the ministers of that destruction to which they think themselves devoted. In this manner, without scruple, are relations and friends separated, most of them never to see each other again.

So it was in South Carolina, and so it had been for two and a half centuries. Although Charleston's auction house would continue to do a booming business into the 1840s, by the time of the American Revolution, most Southern slaves were native-born, and some black families had been living in America for three, four, or even five generations. The Grimké family's slaves, and nearly every slave community in the South, had a singular character that was native to America: the nation's slaves were slaves, certainly, but they were also Americans, even in their chains. Southern slaves spoke an American language, developed a deep and abiding American religion, and carved out a dynamic and unique American culture. These slaves nurtured and advanced a highly complex society, one with its own distinctively American values, traditions, and hopes for liberation.

The white men and women of the South did not fail to notice this, and it frightened them. The families of Europe had come to South Carolina to build a seamless society of highly educated, hardworking, provident, and sophisticated patriot merchants. What they had created instead was two societies, two different *American* societies, one of which lived under the lash. By the beginning of the nineteenth century, the American nation, free of colonial domination and intent on becoming a united republic, was nonetheless inexorably moving toward a fatal division that would turn slaveholders against nonslaveholders. Already, by the end of the American Revolution, it had been clear that the ideals of life, liberty, and happiness were having a significant impact on the American slave, so that slave was pitted against master in an unacknowledged, silent, and largely unseen civil war. It was a rehearsal for the conflict to come.

In the history of America, two actual slave revolts stand out, one led by South Carolina's Denmark Vesey and the other by the Virginia slave Nat Turner. But the true rebellion of American slaves was an everyday event that ran as a violent undercurrent through every particle of society. Slave rebellions were reported in Virginia in 1663, 1687, 1709, 1710, 1722, 1723, and 1730. One slave plot was discovered in Boston in 1638, and another in 1723. In 1712, just three years after the first slaves were sold near Wall Street in New York, nine white citizens were killed by a mob of twenty-three slaves. In 1741, a violent insurrection terrorized New York after a plot to burn the city was uncovered: two slaves were burned alive by a white mob, and eighteen more were hanged. In 1795 in Louisiana, then under French rule, a militia of slaves who had recently had the "Declaration of the Rights of Man" read to them plotted the overthrow of the colonial administration. More than thirty of them were executed.

Other "depradations" were more common. Powerless, outgunned, and shorn of all rights, slaves were completely subservient, but when given the chance, they gave back blood for blood—though not equally. Here and there throughout the South, and continually, single murders of overseers, beatings of trapped slaveholders caught in the wrong place at the wrong time, and burnings of homes and mansions testified to the fact that slaves did not "sing in their chains" but rather attempted, again and again, to tear them off. The best evidence of this comes from the slaveholders themselves, whose diaries record a constant attention to security and to the disciplining of black men and women who showed the slightest rebelliousness: they were "lashed," "whipped," "burned," "maimed," "hanged," "slapped," "cuffed," "struck," "strapped," and "garroted," sometimes publicly, with an approving crowd in attendance. Any Southern city that deserved the name contained a "workhouse" where little actual labor was done, its sole purpose being to provide a place for the punishment (or torture) of those slaves who would not work.

By the beginning of the nineteenth century, the slaveholding South stood virtually alone in its support of slavery. The North (though certainly not all Northerners) had worked for emancipation from the day, in 1688, when a group of four Quakers issued a written statement opposing the slave trade. In 1754, the Quaker yearly meeting had issued a public circular opposing slavery, which had been formally adopted in 1776, with the birth of the Republic. The abolitionist impulse had thereafter spread through the Northern mercantilist class, whose members had willingly freed their servants, having no use for the costs entailed in keeping them. Because the North was blessed with a diverse agricultural base that was not labor-intensive, freeing the slaves became a matter of economics. The result was a flourishing free black population centered in New York, Boston, and Philadelphia.

For the South, the economics of slavery meant profits for rice, tobacco, and cotton growers, whose harvests fueled the economic booms and busts of industrializing England. Southerners had first defended slavery on economic terms, but then, faced with a slaveless North, they had constructed a mythology of slavery that was defended by custom, law, and religion. Nearly all of the myths about race inherited by our own age, and still perpetuated today, have their roots in the myths of slavery: the slaves, Southerners claimed, were ignorant, lazy, shiftless, careless, inept, immoral, and promiscuous, had no sense of family, and could not be educated. A slave was a slave, they said, because custom demanded it, the law dictated it, and God willed it.

The greatest myth, however, was that the slaves were not really Americans at all. They were not, insisted the defenders of slavery (which Southerners themselves called the "peculiar institution"), *like us;* they were *different*. Of course, the Grimké slaves were no more African than the Grimkés themselves were German. A short walk down a well-worn path from the Grimké manor at Belmont to the slave quarters, less than half a mile away, showed just how similar the two seemingly disparate societies could be—for in both places, families raised their children, practiced their religion, and held out hope for the future. In both places, a new and dynamic culture was being born that would be different from any other in the world. But in only one of the two places were people held in bondage.

———

This is a book about four extraordinary individuals and the paths that each of them took on the road from slavery to emancipation and from emancipation to equality. Sarah Moore Grimké and her sister Angelina grew up in the slaveholding South, but they rejected the traditions of their state, their class, and their family to become two of the most prominent and famous champions of abolition. As abolitionists and women, they not only transformed America's views on slavery but also sparked a revolution for women's rights. Their nephews Archibald and Francis Grimké continued their aunts' work into the early decades of the twentieth century, transforming the crusade against slavery into a battle for equal rights, and establishing the foundation of the civil rights movement to follow.

To trace the trajectory of these four lives is to traverse the distance from the Grimké manor to the slave quarters at Belmont, to descend the stairway of the family rooms in Charleston to the basement, where the slaves lived. For while Sarah, Angelina, Archibald, and Francis Grimké all carried the same name, their experiences, their views, their hopes, their travails, and their triumphs were shaped, inexorably, by the color of their skin. We see in their troubles our own; in their triumphs our hope; and in their history, the history of our nation.

PART ONE

The Grimké Sisters

ONE

"They shall be your bondmen for ever . . ."

There was nothing outwardly ostentatious about Charleston society. To primp and preen over their wealth, to lord their position over their "lessers," or to condescend to snobbery—the province of the newly rich—would have never occurred to John Faucheraud Grimké or the other gentlemen sons of South Carolina's great families. Such behavior would have been unseemly, undignified. White Charleston society was instead a world apart, a community of wealth, custom, and privilege built on the English model. Its oldest families, who were descended from the original settlers brought to the Carolinas from Britain in 1669 under the watchful eye of Lord Proprietor Sir Anthony Ashley-Cooper, had become the denizens of a new class of cotton, indigo, and rice wealth. Endowed with such a distinguished pedigree (their ancestors had been sent to the New World by their king, Charles II, himself), they affected what they believed to be the aristocratic manner of their British cousins. Their belief in their way of life, and in their right to live that life as they pleased, formed the central tenet of their faith.

Along the Ashley and Cooper rivers (which join, Charlestonians say, "to form the Atlantic Ocean"), the Pinckneys, Gaillards, Alstons, Draytons, Smiths, Laurenses, Lowndeses, Middletons, Hugers, Rutgerses, and Grimkés built homes with tall wooden doors and ornate black iron gates, behind which well-attired slaves served cool drinks or tended gardens that imitated those of England's noble estates. Everything about

Charleston bespoke its standing as the South's greatest city—if not in size, then in status and stature. By 1800, with a population of twenty thousand—a mere 150 years after its first one hundred families landed at the spit of land named Oyster Point—Charleston was the South's premier port and America's fourth-largest urban area. Its harbor was crowded with ships bound for Britain, France, the Northern states, and Africa. Charleston exported tobacco, rice, cotton, indigo, and lumber and imported textiles, furniture, and slaves.

A visitor to Charleston in 1800 would have been impressed by the city's understated magnificence; it was as subtle and majestic as any mid-size British town but without the seedy clutter. It was only a short carriage ride from the outskirts, down the tree-lined cobblestoned streets and past the homes of Charleston's most affluent citizens, to the center of the city, which was located on a flat peninsula. There, Charleston's banks, dry-goods stores, artisan shops, and law, municipal, and state offices were grouped along two dozen streets that led down to the city park, near the "battery." Young men and women, courting, strolled each summer evening along the waterfront, often accompanied by servants. There were benches in the park, set among oak, maple, and cypress trees planted by the first settlers. If laughter was heard, it was restrained; the more boisterous voices, from the docks, were muted by the long row of offices on the southern side of the city center. On the other side of the city, separated from the affluent homes by a creek, a small group of middle- and lower-class homes jutted up against the modest post office. Nearby were the slave pens, to which men, women, and children from Africa were brought after being quarantined and before being sold to the wealthy planters and those in need of house servants.

One of Charleston's best-known and best-appointed offices (in a nondescript brick building just two blocks from the slave pens) was managed by John Phillips and John Gardner, Rhode Island–born entrepreneurs who hired the captains and leased the ships that transported the slaves to Charleston. In just four short years, between 1803 (when Charleston reopened its overseas slave trade after a legislated hiatus that dated from the end of the American Revolution) and 1807 (when America's international trade in slaves was stopped forever), the firm of Phillips & Gardner reaped a windfall in profits from its imports. In that period, nearly forty thousand Africans landed on Charleston's shores, to be dispatched inland by wagon or sent north along the middle Atlantic coast aboard ships to their new masters. Charlestonians were careful in their trade. Arriving slaves were quarantined for ten days on Sullivan's Island, outside Charleston Harbor, before being transferred to the slave pens. By 1810, the flood of overseas slaves had ended, but the effect was permanent: a majority of South Carolinians were now black, and parts of the state were so inundated by the trade that whites made up only a small portion of the population.

The large home of Judge John Faucheraud Grimké and his wife, Mary Smith Grimké, on Front Street, was a short drive from Saint Philip's Church. When the services ended, the judge and his children, in separate carriages, would ride back to their home and receive guests, as was their Sunday custom. Sometimes, in the evening, the Grimkés would join other parishioners in a special prayer service, or else take part in an event at the central venue of Charleston's civic life, the Old Exchange Building, which looked out over the harbor. The Old Exchange served as the setting for the city's political activity, hosting a regular round of lectures, campaign speeches on patriotic or religious themes emphasizing "right thinking" and "correct morals," and appropriately noncontroversial public discussions about local matters. The Grimké family spent other Sunday evenings calling on close friends at plantations along the Ashley River, northwest of the city, where the Middletons and Draytons had palatial homes. But even as a child, Sarah Grimké, the judge's second daughter and sixth child, preferred teaching Sunday religious classes for slave children to making social visits with her family to Charleston's elite. Sarah was a gifted teacher, though she was frustrated by the fact that she was forced to give her lessons verbally, since Charleston's slaves were forbidden to learn how to read. More comfortable with children than with adults, the nervous young woman became an excellent storyteller. She was at ease with her young charges and believed that their innocence was God's way of reflecting the original state of man.

Christmas, Easter, and Independence Day were the most important holidays in Charleston. For South Carolinians, July 4 was particularly special, and the city took great pride in its festivities. Charleston had suffered grievously during the American Revolution, when the British Army had imprisoned the sons of some of the city's great families in the "dungeon" (preserved for posterity as a museum beneath the Old Exchange Building). On Independence Day, families from South Carolina's up-country plantations would come to Charleston to enjoy the city fair and watch the fireworks that the municipal committee put on around the harbor. The citizenry relived the day when American troops had reoccupied Charleston after Washington's stunning victory at Yorktown. Charlestonians and their up-country "cousins" spread their picnic blankets in the park and greeted old friends as children played and gawked at the soldiers of the South Carolina Militia, resplendent in their uniforms. The militia was the pride of Charleston, a permanent symbol of its contribution to the founding of the young Republic. But even as Charleston celebrated its independence, it took pride in vestigial evidence of its colonial past—streets, lined with trees and six-foot-wide brick walks, that were still named George and King.

The highlight of each July 4 came when Charleston's families gathered in Battery Park to witness the firing of the set of cannons that looked out over the harbor. Just as they had once been fired to stave off Blackbeard, whose pirates had threatened the city in 1718, and the British invaders, whose ships had been spotted outside the harbor in 1780, so now they memorialized the birth of independence, sending their shells out into the middle distance, toward the walls of the fort that guarded the city. This seemingly impregnable gray eminence blocking Charleston Harbor was named for Thomas Sumter, a dashing Revolutionary War cavalryman and friend of John Grimké's. Sumter and Francis Marion, another famous partisan, were the state's premier heroes and, as the "Gamecock" and the "Swamp Fox," the twin icons of its legendary struggle with royalty, having fought the British from their low-country lairs in a series of hit-and-run cavalry raids. Fort Sumter was as much a symbol of Charleston's fighting spirit as the city's homes were symbols of its elegance—and it seemed no less invincible than South Carolina society. Both would stand forever. When the firing of the militia's artillery stopped, and the last of the shells had burst out over the fort, the applause of the onlookers rang into the night, and Charleston's families turned for home, secure in their independence and confident in their future.

The Grimkés and others like them practiced an easy patriotism born of the certainty that no one, ever, could question their right to command the society that their ancestors had created. So assured were they in their position that in 1810, when Sarah Grimké was eighteen, the state legislature (called the House of Commons in a bow to English pretensions) passed legislation granting all white males the right to vote, well in advance of similar measures passed by legislatures in the rest of the country. The real reason for such liberalism was that in South Carolina, the right to vote meant little. Through a series of legislative sleights-of-hand, the administration of the state was firmly controlled by a small group of rich and influential low-country planters, a class to which John Grimké and his family belonged. The legislation merely ensured that the House of Commons would retain its monarchial privileges, claiming the right to appoint all the state's judges, presidential electors, and officeholders, including the governor. The institution of slavery was jealously guarded by the House, since nearly all of its members owned slaves. South Carolina was the nation's only true "slavocracy."

South Carolina's constitution was derived from a unique document of colonial history. "The Fundamental Constitutions of Carolina" was written by Lord Ashley with the help of his personal secretary John Locke. The aristocratic Locke was a learned but unpretentious empiricist Englishman who won immortality by helping to create that most breathtaking of all beliefs, the notion that the people had a right to choose their own government. The constitution drafted by Ashley and Locke was nonetheless at some remove from true republicanism: while it emphasized religious tolerance, which appealed to the French Huguenots (one of Charleston's most prominent lineages), it also established an economic system that encouraged large land grants, which appealed to its English-descended gentry. (Locke, known for his suggestion that some revolutions were necessary, was much less revolutionary than Americans then believed: he held considerable stock in the Royal Africa Company, whose business was the slave trade.) South Carolina's government elected legislators who institutionalized the status of South Carolina's small but affluent nobility. Charleston's citizens constantly celebrated their independence, their love of liberty, and their individual self-reliance, though in fact they were the least disposed to grant those same privileges to anyone else. Charleston was not a city of immigrants, of huddled masses, or of oppressed yearning to be free, nor was it destined to become one. After the initial influx of Huguenots and Englishmen, the town fathers had enacted strict citizenship laws that choked off the flow of new settlers (excepting slaves from Africa), even as they insisted that theirs was a friendly city that would welcome anyone.

For these reasons, Charleston was an anomaly, different not only from the rest of America but even from the rest of the South. During the crush of westward settlement that marked the opening of cotton lands following Eli Whitney's invention of the cotton gin, in 1794, Charleston's elite remained remarkably unaffected by the new South's cotton wealth. Life went on as before, with the exception that those low-country planters who refused to cash in on cotton began to live on borrowed time and borrowed money. But if a handful of Charleston's elite families started to lose their riches, they nevertheless retained their power in the state and city, and their status as South Carolina's leading citizens. The silent, all-knowing, even self-deprecating style that the members of Charleston's elite feigned in imitation of their London cousins stayed firmly in place; they were guaranteed their continued high standing by a system that was, as one aging and disenchanted Charlestonian would later bitterly reflect, "rocked in the cradle of wealth."

Nothing intruded on this easy life. The national government was far away, and the state government solidly in the hands of the ruling class; even slavery itself, while an ever-present reality, seemed a distant concern. In truth, the heads of Charleston's most affluent families had little contact with any but the most trusted of their slaves—those who cooked the family meals or raised the family's children. Few heads of such families ever lowered themselves to the direct, day-to-day management of their plantations. That was left to overseers. Only on rare occasions, when their lives or livelihoods were threatened by precipitously falling profits or, even more unusually, rumors of a slave insurrection did Charleston's ruling fathers intervene in the daily existence of their chattel property.

White women, the ruling matrons of Charleston society, had much more contact with slaves than their husbands, but that contact was of a particular kind. Although white women might be considered the "mistresses" of their domain, they were in fact as dependent on black domestic servants as their husbands were on overseers. House slaves invariably knew more about raising children and disciplining them than the Huger, Pinckney, Smith, or Grimké women, since such matters were left almost exclusively in their hands. So it was, on both counts, that the young male and female progeny of Charleston's elite were planted and pruned to imitate this life-style, trained not as enterprising and creative innovators wedded to the idea of progress, but as "managers" of a status quo that was as fanatically defended as it was universally unquestioned.

In the early 1800s, the Grimké family grew and prospered. John Faucheraud Grimké was as talented and innovative a businessman as had been his paternal grandfather, the silversmith John Paul Grimké. Originally from Alsace-Lorraine and German by birth, the first American Grimké had spoken with a German accent and added an *é* to his name, giving it a French cast. His decision to change the family name, if only slightly, was intended to appeal to the sensibilities of Charleston's most important families, who would not have taken well, he believed, to a name that sounded as German as Grimk. Grandfather Grimké's silver business became one of the most successful in the South, and his products rivaled those crafted by that other famous American silversmith, Paul Revere. Charleston's first families rewarded him handsomely for his unique silver designs and his superior craftsmanship, enabling him to build a jewelry business in the city and to purchase land in the low country to the south. He recovered from a fire that burned his store in 1740 (aided by a loan from Henry Laurens, one of Charleston's most respected civic leaders) and then helped the city fathers rebuild after the devastating hurricane of 1754. John Paul Grimké added to the family holdings and dabbled in the cotton business. He proudly viewed himself as a patriot and was one of the original members of Charleston's Sons of Liberty during the American Revolution. Ambitious, intelligent, and prudent, John Paul Grimké was one of the city's most respected citizens. His grandson John Faucheraud Grimké emulated him.

———

Sarah Grimké admired her father. From an early age she viewed him as the arbiter of her personal morals and the touchstone of her inner strength. She prized the calm propriety with which he approached every crisis. The scion of a most proper Southern family, the grandson of an American patriot, and a descendant of the highly respected Faucherauds, Judge Grimké was a legendary figure even in his youth. As a young man he excelled at his studies, was sent to England to read the law, and took his degree at Oxford. He practiced in London and kept rooms in the Temple. He was a brilliant lawyer and political thinker. In 1774 he was asked by Benjamin Franklin and Thomas Pinckney to join them in signing a petition addressed to King George III, protesting the Boston Port Bill. He proudly agreed to their request and thereafter was viewed as one of the nation's first revolutionaries. Great things were expected of John Grimké.

Grimké had been cutting a wide swath through British society, but when the American Revolution overtook the colonies, he returned to

Charleston, where he raised and trained a company of cavalry. Commissioned as a captain in the Revolutionary Army, he was imprisoned by the British for his disloyalty, then released. Avoiding the loyalist forces, he slipped out of Charleston and joined the army of General Robert Howe. He served as deputy adjutant for South Carolina and Georgia, fought with distinction at the Battle of Eutaw Springs, and then was sent north, where, as a young lieutenant colonel, he witnessed the surrender of Lord Cornwallis's army at Yorktown. He came home from the Revolution a military hero, an accomplished lawyer, a friend of the famous Marquis de Lafayette, and a cosmopolitan political thinker. The war was over, the colonies were free, and a new nation was being born. John Faucheraud Grimké was just twenty-six years old.

Grimké quickly ascended to the top rank of Charleston lawyers. In political circles, his name was regularly mentioned for statewide office. As was his habit then and throughout his life, Grimké ignored the attention, built his law practice, and diligently added to his family holdings. He purchased lots in Charleston, small parcels in the rice country, and land adjoining his family's up-country plantation in the Union District. Called Belmont, this larger cotton plantation in the Appalachian foothills was the jewel in the Grimké family crown. Grimké understood that in the agriculturally fueled mercantilist economy of Charleston, land was the most stable currency and would serve as the best insurance against the wild swings in prices for lowland rice and labor-intensive cotton. He watched over his land carefully and extended his holdings whenever he could. He was a shrewd businessman and investor and was respected for his sound financial dealings.

In 1779, at the age of thirty, John Grimké was appointed to a judgeship and named as a delegate to the state convention that had been called to debate ratification of the U.S. Constitution. Grimké was a conservative who supported state power, but as a veteran officer of the Revolutionary War, he stood with George Washington (whom he greatly admired) and Alexander Hamilton in favor of the Constitution. Like many other South Carolinians, he welcomed the advent of a strong central government, but only after receiving assurances that the smaller states, especially Southern ones such as South Carolina, would be able to retain their unique institutions and traditions. He served with distinction at the ratifying convention and proudly celebrated South Carolina's entry into the new Union.

John Grimké married well, in 1784. Mary Smith was the great-granddaughter of the second Landgrave of South Carolina. A Smith ancestor had saved Charleston from Blackbeard's pirates soon after the town was first settled, and Mary's father, "Banker Smith of Broad Street," was the city's leading financier and its wealthiest citizen. Their line mixed English nobility with Scottish rebels, plantation aristocrats with colonial governors, hardy pioneers with sober patriots. Along with the Draytons, Middletons, and Rhetts, the Smiths dominated Charleston society and South Carolina's political establishment. Robert Barnwell Rhett, Mary Smith's distant nephew (who actually changed his family's surname from Smith in order to be "more Southern"), later became South Carolina's leading voice for secession and an outspoken advocate of "Southern nationalism." Mary Smith Grimké, called Polly by her friends and family, was twelve years younger than her husband but every bit the proper Charleston lady. She was a small woman who spoke often and with animation. With her sharp-edged intensity, strong opinions, and deep religious faith, she was a perfect match for the self-effacing, scholarly Judge John Grimké.

The newly married couple's home was one of the most admired in Charleston. Two winding staircases led up to the massive four-story town house. The first story was set aside for the kitchen, the second for Judge Grimké's offices. The family entertained guests on the third floor and lived on the fourth. To the rear were the slave quarters, which housed cooks, servants, housekeepers, butlers, footmen, seamstresses, laundresses, and parlor maids. The rooms were large and high-ceilinged. Judge Grimké's books were everywhere, lining the walls of his office and walls in the living quarters. Although formal dressers, dining tables, and desks were often imported from England, the family furnished much of the house locally, keeping a nearby furniture-maker busy mimicking the styles of London.

Mary Smith was proud of her husband, who had now begun to take on the accepted role of city and state political leader. He was elected to the South Carolina Parliament, became speaker of the House of Commons, and, with the president of the South Carolina Senate, planned, in 1786, the building of a new state capital, called Columbia, on rolling hillsides bordering the Congaree River. He meticulously laid out the city's streets and sketched in where the capital was to be sited. Columbia was Charleston's bow to the increasing importance of up-country planters, a symbolic confirmation that power was beginning to shift—that while South Carolina was still firmly in the hands of its most affluent families, in Charleston, the state would now actually be governed from its center, at least geographically. When a new state constitution was adopted in 1790, with Grimké's help, low-country power was institutionalized, with disproportionate representation given to Charleston and surrounding parishes. The adoption of the 1790 constitution, with its voting qualifications of land and slave ownership, meant that the state would be safe from the "yahoos" (as Charlestonians called the up-country planters), at least for a time.

But politics was at best a diversion for John Grimké. His life, and his wife's, revolved around the accepted traditions of aristocratic Charleston society. That society was dominated by the Episcopal Church, by the management of plantations (the Grimkés' up-country Belmont holdings demanded special care), by the rearing of children, and, during the long, idle months that separated harvesting from planting, by a series of galas that marked the city's winter season. A quick inspection of Charleston high society in the late eighteenth century shows that the Grimkés were at the center of a Southern urban circle that included some of the South's leading families, many of whom had once been as well known to the silversmith John Paul Grimké as they were now to Judge John Grimké and his young wife.

Soon after he and Polly were married, Judge Grimké began his life's work, a compilation of South Carolina laws that would form the basis of the new state's judicial system. The resulting two volumes (prodigiously titled *South Carolina Justice of the Peace* and *Public Laws of the State of South Carolina*) were to serve as the pillars of the state's juridical structure for many decades to come. While Judge Grimké continued his own impressive practice, his wife bore their children and managed the Grimké home. Their first son, John, was born in 1785, and then Thomas Smith Grimké in 1786, to be followed by Benjamin, Mary, Frederick, and Sarah. Polly Grimké gave birth to fourteen children in all; three died as infants. As the new century dawned, Sarah took her place in a world that was as well ordered as it was predictable. Like all of the Grimké children, she was baptized at Saint Philip's Church in the company of the family's closest friends and relatives.

———

Catherine Birney, Sarah Grimké's close friend, admirer, and first biographer, described the religious life of the Grimké family as one of unwavering devotion. "Judge Grimké, his family and connections," she wrote, were all High-Church Episcopalians, tenacious of every dogma, and severe upon any neglect of religious form of church or household worship. Nothing but sickness excused any member of the family, servants included, from attending morning prayers, and every Sunday the well-appointed carriage bore those who wished to attend church to the most fashionable one in the city. The children attended Sabbath-school regularly, and in the afternoon the girls who were old enough taught classes in the colored school.

The Grimkés were more than simple believers. Unlike many of their acquaintances, who used the church merely to solidify their place in Charleston society, Judge Grimké and his wife were, as family records and testimonies of their close friends show, devout and practicing Protestants who believed in the power of prayer and the threat of sinful temptation. The Grimkés were properly anti-Catholic, the custom having been bred into them through their Huguenot family background and amplified by the then-current disdain for anything that suggested zealotry. Polly Grimké prayed daily with her children, guiding them in their devotions and counseling them in their beliefs in the omnipotence of an ever-present God. The elder Grimkés took their religion seriously enough to imbue their children with constant admonitions to lead lives free of sin, while refraining from passing judgment on others; theirs was a proper, modest, and understated religion, steeped in belief, but without public passion. Their faith was steady, unchanging, and unquestioned.

The same could not be said of Sarah, however. Even as a young girl, Sarah Grimké gained enough of a worldly vision to question her family's beliefs, even as she respected her mother's commitment to prayer. Sarah herself prayed often and believed deeply, but just as she resented being barred from teaching her black serving girl to read, she wondered why it was that God ordained that some would be free and some would not. The Episcopalians at Saint Philip's, where the Grimkés were seen every Sunday, were quite stern on this point, taking as their defense of slavery the words of Leviticus, who counseled that it was a part of God's world and that therefore "the children of the strangers that sojourn among you, of them shall ye buy, and of their families that are with you, which they have begotten in your land: and they shall be your possession. And ye shall take them as an inheritance for your children after you, to inherit them for a possession; they shall be your bondmen for ever."

For those who doubted, good ministers had ready at hand the arguments of Protestant theologians such as Oxford-educated Richard Nisbet, whose "Slavery Not Forbidden By Scripture" (a pamphlet written in 1773) was a touchstone for Christian slaveholders. There were those who disagreed with Nisbet, but he silenced them with accusations of blasphemy, claiming that to deny the righteousness of slavery was to deny that Scripture was the holy writ of God. In the 1770s, Nisbet's broadsides had sparked a bitter theological "war of the pamphlets" that did little to resolve the issue. While Enlightenment theologians held forth on the strength of revealed truths, Nisbet and his allies pressed the attack: asserting that the Bible was wrong about slavery, they adduced, was the same as saying that the revealed word of God was a lie. To this argument, there was no rejoinder. The next logical step was to insist that those who opposed slavery were guilty of heresy or, worse, were atheists, heathens. And that was exactly what happened.

Sarah, as yet unborn, was not privy to this war of the pamphlets, but she certainly understood, even as a child, its major arguments. If belief in God required a belief in slavery, as slavery's advocates implied, then the whippings and beatings that she saw from time to time were not simply something that Christians could tolerate; they were the will of God. Sarah, ever precocious, continued her daily devotions, spent hours each Sunday morning at Saint Philip's, taught Sunday school to black slave children each Sunday afternoon, and returned home to wonder how she could possibly balance the central tenet of her religion's message, to "love others," with its revealed truth, that bondage was an unchangeable condition sanctioned by a loving and just God.

As if to throw all of this into a stark light, Sarah's mother was becoming increasingly intolerant of the behavioral lapses of the Grimké slaves. As Polly grew older and her responsibilities increased, so, too, did her reprimands and petty frustrations. Her handling of the family slaves was unjust and often cruel. She lost her temper more and more frequently and sometimes ordered the slaves to be caned for the slightest infraction. Sarah witnessed many such whippings; as a child of four she saw one so severe that she ran to a ship anchored at Charleston's docks and pleaded with a captain there to take her aboard as a hand. Sarah begged her mother again and again to be lenient with the slaves, but no such mercy was forthcoming. As was the case for many Southern women, the tasks of childbearing and caring for a home and husband took their toll on Polly Grimké, whose intolerance and impatience were obvious to all.

Sarah could not comprehend her mother's impatience and often criticized her lack of tolerance. As she moved into womanhood, her relationship with her mother grew distant and cold. As an adult however, Sarah softened her judgment. She understood the pressures that Southern society imposed upon her mother, and saw how few opportunities she had for personal education and growth. This evolving understanding eventually made its way into Catherine Birney's biography. "As children multiplied," Birney wrote,

> Mrs. Grimké appears to have lost all power of controlling either them or her servants. She was impatient with the former, and resorted with the latter to the punishments commonly inflicted by slave owners. Polly's anger, her lack of emotional control, alienated her children still more from her, and they showed their mother little respect or affection. It never appears to have occurred to any of them to try to relieve her of her cares; and it is possible that she was more sinned against than sinning—a sadly burdened and much-tried woman. From numerous allusions to her in the diaries and letters, the evidence of an ill-regulated household is plain, as also the feelings of the children towards her.

The increasing distance between the Grimké children and their mother was keenly felt by Sarah, who turned for friendship to her brother Thomas. Even as a young boy, he showed flickerings of the brilliance that would mark his life, and though five years older than Sarah, he seemed to understand her better than anyone. They played together as children and shared a love of learning. Later they discussed the law, politics, and religion and engaged in lengthy debates on these topics with their father at the dinner table. The friendship would be a lifelong one. In those early years he shared his schoolwork with her, helped her through his Latin lessons, and defended her right to read their father's law books. But Thomas did not share his sister's outspoken abhorrence of slavery. He listened to her objections and talked with her for many hours on the topic, but his views did not change. Slavery, he believed, was simply a normal part of their lives, as common as the constant call of the tradesmen on Charleston's streets and defensible on the grounds that it actually helped slaves acclimate to their new lives in "civilized" society.

Unformed and uncertain of his future, Thomas supposed that he would follow his father into the law, but he also felt he might make a good minister. Like his younger sister, he had strong religious beliefs. Sarah feared that he would go north to college, but he decided instead to go to the College of Charleston. Sarah saw him nearly every day when she was in the city and listened intently as he explained what he was reading and hearing in college. After two years at Charleston, however, Thomas announced that he had been accepted as a student at Yale. Sarah was heartbroken. After he left for Connecticut, she became increasingly lonely, despite the constant attention of her other brothers and sisters. No one, she thought, could take Thomas's place.

———

Thomas Grimké left for Yale early in 1805. He was relieved to be getting out of Charleston, excited by the challenges that awaited him in the North, and happy to be on his own, away from the everyday cares of the Grimké family. The reality of Polly Grimké's growing intolerance and impatience was becoming more and more public. Sarah blamed herself and vowed to be more helpful to her mother. But there were more salient reasons for Polly's precarious state of mind than the growing independence of her second daughter. Left alone for much of the time while her husband pursued his career, she was simply incapable of managing a household that included ten children and as many servants. Added to these tribulations was the fact that she was pregnant again, with her fourteenth child. She had already had to bury three infants, and caring for, feeding, and teaching the children still at home had become a nearly torturous experience for her.

Polly's greatest challenges, however, were posed not by her children (most of whom she had turned over to "Mauma," the family nurse) but by the household slaves, who demanded as much attention as her family, if not more. Like the much put-upon woman who wrote a defense of slavery for the Southern religious magazine *The Church Intelligencer*, Polly focused on the burdens of being a slaveholder and the almost insurmountable trials that status brought:

> Would you like to stand all day long with a pair of heavy shears in your hand, and cut out coarse negro clothing, till your hand ached with weariness? Would you like to go into the negro houses and stand hour after hour by the bed of the sick and dying, cheering and comforting the poor creature? Would

you like to struggle and wrestle with ignorance, stupidity and
the fearful tendency to immorality—alas! almost inherent in
the negro? All around me, throughout the length and breadth
of the land, are women who do this.

Such self-congratulations were common among white slaveholding
women, who viewed themselves as fonts of intelligence and insight for
a barbarous people whose "immorality" was "almost inherent." For
women such as Mary Smith Grimké, the lack of morals among the slaves
was obvious, for she and other Southern women saw it every day in the
light-colored eyes and fair skin of the children of black slave women. But
as Harriet Martineau, the insightful nineteenth-century British commentator, would write of the Southern system, the problem was not so
much slave "promiscuity" as it was sexual exploitation:

> Every man who resides on his plantation may have his harem,
> and has every inducement of custom, and of pecuniary gain to
> tempt him to the common practice. (The law declares that the
> children of slaves are to follow the fortunes of the mother.
> Hence the practice of planters selling and bequeathing their
> own children.) . . . What security for domestic purity and
> peace there can be where every man has two families, whose
> existence must not be known to each other; where the conjugal
> relation begins in treachery and must be carried on with a
> heavy secret in the husband's breast, no words are needed to
> explain . . . nor to point out the boundless licentiousness
> caused by the practice: a practice which wrung from the wife
> of the planter, in the bitterness of her heart, the declaration
> that a planter's wife was only "the chief slave of the harem."

There is no evidence at all that Judge Grimké had any illicit relationship with his female slaves, but if he did, it would not have been unusual.
The "common practice" of the slave system provided a ready means of
sexual exploitation and produced offspring who, by their very existence,
undermined the myth so commonly accepted in Southern society—that
it was race, and *not* color, that provided the underpinning of slavery.
"Under slavery, we live surrounded by prostitutes, yet an abandoned
woman is sent out of any decent house," Virginian Mary Chesnut later
wrote. "Who thinks any worse of a negro or mulatto woman for being a

thing we can't name? God forgive us, but ours is a monstrous system. Like the patriarchs of old, our men live all in one house with their wives and their concubines; and the mulattos one sees in every family partly resemble the white children. Any lady is ready to tell you who is the father of all the mulatto children in everybody's household but her own. Those, she seems to think, drop from the clouds."

Not all white slave owners, or even most, forced themselves on their slaves; nor were those who did insensible to the effect of their actions on the "domestic peace and security" of either their households or their communities. Charleston's significant population of "mixed-blood" citizens, many of whom were the freed offspring of white-black couplings, was proof of this. The "common practice" might be to overlook the sexual interchange of male slaveholders with black slave women, but it was difficult for the society to ignore the results of such practices. Charleston contained a large population of "free people of color," so common that they were referred to as "fpc's" in plantation society. They came and went as they pleased and, in some cases, even took the names of their former masters; the practice, if Chesnut is to be believed, was more than a simple matter of convenience.

.The Charleston docks served as a depository for these "fpc's." Here, two thousand freed offspring of white-black sexual relations lived in a vibrant, growing, and prosperous society that straddled the ambiguous line between white and black society. Dozens of free "colored" families formed the bedrock of this community, which became so well identified that in the aftermath of the American Revolution, its members established the Brown Fellowship Society, an "exclusive cast[e]-conscious mutual association" limited to "bona fide free brown men of good character." Many of these families worshiped alongside the Charleston elite, including the Grimkés, at Saint Philip's Episcopal Church.

The Brown Fellowship Society was a benevolent association aimed at helping former slaves and their offspring. But it embraced its own distinct color line, excluding free black laborers who were deemed "too black." The organization's leaders never explicitly stated their purpose, perhaps because they did not need to: their society was a way station between the races, a stop for those moving from a black world to a white one. In an economy and society so deeply influenced by the institution of slavery, the Brown Fellowship Society reflected the dominant culture: the truth was that Charleston was a city divided not so much by race as by color, white from black and black from brown. The Grimkés, and certainly Sarah Grimké, could not have failed to notice that the free colored members of Saint Philip's Church had surnames that were familiar to all of Charleston society—Drayton, Huger, and Kinloch—and thus stood as living evidence of the "monstrous system." But as she scanned the brown faces of Saint Philip's, Sarah could at least be reassured in her knowledge that the Grimké men had not used the system for their own purposes. There was not one person named Grimké among the crowd of brown parishioners at Saint Philip's Church. At least not yet.

———

No sooner had Thomas departed for Yale than Sarah gained a new companion. On February 20, 1805, Angelina Emily Grimké, the last child of John and Mary Grimké, was born. She joined a family of six sons (John, Thomas, Frederick, Ben, Henry, and Charles) and four daughters (Mary, Sarah, Anna, and Eliza). Sarah was emotionally overwhelmed by Angelina's arrival, seeing the infant as compensation for Thomas's loss and as a potential lifelong companion who could share her dreams and beliefs. Immediately after her youngest sister's birth, Sarah begged her parents to let her become the child's godmother, pledging that she would do everything necessary, for the rest of her life, to look after her. At first, John and Mary Grimké strongly resisted the idea, but Sarah's constant pleas finally won them over, and when the time came, she stood at the baptismal font at Saint Philip's as Angelina's godmother. She took her responsibilities seriously, spending nearly every minute of every day looking after her "precious Nina." More than a godmother to the child, she became her second mother. For the rest of their lives, Sarah and Angelina Grimké would be nearly inseparable. Years later, Sarah Grimké would recall her sister's christening reverently:

> I had been taught to believe in the efficacy of prayer, and I well remember, after the ceremony was over, slipping out and shutting myself up in my own room, where, with tears streaming down my cheeks, I prayed that God would make me worthy of the task I had assumed, and help me to guide and direct my precious child. Oh, how good I resolved to be, how careful in all my conduct, that my life might be blessed in her.

The advent of Angelina helped break the monotony of the endless rounds of socializing that were expected of Sarah. As the child grew, she began to spend more and more time with her. Just as Sarah called Angelina "my precious Nina," Angelina called her Mother. Sarah took charge of her sister's schooling and religious training, monitored her daily chores, and proselytized to her unremittingly about the evils of slavery. It was a subject on which Sarah was becoming an expert. She knew the name of every Grimké slave and was familiar with each one's family relations, work, medical problems, religious beliefs, and educational status. When her family spent the winter at Belmont, Sarah tended to the needs of these slaves, even as she attempted to ameliorate their workload. As she made her rounds, Angelina, her constant companion, tagged along behind.

Angelina's birth coincided with one of the most difficult periods of Sarah's life. In 1805, at age thirteen, Sarah Grimké was entering young womanhood. In the five years that lay just ahead, she would be expected to learn the traditions and customs of her gender and to begin to take on the role she would fill as an adult female member of the Grimké family. Sarah was painfully aware of what was expected of her, and she was not looking forward to the transition. The customs of Southern society dictated that a young white woman would become an expert in her own "spheres" of raising children, managing a household, planning and hosting social events, and being, in Sarah's words, "a doll, a coquette, a fashionable fool." The pressures on Sarah were intense; her mother insisted that she meet her prescribed responsibilities, all the more emphatically because Sarah continually informed her that she would do no such thing. Sarah's efforts to learn Latin and the law only exacerbated these tensions.

In 1807, Thomas Grimké graduated from Yale and returned to Charleston. Sarah celebrated his homecoming and looked forward to resuming their close relationship. But Thomas was a changed man. Older, more mature, he welcomed the opportunity to participate in Charleston's social season and began looking for a wife. There were other changes as well. While at Yale, Thomas had become a disciple of the college's president, Timothy Dwight, whose evangelism and ideas about educational reform had convinced him that he should become a minister. While Dwight was an outspoken critic of the "deism" then sweeping New England, he was also one of the nation's most prominent social reformers.

Sarah listened closely as her brother told her about his life at Yale, the courses he had taken, the books he'd read, and his work with Dwight. Timothy Dwight had imparted to Thomas his views on the subject of deism (which he judged the most profound danger to the republic), the fulfillment he found in his commitment to a life of service to others (and his growing disillusionment with the overly pious Calvinist traditions of the New England clergy), and his belief in the need for what he called universal education—which placed him at the forefront of the national educational reform movement. With Dwight as his mentor, Thomas Grimké was fully committed to becoming a minister. Sarah was excited to hear these new ideas and sat with rapt attention as Thomas talked about his years in New Haven, but she was disheartened to realize she was no longer her brother's intellectual equal. It was obvious that Yale had given him an education that she herself could never have and could never hope to match. Judge Grimké was also proud of Thomas, but he was not impressed with his ideas. Slowly, inevitably, he reintroduced his son to Charleston society and insisted that he put aside his notion of becoming a minister. It was one thing to believe in educational reform, he felt, and quite another to be a reformer. There was no place for a Dwight disciple in Charleston society or even, the judge made clear, in the Grimké household. Judge Grimké was too sophisticated to directly overrule his son, but he gradually, gently, firmly nudged him back into the life of a Southern gentleman.

Thomas Grimké eventually bowed to his father's wishes, and soon after his return from the north he joined the firm of Langdon Cheves. Cheves was one of the most storied attorneys in the nation, a legendary advocate of Southern nationalism and a man of wit, charm, and rapier intelligence. Impeccably polite and destined for political greatness (as a speaker of the U.S. House of Representatives) as well as controversy (he would back Henry Clay's call for a war with Great Britain in 1812), Cheves molded Thomas Grimké's thinking, teaching him how best to use the intellectual tools that Yale had bequeathed him. Under his tutelage, Thomas set aside his idealism, replacing it with a love of debate and writing that he used to build his reputation as one of South Carolina's most prominent intellectuals. Once set on this course, Thomas Grimké reentered Charleston society, attending every prominent event of the social season of 1809. That July he gave the Independence Oration at Saint Philip's Church, and in 1810 he married Sally Drayton and moved out of the Grimké home on Front Street. Soon after, he established his own law practice in a modest office on Broad Street, where he began to build a career as a politician as well as a friendship with another young lawyer,

Robert Y. Hayne, a fire-breathing defender of "Southern rights." Thomas Grimké's goal was to serve in the state legislature, where he could put Timothy Dwight's reform ideas into practice.

That same year, 1810, found Thomas's sister Sarah Grimké in her second social season.

———

There was not much room for freedom for a young woman in Charleston in those years. The seasons and the migratory travels of the Grimké family determined the pace of Sarah's life. Every November, the Grimkés journeyed two hundred miles to their estate at Belmont, in the up-country Union District of South Carolina, where they stayed until May, relatively isolated from Charleston society with its constant rounds of balls, teas, parties, cotillions, and interfamily visits. In the summer, the family returned to the city, where Sarah was expected to participate in the social whirl and appear as a sophisticated, prim, proper, upright, and smiling young woman. Every young woman looking for a husband had to be "handsome," from "the right family," and "clever." Sarah obeyed the dictates of her family, but inwardly she fumed at the custom. She was convinced that Southern men and Southern society treated all women as commodities.

The only break in the Grimkés' annual winter stay up-country came in February, when Sarah's family returned to Charleston for two weeks, the high point of the "season." During this respite from the boredom of their inland plantation, Judge Grimké attended to his judicial duties while the other members of the family entertained themselves with "Race Week," Mrs. Mitchell King's extravagant ball, the Jockey Club Dinner, and the most eagerly anticipated social event of the year, the Saint Cecilia concert and ball, which all the great families attended. Church events provided further entertainment. Most of the social commerce of Charleston revolved around Saint Michael's and Saint Philip's churches, and Saint Philip's was the scene of the yearly Episcopal Convention, which allowed Charleston's ladies to meet distant relatives. But by far the most important social gatherings took place behind the tall wooden doors of the homes lining the cobblestoned streets that led down to the harbor. Here the gentlemen and ladies of Charleston engaged in the most delicate of dances, introducing their sons and daughters to one another, jockeying for position and status, and trying to make "good" marriages for their children—and for their families.

Sarah Grimké did have at least one suitor around this time, but it ended badly. She wrote in her diary that her brother Thomas had saved her from rushing into an "unhallowed marriage" with a young man by the name of Burke Williams, whom the Grimkés believed to be disreputable and not from an acceptable family. She was crushed to hear of his past from her brother, who said that Williams had already proposed to a number of other young women, apparently for the purpose of luring them into sin. Heartbroken, she spurned the man's advances thereafter, but at a steep emotional cost. This is our only evidence that Sarah was pursued by any man at all during these years. She herself attributed her paucity of suitors to the fact that in her estimation, she was simply too homely to attract the attention of eligible men. This belief, that she was not only a social outsider but unattractive, would plague her for the rest of her life. But in truth, while Sarah became an eager participant in Charleston's courtship rituals in spite of her lack of confidence, she was often guilt-ridden over the "frivolities," the "gaieties and vanities," of dances, balls, dinners, picnics, and walks. She would later look back on this period of her life with amazement, writing about it in her diary as if she had been possessed by a demon:

> I believe for the short space I was exhibited on this theatre, few have exceeded me in extravagance of every kind, and in the sinful indulgence of pride and vanity, sentiments which, however, were strongly mingled with a sense of their insufficiency to produce even earthly happiness, with an eager desire to intellectual pursuits, and a thorough contempt for the trifles I was engaged in. Often during this period have I returned home, sick of the frivolous beings I had been with, mortified at my own folly, and weary of the ballroom and its gilded toys. Night after night, as I glittered now in this gay scene, now in that, my soul has been disturbed by that query, "Where are the talents committed to thy charge?"

In the midst of this season of balls and dances, the Grimkés were faced with their first real test as a family when, in January 1811, Judge Grimké's political enemies began impeachment proceedings against him in the state assembly. Accused of incompetence and threatened with removal from the state court, Judge Grimké, with the help of his sons Thomas and Frederick (who, like Thomas, had been educated at Yale) and the assistance of Charleston lawyer Daniel Huger, planned a vigorous defense. An attempted impeachment of a sitting judge was unusual but not rare in South Carolina, where a perceptible line now divided the up-country landed aristocracy and its "cousins" in Charleston. This division was exacerbated by the petty jealousies that marked the state's highly politicized judicial system. In John Faucheraud Grimké's case, at least, these jealousies exploded into a power struggle born of the desire of a group of increasingly influential young lawyers to make more room for themselves at the top of the judicial system. Grimké himself had committed no substantive misconduct.

His accusers argued that Grimké was too old (at fifty-eight), too opinionated, too strict, and too impatient to remain on the court. The state legislature heard the case in a single day; Huger's defense proved so devastating that the trial was speedily concluded, and Judge Grimké (who still had friends in the chamber from the days when he had been speaker) was acquitted by an overwhelming majority vote. The judge returned to Charleston the next day, vindicated and with his good name intact. But his daughter Sarah noticed that the accusations that had been made against him, though discredited, had taken their toll. He seemed suddenly aged beyond his years.

———

In the spring of 1812, Sarah Grimké attended a lecture given by the Reverend Henry Kollock, a Presbyterian minister renowned for his stirring oratory. She was so moved by the sermon that she determined there and then to lead a life of devotion and service. She shut herself up in her room and turned to the Bible, steeping herself in the words of the New Testament. She pledged to live free of sin and bodily temptations and to reject the soft and easy life that surrounded her. She also told her family that she was leaving the Episcopal Church to become a Presbyterian. Just weeks later, however, she strayed from her pledge and her daily devotions and returned to the rounds of balls and dances. Predictably, perhaps, she castigated herself for neglecting her religious devotions and, in her diary, wrote often of the self-contempt she felt over her "sinful indulgence of pride and vanity." In the summer of 1813, at the age of twenty-one, Sarah took a trip into the up-country with an acquaintance, resolved as ever to "finish my wild career there." At the home of her friend, a young woman from another of Charleston's great families, she once again met the Reverend Kollock. He bore down on her, questioning her about her belief in God, her dependence on prayer, and her decision to return to society. He talked endlessly of the happiness that his religion gave him, of how his faith had given meaning to his life.

They sat together first for hours, and then for hours each day, and while we do not know the exact words that Kollock used with Sarah Grimké, we know that his message had a profound impact on her life. She reiterated her pledge to turn away from "sinful indulgence"; that first night she wrote in her diary that she felt besieged by feelings of inadequacy and "loaded down with iniquity." Returning to Charleston from her visit, she put away her ball gowns and fine dresses and once again dedicated her life to religious study. She was determined to follow Kollock's advice and devote her life to serving others. She started over. She turned down invitations to parties and dinners and attended Bible classes. She later wrote:

> I fed the hungry and clothed the naked, I visited the sick and afflicted, and vainly hoped these outside works would purify a heart defiled with the pride of life, still the seat of carnal propensities and evil passions, but here, too, I failed. I went mourning on my way under the curse of a broken law; and, though I often watered my couch with my tears, and pleaded with my Maker, yet I knew nothing of the sanctifying influence of this holy spirit, and, not finding that happiness in religion I anticipated, I, by degrees, through the persuasions of companions and the inclination of my depraved heart, began to go a little more into society, and to resume my former style of dressing, though in comparative moderation.

Sarah's return to society was short-lived. In 1816, at the age of twenty-four, she once again found the determination to dedicate her life to religious devotion and service. One last visit from the Reverend Kollock confirmed her resolve. She gave up her social life and took on extra duties at her church. Looking back at this time, Sarah would credit Kollock with her transformation, while adding that her commitment to her new life was also the result of the "merciful interposition of Providence." In truth, however, it was not "Providence" that intervened to end her life of "frivolity," but simple human infirmity. That year, the signs of age and exhaustion that Sarah had first seen on her father's face in the aftermath of his impeachment trial worsened. He was ill for a short time, then recovered, then fell ill again. By 1817, his health was in ruins. Exhausted, he was unable to fulfill his judicial duties at all over the next twelve months.

None of Charleston's leading doctors could adequately diagnose Judge Grimké's illness, and the treatments they prescribed had no discernible effect on his health. Perplexed by his patient's worsening condition, the Grimké family doctor recommended that he travel north to Philadelphia to consult with Dr. Phillip Synge Physick, one of America's most eminent surgeons. Judge Grimké agreed but insisted that Sarah accompany him as a nursemaid. She protested vehemently, believing that such a journey would interrupt the new, more devout religious course she had set for herself. It would also take her away from her beloved Nina, then entering her adolescence. But as a devoted daughter, she finally agreed to go with her father to Philadelphia and vowed to nurse him back to health. Judge Grimké was relieved. In May 1819, after several months' preparation, they sailed north.

TWO

"... a stern and relentless God"

Eighteen nineteen was the last year of real peace for America before the debate over slavery became a public and national issue. In that year, there were eleven free and eleven slave states, a deadlock that ensured the safety of slavery where it existed. The most recent addition to the Union, Alabama, kept that delicate balance intact, though even then, just forty-three years after the birth of the Republic, storm clouds were forming on the horizon. In 1819, Secretary of State John Quincy Adams bought Florida from Spain for a paltry $5 million, a transaction that would surely add another star to the glittering slave constellation. But no one could have predicted how decisively, and how soon, the looming controversy would divide the country. Indeed, in 1819, the nation's attention was focused on the "era of good feelings," marked by the restoration of the White House (burned by the British in 1812), the popularity of President James Monroe, and the opening of the Mississippi Valley for settlement. America's favorite sport was squirrel shooting, with teams of four contestants pitted against one another. The frontier moved west to Illinois. In America's schools, children were fascinated by Parson Mason Weems's *Life of George Washington*. In 1819, Abraham Lincoln was ten years old.

John Faucheraud Grimké disembarked in Philadelphia weakened by the strenuous voyage from Charleston and emaciated as a result of the unknown disease that was ravaging his body. A formidable presence in his early years and an imposing and commanding figure as a judge, John Grimké was now almost totally dependent on the wisdom and judgment of his twenty-six-year-old daughter, Sarah. The arrival of the judge and his daughter went unheralded, for while the Grimkés were well known in South Carolina, they were nearly anonymous in the north, especially in the young nation's second-largest city, one of its most cosmopolitan centers. Sarah and her father came to Philadelphia alone, unattended by any of their servants—not that any were necessary: this was to be a short visit, for as Judge Grimké repeatedly assured his daughter, as soon as his condition improved, they would return to Charleston.

Within minutes of their arrival, Sarah tended to their belongings, shepherded her father to a Quaker-owned boardinghouse, and arranged for their meals. She urged her father to rest. Their hosts diligently ministered to their guests and made them feel welcome. Sarah, so long dependent on her father for guidance, realized that he was now incapable of giving her the support she needed. She took charge of the situation, issuing her father preemptory orders, seeing to his needs, and composing the rhythm of their days to fit his illness. Soon they called at the office of Dr. Phillip Synge Physick, the well-known surgeon, who was also an expert diagnostician and one of Philadelphia's leading citizens.

Himself a Quaker, like their hosts, Physick was a kind and gentle man, both thorough and intelligent in his examination, but he could not work miracles. Over a period of several weeks, he attempted to find the cause of Judge Grimké's increasing weakness, but he failed to pinpoint it. Other doctors might have experimented with the standard—if questionable—treatments of the day, but Physick was not a normal physician. Rather than depend on such methods, he prescribed little more than rest and sustenance for his patient and then, when there was no improvement, admitted that he was at a loss. He could find no reason for the judge's illness, he said, and therefore could not prescribe a treatment.

In June, his options exhausted, Dr. Physick advised Sarah that she and her father should retire to Long Branch, New Jersey, on the Atlantic Ocean. Rest and the "sea air," he suggested, might bring her father back to health. But beyond that, he refused to give her even a glimmer of hope for her father's recovery: "His life is in God's hands," he said. Sarah understood then, just three weeks after their arrival, that her father's condition was critical. Although she continued to ignore all signs of his impending death, she knew in her heart that it was very unlikely he would make the return journey with her to South Carolina. Once again, though now thoroughly frightened by the prospect of her father's dying, Sarah made all of the arrangements for their stay on the Jersey shore. At the time, Long Branch was not yet the seaside resort that it would become by century's end; instead, it retained much of its colonial character, despite the few vacationers who came out in mid-July and stayed until the end of August. During those six weeks, families traveled from Philadelphia and New York to rest, lie in the sun, and wade modestly in the ocean. Some homes in Long Branch were rented out to affluent professionals—mostly lawyers and doctors from the nearby cities who were not tied to the land and the endless cycle of planting and cultivation—but for the most part it was still a fishing village whose main attraction was its isolation. The local people prized their solitude and extolled the virtues of a small town built on simple values, where all neighbors were friends and any newcomer was a curiosity.

The Grimkés arrived in Long Branch at the start of the summer and took up residence in a quiet boardinghouse called the Fish Tavern. People came here summer after summer to enjoy the beach, the cool summer evenings, and the prayer meetings in the large common dining hall. While there were guests at the Fish Tavern other than the Grimkés, the tavern's common room and dining hall remained uncrowded until the true beginning of the summer season, and Sarah and her father met few other boarders. Instead, from the day of their arrival, they worked together to defeat the looming threat of John Grimké's unidentified disease.

———

Sarah chafed at being away from home. Much though she loved and admired her father, she was caught up in her own problems and believed that her place was in Charleston, with her family, her Sunday-school students, and her church. She also sincerely felt that it would have been more proper for one of her brothers to make the journey north, as was customary in families such as hers. But no matter what reasons she gave for her hesitation, Sarah knew that her pleadings made her look like a hypocrite: after years of declaring her independence, she was now openly shunning such responsibility—and just at the moment when her father needed her most. Her feelings were mixed, her emotions confused. She felt unprepared and inadequate and feared the challenge that battling her father's illness presented.

Years later, Sarah would concede what her father always knew. Of all of the family, John Grimké understood his daughter better than anyone. Not only could he trust her compassion and intelligence, he also valued her good judgment and her companionship. He was proud of his sons and their professional accomplishments, but Sarah was more like him than any of his other children. During the long hours aboard ship, or while fighting his illness, he needed someone who would tell him the truth about his condition, and if he was to endure a long convalescence, he would need someone to talk with. He had always been able to do that with Sarah, and he prized her quick mind and ready ear. John Grimké also knew that Sarah's unwillingness to accompany him to Philadelphia had little to do with her own inadequacies. He realized that she was reluctant to leave Angelina, her "precious Nina," with whom she had forged a special bond.

Nina, just fourteen years old, was now undergoing her own religious transformation, albeit one due not to long talks with a minister, but instead to the example set by her older sister, protector, and surrogate mother. Like Sarah, Angelina continually questioned the truth of her family's religious beliefs even as she attempted to live the religious life bequeathed her by her mother and father. But unlike her sister, Angelina never felt inadequate to the task, never doubted her own devotion, and was never awed in the face of religious authority. Where Sarah shied away from religious controversy and judged herself imperfect in the face of others' seeming godliness, Angelina sharpened her skepticism and looked askance at Charleston's public displays of religious devotion.

Although the two were devoted friends and close sisters, aside from their chosen plain dress they looked little alike: Sarah was round-faced and short, with few distinguishing characteristics, while Angelina was slightly taller, and thinner, with sharp features. She looked stern and engaged. Sarah was shy and often withdrawn, though she could listen closely to others, a trait that reflected her deep intelligence. The distinctions between the two would harden over the years, with Angelina growing ever more assertive, more outspoken, able to make her voice boom over a crowd. Sarah was just the opposite: at times, even when she spoke in normal tones, her audiences would have to strain to hear her. She was more interested in listening, and her sister in convincing.

There were other differences between the two sisters. Like Sarah, Angelina grew up with slavery; like Sarah, she questioned it at a very early age; and for her, too, the reality of slavery was brought home with brutal poignancy. But unlike her sister, Angelina quickly concluded that slavery did not simply contradict her religious beliefs; it was an absolute wrong that needed to be condemned, an evil to be fought, and an institution that was sickening her family and her state. Even as a young girl, she believed wholly that it needed to be eradicated. At fourteen, Angelina came to a startling conclusion that Sarah, then twenty-seven, had yet to reach: slavery, she believed, was a political problem, not a religious one. The emancipation of black Americans was a matter of political will, not of divine intervention. But where other Southern women viewed the everyday brutality of slavery as an understandable part of life, both Sarah and Angelina were appalled by its practice and emotionally scarred by its presence.

One day, while attending classes at the Charleston Seminary, a private school for the daughters of the city's elite families, Angelina was horrified to see raw, bleeding wounds on the back of a young slave boy who was ordered to open the classroom windows. The deep gashes in his skin, scabbed over and still bloody, ran all the way down his back and his legs. He walked with an uncertain and painful gait, his eyes fearfully darting from one student to another. As he reached for the windows, his face became a mass of pain. When he left the room, his chore accomplished, it was as a limping and frightened animal, humiliated at his status in front of the other children. Angelina fainted at the sight, then committed it to memory. She recounted the incident repeatedly over the years, to anyone who would listen.

It was no surprise, perhaps, that Angelina should share her sister's abhorrence of slavery; after all, she had learned of its evils at Sarah's insistence, as a young student learns from a caring tutor. But Angelina also learned from her older sister in other ways, by mimicking her actions and by showing her own independence. At the age of thirteen, like her father, mother, and siblings before her, Angelina had prepared herself for admission into the Saint Philip's congregation. She spoke with the minister and spent hours in thoughtful prayer. But when the time for her confirmation came, she refused to accept the Episcopal doctrine, informing the minister that after reading the required pledge of obeisance in the Book of Common Prayer, she had become convinced that she did not agree with it. "If, with my feelings and views as they now are, I should go through that form, it would be acting a lie. I cannot do it," she said. The minister was stunned by Angelina's statement and appealed to her family to intervene.

The Grimkés were embarrassed by Angelina's decision, but no

amount of arguing could induce her to change her mind. Polly Grimké was particularly angered and humiliated by her daughter's unexpected pronouncement and came to believe that it had been prompted by the earlier, similar behavior of Sarah, Angelina's godmother. Polly was now faced with the uncomfortable knowledge that two of her daughters had chosen to abandon the family religion. What was more, Sarah and Angelina's actions had inspired gossip among Charleston's population and cast a public eye on all the Grimkés—a scrutiny that had never fallen on the family before. Judge John Grimké and his wife were now the parents of one daughter, Sarah, who had turned to Presbyterianism and another who had done something considerably worse—for after refusing her Episcopal vows, Angelina remained firmly outside *all* of Charleston's religious community.

Mary Smith Grimké's anger and hurt were further deepened by Angelina's announcement that she intended to convene an all-female prayer group comprised of women from all of Charleston's denominations. Such an ecumenical meeting was more than merely unorthodox; it was unheard of. Polly protested and threatened to discipline her daughter, but Angelina refused to obey her mother's dictates, continued in her ways, and called together her religious group. Unable to stop her, and perhaps pleased that Angelina was at least inclined toward religion in *some* form, her mother succumbed to her wishes, just as she had done with Sarah. But the seeds of future strife between Polly and her two daughters were planted. She was confused by their actions and sensitive to the talk about the strange Grimké daughters now making the rounds of Charleston's leading families.

Angelina followed her sister in her deep belief in the value of leading a life free of sin; she followed her again when she judged the Episcopal Church inadequate to meet her religious needs; and she followed her, finally, in deciding to become a Presbyterian. But while she listened carefully, as a child, to her older sister's condemnations of slavery, she took her own path and made her own decisions. Sarah may have condemned slavery as an injustice, but Angelina set out to right the obvious wrong, arguing constantly with her mother over the treatment of the family's slaves and then, during their time at Belmont, their large Union District plantation, sneaking from her room in the middle of the night to take badly needed medicines to slave families. Sarah prayed for guidance on slavery and used the institution as a means of questioning the basic principles of southern Christianity, but she never really confronted the *reality* of slavery. Angelina, in contrast, put her prayers and doubts into action: she refused to own a slave and firmly rejected her mother's suggestion that she take on a serving girl as a personal servant. When Angelina at last agreed to care for a young slave named Kitty, it was only because the girl's behavior had sparked her mother's anger, and Angelina feared for her safety. Unwilling to own the slave or receive wages on her behalf, but also unwilling to return her to her mother—who beat her—Angelina placed Kitty with a "good Christian family" known for being kind to its servants. When Kitty came back to the Grimké family, now more mature and a believing Christian, Angelina returned her to her mother. Kindness, she told Polly, was more than just a word used by well-meaning ministers in Sunday sermons.

Angelina may have learned from Sarah to abhor slavery, and she may well have inherited her religious rebellion from her older sister, but the two were quite distinct in other, more personal ways. While historians often group them together—as "the Grimké sisters"—Sarah and Angelina Grimké in fact looked at the world rather differently. Sarah was emotional, whereas Angelina showed extraordinary calm; Sarah was haunted by self-doubt and feelings of inadequacy, whereas Angelina was self-confident, rebellious, and strong-willed. "[Angelina] was neither so demonstrative nor so tender in her feelings as her elder sister," Catherine Birney later wrote, "and her manner being more dignified and positive, she inspired, even in those nearest to her, a certain degree of awe which forbade, perhaps, the fulness of confidence which Sarah's greater gentleness always invited."

Birney's description of the differences between Sarah and Angelina, though insightful, is incomplete. For as Sarah nursed her father in Philadelphia and New Jersey, Angelina struck out on her own—without, however, having to journey anywhere. Finally free of her sister's influence and emotional hold, Angelina set out on a path that, while influenced by Sarah's in many ways, was also strikingly different. Sarah's introspection and her search for personal salvation found opposites in Angelina's impatience and frustration over her inability to change the world around her. Where Sarah always sought to correct herself—to be more devout, prayerful, and religious—Angelina was always correcting others. Slowly, inexorably, the two grew apart, even as they learned in a way to complement each other. While their public life as famous abolitionist sisters still lay many years in the future, the pattern of their collaboration was well established by the second decade of the nineteenth century.

Even in Charleston, at this early date, Sarah and Angelina Grimké were known as "the Grimké sisters." They were intelligent, strong-willed, and independent.

It is a common pitfall of historians to read meanings into the past that might not have been obvious at the time. Yet in 1819, Angelina's maturity and complex personality began to emerge from the shadow cast by her sister. It would be many years before Angelina would fully take up Sarah's former position as mentor, but the process had already begun. In time, Sarah Grimké would be acknowledged as one of the leading reform thinkers of her age, but her sister Angelina would always be remembered as a crusader.

———

John Faucheraud Grimké died on August 8, 1819, in a small room in the Fish Tavern, overlooking the beach at Long Branch, New Jersey. It was a painful and difficult death, brought on by a debilitating and unknown disease. His body wasted away, his strength slowly ebbed, and his walks with his daughter through the fishing village of Long Branch became shorter and shorter, until they ended altogether and John Grimké was forced to stay in bed. After just a few weeks in New Jersey it was clear that his recovery was beyond hope, as he himself certainly must have known. He waged a valiant battle for life, but years later, in thinking back over this period, Judge Grimké's family would come to the uneasy understanding that when Dr. Physick had recommended that he "take the sea air," it was because he knew that his patient was dying and there was nothing he could do to stop it. It was also at that moment, his family realized, that John Grimké must have concluded that his fate was decided. While he could not know exactly when death would claim him, he resolved to follow his doctor's advice, though it meant he would never set foot in his beloved South Carolina again. He made his choice: he would die not with his family but with his daughter, his most beloved child, by his side.

John Grimké's decision to die in Long Branch, New Jersey, instead of Charleston, South Carolina, was extraordinary. But in understanding why he made this choice, we find clues as to why Sarah and Angelina eventually shunned their native society and its customs to make their own journey north. The world that John Grimké had known was changing. Most of his sons had already left home and begun their own careers. Thomas was now a prominent lawyer in Charleston, John was a doctor, and Benjamin was in Ohio, where he had embarked on a distinguished career as a jurist. The rest of the boys would surely follow in their footsteps. Everyone was well cared for. John Grimké's other daughters were also leading their own lives, marrying and raising their own families. He did not worry about them. His only concern was for Sarah, the daughter he loved most of all. He had once observed that of all of his children, she had the sharpest mind—that if she had been a man, she would have made a great lawyer. John Grimké loved his wife, and he missed her during his time in Philadelphia, but their last years together had been a trial. Polly seemed less and less capable of handling the demands of everyday life. The constant responsibility of raising children and managing a household had taken its toll on the marriage, and she and her husband had grown apart.

John Grimké may have determined to break, finally, with his past—or perhaps he simply wished to spend his last weeks alone with his own thoughts and with a daughter who could share them. Yet in his decision to spend the final months of his life away from his family, we can see a prefigurement of Sarah and Angelina's own search for freedom, and of their own intellectual independence. While scholars, historians, and family chroniclers have been puzzled by the stark break that would divide Sarah and Angelina from the rest of the Grimkés in the years that followed, the sisters' commitment to public service did not emerge full-flowered from the seeds of their own experience; rather, their independence was the result of what they had learned from their father.

John Faucheraud Grimké was a man of great accomplishment and prodigious intellect. Like most other white men of his time and region, Judge Grimké was a landowner, a slaveholder, and a defender of a system that he not only got rich off but also had helped to establish. He never rejected the system or publicly questioned it, but neither is there any hint that he ever defended it as unstintingly as his peers. A believer in the Republic, he did defend the creation of a strong federal structure when others in South Carolina viewed themselves as separate and distinct, a nation unto themselves. John Grimké was proud to be a South Carolinian, but he thought of himself first as an American. He had shared in the birth of the Republic, he had been there to watch Cornwallis surrender at Yorktown, he had befriended Benjamin Franklin, he knew a bit of the world, and he saw America as a unique experiment that, in all crises, must remain united as one nation.

John Grimké was a nationalist in an era when American nationalism was seen by Charleston's intellectual elite as merely a clever conceit that was already becoming passé. The city's aristocracy viewed its privileges and status as special, even God-given, but John Grimké was an exception: he knew better. His grandfather had been a man with a German accent from a French province who came to America with nothing. John Grimké remembered him and would not deign to believe that somehow, out of all others, the Grimkés had been born special. His family was wealthy because its members had worked hard, and he was among the leaders of Charleston's society because that was where his hard work had placed him. Heredity and good breeding meant a great deal, but he knew that riches, possessions, and status were not God-given; they were earned. It was because of this that Judge John Grimké was uncomfortable with the sectionalism preached by Charleston's hereditary upper class, whose philosophical basis—the notion that the elite was chosen by God—was becoming a political fad among the city's leading families. In fact, we can detect in Sarah's father a hint of the same despair that haunted Thomas Jefferson, a man of the same generation, experience, and upbringing.

Grimké shared Jefferson's "extraordinary capacity to sound like an enlightened reformer while upholding the interests of the slave class" (in the words of a twentieth-century historian). The charge is true as stated, for like Jefferson's, Grimké's views on slavery were stereotypically racist. He undoubtedly agreed with Jefferson's judgment regarding what Southerners called the "peculiar institution": "My opinion has ever been that, until more can be done for them [the slaves], we should endeavor with those whom fortune has thrown on our hands, to feed and clothe them well, protect them from all ill usage, require such reasonable labor only as is performed voluntarily by freemen, & be led by no repugnancies to abdicate them, and our duties to them," Jefferson wrote in defense of his position. "The laws do not permit us to turn them loose, if that were for their good: and to commute them for other property is to commit them to those whose usage of them we cannot control."

Unfortunately, Jefferson's words and Grimké's thinking projected emancipation far into the future, when slaveholders would of their own will first educate and then free their slaves. Pressed to predict when exactly the slaves would be freed, Jefferson said he could do nothing but hope for the future: "The concerns of each generation are their own care," he maintained. It is unlikely, of course, that Judge Grimké spent his last weeks reflecting on the nature of slavery; yet there is a sense, unspoken but clearly intimated in the diary kept by his daughter Sarah during her father's long illness, of his dissatisfaction with his own life—as if he understood that something was left undone. If that is true, he was likely the only one who believed it. From relatively modest origins as the grandson of a silversmith, John Grimké had risen to the highest court of his state. He was a widely respected, even beloved, friend and companion to all he met, and a prudent, humble, and well-spoken leader of his community. He was a political giant among his peers, one of the leading men of his state and time.

But he was also independent-minded, and he set out along his own path. While he accumulated wealth and earned his position, his children's lives testified to his values. Tenacious in his religious beliefs, dedicated to his family, and imbued with the values of his culture, John Grimké subtly broke with his peers when he debated points of law with his daughter, refused to punish her for reading and learning, and diligently scolded her for and then ignored her wish to teach slaves the alphabet. Four months after Grimké's death, at the age of seventy, his compatriot Thomas Jefferson (six years Grimké's senior) wrote to John Adams to query him on whether Missouri should be admitted to the Union as a slave state or a free state. The question was then being debated nationally, raising the "awful specter" of civil war. The Missouri controversy reawakened in Jefferson a sense of the betrayal of American idealism that was manifest in slavery; it was, he said, like hearing a "firebell in the night." There is little doubt that Judge John Faucheraud Grimké—lawyer, planter, civic leader, and slaveholder—heard that same bell.

———

Up to the very moment of her father's death, Sarah Grimké desperately attempted, as if through sheer force of will, to nurse him back to health. She planned and prepared his meals; she monitored his exercise; she attended to his every need. When he could no longer feed himself, she fed him. She changed his sheets and his clothes; she bathed him and prayed with him. In early August 1819, when he slipped into a coma, she still refused to give up hope for his recovery and devoted herself to prayer with a greater fervor than ever before. Her father, regaining consciousness only for fitful periods during the last week of his life, saw her in continuous attendance. He cautioned her against hoping for miracles: "Do not indulge vain hopes my child," he said. "I no longer expect recovery nor do I desire it." These words brought an overwhelming end to Sarah's hopes, though throughout the trial she retained her faith.

Two days before his death John Grimké regained consciousness for long enough to talk with his daughter and urge her to leave his bedside, if only to have some respite from her constant attention. At first she refused to go, but he insisted. She walked away from the boardinghouse distraught, but she was finally convinced that her father's death was imminent. Judge Grimké died as he wished, honorably and without complaint, slipping into death in the midst of sleep, with his daughter at his side. In his last weeks, he reaffirmed his religious faith, expressing his belief to his daughter that the flight of his soul would give him his final rest. He was an exhausted man, ravaged by ill health but drained also by his responsibilities.

John Grimké was buried in Long Branch, without the services that would have been accorded him by Saint Philip's Church. In Charleston, Judge Grimké's casket would have been accompanied by his family, all dressed in mourning black. The cortege would have been followed by South Carolina's political leadership, and then by the heads of the families of the upper class to which he belonged. His slaves would have remained at home, except for those few attending to the family at the funeral. A smaller and more private service in the slave church would have remembered the master as a good and kindly man. In Charleston, John Grimké would have been interred alongside his father and mother in the family plot, his grave adorned by a simple headstone. One week after his death, his life would have been extolled in a funeral oration that would be recalled, and repeated, for years after. His sons would have been seated in the front row at the Old Exchange Building as Judge Grimké's colleagues memorialized his service to them, their city, their state, and their country.

The funeral in Long Branch was quite different. Sarah Grimké had made a few friends during her short time in Philadelphia and New Jersey, and they helped her through the burial, but she was otherwise alone. John Grimké was buried, modestly and with little public comment, in the small graveyard of the Long Branch Methodist Church. A local minister uttered words of kind assurance and quoted Scripture, but the ceremony lacked pomp and stature. Few present had known her father. As his casket was lowered into the freshly dug grave, a hot sea breeze blew over the town. The service was short and simple, and when it was over, Sarah retired to the Fish Tavern alone. A few days later, having notified

her mother in South Carolina of her husband's death, Sarah Grimké returned to Philadelphia, where she again took up residence at the Quaker
boardinghouse. She could have booked immediate passage to Charleston, but instead she stayed in Philadelphia for a time to gather her
thoughts and mourn in private.

Sarah did not sail for Charleston until November, three months after
her father's death. It was a momentous journey. During her passage, she
befriended a Quaker family and a charismatic and articulate Quaker
minister named Israel Morris. She was drawn to Morris's powerful personality and impressed by his success as a Philadelphia businessman, devout Christian, father of eight, and influential thinker. His ideas, which
paralleled her own, were compelling and simply stated. He appeared to
have no vices, spoke and dressed modestly, and adhered to a discipline of
self-denial and service to others, a hallmark of the Society of Friends.
Outgoing without being forward, he was unfailingly polite and listened
quietly to the opinions of others. Most important, he seemed to care
about Sarah's ideas and found in her a ready intellectual companion and
avid listener.

While drawn to Morris's ideas and complimented by his attention,
Sarah was initially repelled by his religion and struggled to understand
why it so appealed to him. She admired the Quakers' adherence to their
social principles (their simplicity of manners and dress, their refusal to
argue or proselytize) but questioned their religious doctrines. They were
exotic, hard to comprehend, complex and alien. Sarah seemed most put
off by the Quaker tenet that spiritual truth could be obtained through
self-examination—even though it was precisely the same doctrine she
had adopted for herself, as evidenced by her years of personal searching.
Sarah was also intimidated by the Quakers' belief in public demonstra-
tions of spiritual devotion and by the fact that personal, spontaneous
"utterances of spirit" were required during their weekly meetings. She
had never spoken in public or been overwhelmed by religious inspiration, and she could not imagine a woman's being expected to testify publicly to her most private religious views. Not only was the tradition alien;
it seemed improper, a contravention of the customs and strictures of
proper society.

Despite these qualms on Sarah's part, during the week-long journey to
Charleston, she and Israel Morris became friends. He did not expect her
to become a Quaker, of course, but he asked her to think about the subjects they had talked about and elicited a promise from her that she

would write to him from time to time. He told her that if she ever returned to Philadelphia to visit, or to stay, she was welcome in his home. Near the end of the journey, Morris gave her a copy of the memoirs of John Woolman, a Quaker minister known for his outspoken criticism of slavery and his apostolic message of salvation through personal liberation. Sarah promised Morris that she would read the book and then write to him with her impressions.

———

The home to which Sarah returned in Charleston had been transformed by the death of its master. It was only after his loss that his family realized how much he had been at the center of their lives. Sarah's mother was unable to cope with his death or manage the disposition of the family property. Her impatience with the house servants had not abated, and she was more temperamental than ever. The Grimké brothers, many of whom had their own families and concerns, were of little help.

The strangeness of Sarah's homecoming, though she had been gone for only six months, was matched by the distance she felt from Angelina. While the young girl still referred to her as "Mother," she was less dependent on Sarah now and insisted on making her own decisions. She had struck out on her own in her sister's absence. The two remained close, but distance, time, and the death of their father had changed their relationship. Angelina was still a young girl, only fourteen, while Sarah's nursing of her father through his darkest moments had matured her in ways that she could not have imagined before. Ironically, Sarah's childhood companion, Thomas, seemed to be the only one in the family capable of giving her the guidance she needed as she continued to wrestle with her religious beliefs.

Thomas and Sarah would talk for hours after her return from Philadelphia, just as they had as children. Many of their discussions revisited their most cherished subjects: the nature of God, society, the future of the South, and the terrible crucible of slavery. Sarah was disappointed that Thomas's ideas had not changed; he still argued that slaves were not prepared for emancipation and that to give them their freedom while they retained an inferior economic and social status would be a horrific cruelty. He did not defend slavery, or Southern nationalism, but like many Southerners of his generation, he was incapable of envisioning a society without servants, plantations without field hands, or a democracy without an educated, rich, landed, and white elite.

After many hours of discussion, however, Thomas pledged to his sister that he would try to do something about slavery, even if he could not agree with her contention that the South's slaves should be freed. He had already taken steps in this direction, he told Sarah proudly: while she was in Philadelphia, he had helped to organize the Charleston chapter of the American Colonization Society, an organization founded in 1816 to purchase slaves and resettle them in Africa. The society commanded national attention both through the stature of its founders, who included Supreme Court Chief Justice John Marshall, Kentuckian Henry Clay, and President James Madison, and because of its then-progressive goals. Thomas Grimké became one of its chief defenders and a firm believer in its central philosophy, which held that the slaves should eventually be freed, but also that free blacks and whites could never live side by side in America in peace. By 1820, when Thomas and Sarah were consumed by their conversations on the subject, the American Colonization Society was the most widely accepted vehicle for antislavery sentiment in the nation. Its organizers printed thousands of educational pamphlets, solicited donations from leading philanthropists, recruited a wide-ranging network of supporters, gained the endorsement of legislatures, churches, and Southern planters, and hired relocation agents to begin the work of resettlement.

Sarah's response to Thomas's defense of the American Colonization Society is not known, but it is likely that after hours of discussion with her brother, she began to form a critical response to the society's central idea that whites and blacks could not live together. She believed then, and later, that this tenet was no more than an expression of simple "color prejudice," as she called it. Blacks and whites *could* live together; slavery, no matter how unjust, proved that. Moreover, the prospect of the separation of the races was un-Christian.

Sarah Grimké's ideas were not new. The nascent abolitionist movement saw the American Colonization Society's program as nothing more than an extension of slavery's central crisis: white Americans simply did not believe that black Americans were equal. At best, the society was a well-intentioned monstrosity that in practice would amount to little; at worst, it was a thin veil designed to cover the guilt-ridden consciences of slaveholders. The master-slave relationship, the abolitionists believed, was not the result of a complex economic formula that could somehow be made right through the eradication of black faces in a white population, but a reflection of America's fundamental intolerance. The problem was not that there were black people in America, but that there were slave-holders here.

The disagreement over the American Colonization Society's mission was not, then, merely a dispute about the institution of slavery, or even about whether black people should remain in America. At its heart, the controversy over the program was about national identity; it was about who Americans really were. Black people were different, the society's founders believed, and so should be returned to their native lands. As Sarah later stated it, the trouble with the leaders of the American Colonization Society was that they refused to see what was obvious to her and had been nearly all her life: African Americans were not Africans at all, they were *Americans*. The formulation for Sarah was therefore quite simple. Shipping black Americans to Africa compounded the evil of slavery. It erased the evidence of the sin but not the sin itself; it legitimized the idea that one class of Americans could actually eradicate another.

Thomas and Sarah also engaged in long discussions about religion. Sarah's return to South Carolina reignited the crisis in her beliefs—a crisis that had only been exacerbated by the death of her father, her introduction to the Society of Friends, and the transformations that had taken place within her family. While she firmly put aside the "frivolities" that had so plagued her as a young woman, she was more confused and distracted than ever about her convictions. She felt inadequate, lonely, and incapable of making the simplest decisions. She knew that she had much to offer, but she was unable to find her life's work. Now well past the accepted marrying age, she was trapped by Southern custom, which dictated that an unmarried woman remain with her family—in her case, a family that she now looked on as a group of strangers. She feared she would never be at peace with her religious beliefs, though she questioned them obsessively. At first she believed that the death of her father had solidified her faith, but as time went on, she realized that this was not so. She plunged again into self-doubt and despair, an unhappy woman consigned to the life of a matron in an alien culture. She would later recall of this time:

Tears never moistened my eyes; to prayer I was a stranger. With Job I dared to curse the day of my birth. One day I was tempted to say something of the kind to my mother. She was greatly shocked, and reproved me seriously. I craved a hiding-place in the grave, as a rest from the distress of my feelings, thinking that no state could be worse than the present. Sometimes, being unable to pray, unable to command one feeling of good, either natural or spiritual, I was tempted to commit some great crime, thinking I could repent and thus restore my lost sensibility.

Soon after Sarah's return from the North, Polly Grimké became so worried about her daughter's mental state that she advised her to spend some time away from the family. She made arrangements for Sarah to live with her relatives in North Carolina, far from Charleston and its prying eyes. Sarah agreed to the change of scene, believing that by moving away, if only for a short time, she might well find the solace she so desperately needed. As she explained to her mother, she wanted to reflect on her life and plan what to do next. It had been ten years since Sarah began her prayerful search for the way of life that would suit her best, but despite these devotions, she had failed to find an answer. Now, in the wake of her father's death, the question of what she would do loomed larger than ever.

To the members of her family, who were witnesses to her ongoing spiritual crises, Sarah's trip to visit relatives in North Carolina provided a welcome respite from her disturbing emotional swings. They had tried everything they could think of to cheer her up, but nothing worked. When they told her that she should begin to enjoy life, she answered by saying that "by the sadness of countenance, the heart is made better"— an exasperating answer for a family that was desperately attempting to build a new life after the loss of its most constant guide. Her brother Thomas made light of her persistent self-doubt and her almost obsessive reflections on religion, but he, too, was disturbed by her behavior: "Thee had better turn Quaker, Sally; thy long face would suit well their sober dress," he teased.

———

Sarah Grimké arrived at her uncle James Smith's plantation on the Cape Fear River in North Carolina in the autumn of 1820, and was welcomed openly and lovingly by the Smith family. The plantation, in a then-rural part of the state, was cut off from nearly any settlement. The closest church was a Methodist meeting house where local parishioners gathered each Sunday for prayer and hymn singing. With this one exception, the concerns of Charleston's insulated upper-class society seemed far distant. Because of the small size of the Smith family and the routine of plantation work, Sarah was left with an enormous amount of time on her hands. Her only companion was her cousin Robert Barnwell Rhett, a highly intelligent, outspoken, and confident man whose political celebrity and controversial reputation were still many years off. Rhett and Sarah became friends, but his attentions were not constant. Sarah thought this was just as well; she needed time to think about how to shape her own future.

Among the many books she had brought with her to North Carolina was John Woolman's memoirs, given to her by Israel Morris. While she still rejected Quakerism (when her mother wondered if she might become a Quaker, she answered her firmly, "Anything but a Quaker or a Catholic!"), she remembered her time with Israel Morris fondly and appreciated the kindness shown her by the Quakers she had met in Philadelphia. For many days, then, she read from Woolman's memoirs. Slowly but certainly, the power of his message began to take hold of her. The more she read, the more she began to suspect that membership in the Society of Friends might provide a perfect outlet for her religious views and personal ambitions.

Woolman's memoirs tell the story of an exceptional man, one of the great progressive activists of early American history. Born into modest circumstances, Woolman was convinced of the evils of slavery and opened a tailor's shop in Mount Holly, New Jersey, to support himself and his family while he preached abolition. He traveled throughout the colonies, from New Hampshire to North Carolina, calling for an end to human bondage. His was a radical doctrine: he believed in the equality of all, regardless of color. The stark, almost shocking simplicity of his message commanded the attention of thousands of people. He was not always welcomed warmly in slave societies, but wherever he went, the passion of his beliefs and the intensity of his message drew crowds of listeners. Woolman's central theme was derived from the Gospels: he preached that slavery was incompatible with Christianity, that it was a sin. At the age of thirty-five, he began a journal of his travels, noting his frequent successes and even more common failures. Sarah was entranced by Woolman's simple words, which might well have been inscribed by her. His journey mirrored hers, his doubts were her doubts, his triumphs gave her hope.

Woolman worked diligently to bring his antislavery message into the

Society of Friends, some of whose members were slaveholders. By 1761, the message had begun to take hold. In that year, the Quakers expelled slaveholders from their ranks and promulgated a prohibition barring slave owners from their religion. One of the eighteenth century's true reformers, Woolman also worked to ban the sale of liquor to Native Americans, refused to eat sugar because it was a product of slave labor (a group of his disciples followed his example, launching one of the nation's first boycotts), and wore clothing made from undyed materials (fabric dyes, he said, were unhealthy for the textile workers who handled them). When his writings were published, they were adopted by the handful of organized abolitionists in the American colonies as their official testament, and they would remain, throughout the first part of the nineteenth century, a touchstone for early antislavery activists.

Woolman's book had a profound effect on Sarah Grimké. As a young man, Woolman admitted, he had fallen into "dark entertainments" (as Sarah would have described them) and been attracted to "wanton company." Eventually, however, he wrote, "I was brought seriously to consider my ways; and the sight of my backslidings affected me with sorrow." Woolman described his youth as a rejection of religion, though he knew in his heart that while he rejected God, "I was humbled before him." Every one of Woolman's words seemed aimed at Sarah, who had had many of the same experiences and feelings herself. As he wrote:

> In a while I resolved totally to leave off some of my vanities,
> but there was a secret reserve in my heart of the more refined
> part of them, and I was not low enough to find true peace.
> Thus for some months I had great trouble, there remaining in
> me an unsubjected will which rendered by labours fruitless,
> till at length through the merciful continuance of heavenly
> visitations I was made to bow down in spirit before the Lord.

Unlike Woolman, though, Sarah Grimké had not experienced the mystical, personal revelation that would forever turn her heart to the service of "His word." Still, she longed for the revelation, for a calling, and she began to believe that she might follow in Woolman's footsteps. She would leave her family, her home and state, and set off down the road to sermonize on the evils of slavery, just as he had done many decades before, when he left his business, wife, and children to become a "traveling minister of Jesus Christ."

After two months of reading and rereading Woolman's memoirs, Sarah felt revived. She returned to Charleston and immediately began attending Quaker services. Her mother was, of course, embarrassed by her actions and by the ridicule they sparked among family friends. But Polly did nothing to stop her daughter and even attempted to keep her criticism in check. Her daughter was well beyond her control, a grown woman who could make her own decisions. Sarah's brother Thomas supported her. He gave her books on Quakerism and talked with her about her new religion. Seeking answers to her deeper questions, Sarah wrote to Israel Morris, and they began a lively correspondence. When she wrote him that she might come to Philadelphia, he was enthusiastic and responded that he would gladly open his home to her. She was overjoyed at the prospect of leaving Charleston and increasingly convinced that she should become a Quaker. The Friends' simple rituals, the long and reflective silences of their services, and the personal testaments all had a powerful effect on her own religious views.

At last, when she least expected it, the personal call that Sarah had always hoped for came. Seated quietly in her room, by herself, she heard a voice calling to her, distant and indistinct at first, but then clearer and clearer, and speaking to her at any hour of the day. Finally, the voice gave her a command, instructing her to become a Quaker. She heard the same voice again and again, talking to her and giving her advice, guidance, and confidence. One day the message was overpowering: "Go north," the voice said. "Go north."

She obeyed.

THREE

"He trod the pulpit like a giant ..."

Americans everywhere were hearing voices. No one knew where they came from or when they started, but their call was distinct and unmistakable. Deep in the north woods of New York State, in an area that would become known to historians as the burned-over district (because its towns and villages were visited by the fires of so many religious revivals), men, women, and children began to hear voices calling them to godly service. In the West, itinerant preachers who heard voices gathered thousands together in rural fields to hear a new evangelical message with its call to repentance and service. In the South, where religion was a way of life, people who heard voices heeded the call to repent: they poured from their churches to be rechristened and to rededicate themselves to a life free of sin. Even in New England, staid and fearful since the days when fires burning those "possessed by the devil" had lit the night, ministers summoned their congregants to remake the nation and urged them to follow the "transcendent voice of reason."

Historians call this religious revolution the Second Great Awakening. Its embers were first kindled when the nation moved westward and its pioneers faced new hardships and tragedies on the American frontier. Religion has always been a fundamental part of the American experience, but in the second and third decades of the nineteenth century, its roots reached more deeply into the national psyche than at any time before or since. At the heart of the revival was the sure belief that God's words were written into every human soul, that an all-encompassing deity understood human suffering, and that the promise of salvation was open to all. The Second Great Awakening transformed the way Americans looked at God, and thus transformed the way they lived their lives.

America's first Great Awakening had taken place in the 1730s, during a time of spiritual regeneration. Itinerant preachers conducted open-air revivals for thousands of needy souls. These were new Americans, still under British rule and only recently aware of their uniqueness. They were land-hungry immigrants fearful of the wilderness; women frustrated by their subjugated roles; third and fourth sons whose meager inheritance meant removal to unknown lands; and men who, by the sweat of their unremitting labors, had to pull a living from the soil. Ministers urged their congregants to break away from society's constraints and build a personal relationship with God. People were consumed by this liberating vision. But there were doubters. In New England, stoic and traditional New England, the reaction to this new doctrine of easy salvation was swift and uncompromising. From his pulpit in Northampton, Massachusetts, Jonathan Edwards preached the absolute sovereignty of God, the indispensability of his authority, the autocracy of His grace, and the depravity of man. One could do nothing to change God's will, Edwards said. The fate of a person's soul, he preached, was not in his or her own hands, but in God's. He thundered against sin as his congregation wailed in agonized fits of fear and devotion. He announced that "though He will know that you cannot bear the weight of omnipotence treading upon you, yet He will not regard that, but He will crush you under his feet without mercy; He will crush out your blood, and make it fly, and it will be sprinkled on his garments so as to stain all his raiment. He will not only hate you, but He will have you in the utmost contempt."

Edwards, one of America's most powerful orators, shifted the focus of the Great Awakening from salvation to sacrifice, from the belief in eventual and inevitable redemption to a vision of a harsh and overarching deity whose blood-spattered robes reflected humankind's evil. The austere Puritan message he preached attracted crowds from all over the colonies. Many traveled hundreds of miles to hear his message, as if morbidly fascinated by the dark world he painted. Edwards's call for personal submission and sacrifice changed the way Americans thought about themselves. Many of our fundamental beliefs as a nation come from Edwards: our "work ethic," our sense of national destiny, our preoccupation with monetary success, our belief in the sanctity of family and home, and our obsession with being the first, the best, the greatest nation, and the leader in everything. Edwards was the original "fire and brimstone" preacher, mixing his pounding command to work and pray with a subtle yet unmistakable cynicism: one might be rich, and famous, and successful, he said, and one might even change one's wicked and sinful ways, but in the end, all of it still might mean nothing. His description of hell brought shrieks of despair out of his listeners; a woman in Edwards's congregation, convinced that she had not been born one of the "elect," even committed suicide.

The revolution that Edwards sparked found its counterpoint one hundred years later in the Second Great Awakening. Many reasons have been given for the religious revival that fired the minds of Americans in the early nineteenth century: the dangers that lay waiting in the expanding American territories; the harsh and unforgiving environment that destroyed crops; the sudden and merciless deaths of infants and children from unknown causes and of women in painful and unattended childbirth; the malicious march of disease, infection, and raging epidemics that swept through cities, towns, and villages. Such deaths, so common in that age of rudimentary and sometimes barbaric medical practices (fevers were treated with mercury, headaches with laudanum, pneumonia with scalding gauzes), turned ordinary people into psychological flagellants, into seekers of religious meaning and salvation. Sarah Grimké was hardly alone in her search for a life of religious devotion; for millions of Americans in the early nineteenth century, the need for redemption was as constant as the fear of death.

Perhaps the most important reason for the mass revivals that began in the early part of the century (the largest such revival attracted twenty-five thousand worshipers to Cane Ridge, Kentucky, in 1801, at the beginning of the Second Great Awakening) was a feeling of dissatisfaction with Puritan doctrines. Edwards's message had influenced America's pulpits for decades: there was no escape from God's judgment, for the fate of every soul was already decided. It did not matter how one lived; either one was one of God's "elect" or one was condemned to eternal damnation. But for millions of women who lost babies in childbirth or infancy, the thought that their lost children's souls might burn forever in the unquenchable fires of hell became too much to bear. In Kentucky, Alabama, and Tennessee, where the revival sank its first and deepest roots, women comprised the vast majority of the throngs that greeted the revivalists. Slowly and inexorably, Americans began to reject Edwards's beliefs, replacing his doctrine of the "elect" with one that emphasized personal salvation.

The embers stoked by the mass revival at Cane Ridge finally burst into flame when Charles Grandison Finney, a distinguished lawyer from Adams, a small village in upstate New York, began to preach a new message of individual salvation and universal emancipation from sin. Finney was an unlikely minister. A successful lawyer for many years, he had been raised in a family for which religion was only a passing interest. In 1819, however, he decided that he needed to learn something about the Bible, if only to determine what all this religious fuss was about. He began to attend services at the Adams Presbyterian Church, where he hoped that the local minister could guide him in his Bible study. He expected a creative and erudite explanation of the stories he read there, and a message crafted for the personal needs of the Presbyterian parishioners, but what he received instead was doctrine and ritual. It seemed to him that the minister knew less about the Bible than he did. He rebelled and in the middle of one sermon rose and announced to the congregation, "You have prayed enough since I have attended these meetings to have prayed the devil out of Adams. But here you are praying on and complaining still."

One day in 1821, just months after Sarah Grimké first heard her voice, Finney heard his. Finney's call to the ministry came on a blustery day when New York's trees were in their full autumn regalia. As he walked to his office, he heard a voice ask, "Will you accept salvation today?"

He stopped and answered, "Yes, I will accept it today or die in the attempt."

Instead of continuing on to his office, Finney went into the woods north of town, where he prayed. Another voice interrupted him, and he turned to see a "vision of a prideful heart." He broke into tears: "What! Such a degraded sinner as I am, on my knees confessing my sins to the great and bold God and ashamed to have a human being, and a sinner like myself, find me on my knees endeavoring to make my peace with my offended God." Returning to his workplace, Finney began to speak in tongues and then to sing. He pledged himself to the ministry and "wept aloud with joy and love." He went home, and when he came in to work the next day to see a client, he told him, "I have a retainer from the Lord Jesus Christ to plead his case and I cannot plead yours." With that,

Finney, a latter-day John Woolman, became a "traveling minister of Jesus Christ."

———

Over the next few decades, the story of the conversion of Charles Grandison Finney would become one of the best-known and most frequently repeated stories in America. His call to the ministry was cited by his followers as proof that God had granted a special dispensation not only to Finney and his congregation, but to America itself. Finney's conversion proved that God was not distant and unknowable, but an ever-present, unmediated, and palpable reality. If a well-meaning and honest lawyer in a nondescript town in the backwoods of a new nation could hear the call to salvation and prayer, *anyone* could. The more the story was repeated, the more legendary it became. Finney's message held out hope that a life of sin could be washed away through blunt honesty and self-abasement, and that rewards awaited those who lived lives of accomplishment and discipline. Here was a new religion for a new nation—public, plain-spoken, and open to all.

Just weeks after his conversion, Finney applied for a license to preach as a Presbyterian minister. After a few months of testing his message, he recruited like-minded preachers to his beliefs that salvation was open to all, that ministers who preached the cold, hard teachings of Jonathan Edwards should be condemned, and that sinners should be pursued in factories and fields, not only in churches. The Finneyites set northern New York ablaze with their declaration that salvation was personal, and with their angry condemnation and rejection of ministers who preached that Jesus had died for the sins only of some. Finney's doctrine was explosive and contentious. The more he and his followers renounced the black-cloaked Puritan ministers in their elevated pulpits, the more people roared their approval and flocked to hear the Finneyites preach. In Troy, New York, a Finneyite castigated one local minister by name while his parishioners sat silently approving: "You old, gray headed sinner, you deserved to be in hell long ago," he chided. Soon the message began to spread.

The movement took hold within months of Finney's calling. Hundreds were converted, then thousands. No one, not even the greatest skeptic, left one of Finney's revivals disappointed; his steel-blue eyes, flowing blond hair, imposing frame, and booming voice enthralled those who came to hear his words of hope for a "universal emancipation from sin." Finney was the most powerful orator of his time, as Jonathan Edwards had been of his. One of his followers would later recall Finney's commanding presence:

> While depicting the glories or the terrors of the world to come, he trod the pulpit like a giant. His action was dramatic. He painted in vivid colors. His gestures were appropriate, forcible, and graceful. As he would stand with his face towards the side gallery, and then involuntarily wheel around, the audience in that part of the house towards which he threw his arm would dodge as if he were hurling something at them. In describing the sliding of a sinner to perdition, he would lift his long finger towards the ceiling and slowly bring it down till it pointed to the area in front of the pulpit, when half his hearers in the rear of the house would rise unconsciously to their feet to see him descend into the pit below.

To his drama, Finney added a cult of the common man. He refused to dress in "priestly vestments" and urged his congregants to adopt a life of simplicity and self-denial. Serving as a symbol of this was the "Finney chair," in which sinners would sit for hours in personal anguish as their family and friends looked on. Finney exhorted and pleaded with the sinners to give up their sins, to wash their souls with confession, and to dedicate themselves to a "more useful life." In the midst of these trials women would faint, men would scream, and many, overcome by emotion, would cry out in ecstasy. His goal, he said, was to strip the world of sinners, but his sermons had a much different and more controversial impact: they began to strip established churches of their worshipers.

For this reason, the response to Finney's revival on the part of the traditional clergy was swift and uncompromising. In Troy, a minister urged his parishioners to treat Finney with "little more ceremony than an acknowledged outlaw." One Unitarian proclaimed it a "fact not to be denied or concealed that sound learning, eminent talents and persuasive eloquence, have all been thrown into the shade before the blazing coruscations of the wandering meteors which have shot athwart our moral system." In Connecticut, Lyman Beecher—whose family would do so much to define religion in America in the decades ahead (and whose daughter Harriet Beecher Stowe would write *Uncle Tom's Cabin* nearly thirty years later)—urged church leaders to take steps to counter Finney's teachings, lest his followers "roll back the wheels of time to semi-barbarism."

Finney's religion was an attack on order itself, Beecher argued, and could not be tolerated. "The importance of truth in religion," he stated, "as that which brightens our moral atmosphere, and makes our day, is perhaps more frequently admitted than the importance of order. Truth and order are viewed as if so distinct, as to possess almost nothing in common. What is this but to mistake them? They are near relations, and almost inseparable intimates!"

The power of Finney's message lay in the fact that it held out hope for a personal communication with God unmediated by the stultifying intervention of black-cloaked preachers. The ability to communicate directly with the dead, or with the deity, was a talisman of this message. Hearing voices might be considered odd, or unusual, but it was not viewed as preposterous. Thus, when Sarah Grimké wrote to Israel Morris about her voices, he urged her to listen closely to what the spirits around her were saying. She responded immediately and positively to his advice, asserting that she "saw and communed with spirits, and did not hesitate to acknowledge their influence and to respect their intimations." Her visions and dreams seemed so vivid and so powerful to her that she set them down in her diary. Morris continued to tutor her from afar, and his words gave her solace and strength. When a voice commanded her to travel to Philadelphia and abandon her past, she went; when a voice commanded her to be more devout, she obeyed; and when a voice commanded her to fight slavery, she did that, too.

———

Had she heard it in 1821, Finney's message would have held a particularly strong appeal for Sarah Grimké. But just months before Finney found God in the woods of northern New York, Sarah (accompanied by her widowed younger sister Anna Grimké Frost and her daughter, whose father had died unexpectedly and tragically in Charleston the year before), docked in Philadelphia. She fervently hoped that her prospective conversion to Quakerism and her new surroundings would free her to follow her heart. She knew that in leaving Charleston, she was abandoning her former life, perhaps forever. But she was also single-mindedly dedicated to being of some use to others. With her move to Philadelphia, Sarah believed that she had a chance to fulfill that dream. What she could not have known, or even guessed, was that the ministry of Charles Grandison Finney would eventually help her in that work and make an enormous impact on her life.

Sarah arrived in Philadelphia on May 15, 1821. She found lodgings for her sister Anna and her daughter in the city and then proceeded immediately to Green Hill Farm, Israel Morris's home. A kindly man and a widower with eight children, Morris welcomed Sarah as a member of his family. Although a respected and successful Philadelphia businessman, a responsible and doting father, and a devoted Quaker—outwardly the precise opposite of Sarah Grimké—Morris nevertheless had much in common with her. Like her, he was obsessed by the search for personal salvation and self-worth, though unlike her, he was neither paralyzed by that search nor plagued with doubts as to his own devoutness. On the contrary, his constant religious reflection seemed to give him an energy that Sarah lacked. Morris was a man of stature in his community, widely admired for his views and compassion, and while modest in his dress, as required by his religion, he had an outgoing and attractive personality. He was especially happy to have Sarah in his home, where she could help him look after his children, share his meals, and provide him with engaging and thoughtful companionship. Indeed, there was an immediate attraction between them.

Within a few days of her arrival, Sarah attended services at the Fourth and Arch Street Meeting of the Society of Friends. She befriended Israel's sister, Catherine Morris, who urged her to give herself wholly to the Quaker way of life. Sarah resisted making a final decision, however, out of anxiety over the period of testing that the Society of Friends required; despite the presence of the confident and supportive Israel Morris, she continued to harbor the same feelings of inadequacy that had haunted her during her years in Charleston. She agonized over how she might act during the probationary period, which she saw as an imposing test of her beliefs. She was especially apprehensive about the scrutiny that would be brought to bear on every element of her life. A Council of Elders, charged with making the final decision on her fitness for inclusion in the Society of Friends, would interrogate her on her religious convictions. She resented the idea of this intrusion into her private beliefs. While she wanted to become a Quaker, she told Catherine Morris, she did not want to have every aspect of her beliefs questioned, or every private part of her life opened to inspection.

In the midst of all this, in late 1821, Sarah received word of growing discord in the Grimké household in South Carolina. Her aging mother was becoming ever more impatient, petulant, and intolerant. The family missed the steadying hand of Judge John Grimké, and the status that his position had ensured. Polly felt isolated, ignored, overworked, and abandoned by her children. With her husband gone, the family name did not command the deference that she had once assumed it was owed. Sarah decided to return to Charleston to help her mother, but before she left, she made a startling public display of her faith: "On last Fifth Day [the fifth of the previous month]," she would write in her diary, "I changed my dress for the more plain one of the Quakers, not because I think making my clothes in a peculiar manner makes me any better, but because I believe it was laid upon me, seeing that my natural will revolted from the idea of assuming this garb. I trust I have made this change in the right spirit, and with a single eye to my dear Redeemer. It was accompanied by a feeling of much peace."

But if Sarah's change of dress brought her peace in Philadelphia, and brought joy to Catherine and Israel Morris, it brought only mirth in Charleston. She returned home after six months in the North determined to soothe the frayed nerves of her mother and to give Charleston one last try. But she did not cut her ties with the Morrises, a sure sign that she believed her sojourn in the South would be temporary. She resumed her charity work, taught Sunday School, and attended meetings, but nothing she did seemed to buoy her mother's spirits or improve her own strained relationship with her family. Within a few weeks she knew that her visit was a mistake: not only was her mother more nervous and irritable than before, but the constant comments about Sarah's Quaker dress, her "spinster" status, and her unfamiliar attitudes were nearly intolerable. She determined, therefore, to return to Philadelphia.

Although it would be another ten years before Sarah Grimké began to develop the political philosophy that would have such an enormous impact on the lives of thousands of women, her break with Charleston in 1821 marked the beginning of the end of her uncertainty and self-doubt. If she had not been immediately transformed by the experience of her exile in the North, Sarah Grimké had nonetheless become a new person in Philadelphia. After a season of hesitation, she set herself firmly on the difficult path that would lead her to become a Quaker minister. Year after year she would study diligently to master her new calling and to conquer her fear of speaking in public. It was, she later said, one of the most trying periods of her life. Her new religion required study and reflection; she found the work onerous and doubted her intellectual abilities. "Oh, had I received the education I desired, had I been bred to the profession of the law," she confided to her diary, "I might have been a useful member of society, and instead of myself and my property being taken care of, I might have been a protector of the helpless, and pleader for the poor and unfortunate."

Sarah Grimké's return to Philadelphia in 1822 coincided with the uncovering of what was intended to be the most dangerous and bloody slave rebellion in American history. The conspiracy, hatched in the African Church just outside Charleston, had its inception in a free black church in Philadelphia, where a minister preached "black Christianity," with its message that freedom was at the heart of all religions and slavery was a sin. Slowly, this doctrine of "black Christianity" found its way south, where it had an enormous influence on Charleston's small population of literate freed blacks. Because of its radical preachings, the African Church was barred to slaves and free blacks alike by Charleston's elite, but its most powerful congregant, a carpenter by the name of Denmark Vesey, ignored the ban and gathered recruits to kill white slaveholders. A huge man with a strong hold on his followers, Vesey was a natural revolutionary and a sophisticated and literate political thinker. He had purchased his freedom in 1800, but the emancipation did not extend to his children. The idea that they would grow up in South Carolina in chains filled him with bitterness.

Vesey believed that a clash of the races was inevitable and that the growing controversy over slavery in the North, and the glimmerings of the new abolitionist movement, presaged a conflict between slaveholders and antislavery activists that would end in blood. Any attempt at compromise, he said, would simply postpone the unavoidable contest between blacks and whites in the South. To hurry it along, Vesey recruited a group of followers from his church. One of them had access to a public storehouse in Charleston from which pistols and rifles could be stolen; another had the keys to the city stables, providing the rebels with a ready supply of horses on which to escape the city after terrorizing its inhabitants. The city arsenal, virtually unguarded, was within walking distance of the storehouse, and Vesey believed he could get more guns from there after his insurrection began. Slowly his plans began to take shape and his ring of conspirators grew.

In on the plot were a number of domestic servants, including those of South Carolina's governor, Thomas Bennett. In public, the Bennett house slaves were prominent symbols of slavery's claim to Christian paternalism; they were, as the governor himself later said, a "part of the family." But more than a few of them were willing participants in the Vesey conspiracy and, family or not, were fully prepared to do unto the Bennetts as the Bennetts had, undoubtedly, done to them. One talked casually of murder and rape, later testifying that "when we have done with the fellows, we know what to do with the wenches." Vesey encouraged such hatred, believing it to be the only means he could use to wean his followers from their masters. Charleston's house servants posed the greatest threat to the plot, for they lived better than the field hands. Their ties to their masters, Vesey feared, might make them hesitate or even betray the cause.

The Vesey-led uprising was set to begin on a summer Saturday night, when Charleston would be filled with black families who came into the city from the outlying districts to sell their masters' crops. But Vesey was forced to move up the date of the rebellion by almost a month, from July 2—when the city would be most crowded (in anticipation of the Independence Day celebration)—to June 14. He was concerned lest word of his plot be made public; already there were reports that slave violence would mar Charleston's Independence Day celebration. Such rumors were not uncommon, and sometimes they were not unfounded: three slave plots had already been discovered in South Carolina since the turn of the century. In 1805, a slave plot had been uncovered in Columbia, and in 1816, two planned insurrections had been exposed in Camden and Ashepoo. Vesey knew that Charlestonians were on guard and that his rebellion would surely fail unless he and his followers could achieve complete surprise. There had already been one scare, in May of 1822, just a month before Vesey was to put his plan into motion, when three house servants who knew of the plot told their masters that an insurrection targeting the white population of Charleston was in the works. After an investigation in which one of Thomas Bennett's house servants was named as a conspirator, the city fathers dismissed the report, convinced that the informers were lying.

The men of Charleston's upper class simply could not bring themselves to believe that their slaves would kill them and rape their wives and daughters. Although fears of slave insurrections were commonplace (especially after the 1816 plots), there had been little actual trouble with the slaves of Charleston. The only note of disquiet had come when Congress debated the Missouri Compromise, but even that crisis had eventually passed. South Carolina's John Calhoun believed that the debates of 1820 had resolved the question of slavery forever, by giving Congress the right to regulate slavery in the territories (which meant, as Calhoun understood it, that slavery could be extended) while at the same time protecting the practice in the South. But South Carolinians could not fail to notice the increase in the number of black faces in Charleston and in the state's growing up-country cities. In 1820, for the first time ever, blacks in South Carolina outnumbered whites.

Vesey's plot matured. Relying on a charismatic voodoo minister named Gullah Jack to help keep his recruits in line, Vesey bullied and strengthened the will of his followers. He urged them on by reading them passages from Exodus and talking about what it would be like for them to live as free men and women after the revolt. But three days before his planned insurrection, Vesey was arrested along with most of his followers. As he suspected, a black house servant had betrayed his plan to the authorities, giving them the details and specifying the timing of the attack. The servant's testimony provided overwhelming evidence against Vesey.

Charleston's mayor and the governor called out the militia and began to round up the plotters. On June 17, a special court of five citizens was convened to investigate the conspiracy and try those involved. Vesey proclaimed his innocence. Over the next five weeks, 117 black conspirators would be arrested, and evidence would be gathered against seventy-nine of Vesey's followers. When the extent of the plot was reported to the public, on June 28, the white community was horrified. Vesey was condemned to death; in sentencing him, the court said that he had intended to "trample on all laws, human and divine; to riot in blood, outrage, rapine and conflagration, and to introduce anarchy and confusion in their most horrid forms."

A few white South Carolinians protested. William Johnson, a U.S. Supreme Court justice, doubted there had been any conspiracy at all. He noted that just a few years before Vesey's supposed plot, mass hysteria had swept through parts of South Carolina's Edgefield District, where fears of a slave insurrection had resulted in the lynching and murder of black South Carolinians. Those few who agreed with Johnson's assertion that the plot had been manufactured by whites wanting to "strike terror into the heart of every slave" were silenced by the outraged reaction to reports of the Vesey Conspiracy. Denmark Vesey went to the gallows on July 2, and four weeks later, twenty-two more convicted conspirators were hanged in a mass execution. The African Methodist Episcopal Church in Charleston, where Vesey had taught Sunday school, was slated for destruction.

The Vesey Conspiracy inaugurated a season of uncertainty and violence. Slave regulations were tightened in Charleston and all across the South, while in the North, agitation for emancipation grew. Ohio's legislature adopted a resolution condemning slavery, making it the first state to take that stand, and the American Colonization Society began a national fund-raising campaign to send newly emancipated slaves to Africa. Emboldened by the Ohio resolution, a courageous but otherwise undistinguished newspaper published by Benjamin Lundy began to editorialize on the evils of slavery and the sins of slaveholders. Even Charles Grandison Finney, in the midst of building his revival movement, called on his followers to "aim to be useful" in the fight for the souls of slaves. Finney himself was not an abolitionist, and he firmly cautioned his followers against using their belief in personal salvation to further any political cause, but his words made an impact. Many Finneyites began to translate their leader's call into a campaign against the sin of holding humans in bondage. In Charleston, meanwhile, the horror of the Vesey Conspiracy began to subside, to become, by the middle of the 1820s, little more than a fading memory. Life went on as before, though many Charlestonians continued to wonder whether the mysterious fires that struck a number of the city's businesses in the years following Vesey's execution were set by his followers.

Sarah Grimké was appalled by Vesey's execution and by the increasing violence that she saw in Southern society. She condemned slavery and slaveholders openly and publicly in Charleston. Charlestonians, including many of the Grimké family's closest friends, now viewed her move to Philadelphia as being less a matter of religious conversion than an implicit condemnation of their way of life. There is no question that Sarah was more comfortable in the North. Not only was there a burgeoning free black community in Philadelphia, but Northern women were freer to live their own lives. Some such women, albeit very few, even had their own careers, independent of the wishes of their husbands and contrary to the customs of their society. Sarah needed to look no further than her own Quaker meeting to find women who were leading productive and meaningful lives, among them Lucretia Coffin Mott, one of the most highly respected Quaker ministers in the nation and an outspoken public defender of women's rights and black emancipation.

Sarah admired Mott and tried to emulate her. But the public obligations of Quakerism, including the requirement that members stand "in meeting" and avow the power of God in their own lives, still intimidated her. Sarah was shy and soft-spoken by nature, and her public pronouncements sounded halfhearted and confused. The elders at the Fourth and Arch Street Meeting thought her words shallow and indirect. She sensed their disapproval, but she could not change how she felt, and she found it nearly impossible to conquer her fear of professing her beliefs in front of others. Despite this, she had made enormous progress during her time in Philadelphia; she was now committed to becoming a Quaker minister, and she did not "sit down in meeting in a cold and indifferent state," as she had done when she first entered the Philadelphia congregation. After two years, her commitment to becoming a minister remained undiminished, despite the lack of confidence expressed by the meeting's elders.

Throughout Sarah's first and most difficult years in Philadelphia, Israel and Catherine Morris remained her loyal friends and supporters. They were unfailing allies in her religious goals; they had faith in her abilities. Sarah moved into Catherine's house but was a frequent visitor at Israel's home. She loved his children and viewed his family as her own, caring for the children when they were sick and tutoring them in their studies. She was their constant companion, their surrogate mother. Although her progress toward the ministry was slow and uncertain (she waited vainly to hear the voice of God command her to "rise and speak" in meeting), she found joy in the domestic simplicities of Green Hill and in the plain but homey atmosphere of the Morris house in Philadelphia. She continued to be an eager student and a voracious reader, and she committed her views and beliefs to the pages of her diary nearly every night.

As Sarah spent years in study, contemplation, and learning the ways of the Quakers, she cannot have failed to notice Israel's increasing attentions. She thought him a handsome and appealing man. She was interested in him intellectually and impressed by his kindness, his gentle nature, and his concern for her well-being. She was attracted to him in a way she had never been to any other man, and she looked forward to his visits, confessing to her diary, "I struggle against feelings and temptation

I blush to think of." On September 16, 1826, Israel Morris proposed marriage, but Sarah, confused about her own feelings and focused on her religion, turned him down. It was one of the most difficult decisions she had ever had to make. She was in love with him, but felt inadequate and incapable of returning his affections. Deep down, she was frightened of the responsibilities of marriage: "That was a day of solemn heartfelt supplication that nothing might intervene between me and my God," she wrote. "To the individual there was sufficient attachment, but my soul shrunk from the fearful responsibility of such a situation."

Sarah would have been a wonderful mother to Israel's children, and a loving and caring wife to him. But she feared the obligations that marriage would place on her, including the physical contact it would require. She shrank from such intimacy. She also believed that if she wed, she would end up putting her personal search aside and would find herself trapped by the constraints of marriage, childbirth and child rearing, and keeping a home. Love might conquer all, but Sarah Grimké did not think it could ever replace the goals she had set for herself. Despite her uncertainties about the future, she had not abandoned her dream of becoming a Quaker minister. And secretly, she harbored even larger dreams, of becoming a lawyer or, barring that (it was still, as she well knew, a profession closed to women), a teacher or even a scholar. In 1826, for the first time in her life, Sarah Grimké had finally won the independence she had longed for as a child, and she was beginning to develop the sophisticated political philosophy that would lead, eventually, to her being recognized as one of America's first feminists. At the root of her thinking was the unquestioned belief that in order to accomplish great things (something she herself desperately wanted to do), women had to remain unencumbered by men, children, and marriage. Of all of these, marriage was the greatest temptation; Sarah called it the "snare of Satan." Gerda Lerner, Sarah Grimké's most admiring and most insightful biographer, would identify her deciding to reject Israel Morris's proposal as the moment at which her religious convictions and her political philosophy became fused. It was at this point that her renunciation of personal love was married to her commitment to a life of service to God. As Lerner notes, at the heart of both was Sarah Grimké's deep belief in the efficacy of self-denial:

> Conventional marriage [Sarah believed] meant the lifelong subordination of the woman. Perhaps an unusually strong emotional attachment might have overcome her reluctance, as

it did that of other early feminists. Why her attachment to Israel Morris was not strong enough, must remain a matter for speculation. Perhaps his conservatism and orthodoxy reinforced Sarah's lingering doubts regarding her choice of him. Perhaps he failed to live up to the masculine ideal represented by her father and brother. Perhaps he was indeed the one great love of her life. But after years of practice, resignation came more easily to Sarah than the acceptance of her feelings. Renunciation was the one mode of living she had long practiced; it was—so she had been taught—the road to lasting happiness. No novice nun ever tried harder to make herself a saint. No slave ever proclaimed more loudly the advantages of the chains that bound her.

Sarah Grimké assumed the mantle of spinsterhood for the same reason she had earlier put on the unassuming dress of a Quaker woman: not because she wanted to, but because she did *not* want to. For her, love of God was abhorrence of the self. Happiness was put aside; it was a privilege that could be denied. To deny her love for one man was, for her, to admit her love for God. She conceded as much in her diary: "I have found it very hard work to give him up, had I never known of his love, I did not covet it, it was bestowed to my astonishment for I am unworthy of it. I have even thought if death had taken him from me I could more easily have yielded." Here, as in other instances, Sarah Grimké's diary provides the best evidence of her feelings. For many years after, she would circle September 26, the anniversary of the day Israel Morris proposed to her. She rarely mentioned him by name in her diary, and when she slipped and did, she went back and scratched it out, as if suppressing a great loss. But Israel Morris did not give up. After the shock of Sarah's rejection had subsided (for he seemed confident that she would agree to his proposal), they agreed to remain friends. He bided his time, believing that he could eventually win her over. The match, he was certain, was inevitable, fated.

Sarah felt she could not remain in Philadelphia. While she did not regret her decision not to marry Israel Morris, she thought the temptation of sharing her life with him and his family would be too great to resist. She feared she might accept his next proposal, for it was clear that he had not given up his pursuit. She even went so far as to admit that her rejection might have been ill conceived: "It is a beautiful theory, but my experience belies it, that God can be all in all to man," she later confessed to her diary. "There are moments, diamond points in life, when God fills the yearning soul, and supplies all our needs, through the richness of his mercy in Christ Jesus. But human hearts are created for human hearts to love and be loved by, and their claims are as true and as sacred as those of the spirit."

When a letter arrived from her sister Angelina in late 1827, Sarah had the excuse she needed to leave the Morrises and her other Quaker friends behind. Angelina wrote of her own religious doubts and her decision to leave the Episcopal Church. Sarah immediately booked passage to Charleston, eager to flee Philadelphia and Morris. She arrived in South Carolina on November 22 aboard the *Langdon Cheves*, named for the lawyer who had tutored her older brother Thomas just ten years before. She noted in her diary, "Landed this morning in Charleston, and was welcomed by my dear mother with tears of pleasure and tenderness, as she folded me once more to her bosom. My dear sisters, too, greeted me with all the warmth of affection. It is a blessing to find them all seriously disposed, and my precious Angelina one of the Master's chosen vessels. What a mercy!"

FOUR

"... and blood flowed in streams"

I t was an age of giants. While Sarah Grimké struggled to embrace the rituals and culture of her new religion, Henry Clay, Daniel Webster, and John Calhoun dominated the nation's political life. Henry Clay had authored the famous Missouri Compromise in 1820, then struggled to hold the nation together in its wake, hoping that the agreement had settled the question of slavery forever. In fact, it had done no such thing. "God has given us Missouri," Virginian John Randolph thundered, "and the devil shall not take it from us." In Randolph's opinion, the compromise showed that Yankees were "weak-minded" and that the North would never stand up against Southerners. The Quaker abolitionist editor Elihu Embree disagreed. "Hell is about to enlarge her borders and tyranny her domain," he warned when he learned of Clay's compromise.

In the early 1820s, the first mass-circulation pamphlets calling for slavery's abolition appeared in the North. In 1821, in Ohio, Benjamin Lundy, a diminutive, partially deaf, and indifferently educated former harness maker and devout Quaker, began publishing the *Genius of Universal Emancipation*, the first newspaper to focus on the question of slavery. His ambition had been fired by the sight of slaves being held in Virginia, in chains and slave pens, on their way to bondage further south. The sight "grieved my heart" and "the iron entered my soul," he wrote in explaining his conversion to the abolitionist crusade. Outspoken and controversial in his hatred of slavery, Lundy was a powerful public speaker. Like John Woolman before him, he traveled the countryside as a Quaker prophet, lecturing on the evils of human bondage. He personally broke the bonds of dozens of slaves by convincing their masters to set them free. On the masthead of his newspaper appeared the motto "Let Justice Be Done Though the Heavens Should Fall." Ironically, while Lundy could paint vivid pictures of slavery's evil for his audience, he was not an absolutist and agreed with Clay that its eradication could be and should be gradual.

By the middle of the 1820s, the emancipation movement had taken on an international character. In Great Britain, members of Parliament began considering how best to ban slavery, while British activists mounted a national campaign that energized millions of people in support of immediate emancipation. The British antislavery movement in turn galvanized American abolitionists, who began to call more publicly for emancipation. But despite such growing sentiment, throughout the 1820s the vast majority of American abolitionists agreed with Lundy that emancipation must be gradual, well planned, and rational—not immediate. Benjamin Lundy and men and women like him who abhorred slavery might be committed to the idea that "justice" should be "done," but very few of them really wanted the heavens to fall.

All of that changed, however, in 1828, when Lundy visited Boston on one of his many fund-raising forays. While there he met William Lloyd Garrison, a solid writer and accomplished political thinker with a flair for the dramatic. A lanky, reform-minded Quaker, Garrison was a brilliant newspaperman and editorial writer for the *National Philanthropist*, a pro-temperance newspaper whose slogan was "Moderate Drinking Is the Downhill Road to Intemperance and Drunkenness." Like Lundy, Garrison believed that slavery was a sin, but his friendship with free blacks in Baltimore had turned him against the American Colonization Society and its philosophy of gradualism. He was convinced, instead, that "immediatism" was the only way to defeat slaveholders. Still, Garrison was not a firebrand or a crusader and never fully committed himself to the abolitionist cause—until he met Lundy. Garrison found Lundy's life story fascinating, his energy boundless, and his personal crusade electrifying. Lundy gave him the same message of hope that he gave to other abolitionists: "I shall not hesitate to call things by their proper names, nor yet refrain from speaking the truth," he said. In every way, he was consumed by his mission: "Take right hold! Hold on! And never abandon an inch of ground after it has been taken."

Six months later, Garrison left the *Philanthropist* to dedicate himself to antislavery work. When Lundy returned to New England to promote his crusade and raise more money for his cause and his newspaper, Garrison was at his side. The two men parted company when Lundy decided to carry his antislavery campaign to New York and Ohio before going home to Baltimore, where he would once again take up the fight in the pages of the *Genius of Universal Emancipation*. Whatever the future of their collaboration, Garrison's own course was now laid. He did not wait for Lundy to lead the movement; he set the pace himself. After a short publishing hiatus in Vermont, where he founded and edited a political newspaper, Garrison returned to Boston committed to making abolition his life's work.

On July 4, 1829, Garrison gave the Independence Day address at the Park Street Church on Beacon Hill in Boston. It was not quite what his listeners were expecting. Instead of delivering a turgid and predictable speech filled with standard patriotic phrases and portraits of the "Heroes of '76," Garrison questioned any celebration of independence that did not include black Americans. He told his audience that he was "ashamed" of his country and "sick of all of this hypocritical cant about the rights of man." With his listeners startled to silence, Garrison condemned Independence Day as an excuse for drunkenness and hypocrisy. Rather than carousing, he said, the people of Boston should "spike every cannon and haul down every banner" for shame over the "national sin" of slavery. "I will say, finally, that I tremble for the republic while slavery exists," he concluded. Garrison's speech might be rightly said to mark the beginning of the American abolitionist crusade: while others had worked in the antislavery movement before him, none had done so with as much eloquence, and none had had a program that was so explicit and direct. In August, with his course firmly set, Garrison accepted Lundy's invitation to join him in Baltimore, where they could expend their full energy on publishing Lundy's newspaper.

Garrison left Boston just as David Walker, a free black Bostonian who made his living dealing in old clothes, was writing a pamphlet that would gain national circulation. David Walker's "Appeal to the Colored Citizens of the World" condemned white American hypocrisy, just as Garrison's Independence Day address had done, but Walker added a note of radicalism that even Garrison would have decried. Having been a slave himself, Walker understood slavery's cruelty. But even that, he argued, was nothing compared to the evil promulgated by well-meaning whites who temporized with slave power and compromised with slaveholders. Nor, Walker said, could he excuse the inaction of ignorant and passive black Americans—especially free black Americans—who, to protect their own position, refused to help their brothers. He denounced Clay's colonization plan as a racist hoax designed to postpone the inevitable abolition of slavery: "America is more our country than it is the whites'," he said. "We have enriched it with our blood and tears."

Walker made certain that no one could misunderstand his views. Slaveholders, he asserted, were evil "by their nature" and deserved to be put to death. "I do declare," he wrote, "that one good black man can put to death six white men." He warned that whites bent on killing blacks should set their minds to it, and "do not trifle, for they will not trifle with you." David Walker's "Appeal" was widely read and widely censured. It made its way south and was read on plantations from Maryland to Louisiana; copies were confiscated at all major Southern ports. It is difficult now to assess the pamphlet's actual impact, but its message was a ringing condemnation of Clay and his fellow moderates who said they abhorred slavery but never freed their own slaves: "The whites want slaves, and want us for their slaves, but some of them will curse the day they ever saw us," Walker wrote.

———

While Sarah Grimké had been happy during her years in Philadelphia, she had always regretted leaving her sister Angelina behind in Charleston. Her journey back to South Carolina in 1827 was ostensibly intended to renew contact with her mother and the rest of the family, but she was also curious about Angelina's growth and intrigued by the letters she had written to her about her religious life. Sarah feared that if Angelina stayed in Charleston, she would lose her independence and come under the influence of Polly Grimké, her other sisters (especially Eliza and Mary), and her more traditional brothers (including Henry and John). In fact, she need not have worried on this score.

Sarah had left her mark on her sister. Like her, Angelina was committed to following her own path and viewed slavery as an evil. In 1826, at the age of twenty-one, she had abandoned the Episcopal Church and converted to Presbyterianism, just as her sister Sarah had done before her. "O, my dear mother," she wrote to Sarah at the time, "I have joyful news to tell you. God has given me a new heart. He has renewed a right spirit within me. This is news which has occasioned even the angels in heaven to rejoice; surely, then, as a Christian, as a sister and my mother, you will also greatly rejoice. For many years I hardened my heart, and would not listen to God's admonitions to flee from the wrath to come. Now I feel as if I could give up all for Christ, and that if I no longer live in conformity to the world, I can be saved."

If Angelina followed the same general path as Sarah, her views were nonetheless more independent and less introspective than her sister's. There was more joy in Angelina's life, and less "wormwood and gall." Where Sarah viewed religion as a means to self-discipline, Angelina looked at it as an instrument of instruction; where Sarah constantly questioned her own piety, Angelina questioned the piety of others. Angelina saw her own doubts, failures, and desires not as manifestations of her inherent sinfulness, but as lessons to be learned on the road to salvation. She attempted to mold her religion to suit her life. She did not convert to Presbyterianism because she thought its ritual was more demanding or its liturgy inherently more rational; she knew better. Rather, her reason for converting to Presbyterianism was a practical one: the religion suited her, and she said so, though she sensed that Sarah might not approve.

> The Presbyterians, I think, enjoy so many privileges that, on this account, I would wish to be one. They have their monthly concert and prayer-meetings, Bible-classes, weekly prayer-meetings, morning and evening, and many more which spring from different circumstances. I trust, my dear mother, you will approve of what I have done. I cannot but think if I had been taking an improper step, my conscience would have warned me of it, but, far otherwise, I have gone on my way rejoicing.

The differences between the two sisters were revealing. Angelina was willing to concede, with Sarah, that she was a "poor and miserable sinner," but having acknowledged that, she refused to act like one. For Angelina, religion was an experiment; for Sarah, a test. For Angelina, devotion and prayer were tools to be used in the search for personal happiness; for Sarah, they were weapons in her fight against temptation. There were moments, of course, when Sarah could believe, and write, that "human hearts are created for human hearts to love," but such thinking was rare for her; it was celebrated, however, by Angelina. The younger Grimké enjoyed her religion and understood, without actually acknowledging the thought, that church provided one of the few social outlets—or "privileges," as she called them—that Southern women could enjoy. She was prepared to take advantage of that opportunity.

Angelina was content in the Presbyterian Church and anxious to show Sarah her newfound devotion when the latter returned home in 1827. But just six months later, undoubtedly under Sarah's influence, Angelina would conclude that her new religion did not measure up to her expectations after all. Sarah did not purposely attempt to sway her sister, but her commitment to religious sacrifice and personal service surely influenced Angelina's thinking. Shortly after her arrival, at the very beginning of 1828, Sarah wrote in her diary, "This morning my dear Angelina proposed destroying Scott's novels, which she had purchased before she was serious. Perhaps I strengthened her a little, and accordingly they were cut up. She also gave me some elegant articles to stuff a cushion, believing that, as we were commanded to lead holy and unblameable lives, so we must not sanction sin in others by giving them what we had put away ourselves."

Angelina followed Sarah's example, and admired her, but she also had an overwhelming sense that destiny had chosen her for some great work: "I have no idea what it is, and I may be mistaken, but it does seem that if I am obedient to the 'still small voice' in my heart, . . . it will lead me and cause me to glorify my Master in a more honorable work than any in which I have been yet engaged." Shortly after writing this in her diary, in the spring of 1828—just as Sarah decided to end her visit to Charleston and return to Philadelphia—Angelina Grimké resolved to become a Quaker. Sarah left her sister at home once again, pleased that her influence on her was secure—that she was still "Mother," and that Angelina once more thought of her as her guide and light. That summer, Angelina would "untrim" her bonnet ("I do want, if I am a Christian, to look like one," she said) and exchange her pretty Presbyterian dress for a Quaker's garb ("The first thing I gave up was a cashmere mantle which cost twenty dollars"). While not yet fully convinced of the worth of Quakerism, she believed that her sacrifice proved there were great things in store for her.

——————

If Angelina believed that Sarah's public displays of devotion had acclimated Charleston to the strange ways of the Grimké sisters, she was soon proven wrong. Where Sarah's conversion had occasioned constant comment, even snickering, Angelina's decision sparked widespread criticism. In the summer of 1828, she was visited, in succession, by the Reverend McDowell, the Presbyterian Church's committee of leading women, and a number of longtime family friends. All pleaded with her to rethink her resolve, just as congregants of Saint Philip's had done nearly eighteen months earlier. "My friends tell me that I render myself ridiculous, and expose the cause of Jesus to reproach, on account of my plain dressing. They tell me it is wrong to make myself so conspicuous. But the more I ponder on the subject, the more I feel that I am called with a high and holy calling, and that I ought to be peculiar, and cannot be too zealous," she wrote to Sarah.

For several months, Angelina diligently walked through Charleston's streets to the modest Quaker meeting house, where she joined the small congregation comprising two elderly and feuding men. Her attendance at these services soon became the occasion for further taunts from proper Charlestonians, for no honorable Southern lady would ever dare be alone with two men, no matter what their age. Angelina ignored the ridicule, held herself proudly as she marched to and from the meeting house, and was met at home by a chilly reception from her mother. Polly was by turns angered and disappointed by Angelina's actions. She believed, justifiably, that yet another daughter was lost to the High Episcopal traditions of the Grimké family. Old now, and alone, she became increasingly bitter. She turned away from Angelina and blamed Sarah for the family's troubles.

The gossip sparked by Angelina's attendance at the Quaker meeting had little direct effect on her: the more she was ridiculed, the more committed she became to her new religion. But as the pressures mounted on her from both family and friends, her health deteriorated. After a flurry of letters to Sarah, she decided that she should follow her sister north, commenting hopefully that given the hostility she faced in Charleston, the visit might turn into an extended stay—even though she knew in her heart that it might mean abandoning Charleston, her family, and her friends forever.

Sarah was overjoyed at the news that Angelina planned to join her, but she worried that her influence on her younger sister might be misinterpreted. Fearing that her victory might be viewed as evidence of a "sin of pride," she vowed to herself and to Angelina that she would no longer attempt to sway her sister's religious views. Once again, the voices she heard provided a powerful inducement. "My beloved Angelina arrived yesterday," she wrote in her diary on July 13, 1828. "Peace has, I believe, been the covering of our minds; and in thinking of her today, and trying to feel whether I should advise her not to adopt immediately the garb of a Quaker, the language presented itself, 'Touch not mine anointed, and do my prophets no harm.' So I dared not meddle with her."

Angelina stayed with Sarah at Catherine Morris's home during the summer of 1828 and became more and more convinced that she should become a member of the Philadelphia meeting. But by summer's end, adhering to a pattern set years before by Sarah, she decided to return to Charleston to try to soothe her mother's hurt feelings over her sudden departure. She wrote Polly that she hoped her stay would be pleasant and free of the recriminations that had followed her abandonment of Saint Philip's. She arrived in the late-summer heat and took up where she had left off, walking every day to Charleston's Quaker meeting house. But the visit only reinforced her conviction that she had to leave the South.

What disturbed her most was not just the brutality of slavery (a constant feature of her diary entries) but the economic hardships it caused and the hypocrisy it engendered. The Grimkés, as she repeatedly noted, lived in the midst of plenty while others had nothing. Her family was "raised so far above the poor" as to make it difficult for her to live in "plainness and simplicity." Her simple Quaker dress, worn to show that she was not like the rest of her family, was deemed an affectation in Charleston. Still, it was not the rude remarks or the insulting stares that she feared, but rather the judgment of Charleston's poor white and slave populations: "The Lord's poor tell me they do not like to come to such a fine house to see me; and if they come, instead of being able to read a lesson of frugality, and deadness to the world, they must go away lamenting over the inconsistency of a sister professor."

Angelina turned her anger and frustration on her mother. They argued about slavery, they argued about religion, they argued about Sarah and the rest of the family; they even argued about Polly's decision to have the drawing room repainted. Angelina was embarrassed by her mother's extravagance. When the drawing room was finished, Polly Grimké invited her friends to tea. Angelina joined them for a short time but left, rudely, before the visit was completed. She deeply resented her mother and condemned her for continuing to live a life of comfort in the midst of poverty, and for her defense of slavery. The household spiraled down into charges and countercharges of who was responsible for what: Angelina accused her mother of impiety, and Polly responded that she no longer understood her daughter, adding bitterly that her actions were a constant subject of gossip in the community. Angelina recounted this contentious exchange in a breathless diary entry:

> I spoke to her of how great a trial it was to me to see her living in the luxury she did, and explained to her that it was not, as she seemed to think, because I did not wish to see brother John and sister Sally [two neighbors] that I was tried at their dining here every week, but it was the parade and profusion which was displayed when they came. I spoke also of the drawing-room and remarked it was as much my feeling about that which had prevented my coming into the room when M.A. [these initials were used by Angelina to hide the visitor's identity] and others drank tea here, as my objection to fashionable company. She said it was very hard that she could not give her children what food she chose, or have a room papered, without being found fault with; that, indeed, she was weary of being continually blamed for everything she did, and she wished she could be let alone for she saw no sin in these things.

The argument continued until finally Polly let loose the emotions and resentments she had been choking back for so many years. She was distraught, embittered, and confused about Sarah and Angelina's religious beliefs. In a rage, she accused Angelina of judging her too harshly and of acting as if her beliefs were truer, more devout, and more blessed than Polly's. Angelina, she said, now condemned everything around her in the Grimké household and in Charleston. Yet when she was a child she had said nothing, but only enjoyed the benefits and privileges of their lives. Polly's charges reflected the views of most of Charleston, including the family's friends, and her criticism hit its mark. The resentment focused not just on Sarah and Angelina's religious feelings or their decision to change churches (while not common, such conversions were not unique in the community), but also, and more particularly, on the sisters' obvious and public display of piety. Angelina, in a rare of display of fury, reminded her mother of the incident involving the slave girl Kitty, who had likewise once been the focal point of Polly's wrath. She intended to wound her mother by bringing up her treatment of the slave girl, and she succeeded.

> I remarked that true believers had but one leader, who would, if they followed Him, guide them into all truth, and teach them the same things. She again spoke of my turning Quaker, and said it was because I was a Quaker that I disapproved of a great many things that nobody but Quakers could find any harm in. I was most roused at this, and said with a good deal of energy, "Dear mother, what but the power of God could ever have made me change my sentiments." Some very painful conversation followed about Kitty. I did not hesitate to say that "no one with Christian feelings could have treated her as she was treated before I took her; her condition was a disgrace to the name of Christian." She reminded me that I had advised the very method that had been adopted with her. This stung me to the quick. "Not after I professed Christianity," I eagerly replied, "and that I should have done so before, only proved the wretched manner of my education."

———

The break was now complete. Angelina and her mother attempted to bridge the gulf that separated them (with Polly agreeing, reluctantly, to observe a silent time with her daughter before each evening meal, a Quaker tradition), but their argument could not be forgotten. "I sit in silence with dear mother," Angelina wrote, "but feel very sensibly that she take no interest at all in it; still, I do not like to relinquish the habit, believing it may yet be blessed." Their bitter exchange proved a continuing source of ill feeling. Angelina expressed no remorse for her angry response to her mother's despair over the loss of her daughters and their decision to move north; she simply did not understand how her own actions and Sarah's, and their rejection of the traditions of their family's church, had affected Polly. What she did not realize was that those actions and that rejection amounted to a repudiation not only of what the Grimkés represented in Charleston, but of Polly herself. It was a personal condemnation, and it was very deeply felt.

Angelina had her own views on the matter. She believed that her break with mother, and with the rest of her family, had nothing to do with religion or attitude or life-style; instead, as she wrote in her diary, all of the anger and bitterness she felt came down to the fact that the Grimkés—and their society, their friends, their city, state, and region—tolerated, defended, and even *promoted* slavery. The defense of the practice was at the root of all evil, "for so acute have been my sufferings on account of slavery," Angelina wrote, "and so strong my feelings of indignation in looking upon its oppressions and degradations, that I cannot command my feelings in speaking of what my own eyes have seen, and thus, I believe, I lost the satisfaction I should otherwise have felt for speaking the truth." Common, everyday oppressions that she would scarcely have noticed years before now took on enormous importance.

Angelina found herself intervening more and more in the slave question. At first she responded by closing her eyes to these evils, but then she would plunge immediately into remorse over her own lack of conscience; she reacted to that remorse and to her pangs of conscience by placing herself between slaveowners and slaves. She was caught between the desire to flee South Carolina and the feeling that she had somehow to confront the "horrible institution" in her home state. Both options filled her with dread. During her time in Charleston, even before her final break with her mother, the issue of slavery began to replace the issue of religion in Angelina's life, and gradually she became convinced that the "still small beating" of her heart was leading her into a personal crusade against the "peculiar institution." Overwhelmed by the evil she observed around her and imprisoned by a feeling of impotence in the face of the power of her state's customs, Angelina turned to her diary. Her vivid first-person accounts of the daily life of slavery in Charleston would provide the grist for her later, more revolutionary abolitionist writings. These were the bedrock experiences on which she would build her personal crusade against slaveholders, slavery, and "the slave power."

> Whilst returning from meeting this morning, I saw before me a colored women who in much distress was vindicating herself to two white boys, one about eighteen, the other fifteen, who walked on each side of her. The dreadful apprehension that they were leading her to the workhouse crossed my mind, and I would have avoided her if I could. As I approached, the younger said to her "I will have you tied up." My knees smote together, and my heart sank within me. As I passed them, she exclaimed, "Missus!" But I felt all I had to do was suffer the pain of seeing her. My lips were sealed, and my soul earnestly

craved a willingness to bear the exercise which was laid on me. How long, O Lord, how long wilt thou suffer the foot of the oppressor to stand on the neck of the slave! None but those who know from experience what it is to live in a land of bondage can form any idea of what is endured by those whose eyes are open to the enormities of slavery, and whose hearts are tender enough to feel for these miserable creatures. For two or three months after my return here [from Philadelphia] it seemed to me that all the cruelty and unkindness which I had from my infancy seen practiced toward them came back to my mind as though it was only yesterday. And as to the house of correction, it seemed as though its doors were un-barred to me, and the wretched, lacerated inmates of its cold, dark cells were presented to my view. Night and day they were before me, and yet my hands were bound as with chains of iron.

Angelina Grimké's understanding of the institution of slavery was not yet as sophisticated as it would become over the next few decades. In later years she would be horrified by the ignorance she had displayed in referring to black Americans as "these miserable creatures," but in 1829 her political thinking had not yet evolved to the point where, as she would do at the height of her intellectual powers, she could identify racism—or, more properly, "color prejudice"—as the real evil at the heart of slavery. She sensed it (the thing she would later label "this funda-mental truth"), yes, but for now she looked on slavery as an institution that bound *her* as much as it bound the servants and field hands around her: "The suffering of mind through which I have passed has necessarily rendered me silent and solemn," she wrote.

Caught between two alternatives, to flee or to fight, Angelina Grimké was now convinced that, acting alone, she could do nothing to overthrow the power of the slave institution. But unlike her sister Sarah, who had fled to Philadelphia to find God, Angelina did not conclude that she needed to become more religious or more devout. Rather, she viewed her escape from South Carolina as an emancipation from a political system that she believed she could not hope to defeat: "Sometimes I think that the children of Israel could not have looked towards the land of Canaan with keener longing than I do to the North. I do not expect to go there and be exempt from trial, far from it; and yet it looks like a promised land, a pleasant land, because it is a land of freedom; and it seems to me that I would rather bear much deeper spiritual exercises than, day after day, and month after month, to endure the countless evils which incessantly flow from slavery."

In the autumn of 1829, spurred on by Sarah's letters, Angelina decided to leave her family and her home state. But before her departure, she attempted to mend the rift that had opened between her and her mother. She was successful this time, in part because of Polly's willingness to admit that slavery might be wrong, an acknowledgment that must have cost her dearly. Angelina did not question her mother's feelings, and evidently it did not occur to her that Polly's concession might have been issued as a last attempt to win the love of a daughter who was about to abandon her. Instead, Angelina took pride in her mother's admission and left Charleston convinced that she had scored at least a modest victory in the fight against her family's greatest sin.

———

Angelina made her home in Philadelphia with Sarah and Catherine Morris and, under Sarah's influence, turned her attention to her new religion. She now became aware of her sister's difficulty in meeting the onerous challenge of being a good Quaker. While Angelina had been wrestling with slavery in South Carolina, Sarah had been contending with her own lack of religious confidence. Standing in meeting to give personal testimony still seemed like torture to her, and her tentative attempts at public prayer were met with barely concealed scorn on the part of the Fourth and Arch Street Quakers. "I think no criminal under sentence of death can look more fearfully to the day of execution than I do towards our Yearly Meeting," Sarah wrote in her diary.

Angelina was more confident and less intimidated by the Quaker hierarchy than her sister. Both women regularly broke with Quaker tradition by praying aloud in private devotions and sprinkling their bonnets with bits of color. Sarah's inability to be as articulate and forceful as other Quakers was her crucible, for gaining and keeping the attention of congregants and speaking movingly "in meeting" was an absolute, if unstated, requirement of those who would judge her fitness as a Quaker as well as her fitness for the ministry. There was a certain prejudice common at the time that influenced her congregation against her, in that those who stuttered or were shy were thought to be less filled with the spirit than those to whom public speaking and public devotion came easily.

Quaker ministers were expected to speak quietly but forcefully of the power of belief and faith; simple shyness was considered a sure sign of doubt.

Angelina was one of those for whom public speaking was almost second nature. But her ability to stand and speak of her religious views placed as many burdens on her as the opposite trait did on Sarah. Although she did not yet admit it publicly or even in private, Angelina found the requirements of Quaker piety contrived and the traditional obeisance to the Quaker hierarchy irrational. In mid-1830, when she had been in Philadelphia for less than a year, she attributed these beliefs (much as Sarah had done some years before) to the influence of the devil: "I have passed through some trying feelings of late about becoming a member of the Friends' Society. Perhaps it is Satan who has been doing all he could to prevent my joining, by showing me the inconsistencies of the people, and persuading me that I am too good to be one of them," she noted in her diary.

Still, Angelina put aside her doubts, in large part out of devotion to her sister. But she was not yet a convinced Quaker, nor would she ever be. She was, as she herself readily admitted, "full of rebellion." It did not help that the Quakers were silent on the subject of slavery. While John Woolman, Benjamin Lundy, and William Lloyd Garrison (the latter two not yet known publicly for their abolitionist views) were both Quakers and abolitionists, Quaker doctrine dictated a strict separation between the secular lives of church members and the requirements of church beliefs. Although individual Quakers were required to give up their slaves, most members of the Society of Friends were gradualists, and a number were well known for their support of the American Colonization Society.

If Angelina felt any resentment at having escaped the South only to join a religion that remained silent on the question of human bondage, she gave no indication of it in her writings. But when Sarah went to see their mother in South Carolina in 1832 (her fifth such visit), Angelina returned to the festering subject in a letter she sent to her sister in Charleston: "I am not at all surprised at the account thou has given of Carolina, and yet am not alarmed, as I believe the time of retribution has not yet fully come, and I cannot but hope that those most dear to us will have fled from her borders before the day of judgment arrives." Sarah came back to Philadelphia similarly convinced that a great explosion over slavery was inevitable. Both sisters were troubled by how unconcerned their small and insulated religious community seemed to be about what they believed was a highly volatile issue—one that not only would turn Americans against one another but might well turn slaves against slaveholders.

South Carolina plantation owners had long scoffed at such speculations, as they had done just before the discovery of the Vesey Conspiracy. But in the summer of 1832, Southerners had been awakened from their complacency by news of a bloody and terrifying slave insurrection in southeastern Virginia, led by a black man named Nat Turner. Ironically, Nat Turner was much like the Grimkés, Charles Finney, and hundreds of others who answered the call of the voices that spoke to them distinctly of redemption and salvation. Like the itinerant preachers whom he unknowingly mimicked, men such as Woolman and Lundy and Garrison, Turner sought to cleanse the temple of the sin of slavery and lead his people to a New Jerusalem of emancipation and salvation. But the means he used to that end were different. Where other men and women sought salvation through prayer, Turner sought it through bloodshed. And where the tools of the nation's preachers were their devotion, the Bible, and their faith in God, Nat Turner's tools were knives, hatchets, and guns.

———

Born a slave in 1800, Turner became a valued and talented worker for a succession of owners in rural southeastern Virginia, who prized his skills as a carpenter, blacksmith, and ready field hand. Turner was also well respected by the black community of Southampton, Virginia, where he preached a Baptist liturgy of personal service and obedience to God in sermons that were both powerful and popular. After his master allowed him to preach at other nearby black churches, his reputation spread, and soon he was invited to give sermons at churches far from home. Turner was an intelligent and articulate man who believed deeply in the Gospel; he knew it as well as many, and better than most. "The Spirit" was so deeply embedded in him that slaves from all over southeastern Virginia came to hear him speak. Eventually his commitment to his religion overcame all other concerns: he was consumed by it and admitted that his "visions and voice" made him almost useless as a worker. "To a mind like mine, restless, inquisitive, and observant of everything that was passing, it is easy to suppose that religion was the subject to which it would be directed; and, although this subject principally occupied my thoughts, there was nothing that I saw or heard to which my attention was not directed," he would later claim. Turner taught himself to read and reason and was so clever that other slaves, when planning a theft or "going on any roguery," turned to him as a master strategist.

Turner was deeply devout, literate, and articulate, but he felt he was different from others. He therefore "studiously avoided mixing in society" and "wrapped" himself in mystery. Devoted to prayer and fasting, he isolated himself. His seclusion brought him closer to God—so close that he could almost hear his voice. And then God spoke so clearly that Turner was pledged forever to obey him. "As I was praying one day at my plough," he explained, "the Spirit spoke to me, saying 'Seek ye the kingdom of heaven, and all things shall be added unto you.' I was greatly astonished, and for two years prayed continually, whenever my duty would permit; and then again I had the same revelation, which fully confirmed me in the impression that I was ordained for some great purpose in the hands of the Almighty."

As Turner was praying one day, it came to him that it was not the intention of God that he should remain a slave. Hearing God's voice and obeying his summons, he began to prepare for the "great day of judgment." He traveled through Virginia, telling other slaves about his visions and recounting to them his conversations with God. His communion with "the Spirit" revealed "the knowledge of the elements, the revolution of the planets, the operation of the tides, and change of the season." One day, during his meditations, Turner had a revelation, "a vision—and I saw white spirits and black spirits engaged in battle, and the sun was darkened—the thunder rolled in the heavens, and blood flowed in streams." Thereafter he began to notice signs and symbols laid out for him in nature: lights in the sky, and "the Savior's hands, stretched forth from east to west."

> And I wondered greatly at these miracles, and prayed to be informed of a certainty of the meaning thereof; and shortly afterwards, while laboring in the field, I discovered drops of blood on the corn, as though it were dew from heaven, and I communicated it to many, both white and black, in the neighborhood. . . . And now the Holy Ghost had revealed itself to me, and made plain the miracles it had shown me; for as the blood of Christ had been shed on this earth, and had ascended to heaven for the salvation of sinners, and was now returning to earth again in the form of dew . . . it was plain to me that the Savior was about to lay down the yoke he had

borne for the sins of men, and the great day of judgment was at hand.

The "great day of judgment" was August 21, 1831. In the early afternoon of that day, Turner met with six of his friends on the farm of his owner, Joseph Travis. They had planned a barbecue. Eleven hours later, well after sunset, Turner climbed onto the upstairs porch of his master's house, entered through a window, carefully and quietly walked down the stairs to the front door, and unlatched it to let in his fellow conspirators. There they murdered Travis, his wife and child, and two of his apprentices. Turner would later say, "The murder of this [Travis's] family, five in number, was the work of a moment, not one of them awake; there was a little infant sleeping in a cradle, that was forgotten, until we had left the house and gone some distance, when Henry and Will returned and killed it; we got here, four guns that would shoot, and several old muskets, with a pound or two of powder." The band then walked six hundred yards to the farm of Salathel Francis, whom they hailed from his front yard; Francis came to the door and was immediately killed. The family's throats were cut, and their bodies left headless. The band next murdered Mrs. Reese "in her bed." The killing continued at other nearby farms, where the members of the white families were dispatched one by one, often by the blow of a broadax. "A general destruction of property and search for money and ammunition, always succeeded the murders," Turner later testified.

The murders were premeditated, brutal, and unmerciful. Turner led his band on a path of slaughter, killing all the white people he could find; one family they dispatched included ten children. At each stop, Turner would free the slaves owned by the his victims and urge them to join his group; many did, vowing to kill slaveholders wherever they found them. Many of his men were now mounted on stolen horses. With little apparent thought of escaping from the militias that were sure to be summoned from the surrounding countryside, Turner instructed his rebels to kill every white they saw. Over a period of nearly three days, the band, which had grown by then from a nucleus of seven to some seventy or eighty slaves in all, would kill fifty-seven white people.

After murdering the white families that were neighbors to the Travises, and a number of others in the area surrounding thickly wooded Southampton, Virginia, Turner ordered his rebels to seize the county seat, at Jerusalem. They marched and rode toward Jerusalem, killing as they went. The killing was done almost mechanically. In some instances, slaves who had lived and worked side by side with their masters for years turned on them and their families without hesitation. While some of Turner's recruits would later claim to have felt sorry about the murders, few showed any true remorse. Turner and his band did little to hide their actions; they planned to march on Jerusalem, find food and ammunition, and continue their uprising. Turner believed that more slaves, freed from their fleeing masters, would provide ready reinforcements for his swelling army.

Almost two full days after the first murders, however, Turner's band was intercepted on the road leading into Jerusalem by a white militia. The two groups exchanged fire, and Turner's poorly disciplined rebels fled down the road and into the woods. A core group around Turner stayed together and faced the militia again on the morning of August 23; the militia broke up and disarmed the band, but Turner himself escaped his captors and ran into the woods. After his escape, and the final victory of the white militia, thirteen slaves were immediately hanged. Several months later, their leader was captured near the Travis home. Turner was given a quick trial and, like his coconspirators, executed by hanging, on November 11, 1831.

———

Nat Turner's rebellion stunned the nation. In its aftermath, the South reacted by imposing new and tighter restrictions on the movement of slaves, and a chorus of voices condemned the North's nascent abolitionist movement. A number of influential Southern commentators believed that David Walker's "Appeal" had sparked Turner's murderous campaign, reflecting the widely held view that the region's slave population would remain quiescent if only it were left alone by Northern meddlers. Indeed, Turner was an unlikely rebel, as a slave given almost total freedom of movement by his owner and evidently not mistreated. But as with Denmark Vesey, the taste of freedom Turner got, and his obvious intelligence, worked against the slave system; no matter what privileges a slave might enjoy, slavery remained an institution based on human bondage, on the ownership of one human being by another. No "privileges" could ever erase that fact.

It was not so much the hatred of oppression as the hope of freedom that fired the imaginations of Denmark Vesey and Nat Turner. Both were preachers, and both were allowed to travel freely, often far from their masters' homes. This, in the end, was the problem, for both were respected in their community, both were literate, and both chafed against the loosest of ties that bound them. They were not brutalized or physically abused, but both knew that a better life was possible, and given the chance, they gambled that they could win it. In each case, the response of the white community to the uprising was the same: South Carolina moved to strengthen the line between slave and free, making black men and women wholly the one or wholly the other.

The Turner Rebellion energized the South's most conservative forces. Even as white planters continued to deny that their slaves caused problems, they moved quickly to tighten slave codes. Once—it seemed now in the distant past—many of the South's most influential voices had called for gradual emancipation. But the cotton boom, the sudden profitability of the region's internal slave trade, and the growth of a distinctive, and elitist, Southern culture all reversed that trend. Calls for emancipation were now few and, when heard, quickly silenced. Even in the North, support for emancipation was isolated, as the vast majority of Northerners were simply unconcerned with the issue: slavery was a distant problem that had no impact on them. While Northerners might agree that slavery was ultimately wrong, most felt it was an issue that the South must decide.

That was not true for Sarah and Angelina Grimké. Although the establishment of the American Anti-Slavery Society, the spread of abolitionist publications, and the seemingly endless congressional debates on the question went without comment from either sister, both women's diaries and letters were consumed by the matter and had been for many years. But neither sister had yet formed a plan of action that would put them in the middle of the antislavery debate. Moreover, both were involved in a religion that strongly disapproved of such controversial political views. As a result, Angelina and Sarah turned their energies to perfecting their religious views and shaping their religious devotions. As the two sisters continued to question their religious commitment and the ability of the Society of Friends to meet their needs, they remained almost insensible to the rising clamor around them. Even the most profound and famous national exchange on the subject, the Lane Seminary Debates of 1834, did not command their attention. They could not know it then, but the leader of that debate and its chief organizer, Theodore Dwight Weld, would eventually play a central role in their lives and thinking.

FIVE

"The ground on which you stand
is holy ground..."

Years after he attended Hamilton College, in upstate New York, Theodore Dwight Weld was still remembered as one of the school's most able students. A brilliant speaker and gifted thinker, Weld was descended from Thomas Welde of Boston, one of the original trustees of Harvard College. He was steeped in the religious heritage of his family, which moved to New York from Connecticut in the early 1820s, bringing the storied history of the Welds with them. The Welds had been among the nation's first "revolutionary Puritans," ministers whose firebrand sermons had set the course for New England's tradition of straitlaced rectitude. Religion was the central pillar of the family's life. Weld's mother, Elizabeth Clark, was a descendant of Jonathan Edwards; his father had followed a traditional path to the pulpit, from Andover Academy to Harvard and thence to a permanent appointment in a large and powerful church in Hampton, Connecticut.

Unfortunately for Theodore's father, Ludovicus Weld, things in Hampton were not what they had once been. By the early 1820s, the two-hundred-year reign of unquestioned Puritan fealty was nearing its end in New England. Hampton was symbolic of this malaise. A steady increase in the number of Baptists had undermined the town's Congregationalist monopoly, and a strong Unitarian movement threatened to dethrone Ludovicus from his position as Hampton's most respected minister. Such developments would have been unheard of just a generation before, but church attendance had dropped since then, and swearing, immodest dress, adultery, and heresy were rife. Theodore's father battled "Satan's course" (as he called it) through a series of personal visits to his congregants, during which he pleaded with them to return to their church. He blamed Thomas Jefferson and other "Jacobeans" for the wholesale flight from Calvinism, but no amount of thunder could shift his congregation's course. Eventually, plagued by ill health, he gave up entirely and moved the family west to Fabius Township, near Syracuse, New York.

Theodore attended Andover and then Hamilton College. While he planned to follow in his father's footsteps and join the ministry, the two were quite different in temperament. During Theodore's time at Andover, his volatile personality and his desire for adventure led him into a career as a lecturer on mnemonics, or the "art and science of memory." While still only a teenager, he was a great success. For two years he traveled from town to town in New England and New York, perfecting his presentation. After a childhood under the obdurate rule of his father, who had shown him little affection, Theodore found that his intelligence, command of the language, and unique empathy for the plight of others gave him a power and popularity that his father had never been able to claim. Eventually, however, he turned from this rather frivolous course and began to think about entering the ministry. He returned to his family's new home in New York and, though not actually enrolled at Hamilton (he wanted to take some time to reflect on what he should do next), took rooms at the school and attended a number of classes.

At Hamilton, Weld was a giant, a commanding speaker and a natural leader. His fellow students looked to him not only for intellectual guidance but also for religious counsel. He was captivated by religious questions and seemed to his peers to have an almost personal, intimate relationship with God, but he never wavered from his father's faith. He advised others to ignore the "charlatans" and "false prophets" of the growing New York revival movement, scoffing at his sister, Elizabeth, when she extolled Charles Finney's message after attending one of his sermons. He ignored the pleadings of some Hamilton students who had become Finneyites: "My father," he said, "was a real minister of the Gospel, grave and courteous, and an honor to the profession. This man is not a minister, and I will never acknowledge him as such."

Undeterred by this criticism, Theodore's sister continued her campaign. "We had heard of the revival at Utica," she wrote him in February 1826, "[and] hope our friends there will be sharers. We hope and pray too that our dear Theodore may not be left to witness, to wonder, and perish." Perhaps inevitably, Weld agreed to attend a Finney sermon, if for no other reason than to show that he would not bend under the man's power. Finney, who had heard of Weld's influence among the students at Hamilton, looked forward to converting him. During his Utica sermon, Finney seemed to speak directly to Weld, fixing him with his intense gaze and striding toward him from the stage. "And yes!" he shouted at one point, his finger descending toward Weld, "You'll go to college and use all your influence against the Lord's work." The next day, apparently unaffected by the sermon, Weld encountered Finney at a local store. This time he criticized the revivalist to his face, lecturing him for over an hour in public. A crowd gathered to witness the confrontation. Finally, after a long moment of silence, Finney spoke: "Mr. Weld," he asked, "are you the son of a minister of Christ, and this is [sic] the way for you to behave?"

Weld would subsequently admit to being "so ashamed" by his behavior that he "could not live." He fled the scene, leaving Finney standing on the sidewalk, but later he walked to the man's home to apologize for his actions. When Finney came down the stairs, he spotted Weld waiting for him just inside his door and said, "Ah is it not enough? Have you followed a minister of the Lord Jesus to his own home to abuse him?" Weld was abject. "Mr. Finney," he began, "I have come for a very different purpose . . . ," but at this point Finney threw his arms around him and "dragged him into the parlor." There they both fell on their knees "sobbing and praying, sobbing and praying." It was an overpowering moment, filled with more religious emotion than Weld had ever before felt. But still he would not convert. That night he paced back and forth in his room, and the next morning, as he later testified, "an invisible force crushed me to the floor and a voice called upon me to repent." That same evening, he stood in front of Finney's congregation and confessed his sins. He pledged himself to Finney's crusade. He was converted.

————

Throughout 1827, Theodore Weld traveled the back roads of New York as Charles Finney's most trusted lieutenant. He brought to his ministry the same power and compassion he had once used to such great effect as a lecturer on mnemonics. As he spoke, he began to reshape Finney's message, adding to his promise of salvation a call for crusading reform. Weld's was an unusual approach, for he himself was not a born reformer.

He rejected the notions of apocalyptic political revolutionaries as adamantly as he had once rejected Finney, and insisted that he did not want to remake the world; he wished only to save souls. But he also contended that the best way to do that was to mark out a new future for the nation, a future that would depend on religious devotion coupled with a strong commitment to good works.

In the winter of 1827, in pursuit of this program, Weld met in Boston with Lyman Beecher, the most respected religious voice of his era. Beecher, Weld knew, was far more than America's preeminent preacher; he seemed also to embody all of the nation's moral ideals, in representing the established clergy, who looked to him for leadership. Weld hoped to forge an alliance between Finney and Beecher and thereby to create a single entity—a whole that would couple Finney's charisma to Beecher's credibility even as it linked the impetus of the new movement with the traditional power of the American clergy. While the meeting would not result in a firm reconciliation between the "Eastern" Beecherites and the "Western" Finneyite revivalists, the two camps would start cooperating in building a religious movement that would not destroy itself over questions of ritual and doctrine. Weld insisted to Beecher that he and Finney had much in common, including a zealous desire to remake America. Beecher listened closely and agreed that he shared that goal. He reluctantly acknowledged that he, too, saw that Finney's religious movement might be transformed to address society's problems. Weld was pleased by the meeting, and when he left Boston, he felt confident that he would meet Beecher again.

For Weld, the challenge was to transform the zeal of Finney's call for religious devotion into a push for spiritual freedom that would have a discernible impact on American life. In Weld's mind, the two—religious devotion and spiritual freedom—were inseparable. Americans, he believed, were not so much lacking in religious fealty (a problem best addressed by a liberal dose of devout prayer) as enslaved by their undisciplined desires. Accepting Finney's new Christian message meant not only engaging in a personal dialogue with God, but also freeing one's soul from the feast of temptation, from Satan's grip. Weld was convinced that the towns in which he preached were battlegrounds where God and Satan faced each other every day, in constant combat for the soul of America. Weld's message fit neatly into Finney's conception of a new and more moral church, but Weld went much further than his mentor was willing to go. In battling orthodoxy, Finney's disciples attempted to build new "modes and norms" of worship, following his belief that by bringing his ministry into America's streets, he could drive Americans back to their churches, where they belonged. Weld reversed this formula: he wanted to drive Finney's newly devout converts *out* of the churches and revival tents and *into* the streets, where their commitment to human perfectibility would spur social change.

Finney's critic Lyman Beecher agreed with this view. He was pleased to hear that Weld understood the connection between Finney's criticism of orthodoxy and the establishment of broad-based social reform activities. Beecher himself was working quietly to bring his own message of salvation into America's nascent reform movements. He had preached on the evils of alcohol for many years, even to the point of taking his message into mission houses in New York and Boston. That was where the Finneyites had to go, he argued, for what could they accomplish by pushing for church reform? That had been done many times before, and it had failed. The point, Beecher thought, was to remake human souls, and thereby transform America.

Staid, conservative, disciplined, and upright Lyman Beecher was something of a revivalist himself. He believed that America could become a "Republic of God," and while he faithfully adhered to his nation's first (unstated) political commandment—dictating the strict separation of church and state—he told his congregants that the "great commotions and distress of nations" that the world was then seeing would unquestionably lead to the "spiritual, universal reign of Christ on earth." Beecher believed that a time of troubles and blood would precede America's national salvation, much as the Passion had preceded Christ's ascent into Heaven. God's triumph was inevitable, but it would be bloody. America's soul would be seared by the coming conflict.

Beecher's pulpit-thumping sermons on America's destiny and his quiet but pointed temperance crusade had a profound effect on Theodore Weld. Just four years after his conversion, Weld was known as one of the most powerful temperance speakers in the nation. There were others, but none tied sobriety, spiritual development, and national pride into a single message. Weld's temperance campaign helped keep Finney's revival alive. That was a concern, for as Weld admitted, the hotter the fires of a revival burned, the more quickly they seemed to burn themselves out. By 1830, the flames of the Finney revival were cooling; even in upstate New York, Weld noticed a dampening of the religious fervor that Finney's crusade had stoked. "The state of feeling in Oneida County is dreadfully low," he wrote to Finney at one point. "Christians have talked themselves to death." The problem, as Weld saw it, was that the Finney crusade was becoming more of a business than a holy calling. He even criticized Finney personally, saying that he ran revivals as "a sort of trade, to be worked at so many hours every day and then laid aside." Weld wanted more. He wanted what Beecher wanted: a "Republic of God."

After much soul searching, Weld decided that the best way to keep the revival going was to renew the effort to build a relationship between Finney's religious movement and Beecher's call for social reform, with an emphasis, this time, on combining religious education with practical work. His purpose was to draw a distinction between Finney's followers and the ill, old, and infirm leaders of orthodoxy. Under Weld's guidance, marrying manual labor to education became something of an obsession for Finney's followers, and the idea took hold, as well, of the public's imagination. Study, exercise, religious devotion, and hard work, it was thought, cleared the mind and made straight the path to God. When Hamilton College rejected Weld's proposal to establish a manual labor program, Finney's followers left the school to join the newly formed Oneida Institute, which offered a curriculum of divinity studies supplemented by a strict daily regimen of manual labor.

Oneida was literally built from the ground up: its students laid its bricks and mortar and landscaped its walks and parks. For Oneida's students, the institute symbolized a revolutionary shift in religious practice, combining piety with a robust engagement in the world. The purpose of the work institute was not simply to prepare young men for the ministry, but to prepare them to spread the word of the revival among the unconverted—the shopkeepers, merchants, seamen, and farmers of America—who needed the Word of God most. How could ministers reach such people if they themselves had never planted or harvested crops, if their backs had never been bent by loads, their fingers never callused by constant work? Oneida was built almost overnight, with Weld as its spiritual leader. But almost as soon as the work was begun, he began to look for new challenges.

In 1831, after turning down several offers of leadership positions from local congregations, he accepted philanthropist Lewis Tappan's invitation to become the general agent for the newly formed Society for the Promotion of Manual Labor in Literary Institutions. The job would take him south and west, into Pennsylvania and Ohio, and keep him in touch with Tappan and his brother Arthur, the richest and most progressive philanthropists in America. The Tappans were known for supporting crusaders and causes, having given money to everything from the temperance movement to a home for "wayward" women. Convinced Christians, like Weld, they were firm believers in Finney's message and advocates of the labor and education movement symbolized by the "Oneida Revival." As part of their mandate to Weld, they asked that he find a suitable school where the ideals of Oneida might be planted in a new National Manual Labor Institution in the "wilderness." After months of traveling, Weld sent the Tappans his final, meticulously written report. He said that the small Lane Seminary, in Cincinnati, would be the ideal location for the Tappans to carry on the mission begun at Oneida.

———

Originally founded by two New Orleans businessmen, the Lane Seminary provided a traditional education to the young men of southern Ohio. In 1832, when Weld visited the campus, Lane was run by F. Y. Vail, a soft-spoken and talented teacher who spent more time raising money for his school than actually teaching. Lane desperately needed the infusion of funds and new students that Weld, and the Tappans, were offering. Recasting the Lane curriculum to include a manual labor component was a small price to pay to ensure the school's survival. For Vail, the appearance of Theodore Weld was a godsend. For Weld, in turn, Cincinnati seemed the perfect setting for a new manual labor crusade; here, he could prove his belief that the future of the revival movement lay in the new lands of Ohio and the West. Overjoyed by his discovery of Lane, he urged Finney and three dozen of his Oneida disciples to join him. He viewed the place as the cradle of a new crusade that would finally banish the devil from the soul of the nation. "Satan's seat," he told Finney, could be conquered only in the West—not by "working the lever" in Boston, New York, or Philadelphia. "Kindle back fires, back fires, back fires far and wide, let them stretch over the interior then while you are engaged there the cities are preparing fast; when ripe—at the favorable nick of time—give the word—rally your forces and in the twinkling of an eye make a plunge—and they are a wreck," he promised.

The twentieth century's peasant-based national liberation movements, its cultural revolutions and messianic calls for the remaking of humanity, would have fared well under Weld's leadership. His pronouncements to Finney were nearly revolutionary, and slowly he began to infuse his religious rhetoric with an increasingly specific political message. If the revivalists could win the countryside, he argued, then the cities ("Satan's domain") would surely follow. The conquest would be complete. Steeled by the harsh realities of the frontier, strengthened by working on the land, and purified by the West's wilderness paradise, Lane's seminarians would rekindle the fading fires of Finney's revival—and remake America. But much to Weld's disappointment, Finney said he preferred to stay in the East. Saddened, even disillusioned by this response, Weld immediately asked Finney's former antagonist and constant critic Lyman Beecher if he would come to Cincinnati to lead the school. It seemed a natural choice. By now Beecher was almost fully reconciled with the Finneyites and, having made his name in New England, was looking for a new pulpit and cause to expand his already considerable reputation.

Fired by the same vision as Theodore Weld, Beecher welcomed the challenge of leading a new school that would take a novel approach to both education and religion. After visiting Cincinnati, he set about the task of restructuring Lane's curriculum, hiring new teachers, and, most important of all, raising badly needed funds to keep the school's doors open. Even with the addition of Weld's Oneida disciples, Beecher knew that the work would tax his every resource. Self-certain and, to a measure, self-absorbed (he never questioned his own rectitude), Beecher was nevertheless a formidable figure. He was every bit the minister, with an imperious presence, bushy eyebrows, and a hearty and stolid greeting. People knew when Lyman Beecher entered a room, for his voice commanded attention. Only a man of his stature and convictions could make Lane successful. Beecher was perfect for the job: not only did he have an enormous network of supporters and potential founders, but he also shared with Weld the belief that the final struggle with Satan would be waged in the nation's new frontier lands. "If we gain the West," he told his congregation upon his departure, "all is safe; if we lose it, all is lost."

Catherine Beecher, one of Lyman Beecher's talented daughters, agreed with her father, asserting that Ohio's fertile lands symbolized its potential. With just a little labor, the revivalists could "bring forth an hundredfold more" there than they could in the "fixed, steady unexcitable soil of New England," she said. Catherine Beecher was thrilled at the prospect of her father's challenge in the West. An educator herself, and the head of a seminary for young women in Connecticut, she could see the fast-forming outlines of a national reform movement. She maintained friendships with a number of Philadelphia Quakers who might help—young women who, when called upon, could energize the support (and the potential funds) of their community. One of these Quakers was Angelina Grimké, with whom Catherine had a pleasant and increasingly intimate correspondence. Angelina came to visit her Hartford Seminary and returned to Philadelphia convinced that she could take part in this new movement as a teacher at Catherine's side. She was impressed with Catherine Beecher, viewing her as a woman with a distinct sense of religious devotion who was also committed to putting her religious beliefs into practice. Before such efforts, Angelina thought, the devil himself might shrink in cowardice.

Weld and his group of Oneida disciples traveled west to Cincinnati in time for the fall term of 1832, prepared to begin the great experiment of bringing God to the wilderness. Lyman Beecher, as the head of the new seminary, welcomed the students and began the actual work of teaching, which had to succeed before anything else. Beecher took pride in his position, but the real spiritual leader of the student body was twenty-nine-year-old Theodore Dwight Weld. The new core of Oneida men mixed well with the Lane seminarians, but there was never any question as to who was in charge: a new faculty was chosen by the students, who were careful to pick only those who believed in the worth of combining education with labor. The students kept their ranks undiluted by skeptical outsiders, fearing that Lane, like Oneida, might be diverted by an infusion of what they saw as the staid and traditional educational practices of the East. Their sense of purpose was reinforced by letters from those they had left behind in New York: "Oneida has lost the spirit which she once possessed," one such student wrote dejectedly. "Her soul has gone."

In late 1832, Weld traveled to Hudson, Ohio, to lecture on temperance at Western Reserve College. He drew good crowds wherever he went, but he was especially welcome in Hudson, where some of the nation's most outspoken abolitionists, including a trio of Western Reserve professors—Charles Storrs, Elizur Wright, and Beriah Green—had created a hotbed of antislavery sentiment. Storrs, Wright, and Green were supporters of William Lloyd Garrison's doctrine of "immediatism," and they descended on the charismatic Weld, hoping to win him to their cause. His enormous influence, his volatile speaking style, and his brilliant organizing techniques would be a boon to the abolitionist cause, they believed. Their message to him was straightforward, but powerful: slavery was a sin. Satan, they said, was being loosed on a prayerful nation, but not merely through the temptations of desire and alcohol. Men and women in chains were a blight on the soul of America. The Republic, they argued, could never hope to win salvation, could never truly save its own soul, without emancipation.

The meeting in Hudson shook Weld's faith in his seminary's simple goals. Combining education, godliness, and work was a revolutionary idea, but it needed a purpose; harvesting new souls was essential to begin the work of building a godly republic, but it had to be for some cause. Weld isolated himself from the other Lane students to think about these issues, and then, within a month of his visit to Hudson, he pledged himself to the abolitionist cause. Weld realized that abolitionism provided a fertile battleground on which to deploy his new revivalist soldiers. "I hardly know how to contain myself," he wrote to Elizur Wright in January 1833. "If I was not positively pledged for two or three years to come, and if I had finished my education, I would devote myself to the holy work, come life or death." To William Lloyd Garrison, who invited him to attend the founding convention of the American Anti-Slavery Society (AAS) in December 1833, Weld explained that he supported immediate emancipation because of his belief in the "great bottom law of human right, that nothing but crime can forfeit liberty." While Weld had to decline Garrison's invitation, he told him he would be there in spirit. In the meantime, he said, he would attempt to open a new front for the abolitionists in southern Ohio by candidly discussing the topic at the Lane Seminary. He wrote to the abolitionist Amos Phelps that he believed the "proximity of Cincinnati and the whole eastern line of Ohio to slaveholding states has thus far muzzled men both in public and private upon the subject of slavery." Weld promised he would soon change that, and pledged that Phelps could "expect to hear from this Institution—a more favorable Report." He had a plan, he said, that would make Phelps proud of Lane's commitment to abolitionism.

————

Weld's plan was a modest one: he proposed that Lane's seminarians simply begin to talk openly about slavery, in informal meetings. These discussions, he believed, would soon take on a life of their own. But they needed to be organized around a single issue. So Weld posed a question to his fellow students that he said they should consider. It seemed simple enough: the question was whether slavery should be abolished gradually, through a return of the slaves to a new homeland in Africa (the alterna-

tive supported by an overwhelming number of Weld's fellow seminarians), or all at once, immediately. Having planted these first seeds, which
were meant to capture the attention of his fellow students without causing controversy, Weld suggested that a public discussion be held on the
topic. He was hoping that the question could be debated before the end
of 1833 in a formal setting, but at the insistence of the school's colonization advocates, he agreed to postpone any public debate until at least the
beginning of 1834. This would give the two sides time to prepare their
arguments, and the advocates of colonization a chance to clarify their position. In the meantime, Weld and a small group of his followers (a growing contingent of Lane students) continued their own, more personal,
crusade: "We early began to inculcate our views by conversation, upon
our fellow-students," he later wrote. "Those of us who sympathized together in our abhorrence of slavery selected each his man to instruct, convince and enlist in the cause. Thus we carried on one after another, and,
before ever we came to public debate, knew pretty well where we stood."

As Weld summarized it, Lane's students would focus on two questions in their public debate. First, "Ought the people of the Slaveholding
States [to] abolish Slavery immediately?" and then, "Are the doctrine,
tendencies and measures of the American Colonization Society, and the
influence of its principle [sic] supporters, such as [to] render it worthy of
the patronage of the Christian public?" Weld negotiated with the colonization faction on the time and place of the debates. The two sides concluded that they would take place at the seminary for two and a half
hours on successive evenings over a period of nine days, to begin in February of 1834. In fact, the debates would last for eighteen days, with
some sessions going on for many hours. The public began to take notice
as word of the "Lane Debates" spread through Cincinnati and the rest of
Ohio. Reports of the proceedings were followed closely by the newspapers and the religious community.

Weld began the debates with a long disquisition on the nature of slavery, and from then on he dominated the discussions, building his case for
immediate emancipation point by point and responding, when necessary, to the arguments of the pro-colonization faction, the overwhelming
majority of whose members were from the South. In his presentations, he
drew on Scripture and religious practice to shame the Southern seminarians. But in the end it was not Weld's overpowering presence that transformed the debates or drew increasing public attention; rather, it was the
conversion of Lane's Southern students. By the last day, every student

present had been converted to immediatism, and under Weld's leadership, the formation of a Lane Anti-Slavery Society was announced.

The Lane Debates were electrifying and controversial. That some of the nation's leading divinity students (and the chief lieutenant of its most famous revivalist) should have concluded that slavery was a sin, and that in the eyes of God, black men and women were equal to whites, was shocking. The conversion of the Southern divinity students, too, was dramatic and unprecedented. And even more stunning was the outright condemnation of colonization plans, without reservation. The majority of Americans who opposed slavery, even those who appeared to take a radical position on the issue, simply did not believe that immediate emancipation was possible; even to suggest that it was, they knew, was to court trouble. People wanted a change, but a comfortable one, a slow and gradual shift away from the practice of keeping others in chains. The truth was that in 1834, most antislavery activists believed that the continuation of slavery was actually preferable to immediate emancipation—that if slavery could not be eliminated gradually, through the resettlement of black Americans, then it should not be eliminated at all. Weld attempted to answer this argument, and to counter the fears it was based on, by writing a constitution for the Lane Anti-Slavery Society that moderated the doctrine of "immediatism." Slaves would not be turned loose on the nation "to roam as vagabonds and aliens" and would not be "invested with all political rights and privileges" enjoyed by whites. Emancipation would not mean the end of white political dominance, Weld promised. But it would mean the extirpation of the nation's greatest sin. Emancipation would cleanse America's soul.

Weld's calming words had little effect, for the controversy generated by the simple fact that a debate on slavery had taken place was still reverberating through the North. Nor could Weld have stopped the movement he had begun, even if he had wanted to do so. After forming their antislavery society, Weld and his fellow students promoted black learning and dispatched abolitionist activists into Cincinnati's black community. "We believe that faith without works is dead," Weld wrote to Tappan, in typical Finney fashion. "We have formed a large and efficient organization for elevating the colored people in Cincinnati—have established a Lyceum among them, and lecture three or four evenings a week, on grammar, geography, arithmetic, natural philosophy, etc." Even in promoting this work, Weld was not typical of his fellow abolitionists, many of whom espoused openly racist views: emancipation was a good political cause and an effective organizing tool to revive the waning power of the Finney revival, they believed, but that was all—it had nothing to do with equality. For many diehard abolitionists, black inferiority was a given. But for Weld, the belief in black inferiority was as bad as slavery itself; it was in fact its root cause.

The Lane Debates drew a great deal of public comment, most of it negative. Weld was widely condemned, and Lane's students were suspected of being radicals. Even in Cincinnati, there was a backlash. The people of the city prided themselves on their tolerance and Western values, and they felt Weld had gone too far; he was not one of them. For Cincinnatians, the sight of Lane students working in the black community was scandalous, intolerable.

In the national press, which followed the Lane Debates in great detail, Weld was accused of "folly," "madness," "vanity," "ambition," "self-complacency," and "total contempt of law and public sentiment." The great fear that his movement occasioned was contained in one word, *amalgamation*, which was code for the mixing of the races. The concern was that black men might someday be able to court and marry white women and "pollute them" with "their seed." Lyman Beecher, ever the prudent and patient graying eminence of America's religious orthodoxy, counseled patience and restraint and attempted to dampen Weld's enthusiasm for immediatism. He admired Weld and looked on him almost as a son, but he could not endorse his views on this matter; privately, Beecher feared that the abolitionist crusade would overshadow his own religious work and divert the students from their main course of studies. Unable to stop the Lane Debates, Beecher instead dedicated himself to publicly shrugging off their ultimate impact. The debates simply showed that young people, he seemed to say, thought they could change the world by wishing it so; they were impetuous, as they should be. But this strategy—of treating the debates as so much hubbub in a seminary dedicated to serious study—did not work. Faced with a rising public clamor, Beecher decided that Lane needed to act quickly to put the controversy in the past. When the school's board of trustees attempted to contain the fury over Weld's activism by barring any further debate on abolitionism at Lane and then censuring him for his actions, Beecher supported the measures. The school itself, he believed, was more important than the issue of slavery, and certainly more important than Weld.

The board's action, designed to end the controversy caused by the debates, was a terrible miscalculation; it transformed the debate over slavery into a debate over the right to free speech. It energized Lane's new abolitionists and turned them against the school. In response to the board's decision, the new antislavery crusaders openly, proudly, and ostentatiously walked the streets of Cincinnati with free blacks, their families, and their own wives, mothers, and daughters—in obvious defiance of the seminary's leadership. Beecher met with the students, pleaded with them to act reasonably, and urged them to take into account what effect their actions might have on Lane's future. "If you want to teach [in] colored schools," he told them, "I can fill your pockets with money; but if you will visit in colored families, and walk with them in the streets, you will be overwhelmed." Weld ignored Beecher's warning and encouraged the students to increase their activities in the black community. It was not only a test of his leadership but an experiment in political action, for in defying the Lane authorities, Weld was developing an entirely new and attractive vocation that had not existed in the nation since the days of the American Revolution: mass political organizing around a single reform ideal. Lane's trustees responded by threatening Weld with expulsion, but he was not intimidated. He circulated a manifesto urging support for his position and defiance of the board:

> Is research to be hoodwinked, and debate struck dumb, and scrutiny sabotaged, and freedom of speech measured by the gag-law, and vision darkened, and sympathy made contraband, and vigilance drugged into slumber, and conscience death-struck in the act of resurrection, and moral combination against damning wrong to be forestalled by invocations of popular fury? . . . What! think to put down discussion in eighteen hundred and thirty-four! and that, too, by the dictum of self-clothed authority! Go, stop the stars in their courses, and puff out the sun with an infant's breath. . . . Slavery with its robbery of body and soul from birth to death, its exactions of toil unrecompensed, its sunderings of kindred, its frantic orgies of lust, its intellect leveled with the dust, its baptisms of blood, and its legacy of damning horrors to the eternity of the spirit—Slavery, in this land of liberty, and light, and revivals of millennial glory—its days are numbered and well-nigh finished. . . . The nation is shaking off its slumber.

On August 20, 1834, the executive committee of the board of Trustees of Lane Seminary recommended that all student societies be banned, that students be required to submit all public statements for review before their release, and that the faculty and administration exercise their powers to approve the immediate expulsion of any student violating these rules. Traveling in the East, Beecher wrote to ask the executive committee to modify its statement, which was bound, he thought, to exacerbate the division between the students and the administration. He then reassured Lewis Tappan that all would be well as soon as he could get back to Cincinnati and calm everyone down. Tappan was not mollified, nor did he respond in exactly the manner that Beecher had expected: the philanthropist was not worried about his investment, but rather concerned about temporizing with evil. "If you, doctor, were a thorough Anti-Slavery man, how easy it would be for you and Mr. Weld to go on harmoniously," he hinted. Beecher objected to Tappan's criticism, insisting that he *was* a strong abolitionist, and that he, like Weld, "wished to have the colored people raised here." But, he said, he refused to second the position that "they shall be elevated here." Beecher's son-in-law, Calvin Stowe, agreed and sided with the faculty in endorsing Lane's new regulations, then went home to argue his position with his wife, Lyman's daughter Harriet. An admirer of Weld, she was less convinced.

In October of 1834, Weld and his followers decided to leave Lane in protest rather than submit to the board's rules. As a parting barrage, they published "A Statement of the Reasons Which Induced the Students of Lane Seminary to Dissolve Their Connection with That Institution." The dramatic walkout occurred just after the first week of October. It stunned the community and all but destroyed the seminary. Most of the students, all followers of Weld, enrolled at a small and unknown college in nearby Oberlin, Ohio, where Charles Grandison Finney (who, in the midst of the hubbub, had decided that he should come west after all) served as the head of the theology department. Oberlin invited Weld to join its faculty; he rejected the offer. "The Providence of God has for some time made it plain to me that the Abolition of Slavery and the elevation of the free colored race have intrinsic demands upon me superior to every other cause," he wrote to the Oberlin trustees.

At the end of 1834, Weld accepted a position as the antislavery agent in Ohio for the American Anti-Slavery Society. His newest friend, former Kentucky and Alabama slaveholder James G. Birney (whom Weld had convinced to free his slaves and become an abolitionist activist), heard of the appointment and silently and privately celebrated Weld's addition to the movement: "I give him one year to abolitionize all of Ohio," he wrote in his diary. All through that winter, Weld traveled the back roads of Ohio, crusading on the slavery issue. Wherever he went, he drew large crowds of people intent on meeting the now-famous man and hearing his message. Other former Lane seminarians followed his example, preaching the new "Gospel of Emancipation" in New York and Pennsylvania. Spring came early in 1835 to the Ohio Valley, and still the public turned out in overwhelming numbers to hear Weld speak. Thousands flocked to the abolitionist banner. Weld believed that if recruiting continued a such a rate, the antislavery movement could not fail. All it needed to succeed was one more push, one more season of meetings and organizing.

The great abolition summer of 1835 was to have been the high-water mark of the antislavery movement, but instead it marked the beginning of an antiabolitionist backlash, a reaction not only to fears raised by the "Lane Rebels," but also to the American Anti-Slavery Society's mailing program—a political appeal against slavery combined with a fundraising circular, carefully aimed at one million Americans, including prominent Southerners. The Tappans met with Garrison at the beginning of the year to map out the campaign, which would cost thirty thousand dollars (at the time, an amazing sum for such an enterprise) and be the first of its kind in American history. If successful, the mailing would raise public consciousness about the evils of slavery, swell the society's national coffers, and bring in thousands of new members, extending the organization's political reach into grass-roots America. The Lane Debates, the AAS mail campaign, the continuing popularity of antislavery speakers (who seemed to appear out of nowhere to take the pulpit in any small town), and, of course, rumors that Weld, Garrison, and their followers wanted to "amalgamate" blacks and whites all combined to fuel the fires of racial hatred.

In Nashville, Tennessee, Amos Dresser, a participant in the Lane Debates, was chased down, captured, tied up, and given twenty lashes in a public market. Even New England, the heartland of the abolitionist movement, saw its share of hatred and violence. In Canaan, New Hampshire, townsmen hitched one hundred oxen to the interracial Noyes

Academy and dragged the building from the town. In Boston, after British abolitionist George Thompson spoke before a large antislavery audience at Julian Hall as a culmination of his American speaking tour, he needed to be protected from a violent lynch mob that had gathered outside. Another crowd disrupted a speech by abolitionist Samuel J. May by throwing eggs at him. Several days later, the poet John Greenleaf Whittier was mistaken for George Thompson and chased with brickbats through the streets of Concord (causing Garrison to decry the town as that "misnamed place"). One week later, Garrison arrived at work in downtown Boston to find that a gallows had been erected on the street outside his office; there was a note attached from "Judge Lynch." In New York City, rumors spread that assassins had been dispatched from New Orleans to murder Lewis and Arthur Tappan, the brothers whose largesse had helped to spark the abolitionist movement.

In Southern ports, mail sacks were seized and antislavery literature was publicly burned. In Charleston, an antiabolitionist mob (led by Grimké family friend and leading Charleston lawyer Robert Y. Hayne) hanged Garrison and the Tappans in effigy; three thousand Charlestonians cheered the mob on, then danced in lines around the bonfire. In Virginia, Senator (and future President) John Tyler rechristened the greatest abolitionists "Somebody" Garrison and "Mr. Foreigner" Thompson and accused them of "patting the greasy little fellows on their cheeks and giving them most lovely kisses." The federal government, stunned by the public backlash against the abolitionists, reacted by declaring that abolitionist literature would not be delivered in defiance of "community standards." President Andrew Jackson called the abolitionists' tracts "unconstitutional and wicked."

New England's well-organized abolitionist community struck back. At the end of the summer, Garrison and his closest colleagues announced that George Thompson would address the first-anniversary meeting of the Boston Female Anti-Slavery Society, to be held on October 14. The city responded by closing its doors: no church or meeting hall could be found to host the event. In desperation, Thompson's appearance was postponed by one week and moved to the smaller AAS headquarters, on Washington Street, not far from the office of *The Liberator*, the nation's leading abolitionist newspaper, which Garrison founded and edited. The antiabolitionist mob was ready, its numbers swelled by a handbill circulated through the streets of Boston:

THOMPSON
THE ABOLITIONIST!

That infamous foreign scoundrel, THOMPSON, will hold forth *this afternoon* at the *Liberator* office, No. 48 Washington street. The present is a fair opportunity for the friends of the Union to snake Thompson out! It will be a contest between the Abolitionists and the friends of the Union. A purse of $100 has been raised by a number of patriotic citizens to reward the individual who shall first lay violent hands on Thompson, so that he may be brought to the tar-kettle before dark. Friends of the Union, be vigilant!

Although the street address provided was wrong, the sentiment expressed in the broadside was unmistakable. But the meeting went forward in spite of this threat. On the afternoon of October 21, a crowd formed outside the AAS offices, and a group of antiabolitionists blocked the doors to the organization's auditorium, which was festooned with abolitionist banners. Mary Parker, president of the Boston Female Anti-Slavery Society, with Garrison at her side, opened the meeting with a reading from Scripture, followed by a prayer. As the secretary of the society rose to read her report, Boston's mayor ran into the hall and urged the women to go home, warning that he could not be responsible for their safety if they stayed. "If you go now, I will protect you," he announced, raising his voice so it could be heard over the noise of the crowd. The room was cleared, and the abolitionists spilled out into the street, where a cordon of police greeted them.

As the women were escorted up Washington Street by a phalanx of Boston's constables, Garrison remained in the building, apparently unaware of the danger he faced. His attention was finally caught by the shouts of the mob that had gathered outside the building. Some called for him to be lynched, while others urged their fellows to "turn him a right nigger color with tar." Garrison decided to make his escape by climbing out a window and onto the roof of a nearby shed. As the mayor was attempting to calm the crowd in the street, someone spotted Garrison, who jumped down from the roof and fled into an alley, chased by an antiabolitionist gang of stevedores, shopkeepers, and sailors from the nearby docks. He ducked into a carpenter's shop and hid in an upstairs room, behind a door barred by a piece of wood, but it was no barrier against the mob.

Captured, finally, by a group of ruffians, Garrison was tied up with rope and dropped from a window, sacklike, into the arms of the waiting crowd, a humiliating and frightening moment for the proud editor. The police could do little to help him. Fortunately for Garrison, two sympathetic workmen below shielded him from the rain of blows and hustled him back up the alley toward Boston Common and City Hall, where they found a covey of police officers as well as the mayor, Theodore Lyman. Garrison was escorted into Lyman's office while the police attempted to quiet the growing and angry crowd. Fearing that the officers would be overwhelmed by what was now a lynch mob, Lyman suggested that Garrison be smuggled from his office in disguise. Dressed "in a borrowed coat and pantaloons," as Garrison's biographer Henry Meyer would dryly note, Garrison was taken from the building and deposited for his own safety in the Leveritt Street Jail, just a few blocks from his home on Washington Street. He was finally safe, if utterly shaken by his brush with death.

In jail, Garrison took stock of the day's events. What he had witnessed on the streets of Boston filled him with fear, but he also took pride in knowing that he had succeeded in his goal. Having begun with modest resources and few hopes just four years before, Garrison had become an icon of the abolitionist cause, and his newspaper, *The Liberator,* was the leading voice of the movement. Garrison now imagined himself at the center of the great crusade, as its great martyred leader. With an eye to posterity, he wrote the following inscription on the jailhouse wall:

> William Lloyd Garrison was put into this cell on Wednesday afternoon, October 21, 1835, to save him from the violence of a "respectable and influential" mob, who sought to destroy him for preaching the abominable and dangerous doctrine that "all men are created equal" and that all oppression is odious in the sight of God. Hail Columbia! . . .

Everywhere, it seemed, the abolitionist crusade was facing new challenges. Abolitionists had once been viewed as marginal and harmless radicals, but as their influence grew, so did antipathy toward their program. If the revulsion of Northerners was inspired by racial fears, stronger forces were at work in the South. There, not only abolitionists (who were actually very few in number) were suspect; so, too, was anyone viewed as compromising with Northerners, including Angelina and Sarah Grimké's brother Thomas.

———

In September 1834, Thomas Grimké went to see his sisters in Philadelphia. His visit was much anticipated. Both Sarah and Angelina had exchanged numerous letters with him; they had fond memories of Thomas from their childhood, and as adults they admired his honesty and intellect. There was indeed much in him to admire. Thomas Smith Grimké was a nationally known politician; unfortunately, he was infamous in the South, where many of his political colleagues looked on him as a traitor. As the state senator representing Charleston, Grimké had stood alone in the South Carolina legislature when, in 1832, it voted to call a statewide convention to consider nullifying the federal "tariff of abominations," a tax on cotton goods imported into the United States—which hurt Southern cotton growers. South Carolina planters saw the tariff as a Northern attempt to drive down cotton prices and put them out of business. When the delegates of the special convention voted to forbid the collection of duties in the state, Grimké wrote a letter to U.S. Senator John Calhoun, asking him to shift his position and stand with the Union. The letter was reprinted in South Carolina's leading newspapers and nearly cost Grimké his life.

One night, almost immediately after the publication of his letter to Calhoun, a mob descended on Grimké's home to call him to account. He appeared, unarmed, on his front porch and proclaimed himself willing to die for the Union. He looked out at the crowd defiantly. During the debate that followed, the would-be lynchers dispersed—not because they were persuaded by Grimké's arguments, but because they did not have the stomach to hang one of the state's most prominent politicians. Thomas Grimké remained defiant, and one of the state's leading Unionists. Hearing of the incident, Angelina wrote to reassure him that though he was in the midst of danger, she was "comforted in believing that my kingdom is not of this world, nor thine either, I trust, beloved brother." Sarah was more circumspect and more frightened: "My fears respecting you are often prevalent, but I endeavor not to be too anxious," she confided in a postscript to Angelina's letter. "The Lord is omnipotent, and although I fear His sword is unsheathed against America, I believe He will remember his own elect, and shield them."

Thomas calmed his sisters' fears, telling them that their family's friends and his own trust in the future would save him from danger. While Charlestonians might disagree on political matters, he said, the ties that bound South Carolinians together could never be broken. The mob that had approached him in the night was not to be feared but rather educated; that was his responsibility, and he took it seriously. Surely, he said, the state would understand the value of compromise and find a way to temper its views. Events proved him right. President Andrew Jackson condemned South Carolina and dispatched warships to enforce the tariff, but at the worst moment of the crisis, Henry Clay intervened and proposed a compromise: the tariff would stay in place for the time being, but it would slowly be reduced until it was eliminated entirely. Clay's compromise satisfied South Carolina's secessionists; the crisis passed, and the controversy over Thomas Grimké's defense of the Union faded.

Thomas stayed with his sisters in Philadelphia for several days. He talked about his involvement in the American Colonization Society and his belief in pacifism. He brought them greetings from the rest of the family and asked about their commitment to their new religion. He took an interest in everything about their lives. Sarah and Angelina approved of his pacifism, but they were blunt in their condemnation of his leadership role in the colonization society. They argued strenuously for immediate and complete emancipation; only that, they said, could wipe away the stain of slavery. Before leaving for Ohio to visit his brother Benjamin, Thomas promised his sisters that he would study the issue. In early October 1834 he traveled west and on his arrival delivered a speech at the Ohio College of Teachers. That same evening, he fell ill with cholera. His condition worsened the next day, and Benjamin was summoned to his bedside. Thomas Grimké died on the morning of October 12, 1834, far from home, just like his father before him. Sarah and Angelina were nearly inconsolable. They wrote a memorial to him and sent it south to be read at his funeral.

It was a season of death for the Grimké sisters. Just weeks before their brother Thomas died, Angelina had suffered the loss of Edward Bettles, a man she believed she was destined to marry. Bettles had been introduced to Angelina shortly after she first arrived in Philadelphia, and he had begun to call on her in 1831. His interest was obvious and recipro-cated by her. Their relationship grew, though it was interrupted over the years by a number of disagreements. After Angelina visited Catherine Beecher's seminary in Hartford, Edward stopped calling on her, appar-ently disapproving of her plans to leave Philadelphia. In January 1832, however, he resumed his visits, to her great joy. In May 1834, trying to find a way to be close to him, she had agreed to nurse his cousin, who had fallen victim to Philadelphia's second cholera outbreak in five years. The Quakers were very active in nursing the sick, often placing themselves in great danger. Eventually the epidemic would run its course, but not be-fore taking the lives of more than nine hundred people in the city. Among these was Edward Bettles, who fell ill on September 23, 1834, and died less than a week later.

Bettles's death had a profound effect on Angelina. Like Sarah, she was now convinced that she would live out her life as a spinster. She stopped writing in her diary and never again mentioned Edward's name. Sarah did the same with her brother Thomas after he died in Ohio. The future must have seemed like a wasteland to both of them. In late 1834, both women (Sarah was now forty-two, Angelina twenty-nine) were unmar-ried and estranged from their family, and to make matters worse, both were weary of the obligations that the Fourth and Arch Street Meeting placed on their lives, and angered by the Quakers' isolation from the rest of the nation. When Angelina asked a member of the Quaker meeting about the religion's views on slavery, she was told to bring her concerns before the Committee on Suffering. Dissatisfied with that answer, An-gelina began to attend abolitionist meetings and to subscribe to anti-slavery publications, including William Lloyd Garrison's *The Liberator*. On March 3, 1835, she attended abolitionist George Thompson's lecture on slavery at Philadelphia's Presbyterian Church.

Thompson's speech inspired Angelina, who soon became obsessed with the abolitionist movement. It was an exciting and feverish political time; the whole nation seemed suddenly to be talking about slavery. For Angelina, the Quakers' position on the issue—or, as she saw it, their *si-lence* on the issue—was stifling. She now doubted that her chosen reli-gion was as dedicated to reform as she had once believed. To rid herself of these doubts, and to give herself some time to recover from the death of Edward Bettles, Angelina decided to spend the summer of 1835 with a close friend, Margaret Parker, in Shrewsbury, on the New Jersey shore. Shrewsbury provided a needed respite for her, a place where she could gather her thoughts, plan out her future, and talk things over with a trusted friend.

Angelina continued to read antislavery publications and spoke of the issue often with Margaret Parker. She tried to interest her sister in it as well, but that was a difficult proposition: while Sarah fervently opposed slavery, she was concerned that the elders of the Fourth and Arch Street Meeting would disapprove of Angelina's views. Angelina did not want to disappoint Sarah, and she, too, feared the reaction of other Quakers to her new interest in the abolitionist movement. But she wanted to join the national crusade. She believed passionately in the abolitionist cause and admired men who, like Garrison and her brother Thomas, stood against mobs and spoke against public convention on behalf of what was right. Only Sarah, and her concern for Sarah, kept Angelina silent. Still, she railed against her prison of conscience in the pages of her diary: "What to do? What to do?" she asked herself over and over.

In the pages of *The Liberator*, Angelina read of the antiabolitionist riots sweeping the North and of the burning of abolitionist literature in Charleston and across the South. Even before nearly losing his life in "The Boston Riot" (as he would later officially name it), Garrison penned an editorial in *The Liberator* condemning mob violence. He pleaded that George Thompson be allowed a fair hearing; he appealed for public calm and urged the people of Boston, where the fires of liberty in America had first been lit, to defend a man's right to speak in public.

Angelina was overcome by Garrison's eloquence; she had to do something, she felt, to show her support. A private letter from her might help the cause, she believed, and it could be sent without jeopardizing her position with the Philadelphia Quakers. She immediately sat down to write out her views. Addressing her letter to Garrison himself, she summed up her background and experiences as a daughter of respectable slaveholders and urged him on in his crusade. She supported the abolitionists, she said, because slavery was evil, a sin. She condemned violence and praised the courage of the abolitionists. She had never done anything like this before, but now, fired by conviction, she poured out her feelings. Hailing Garrison as "Respected Friend," she wrote:

> I can hardly express to thee the deep and solemn interest with
> which I have viewed the violent proceedings of the last few

weeks. Although I expected opposition, I was not prepared for
it so soon—it took me by surprise—and I greatly feared abolitionists would be driven back in the first outset, and thrown
into confusion. Under these feelings I was urged to read thy
Appeal to the citizens of Boston. Judge then, what were my
feelings on finding that my fears were utterly groundless, and
that thou stood firm in the midst of storm, determined to suffer and to die, rather than yield one inch. . . . The ground on
which you stand is holy ground; never, never surrender it. If
you surrender it, the hope of the slave is extinguished. . . . If
persecution is the means which God has ordained for the accomplishment of this great end, EMANCIPATION; then . . .
I feel as if I could say, LET IT COME; for it is my deep,
solemn deliberate conviction, that this is a cause worth dying for. . . .

Garrison was overwhelmed by Angelina's letter and published it in
the August 30 issue of *The Liberator*. In a short prefatory essay, he introduced its author as the sister of "the late Thomas Smith Grimké of
Charleston." He predicted that it would be reprinted and passed from
hand to hand. Several weeks later, a friend told Angelina that her status
as a Quaker was in danger and that she must immediately repudiate the
letter and reject the teachings of Garrison; *The Liberator*'s editor was a
disreputable fanatic, her Quaker friend insisted. Angelina refused to take
either action and looked to her sister for support. But even Sarah seemed
to turn against her, telling her that the letter had been ill conceived and
would bring her nothing but grief. Seeing the trouble she had caused,
Angelina despaired. "To have the name of Grimké associated with that
of the despised Garrison seemed like bringing disgrace upon my family,
not myself alone," she would later write. "I cannot describe the anguish
of my soul. Nevertheless, I could not blame the publication of the letter,
nor would I have recalled it if I could."

Angelina did not know it then, but even as she suffered public condemnation, other forces were at work. Within the month, several religious publications reprinted her letter, including the influential *New York
Evangelist*. The outpouring of support was obvious in successive issues
of *The Liberator*, where letters from the abolitionist community praised
Angelina's courage and called her the new light of the movement. One
reader maintained that her letter had done more for the cause of aboli-

tionism than all the speeches of the movement's leaders combined, and indeed, its impact was considerable. In the North, Angelina Grimké's letter was read and reread as testimony to slavery's brutality and as a sign of hope that other Southerners might one day, like her, come to their senses. In mid-October, Garrison published the letter in a volume with his own article on the Boston Riot and an abolitionist poem by John Greenleaf Whittier. He called the compilation *Slavery and the Boston Riot*.

Angelina Grimké was now famous: against her will, she had been thrust to the forefront of the abolitionist cause. But she welcomed the attention. Six years before, while still in Charleston, she had written one of her most telling and most uncomfortably personal diary entries about her hopes for her life. It was on the same day that she witnessed a slave woman threatened by two young white men:

> . . . It seemed as though the very exercises I was suffering under were preparing me for future usefulness to them [South Carolina's slaves]; and this,—hope, I can scarcely call it, for my very soul trembled at the solemn thought of such a work being placed in my feeble and unworthy hands,—this idea was the means of reconciling me to suffer, and causing me to feel something of a willingness to pass through any trials, if I could only be the means of exposing the cruelty and injustice which was practiced in the institution of oppression, and of bringing to light the hidden things of darkness, of revealing the secrets of iniquity and abolishing its present regulations. . . .

After the publication of her letter, Angelina defended herself to Sarah. "I remember how often, in deep and solemn prayer, I had told my Heavenly Father I was willing to suffer anything if I could only aid the great cause of emancipation." Now, in the waning months of 1835—in an environment where abolitionists were being dragged from their homes and beaten, where their literature was being burned, and where the lives and homes of free blacks were being threatened with destruction—her prayers were answered.

PART TWO

The Grimké Family

"... lift up thy voice like a trumpet ..."

The attacks on Northern abolitionists that had marred the "abolition summer" of 1835 continued into the fall. A Boston clergyman named Amos Phelps was almost killed while giving an abolitionist lecture in Connecticut; the British abolitionist (and Weld's mentor and best friend) Charles Stuart was attacked in western New York; and threats persisted against William Lloyd Garrison. The "Lane Rebels," and most particularly the abolitionist triumvirate of Theodore Weld, Southerner James Thome, and Ohioan Henry B. Stanton, were targeted for special attention: nearly everywhere they went, they were greeted with jeers, pelted with eggs, or threatened with tar and feathers. Weld was not surprised by the attacks and remained optimistic that the abolitionist cause would inevitably triumph. As he wrote to Southerner James Birney:

> *One year ago* there were but three newspapers in the United States which advocated the immediate emancipation of the slave and deprecated the doctrines and influence of the [American Colonization Society]. Now there are between thirty and thirty-five. A year since all the Editors advocating immediate Emancipation, circulated less than four thousand papers weekly. Now Em. circulates weekly about eight thousand. A year since there were not more than three or four

Anti-Slavery Societies in the Country. *Now* there are about
two hundred.

The Grimké sisters' view was not nearly so sanguine. Caught between
the disapproval of their Quaker congregation in Philadelphia and their
frustration over their own inability to be useful to the antislavery cause,
Sarah and Angelina read of the mounting attacks with a growing sense of
alarm. The enemies of abolitionism were everywhere, fueled both by the
concern that the issue might divide the nation and by their own racial
prejudice. It was this latter that Angelina, in particular, was quick to recognize. To allay their fears that they, too, would be targeted, the sisters
began a relationship with the Philadelphia Female Anti-Slavery Society.
Formed in 1833, the society numbered among its members some of
Philadelphia's leading Quakers, including Sarah's friend Lucretia Mott,
a Quaker minister and mother of six, and two activists named Lydia
White and Sydney Ann Lewis.

The sisters were wise to look for support among abolitionist activists.
In the few short years that the movement had been prominent, it had
successfully organized a far-flung network of activists who provided the
cause with a coordinated political program and a universally accepted
ideology. While the abolitionist cause was not nearly as well organized in
1835 as it would become in the years immediately following, its growth,
appeal, and central message were already well established. Its leadership
included some of the most dedicated and intelligent political thinkers in
the nation, as well as a number of prominent Quakers.

While still small in number—and well outside the mainstream of their
religion—a growing core of dedicated and outspoken Quakers took pride
in the fact that their early antislavery organizing efforts had provided the
major impetus for the establishment of a national abolitionist movement.
In 1827, Quaker Elias Hicks had founded the Free Produce movement,
which advocated boycotts of slave-produced goods, and the Free Produce Society of Pennsylvania had in turn fostered a schism between
Hicksite and orthodox Quakers—that is, between a reformist wing of the
Society of Friends and those who advocated a strict separation between
political and religious work. The Hicksites had attracted some of the society's most innovative thinkers, including James Mott, Isaac Hopper,
and Thomas Shipley, all of whom would become leading abolitionists. As
a result of their work, Philadelphia had become a hotbed of abolitionist
sentiment and the spiritual center of the abolitionist movement.

The formation of the Free Produce Society had accelerated efforts to establish a national antislavery coordinating body. While the group of New York activist reformers around Lewis Tappan looked with suspicion on the idea of a national organization (they feared that "Garrisonians" from New England would insist on the adoption of a radical platform with narrow appeal), the move to form a coordinating body of abolitionist activists gained widespread support throughout the early 1830s. The leaders of the three wings of the abolitionist movement—the New York reformers (under the leadership of philanthropists Arthur and Lewis Tappan), the New England antislavery radicals (under the leadership of William Lloyd Garrison), and the Philadelphia Quakers (led by Hicksites in the Free Produce movement)—were finally able to resolve enough of their differences to hold an organizing convention of the American Anti-Slavery Society in Philadelphia in 1833. Among the sixty-three delegates to the convention were a core group of free black activists as well as a large number of women.

The organizing meeting of the American Anti-Slavery Society had convened on the morning of December 4, 1833, at the Adelphi Society Hall on Fifth Street in Philadelphia. The Adelphi Society, in the heart of the black community, had provided the only meeting hall made available to the "amalgamationists" (as they were pointedly described by polite Philadelphia society). The meeting offered an antislavery forum for a range of widely divergent political views: in attendance were evangelical Christians from New York, black artisans from New England, revivalist ministers from Ohio, free-labor advocates from Oneida, Quaker women from Philadelphia, and Boston firebrands. John Greenleaf Whittier described the scene: "Looking over the assembly, I noticed that it was mainly composed of comparatively few young men, some in middle age, and a few beyond that period. They were nearly all plainly dressed, with a view to comfort rather than elegance. Many of the faces turned towards me wore a look of expectance and suppressed enthusiasm; all had the earnestness which might be expected of men engaged in an enterprise beset with difficulty and perhaps with peril."

Beriah Green, the president of the Oneida Institute and an ordained minister, had begun the meeting by reciting from the Bible (Isaiah 58:1): "Cry aloud, spare not, lift up thy voice like a trumpet, and show my people their transgression, and the house of Jacob their sins." Despite the differences among the delegates, the meeting was surprisingly cordial, with everyone focused on the "great crusade" that lay ahead, and nearly all the factions finding common political ground in their desire to launch an organization that would institutionalize the antislavery movement. After three days of meetings, the convention adopted a "Declaration of Sentiments" that called for immediate emancipation and pledged that the new organization would "secure to the colored population of the United States all the rights and privileges which belong to them as men and as Americans." With that the delegates adjourned, confident that the organization they had established would become the immediate focus of the nation's antislavery efforts, and that with a little effort, thousands of Americans would flock to the AAS banner. With the talk of human freedom ringing in their ears, they were certain that eventually the scourge of human bondage would be defeated forever.

The Tappan brothers, Lewis and Arthur, who had funded the meeting and been its major organizers, understood the obstacles they faced: the movement was short on funds (a problem they could solve), long on rhetoric (in much abundance, especially in Philadelphia), and in danger of falling apart even before it was really established. Still, the Tappans forged ahead, taking steps to put the organization on a sound footing. Their first act was to bring Elizur Wright, the modest but clear-thinking Western Reserve professor, to New York as the AAS's corresponding secretary. He was given almost total control of the society's finances and instructed to run it like a business. AAS chapters needed to be formed, the Tappans said, and members needed to pay *dues*; after all, political organizing required more than just good intentions, it required *money*. The Tappans then recruited "Lane Rebel" Theodore Dwight Weld as the AAS's first "antislavery agent." Mercurial and impossible to control, Weld nevertheless had the kind of fervent dedication the Tappans admired. True, he was opinionated, independent, and self-absorbed—but he was also an organizing genius. The Tappans and the AAS desperately needed him.

In the decades that followed, the original sixty-three organizers of the American Anti-Slavery Society would fondly recall the camaraderie and common purpose that had energized their discussions during the conference in Philadelphia. They would imbue their Declaration of Sentiments with an almost mystical quality, akin to that of the Declaration of Independence. It was, they would say, something that all of them had universally believed. Of course, this perspective was to come years later, when the passage of time had dimmed the controversies, political divisions, and headstrong personalities that once dominated the abolitionist movement. In fact, that the members of the AAS could even agree on a document such as the "Declaration of Sentiments" was something of a miracle. Already, by the end of the Philadelphia meeting, despite their efforts and intentions to join forces, the two major factions of the new antislavery organization were separated by deep and abiding differences, though they were conveniently and carefully papered over at the time. While the New England Garrisonians wanted to push the movement toward a more radical position, believing that equality as well as emancipation must be the inevitable outcome of their struggle, Lewis Tappan's group of New York reformers favored a more incremental and gradual approach to eradicating slavery. They believed that someday the AAS would have to be transformed from a marginal organization into a popular and accepted political movement with broad public appeal.

Their dispute was over the use of the term "immediate." For while Tappan and his Protestant reform cadre agreed that there should be an "immediate" end to slavery, they did *not* agree that black Americans could be placed on equal footing with whites, and even if they *had* agreed, they would never have adopted such a program in an environment in which abolitionists were being stoned for saying much less. Instead, the Tappans spelled out what *they* meant by "immediate" emancipation in a formula that in the years ahead would be lost on Southerners and virtually ignored in the North. Yes, they said, the AAS wanted immediate emancipation, but it was to be "gradually obtained." Garrison was enraged by the formulation and condemned the program of gradualism as naive and compromising, even going so far as to imply that such a compromise was a sin as great as that of slavery itself. Garrison was convinced that color prejudice formed the bedrock of slave society and that *its* defeat, and not just slavery's, had to be the ultimate goal of the abolitionist crusade.

But if Garrison was more sensitive to the obvious inequalities in the American Republic, he was much less realistic about how to go about solving those inequalities, and therefore much less effective, than the politically minded Tappans and their group of New York reformers. Lewis and Arthur Tappan and their followers had a keen sense of what could and could not be expected of the American public. Lewis Tappan, in particular, anticipated a long and difficult political battle over the question of slavery. While he believed that the abolitionist cause would ultimately triumph, he knew that it might take years or even decades of hard work, detailed organizing, and fund-raising to bring the American people to the point where they would fight slavery. And it would be many more years after *that* before anything like full equality for America's black population could even be imagined. Unlike Garrison, Tappan was a patient man.

It is because of this division that the Philadelphia abolitionist meeting of 1833 is remembered as a seminal event in abolitionist history—not simply because it gave birth to the AAS, but also because of the dynamic political forces that it spawned and set loose on American society. In the decades following the Civil War (which itself was still, on the day the AAS was founded, twenty-seven years away), women, working-class men, and free blacks would look back at the Philadelphia meeting as the starting point of their own struggles. The abolitionist movement was about slavery, certainly, but it also attracted the hopes of all the nation's marginalized populations and provided a forum for the disenfranchised of all classes. This is true in spite of the fact that though free blacks from New York, Boston, and Philadelphia attended the convention, and three black delegates affixed their signatures to the final declaration, black leaders had little voice in the attendant debates and were never mentioned as possible leaders in the newly founded American Anti-Slavery Society. Their representation was titular; it was "white folks," it was commonly thought, who must take the lead.

Women, too, were shut out of AAS leadership, nor were they allowed to vote on AAS resolutions—this despite the fact that women comprised more than one third of the convention's delegates. Lucretia Mott, who spoke from her seat in the Adelphi Society Hall balcony—her raspy but firm voice clearly audible above the murmurs below—proved to be influential during the convention's proceedings. She offered several resolutions that were adopted by the delegates, but she was silenced on important issues and, though she, too, signed the declaration, was assigned no role in the workings of the AAS. As a result, just days after the conclusion of the AAS meeting, Mott and the other women delegates formed their own society. The Philadelphia Female Anti-Slavery Society dedicated itself to the same principles as the AAS, but its goal was to build an antislavery movement among the most powerful, and untapped, political resource in the nation: American women.

From its inception, the Philadelphia Female Anti-Slavery Society distanced itself from the AAS in a number of important respects. Among its members was a group of well-known black women who, because of both their color and their gender, were all but barred from AAS proceedings. The young Forten women, from a prominent Philadelphia free black family, attended the new society's organizing meeting, as did Harriet Forten Purvis (also from the well-known Forten family), the wife of an influential and wealthy black businessman. Black Quaker abolitionists Grace Douglass and her daughter Sarah were also there. (Sarah Douglass would become Sarah Grimké's lifelong friend and correspondent, and would provide us, through her letters, with one of the most remarkable commentaries ever written on American life in the nineteenth century.) Likewise included among the delegates were women who would later become dominant voices in the movement for women's rights as well as a number, mostly Quakers, who were strong believers in political reform: Abba Alcott, Lydia White and Sydney Ann Lewis (who led the Free Produce movement), Sarah Pugh (a Hicksite schoolteacher), and Esther Moore.

The political and social implications of forming a female antislavery society were not lost on its organizers. Mott had already brought down on herself the wrath of the Society of Friends for her outspoken advocacy of abolitionism; now she and her followers were subjected to public ridicule. Each day of their meeting, a group of Philadelphia men appeared to heckle them, and the city's newspapers called the convention "frivolous" and unnecessary. One paper urged the women to return to their homes, to their own "sphere," where more useful work awaited them. The delegates were well advised to be worried by such criticism, for their decision to organize separately from the AAS had enormous repercussions. That women could organize to work for black emancipation meant, ultimately, that they might one day organize for their *own* emancipation. The AAS's decision to bar women from its ranks because political action was not in their "sphere" (as the term was then so delicately used) suggested to Mott, and many others, that the AAS leadership was as much interested in guarding its prerogatives against women as slaveholders were in guarding theirs against slaves.

But Lucretia Mott, for one, would never have put this so explicitly in 1833. She was open, well-intentioned, and bluntly honest—not naive but guileless. She could not have imagined that it would be the Philadelphia Female Anti-Slavery Society (and not the male-dominated AAS) that would provide the seed corn of a well-defined American political reform impulse—an impulse that was to continue from 1833 into the twentieth century and beyond. Its two most prominent political and social off-shoots would be the late-nineteenth-century formation of the suffragist movement and the establishment of a distinctive and powerful black po-litical culture. The beginnings of both the feminist and the civil rights movements date from Mott's decision to form a separate abolitionist so-ciety led by women. Lucretia Mott's influence in giving voice to this re-form impulse was equaled only by that of the Grimké sisters—who joined the Philadelphia Female Anti-Slavery Society shortly after its formation.

It is difficult to gauge the precise influence of Mott on Angelina and Sarah Grimké, but her views were undoubtedly significant, reaching the sisters at a time when they were both having difficulty dampening their own political opinions to meet the requirements of the Society of Friends. Mott, the daughter of a China trade captain, led by example. She would not wear cotton or eat sugar (both products of a slave economy), believed that men and women were equal in the eyes of God, refused to curb her political views in meetings of the Society of Friends (and criticized her fellow Quakers for their intolerance), rejected the primacy of the soci-ety's Committee of Elders (a constant source of irritation to its members, left unexpressed because she simply would not listen), and was an early advocate of abolitionism. She believed that women should vote, hold of-fice, and lead the nation; she thought they would make better politicians than men. She was, as she later wrote, "so thoroughly imbued with women's rights that it was the most important question of my life from an early day." It was under her guidance, and with her blessing, that Sarah and Angelina Grimké were finally able to escape the suffocating orthodoxy of Philadelphia's Fourth and Arch Street Meeting and become leading voices in the antislavery movement, as well as influential figures in the nascent campaign to win equal rights for women.

————

While many viewed Philadelphia as a hotbed of abolitionist sentiment, the Grimké sisters saw it only as a prison. After Angelina's letter to Wil-liam Lloyd Garrison appeared in *The Liberator*, the sisters met with a chilly reception at the Fourth and Arch Street Meeting. They were also unwelcome, now, in Catherine Morris's home, especially since Angelina had questioned her about the society's policy of making its black congre-gants sit on separate benches during Quaker services. (The two sisters moved out of Catherine's house soon after Angelina's letter was published.) Catherine was shocked and dismayed by Angelina's query. She said that she agreed with the seating practice, that there were firm reasons for the existence of the "colored bench," and that such questions should not even be asked. She believed in the efficacy of "silent witness," the practice of leaving change to conscience and good works. Sarah and Angelina accepted Catherine's reasoning, but they found the Fourth and Arch Street Meeting's services increasingly stifling, and they resented the disdainful looks and verbal reproaches they received during their own public shows of devotion. Angelina was angry; Sarah felt rejected. Both felt they were being treated as outsiders.

Embittered by and alienated from their own meeting, the sisters eagerly accepted an invitation to visit a number of Rhode Island Quaker congregations in early 1836. "The Friend of sinners opened a door of escape for me out of that, city of bonds and affliction," Sarah wrote in her diary. She was deeply relieved. The sisters sailed to Rhode Island and were warmly greeted by the Quaker community in Providence. They were feted and escorted about as honored guests, and were surprised to discover that their views on slavery, while not widely known, were respected among a small group of friends. They listened attentively and appreciatively as the congregants of the Providence Society of Friends lectured them on boycotting slave products, and they were exhilarated by the respectful responses their ideas occasioned. Angelina's authorship of *The Liberator* letter made her something of a celebrity in Providence. During her stay, she was visited by a number of New England abolitionists and was even invited to lecture on slavery to Quaker women in Massachusetts. She turned down the invitations, claiming that her responsibilities called her back to Philadelphia. She understood clearly that she was not yet ready to assume a public role: she had not yet found her voice.

In the summer of 1836, Sarah and Angelina lived apart. Angelina once again vacationed in Shrewsbury, while Sarah took up residence with a Quaker friend in Burlington, New Jersey. For both sisters, the separation seemed to symbolize the exile they felt from their faith. Sarah was especially disturbed, and even embarrassed, by the cold reception she and Angelina continued to be accorded; Angelina, for her part, was not so much disturbed as angered by it. As Sarah continued to ponder how best to mend relations with Philadelphia's conservative Quaker society (going, as always, through a period of self-doubt and questioning), Angelina was moving in the opposite direction—toward an outright rejection of

Quaker orthodoxy. "I feel no openness among Friends," she wrote to Sarah during the long summer of 1836. "My spirit is oppressed and heavy laden, and shut up in prison. What am I to do? The only relief I experience is in writing letters and pieces for the peace and anti-slavery causes. My mind is fully made up not to spend next winter in Philadelphia, if I can help it. I know not what is to become of me. I am perfectly blind as to the future."

It was her anger that had compelled Angelina to return to Shrewsbury; she believed that there was nothing left for her or her sister in Philadelphia. Yet she knew that her stay on the New Jersey shore was only temporary. She felt as if something were calling her to a new "mission," but she did not yet know just where it would take her. Sarah was concerned by Angelina's talk of a mission and wondered how the two of them could hope to live in the years ahead. She felt increasingly cut off from her Quaker friends (from whom in addition to a small stipend left to them by their father they gained shelter and sustenance), and rejected by the Fourth and Arch Street Meeting's Council of Elders; her dream of one day becoming a Quaker minister now seemed out of reach. Even the possibility that she and Angelina might one day be employed as teachers seemed unlikely, for Angelina had rejected Catherine Morris's suggestion that she establish a Quaker school. "I cannot think of acceding to it because I have seen so clearly [that] my pen, at least, must be employed in the great reformations of the day, and if I engaged in a school, my time would not be my own," Angelina wrote to Sarah. "No money that could be given could induce me to bind my body and mind and soul so completely to Philadelphia."

Sarah was alarmed by this: Angelina's writing, no matter how well meaning, was not yielding an income, and her views on slavery and on Quakerism were driving away the only friends they had. Sarah looked on her sister's "mission" as so much talk. While Angelina had begun several essays, she had put them aside in favor of a more solitary study of the Bible, a task for which she would surely not be paid. Above all, Sarah feared that a distance was opening up between her and Angelina, an emotional separation that would continue to draw them apart. It was not only Angelina's growing disenchantment with Quakerism that worried her; she also sensed that her sister was about to set off down an unknown path fraught with dangers and perhaps impoverishment. She was not sure she could follow her. "My beloved sister does indeed need the prayers of all who love her," she wrote to her friend Sarah Douglass. "Oh! May He who laid down his life for us guide her footsteps and keep her in the hollow of His holy hand. Perhaps the Lord may be pleased to cast our lot somewhere together. If so, I feel as if I could ask no more in this world."

As she had done all her life, and as Sarah had instructed her, Angelina waited for a "call"—a signal that God had a plan for her. She never lost faith in the power of prayer, the power of faith itself, nor did she ever lose faith in the clear sound of her own "inner voice," or her sense of destiny. God, she believed, had intended her to come north to do *his* work. The fact that her call had not yet come did not mean that her destiny was undecided. *He* would decide, and in his own time. So while waiting, she undertook a close study of the Bible. She hoped to prove that what she had been taught as a child was untrue, that slavery was *not* defended by Scripture.

A few days later, in the middle of the summer, Sarah wrote to Angelina, half pleading that she reconsider the invitation to lecture on slavery in Massachusetts. Sarah wanted her to accept; that way at least *something* would be decided about the future, and they could get away together, and be among friends. Angelina answered her curtly: she would not go to New York, or to Massachusetts, or anywhere else, but would stay in Shrewsbury with Margaret Parker. Her friendship with Parker had blossomed, and she enjoyed her company. The two women held many of the same views and took pleasure in their religious discussions. Angelina shared her doubts about Quakerism with Parker, who did not always agree but was always willing to listen. The conversations often lasted all day, as the women exchanged ideas and Angelina read aloud from the Bible.

One week after receiving Sarah's pleading letter, just as the summer heat was at its most intense, Angelina appeared at breakfast with a broad smile on her face, eyes brimming with tears. "It has all come to me," she announced. "God has shown me what I can do; I can write an appeal to Southern women, one which, thus inspired, will touch their hearts, and lead them to use their influence with their husbands and brothers. I will speak to them in such tones that they *must* hear me, and, through me, the voice of justice and humanity."

That same day, Angelina got a letter from the abolitionist Elizur Wright, secretary of the American Anti-Slavery Society, asking her to come to New York to speak to women about slavery. Wright was convinced that such meetings, in homes and churches, could bring hundreds, if not thousands, of women into the antislavery movement. Angelina was complimented by Wright's invitation, but she was far too nervous about and uncertain of her own talents to accept it; and besides, she was already at work on her "appeal." She politely turned Wright down, but she expressed her most basic fears to Sarah: "The bare idea that such a thing may be required of me is truly alarming," she wrote, "and that thy mind should be at all resigned to it increases the fear that possibly I may have to do it. It does not appear by the letter that it is expected that I should extend my work *outside* of our society. One thing, however, I do see clearly, that I am not to do it *now*." She put aside Wright's letter and instead began to write. She called her essay "An Appeal to the Christian Women of the Southern States."

Angelina Grimké wrote her "Appeal" in two weeks. She explained to Sarah that her goal was to "endeavor to undeceive the South as to the supposed objects of antislavery societies, and bear my full testimony to their pacific principles; and then to close with as feeling an appeal as possible to them as women, as Christian women, setting before them the awful responsibility resting on them at this crisis; for if the women of the South do not rise in the strength of the Lord to plead with their fathers, husbands, brothers, and sons, that country must witness the most dreadful scenes of murder and blood." Angelina meant her "Appeal" to be an emotional call, but its central message was taken from her study of the Bible: the belief that slavery was a sin, that human bondage was not defended by a dark and vengeful God, and that freedom was a blessing that held out the promise of salvation.

Angelina was confident that Wright and the AAS would publish her "Appeal"—perhaps, she said, in a pamphlet form of "a dozen pages, I suppose." She suspected that it would have a great effect, "for I well know my name is worth more than myself, and will add weight to it. Now, dearest [Sarah], what dost thou think of it? A pretty bold step, I know, and one of which my friends will highly disapprove, but this is a day in which I feel I must act independently of consequences to myself, for of how little consequence will my trials be, if the cause of truth is heeded ever so little. The South must be reached."

Angelina finished her essay at the end of July and included it in a letter she sent to Elizur Wright on August 1, 1836. Less than two weeks later, Wright penned his reply to her, agreeing to publish the "Appeal" as a pamphlet. "Oh that it could be rained down into every parlor in our land," he wrote. "I know it will carry the Christian women of the South if it can be read, and my soul blesses that dear and glorious Savior who has help[ed] you to write it." The resulting pamphlet, thirty-six pages in length, was published in October. It gained immediate recognition as one of the most profound antislavery documents published up to that time; its message was unique. While its appeal was emotional, religious, and heartfelt, its novelty lay in the fact that it had been written not simply by a woman (there were, after all, a number of well-known women writers in the North at the time), but by a *Southern* woman. It possessed a credibility, and would acquire a notoriety, that few other antislavery publications achieved.

It greatest value, however, was that it bluntly called women— Southern women—to political action, stating plainly and persuasively that their voices, when raised, would have a much more profound moral impact than the voices of men, whether slaveholders or abolitionists. Difficult though it is to believe now, the idea that women could change society was then viewed not merely as novel or odd, but as revolutionary, even scandalous. The idea struck at the heart of the nation, at its foundation, and at those who ruled it. Even more compelling was Angelina's purposeful, and personal, style. "It is because I feel a deep and tender interest in your present and eternal welfare," she wrote, "that I am willing thus publicly to address you." It was as if she were talking to her family and friends in a Charleston parlor. She intimated, broadly, that the question of slavery was for women to decide: "Be not afraid then to read my appeal, it is not written in the heat of passion or prejudice, but in that solemn calmness which is the result of conviction and duty. It is true, I am going to tell you unwelcome truths, but I mean to speak those truths in love. . . ."

Angelina understood her audience as well as, and perhaps better than, any Northern woman could. Her appeal was religious, for Southern women were religious; her tone was conversational, for Southern women talked, mostly to one another; and her reasoning was intelligent, even learned, because the Southern women she knew (the wives of men who owned slaves) were educated and well read. Her argument was derived from the Bible, because it was the "ultimate appeal," but the notion that slavery was a *sin*, which stained the sinner, was very much her own. "It has been justly remarked that 'God never made a slave,' he made man upright, his back was not made to carry burdens, nor his neck to wear a yoke, and the man must be crushed within him, before his back can be fitted to the burden of perpetual slavery; and that his back is not fitted to it, is manifest by the insurrections that so often disturb the peace and security of slaveholding countries," she noted.

Warming to her subject, she reminded Southern women of their special place in history and of their unique influence. She had a talent for drawing visions from her religion that would have a special resonance in the South, images imbued with a cadence she had learned as a girl in Charleston. This "Appeal" to "Southern Women" was not actually written for Northerners; Angelina Grimké *intended* to reach her stated audience. Like any good writer, she could see her readers in her mind's eye as she committed the words to paper. That was what gave her words their power.

And who last hung around the cross of Jesus on the mountain of Golgotha? Who first visited the sepulchre early in the morning on the first day of the week, carrying sweet spices to embalm his precious body, not knowing that it is incorruptible and could not be beholden by the bands of death? These were *women!* To whom did he first appear after his resurrection? It was a *woman!* . . . But this is not all. Roman women were burnt at the stake, their delicate limbs were torn joint from joint by the ferocious beasts of the Amp[h]itheatre, and tossed by the wild bull in his fury, for the diversion of that idolatrous, warlike, and slaveholding people. Yes, *women* suffered under the ten persecutions of heathen Rome, with the most unshrinking constancy and fortitude; not all the entreaties of friends, nor the claims of new born infancy, nor the cruel threats of enemies could make them sprinkle one grain of incense upon the alt[a]rs of Roman idols. Come now with me to the beautiful valleys of the Piedmont. Whose blood stains the green sward, and decks the wild flowers with colors not their own, and smokes on the sword of persecuting France? It is *woman's,* as well as man's? Yes, *women* are accounted as sheep for the slaughter, and were cut down as the tender saplings of the wood.

No more emotional and powerful appeal against slavery would be written by anyone, then or later. Angelina Grimké's "An Appeal to the Christian Women of the Southern States" was a tour de force. Its reception in the South was predictable: of the thousands of copies that were printed, hundreds were burned on the docks of Charleston, confiscated in New Orleans, and suppressed in Richmond. Its call to action went largely unheeded by Southerners, as Angelina herself had gloomily predicted. But the "Appeal" had a tremendous impact on Northern women, who read in its words a message that held more optimism and hope for their own lives than any other they had ever heard. For if Southern women could be enjoined to unite in a holy crusade, then so could they; and if Southern women could attain a powerful influence by expanding their own "sphere" of house, home, and hearth, well, then, so could they. The differences between Northern women and Southern women were not significant, for abolitionists were attacked in both regions, and violently.

In Charleston, meanwhile, Angelina's "Appeal" brought unwanted attention to her family. The mayor paid a courtesy call on her mother; after a few customarily polite remarks and questions about family, friends, and her health, he suggested to Polly that Angelina not make an appearance in Charleston, for if she did turn up, he said, she would be loaded aboard the same boat that had delivered her, and returned to the North. This anecdote, when related to Angelina, must have brought a smile to her face: she had no intention of returning to South Carolina—not then, or later, or ever. Instead, with Sarah, she planned to break permanently with Philadelphia and the Philadelphia Quakers and travel to New York, where both sisters could dedicate themselves to serving the antislavery cause.

———

Theodore Weld had proved James Birney right in his prediction that he would "abolitionize" all of Ohio in one short year—or almost. Beginning in Ripley, in the southern part of the state, Weld moved on to West Union, then to Hillsborough and Greenfield. Early 1835 found him in Concord and Frankfort, and in the spring he converted Circleville and Bloomingsberg. In April, after being turned away from Zanesville by a mob, he organized the Ohio Anti-Slavery Society, which held its first convention in Putnam. In May he traveled into eastern Ohio, and in June he found himself in Cleveland. Later that month he lectured in Ravenna, Elyria, and Oberlin. In the abolition summer of 1835, following the mandate of the newly formed American Anti-Slavery Society, he left Ohio for his home state of New York.

Weld thought of himself as the John the Baptist of the antislavery movement: he dressed simply, took his meals with friends he met along the way, and slept where fate dictated. Some towns were more difficult to "abolitionize" than others. He gave eleven lectures in Ripley without seeming effect, but after he left, the town formed a strong antislavery chapter. In Circleville, an antiabolitionist mob pelted him with rocks; in another town, his meeting had to be moved from the courthouse to the schoolhouse and back again. The work was hard, but it absorbed him. Part mnemonic salesman, part learned professor, part minister, part revivalist, he took whatever time he needed (whether with just one person or with hundreds) to bring the reality of slavery to life.

Weld appealed to his audiences' emotions. He described, in vivid detail, the "bent backs," "chained and groaning humans," and "manacled field hands" of the slave states; these were always his reminders of the everyday reality of slavery. But most of his talks focused on the "yearning for freedom in the heart of every slave." His message inspired powerful feelings, especially among women, who likewise yearned for freedom. It was an age of sentiment and sentimentality: emotions were felt, and deeply. "I have slept since you left us, but not in peace," one abolitionist woman wrote to him after his appearance in Cleveland. "I am moved like a quivering touch of a lacerated limb, the convulsive throb of a crushed bosom, the sinking ebb of life's last tide, and the bursting throe of revivification."

Weld's emotional appeal concentrated most strongly on the *sin* of slavery, and less on the inequality that the institution represented. He was a political realist. People, he knew, would come to hear him speak of unspeakable acts, they would listen enraptured to his stories of slaves who made harrowing escapes to freedom, and they would be thrilled by his vision of the burden of sin's being lifted from the backs of white sinners. But his listeners, he realized, were not interested in discussions of equality and freedom, or in the dream of one world unburdened by chains. The politics would come later. Weld preached emancipation as if from a pulpit, because he knew that as much as the men and women of the North hated slavery, they also feared black equality. His followers agreed. His talks combined Finney's thunder with the promise of God's salvation—a feint here, a dodge there, but always and everywhere the same message: slavery was an intolerable sin, a blot on the human spirit, a stain on the soul of the nation. "In discussing the subject of slavery," he said, "I have always presented it as pre-eminently a moral question, arresting the conscience of the nation, and rolling upon it its infinite claims—the accumulated pressure of myriad wrongs and woes and hoarded guilts. As a question of politics and national economy, I have passed it with scarce a look or word, believing that the business of abolitionism is with the heart of the nation, rather than with its purse strings."

Describing this one-man crusade, Lewis Tappan observed that "a man like Weld thinks the center of the world is where he acts." Weld himself would not have resented the comment. While others of the Lane Rebels were also dispatched as "agents" by the AAS, none was as single-minded as the Connecticut preacher's son, and none was as undeterred. The AAS's leadership always enjoyed his written reports, for they exuded self-confidence. Tens of thousands of Americans were now joining the antislavery cause, Weld wrote. Within five years, he said, more than half a million slaves would be freed, and one and a half million within a decade. He had reason to be optimistic, for wherever he lectured, and in spite of the stones and threats, he drew large crowds. He was magnetic. People flocked to hear him speak, though some of them did not even care about slavery—they were entranced, instead, by his revivalist style, and consumed by the lightning thrusts of his arguments.

Despite Weld's enormous success, Elizur Wright, the former professor turned administrator (who, as secretary of the American Anti-Slavery Society, was charged with supervising the organization's fieldwork), remained skeptical of his argument that the AAS should "abolitionize" the countryside and ignore the cities. Wright wanted to mount a national urban crusade focusing on New York, Boston, and Philadelphia. Like Weld, Wright saw the abolitionist crusade as a political movement, and like him, he was very religious, but he differed from him in emphasizing the primacy of "political transformation" over "moral reformation." Wright and the Tappans dreamed of building a national organization that could take on the political establishment. Weld scoffed at this notion, believing that political work should be saved for the future. It was important, he agreed, but it was not what *he* wanted to do. When Weld was invited to attended the yearly convention of the AAS, he skewered

Wright and the Tappans for their "ostentatious display" and called the meeting a "sham and show off" that would find the antislavery establishment "sailing round in Cleopatra's barge" (in our own day, Weld would have referred to the Tappans and Wright as "limousine radicals").

Ever tolerant, ever patient (after all, Weld was the AAS's best field agent), Wright pushed Weld to apply his genius more to national organizing and less to "stump speaking." Weld responded that he was most effective where he was: "I am a Backwoodsman—can grub up stumps and roll logs and burn brush heaps and break green sward," he wrote. "Let me keep about my own business and stay in my own place." Wright was exasperated. "Has an agent a right to be more 'egotistical' to one of us than to the public?" he asked Weld in an unusually blunt letter. Weld maintained his independence and ignored Wright's criticism, insisting, "A *stump* is my throne my parish my home—My element the *everydayisms* of plain common life." But Wright did not give up. Slowly, he was moving Weld east, where the AAS could best use his talents—as a national organizer and political figure, not as some backwoods peddler of moral snake oil. Wright was confident: after Ohio, Weld would "abolitionize" upstate New York, and then he would come south, to New York City. That, Wright believed, was the great prize, the diamond in the antislavery crown.

New York was not Ohio. In 1836, Ohio was still the frontier, its political establishment and its traditions not yet defined. New York's political establishment, by contrast, was well organized, sophisticated, and tough. Its political leaders did not take kindly to the "everydayisms of plain common life" and ridiculed anyone who believed that New York's great masses could be converted by someone who spoke to them while standing on a stump. Antiabolitionist agitators knew that Weld was coming; they had watched him in Ohio and now mounted a campaign aimed at undermining him at every turn. New York's legislators could do little to stop Weld on his home ground upstate, where Charles Finney had first stoked the fires of the Great Revival, so they bided their time and waited for him to move east. They had plans for him, and they beckoned him on, plotting to undo his crusade on their own ground—in Albany, or perhaps in Troy.

Weld himself remained unconcerned. Not only was upstate New York a seat of abolitionist sentiment; it was also shot through with "stations" on the Underground Railroad, the legendary, and spontaneous, national movement that helped escaped slaves make their way to Canada and freedom. Although no one knows precisely how many slaves were surreptitiously ushered north in the five decades before the Civil War, thousands probably made use of the "station masters," "conductors," and "engineers" of the system—the farmers and artisans, in upstate New York especially, who secreted slaves and slave families in their haylofts and cellars, defying slave catchers and local antiabolitionist constables alike.

Unaware of the forces gathering to oppose him, Weld believed that the birthplace of Charles Finney's religious revival would almost certainly yield a bounteous harvest of antislavery activists. The first few months of his mission proved him right. Hundreds attended his lectures at the Bleecker Street Church in Utica, which netted the AAS six hundred novice abolitionists and half a dozen new AAS chapters. Twelve hundred citizens signed petitions against slavery in upstate New York in a single three-day period. "The Lord is with us—truth tells. Mob dead, buried, and rotten. Shall probably lecture here sometime longer. Go next to Rochester," Weld wrote to Lewis Tappan. But all was *not* well; the mob was far from "buried." As Weld crusaded, New York's antiabolitionist activists planned their response: the issue was not slavery, they maintained (why argue with Weld on an issue he knew so well?), but "amalgamation." For wherever Weld went, he insisted on inviting free blacks to hear him.

Tappan was uncertain about this part of Weld's philosophy; he himself believed that while recruiting free blacks and opening black schools, visiting black churches, and even allowing black men and women to be part of interracial choirs during antislavery lectures was good politics *inside* the movement, it exposed free blacks to targeting and victimization *outside* it. Tappan remembered what had happened in Cincinnati, when white Lane seminarians had mixed with free blacks in the black community and in so doing harmed the very people they intended to help. It was not the abolitionists who suffered at such times, Tappan knew, but free blacks: black homes were burned, black businesses looted, and black men and women attacked, while the white abolitionists remained untouched. Tappan did not approve of the fact that good reformers never seemed to suffer the most violent consequences of white hatred; the point, he argued, was to *help* black people, not hurt them.

Weld chided Tappan for his uncertainty and castigated the AAS's leadership for its stated policy of "elevating" free blacks—a policy that he said amounted to "Great cry and little wool." Outspoken though Weld was, he would brook no criticism of his own views or actions. So when Tappan censured him for allowing white antiabolitionist forces in Ohio to intimidate free blacks (and, in so doing, recalled Weld's own refusal, once, to walk down the street with a black woman), Weld snapped that Tappan could not have it both ways. First he wanted the abolitionists to bar blacks from their meetings out of fear for their safety, and now he was criticizing Weld for refusing to walk with a black woman—all without knowing the facts. Weld's response, as damning as it was eloquent, was circulated within the abolitionist community, to be repeated and used to great effect in abolitionist speeches. He told Tappan:

> As to my feelings towards the Colored people, suffice it to say while I was at Lane Seminary my intercourse was with the Colored people of Cincinnati I think if may say *exclusively*. If I ate in the City it was at *their* tables. If I slept in the City it was at *their* homes. If I attended parties, it was *theirs—weddings—theirs—Funerals—theirs—Religious meetings—theirs*—Sabbath schools—Bible classes—theirs . . . I was with the Colored people in their meetings by day and by night. If any one wishes to know what my *principles* and *practice* have been and are as to Intercourse with the Colored people, I say let him ask the three thousand colored people in Cincinnati and if he ask it soberly they will laugh in his face. But, says brother Tappan, would you "have walked arm in arm with a Colored lady at mid-day down main street in Cincinnati?" Answer No. Why!? . . . Because to do it would bring down a storm of vengeance upon the defenceless people of Color, throw them out of employ, drive them out homeless, and surrender them up victims to popular fury.

The dispute boiled, then simmered, and finally cooled. Tappan did not want to offend Weld; he was too valuable. In May, Weld moved on to Troy, the scene of much antiabolitionist agitation. He did not know it, but New York's political establishment was lying in wait for him. Members of the New York legislature who opposed his views had seeded Troy with reports that the abolitionists were attempting to incite slaves to insurrection. They played on "amalgamationist" fears and spread rumors about abolitionist men's consorting with black women. The most scurrilous, most emotional, and wildest reports concerned Weld's activities in Ohio, where he had been greeted with stones, his enemies said, and run out of towns. He had disrupted the peace of communities and been seen with black women. Blithely unaware of this controversy, Weld approached his task in Troy as he had in southern Ohio, by bringing together small groups in churches to dampen antiabolitionist sentiment. It did not work. In mid-May, Weld was greeted at a local church by a brick-throwing mob. He was forced to move the meeting to another church, but with fewer attendees: the antiabolitionist mob succeeded in intimidating some of his likeliest converts. He forged on, asking the Troy police for protection. But twice during the lecture that followed on his second day in the city, a large mob (including at least one Troy policeman) broke into the church and attempted to rush the pulpit.

"Stones, pieces of brick, eggs, cents, sticks, etc. were thrown at me while speaking," he later wrote. As he had done in Ohio, Weld went on, attempting to lecture on successive nights, but always straining to be heard over the shouts of an angry crowd. His life was threatened. Each time, when he had finished speaking, he was shoved, pushed, jostled, and punched by a group of ruffians, brought together specifically for the purpose of breaking up his meetings. Elizur Wright wrote to Weld urging him to give up on Troy, saying he was in too much danger there. Writing from Boston, William Lloyd Garrison agreed. He argued that Weld would do more good by coming to a yearly antislavery meeting in Rhode Island: "What is Troy compared to the nation?" he asked. Weld fought on, but the mobs only grew. Finally, the mayor (who had actually helped foster the discord around Weld) ordered him out of the city. Weld protested and said he intended to stay, but the mayor threatened to have him arrested. Weld eventually left, feeling and looking defeated. Troy was a setback. It was the first time Weld had ever failed to "abolitionize" a city.

Despite this failure, Weld's reputation was enhanced by his crusade in New York. He brought hundreds into the abolitionist movement and, in the face of overwhelming and sometimes violent opposition, built a nascent grass-roots political movement and seeded a national organization. Still, he was stunned by the ferocity of the crowds that had gathered to oppose him in Troy. The shouts of the antiabolitionists, and the hatred in their eyes, had a discernible impact on his emotions: he was perceptibly and, many thought, permanently shaken. The experience convinced him to heed the call of Elizur Wright and the rest of the leadership of the American Anti-Slavery Society. These men were convinced that, impressive though their organizing efforts had been to date, they had not yet brought their movement into the mainstream. It was time, they argued, to build a network of national agents who could take the cause into America's homes. Weld did well in the field—brilliantly, in fact—but what the AAS needed was dozens of Welds. In the wake of his Troy failure, Weld agreed.

In July 1836, Weld met with the Tappan brothers and Elizur Wright in New York to map out a comprehensive national antislavery strategy. Weld insisted that his approach, of focusing on the countryside, was the correct one, and for the first time ever, Wright concurred. But the Tappans and Wright argued that more and better-trained agents were needed in the field, and that Weld, and no one else, should train them. Weld conceded the point but asked to be given three months to find new recruits and develop a training program for them. In effect, Wright and the Tappans charged Weld with the responsibility of reorganizing, training, and then monitoring the entire AAS agent system. In November, after three months of preparation that included interviewing potential new antislavery agents (to weed out the faint of heart and, as Weld said, the mere "propagandists"), Weld summoned thirty-nine of what he hoped would eventually be "the seventy" (the number of "helpers of the apostles" in the early church) to New York for an agents' convention. Among their number were Sarah and Angelina Grimké.

SEVEN

"... we will go and work together"

S tudents of history tend to draw a direct causal line linking early antislavery agitation and the growth of the abolitionist movement to
the coming of the Civil War and the drafting of the Emancipation
Proclamation. But in fact, no such line can be drawn. The antislavery
movement was much more a process than it was a deep and broadly
based public crusade; its expansion depended on a number of disparate
and complex factors. The agents who met in New York in 1836 represented a variety of political and social beliefs. That they could gather at
all was miraculous; that they assembled as a result of their early accomplishments was a myth. Of the thirty-nine antislavery agitators who
came together in New York, only three could claim any real previous success: Southerner James Thome, Ohioan Henry B. Stanton, and mnemonics lecturer Theodore Dwight Weld. All of them had once been Lane
Rebels.

The abolitionist movement was more than a melding of discrete political causes; it also brought together political enemies. The founding
convention of the American Anti-Slavery Society, in Philadelphia, had
been dominated by New England Garrisonians and New York reformers,
but in the fall of 1836, that original group was expanded to include
Philadelphia Quakers, exiled Southerners, and even—with the appearance of the Grimké sisters—former slaveholders. The AAS was an odd
stew. Its chief backers, the Tappan brothers, a pair of rich dry-goods

retailers, crusaded against every major depravity then rife in New York—prostitution, drunkenness, child abandonment, organized banditry, graft—and established benevolent associations to answer every evil: a woman's home, a temperance association, an orphanage, Bible reading groups, neighborhood associations. They were Protestant reformers, with a sword in one hand and the Bible in the other.

Boston's Garrison thought the Tappans naive and touched by vanity. He mistrusted them, in essence, because he believed that in arguing for a more clearly political approach to the problem of slavery, they were seeking power. Garrison did not want power; rather, he wanted to inaugurate the Kingdom of God in the United States of America. While nominally a Quaker, Garrison, like those around him, was schooled in the ways of New England Puritanism. Confident, outspoken, impatient, fiercely independent, quick to judge and even quicker to condemn, mistrustful of government and of *any* organization, Garrison and his cohorts were not interested in arguing the merits of their case; they *knew* they were right. Garrison brought his rapier wit and hammering logic to the pages of *The Liberator*. His editorials made his colleagues wince, but he would not compromise his own beliefs or curb the power of his pen. He invented the language of abolition and perfected an invective of moral rectitude, calling historian George Bancroft, that icon of American history and symbol of great learning in the new Republic, an "ambitious, unprincipled time-serving demagogue, who would sell his country as Judas sold his Lord." Garrison likewise referred to Henry Clay, the "Harry of the West" and perhaps the most beloved political figure of his age, as a "pitiable object . . . an awful curse." Garrison even turned his wrath on the great Daniel Webster, labeling him a "lick spittle of the slaveholding oligarchy" (John Greenleaf Whittier would mimic Garrison by calling Webster Ichabod in his poem by the same name). How could anyone respect Garrison, that hawk-faced, hatchet-headed, severe, black-suited eminence who fairly breathed fire? But the New England abolitionists followed him because he was ferocious and because he was brilliant; and they supported him because, when all the arguments had been heard and the votes taken, he was right: slavery was a stain, a betrayal, a sin.

Garrison's language astonished the Philadelphia Quakers. Bred to tolerance (the Society of Friends might disapprove of some of its members' opinions, but it never directly silenced them), they were soft-spoken, highly disciplined, and imbued with a sense of unquestioned moral authority. The Quaker abolitionist message held primacy even among the most outspoken antislavery voices. John Woolman had nearly single-handedly brought the issue into the national conscience a century before, and since then, the Quakers had arguably done more for the cause, through the establishment of their Free Produce movement, than all the calls for "immediatism" put together. Lacking any desire for personal preferment and regularly eschewing the opportunity for personal gain, Quakers were the glue of the abolitionist movement, the least likely of its supporters to build on animosities, to be schismatics. The Quakers, not Garrison, provided the abolitionist movement with its religious message, its view of the future, its tolerance, its hope, and, ultimately, its way past the divisions that many Quakers feared would bloody the nation. And many of the most prominent Quaker abolitionists were women.

All of these factions—Boston Puritans, New York reformers, and Philadelphia Quakers—had been brought together by the Second Great Awakening and the frontier religious revival it had sparked. Themselves mesmerized by Finney and his followers, the Tappans had looked with wonder at the hundreds and thousands who flocked to hear his message. The great abolitionists had been trained by Finney, and the greatest abolitionist orator of them all, Theodore Dwight Weld (now known as the "thunderer of the West"), had once been his top lieutenant. Weld's mission at the Lane Seminary had provided the AAS with the infusion of young blood it so desperately needed in the wake of its organizing convention in Philadelphia in 1833. Weld, Thome, and Stanton (the great triumvirate of the Western revival, and the most talented and sought-after abolitionist speakers) formed the core of the AAS's organizing initiative. Although the society had printed millions of antislavery pamphlets in the two years since its founding, almost all AAS officers agreed that the "pamphlet campaign" had failed. It was Weld and his colleagues who had built the abolitionist movement, and it was they who now began the long and arduous task of training its most important agents. Catherine Birney, the Grimké sisters' earliest biographer, described these first organizers:

> Working with common purpose, these men were of varied accomplishments and qualities. William Jay and James G. Birney were cultured men of the world, trained in legal practice and public life; Arthur Tappan, Lewis Tappan, John

Rankin, and Duncan Dunbar, were successful merchants; Abraham L. Cox, a physician in large practice; Theodore D. Weld, Henry B. Stanton, Alvan Stewart, and Gerrit Smith were popular orators; Joshua Leavitt, Elizur Wright, and William Goodell were ready writers and able editors; Beriah Green and Amos A. Phelps were pulpit speakers and authors, and John G. Whittier a poet.

Weld began to train the new group of agents in the techniques he had learned in Ohio, Pennsylvania, and upstate New York by conducting two and sometimes three intensive and exhausting daily sessions at the AAS headquarters in New York City. The training commenced on November 15 and lasted until December 2, with many of the sessions going on into the late hours of the evening. Weld posed the questions that the agents would face in the field, and then provided the answers: What was slavery? Why didn't the abolitionists take their campaign into the South? Hadn't the Hebrews of the Bible had slaves? Hadn't Saint Paul defended slavery? Was slavery a sin? Why didn't the abolitionists support colonization? Did abolitionists "consort" with free blacks? The Grimké sisters—not officially listed among the future "seventy," but invited to attend the sessions by Weld himself—were awestruck by the proceedings and became Weld's most apt and dedicated pupils. To Angelina, it seemed clear that among all the great men who surrounded her, the true leader of the movement, and its most powerful voice, was Theodore Dwight Weld.

In many ways, Angelina and Sarah Grimké's journey from Philadelphia to New York was even more difficult for them than their exile from Charleston. Sarah in particular was loath to make a final break with their friends in the Fourth and Arch Street Meeting, and she believed that Angelina's growing involvement in the antislavery movement would only bring her grief. But she was not insensible to her sister's pleadings, issued from Shrewsbury, that she reconsider her views and join her there to discuss their common future. Sarah relented: she would follow Angelina wherever she led, though she was still heavy-hearted over what now appeared to be a definitive rupture with their Philadelphia Quaker friends. Like Angelina, Sarah was forced to leave not just her religion but the only people she knew well in the North. At age forty-four, Sarah Grimké was starting over again.

Angelina shared her older sister's doubts. She was especially upset about their break with Catherine Morris, their dearest friend in Philadelphia. "Her disapproval, more than anything else," Angelina wrote, "shook my resolution." In Shrewsbury, the two sisters spent many days trying to decide what to do. Angelina wanted to devote herself to antislavery work in New England, focusing on the Free Produce movement and specifically on organizing a boycott of Southern cotton. She put aside this plan when she was told that even the Quakers of New England opposed her coming there, believing she had little chance of success. Catherine Morris wrote that she would need a "certificate" from the Fourth and Arch Street Meeting to make the trip. While Angelina dismissed Morris's warning—"I have realized very sensibly of late that I belong not to them," she retorted—she decided it would be better for her to accept the AAS's long-standing invitation to come to New York and speak to women about the antislavery cause.

When the New York agents' meeting adjourned, after nearly three weeks of daily training sessions, the Grimké sisters set out on a personal crusade against slavery. Sarah was a willing and newly energized participant. She had begun to feel something in New York that she had not felt for many years: she was, finally, fully at ease with the choice she was making, and felt more self-confident and self-assured than she had in a very long time. Gone was her fear that her beliefs would stir up bitterness; gone, too, were the religious self-doubts that had plagued her for two decades. After the agents' meeting ended, she followed her sister's lead and wrote a special appeal of her own. Sarah, however—as seemed most appropriate to her temperament—addressed *her* plea to Southern clergymen.

Sarah Grimké's "An Epistle to the Clergy of the Southern States" had as subtle an impact on Southerners as Angelina's address had had on Southern women. After its publication by the American Anti-Slavery Society, in December 1836, it was banned in Charleston and confiscated in every major city of the South But like Angelina's "Appeal," it was also widely read. Sarah had picked her target well. Many among the Southern clergy, she knew, had long been calling for a public debate on slavery, but had been silenced by public opinion and political force. Like Angelina, Sarah spoke to her audience as a native Southerner and not a Northern abolitionist. "A solemn sense of duty I owe as a southerner to every class of the community of which I once was a part," she wrote, "likewise impels one to address you, especially, who are filling the important and responsible station of minister of Jehovah, expounders of the lively oracles of God."

Sarah's letter was learned and detailed, and it struck at the heart of the Southern belief that the "peculiar institution" was blessed by Scripture. To prove that her own arguments were taken from that source, she established her credentials as a reader of the biblical text in its original language. She argued, for instance, that the correct translation of a selected passage in the Old Testament proved that Abraham had not had slaves; she called the assertion "a mere slander." (That the Bible was literature and not the literal word of God was not something that Sarah, or any of the Southern clergyman she addressed, believed, much less discussed. So basing her argument on the actual translation of a passage was more than important; it was critical.) In remembrance of her childhood, Sarah castigated Southern ministers for launching a crusade to distribute copies of the Bible "to the heathen" even as they denied their slaves the right to read it. Finally, delicately, she alluded to the sin that stalked too many Southern households, where men took advantage of black slave women and willingly participated in (using Mary Chesnut's phrase) "a sin we cannot name."

The reputation of Angelina and Sarah Grimké, and their emergence as new leaders in the abolitionist movement, commenced with Angelina's "Appeal" but became solidified by Sarah's epistle. In the aftermath of the agents' meeting, therefore, it seemed only natural to invite them to help establish the Female Anti-Slavery Society, comprised mostly of New York women and conceived as an adjunct to the AAS. At the urging of the Tappans, Wright, and Weld, Angelina and Sarah resolved to speak to small groups of women interested in the subject. They began with a series of parlor meetings set up by women in their homes in New York City. Angelina and Sarah would appear, speak, and then answer questions. More often than not, these meetings lasted for hours, and while they attracted only a limited number of women, they were critical in cementing the foundation of the abolitionist and, later, the women's rights movements. They served as the political laboratory for what was to follow.

The appeal of the Grimké sisters was immediate, and soon enough, no "small parlor" could hold their audience. Their insistence on speaking to other women on such a controversial and blatantly political topic as abolition caused a minor sensation at the headquarters of the AAS, despite the support they received from that organization's leadership. There were fears, bluntly stated, that Angelina and Sarah would call so much attention to themselves as to undermine the abolitionist crusade. They, and not slavery, it was said, would become the focus of public attention. More pertinent, though never stated, was the fear that in speaking out on a publicly controversial subject, the Grimké sisters would instill in women the idea that the "political sphere" (that is, men's sphere) was actually open to them. There was also a growing wariness among antislavery leaders about abolitionism's real problem and its greatest weakness: its inability to attract the American mainstream. The majority of Americans, it was thought, might well be offended by the Grimkés and persuaded that they were the "new Fanny Wrights"—a reference to the famous feminist Scotswoman who toured the U.S. in the 1820s, lecturing on equal rights for women, and formed a socialist labor colony in Tennessee. Her behavior had been widely condemned as unseemly.

At the end of December 1836, Sarah and Angelina Grimké made their first public (non-parlor) appearance, addressing an audience of more than three hundred women on the subject of slavery. Angelina spoke for forty minutes about her own experiences and beliefs before yielding the floor to Sarah ("dear sister did her part better than I did," Angelina would testify), and then both answered questions. The meeting lasted for two hours. The Grimké sisters' appearance had a profound impact on the antislavery movement, because while the Philadelphia Female Anti-Slavery Society, the Female Anti-Slavery Society (of New York), and dozens of other women's antislavery groups all recruited women for the cause, female abolitionists had yet to find their voice. The Grimké sisters spoke for them. But these "lectures" had other, much more revolutionary effects as well.

Just as many of the male leaders of the AAS feared, the Grimké sisters' activism had ramifications that could divide their movement and divert the efforts of its largest group of supporters, women, to another cause. They had reason to worry. Throughout January 1837, the public lecture series continued, drawing unexpectedly large crowds; the AAS gained hundreds of converts. Women became the most able and effective workers in the antislavery movement, giving their time and personal resources to petition drives and pamphlet campaigns. Sarah had never been happier; like Angelina, she had found her calling. "I would not give up my abolition feelings for anything I know," she wrote in a postscript to one of

Angelina's letters. "They are intertwined with my Christianity. They have given a new spring to my existence, and shed over my whole being sweet and hallowed enjoyments."

———

Nearly all of the AAS's leaders in New York, and the leaders of chapters in New England, Pennsylvania, and Ohio, knew their program was modest, but that was how they intended it to be. They did not want to call for a revolution (with the exception of Garrison, of course, who used the word whenever an audience appeared); they did not want to spark a slave insurrection in the South (the prospect of such an event horrified them); they did not want to win equal rights for black people (they simply did not believe that black Americans were "ready" for equality); and they did not want to foment violence against slaveholders (nearly all AAS leaders were pacifists). They believed that their program was enlightened, persuasive, moral, and blessed by an all-powerful deity. Most abolitionists advocated "immediate emancipation, gradually obtained," because they supposed that that objective would attract converts to their cause. Nevertheless, the vast majority of the American people, in both North and South, still looked on the abolitionists as fanatics.

Weld, the Tappans, Garrison, Wright, Stanton, Thome, and the Grimkés—all of them powerful speakers and highly motivated organizers—had made great strides in putting their message before the public. But at the end of 1836, they agreed that even after all their work, few Americans really gave slavery any thought, and fewer still were inclined to lend their voices (or empty their pockets) on behalf of the movement. There had, however, been one notable victory: in the two years since the founding of the AAS, slavery had become a national issue, an accepted part of the nation's political discourse. In this, the abolitionists had been best served by their enemies. Enraged by the abolitionists' program and threatened by their attempts to win the public over to their views, Southerners commonly portrayed the antislavery activists as "incendiaries," "instigators," "fanatical crusaders," and "cold-hearted, base and malignant libelers and calumniators." They were in fact none of those things, but the more the Southerners said they were, the more other Northerners began to doubt it; and the more those Northerners listened to the arguments of the abolitionists, the more sense they made. If Southerners did not build the abolitionist movement, they certainly played a major role in bringing its message before the public.

In the first session of the Twenty-fourth Congress, in December 1835, freshman congressman James Henry Hammond of South Carolina had stood alone on the floor of the House of Representatives and demanded that his colleagues refuse to "receive" a petition from 172 women of Maine asking the United States government to outlaw slavery in the District of Columbia, a petition sent to the House as part of the AAS's antislavery petition drive. Hammond's demand was unprecedented: never before had a petition *not* been received by the House, though most petitions were politely laid aside after being duly noted by congressmen intent on humoring their constituents. Hammond would have none of that. Antislavery petitions, he said, were an insult to the South. It would not be unconstitutional for Congress not to receive a petition, he contended, because it was not as if the petitioners had been denied their right to assemble and ask for signatures; Congress had the full right to dispose of such business as it wished.

Hammond's proposal was founded not on some fine point of parliamentary privilege or little-used technicality in the House rules, but rather on his own antipathy toward abolitionists, his defense of slavery, and his perceived need to impress his Southern colleagues with his Southern patriotism. That Hammond hated abolitionists was made clear to all, however, not just to his fellow Southerners, as he spewed invective:

> And I warn the abolitionists, ignorant, infatuated, barbarians as they are, that if chance shall throw any of them into our hands he may expect a felon's death. No human law, no human influence, can arrest his fate. The superhuman instinct of self-preservation, the indignant feelings of an outraged people, to whose hearth-stones he is seeking to carry death and desolation, pronounce his doom; and if we failed to accord it to him we would be unworthy of the forms we wear, unworthy of the beings whom it is our duty to protect, and we would merit and expect the indignation of offended Heaven.

"Abolitionists," Hammond thundered, could be "silenced in but one way—Terror—Death." Hammond, all six foot one of him (a giant in those days), was a newly rich South Carolinian, having married into a landed family and thence inherited the management of its holdings. He was a brilliant lawyer and orator, and as purely Southern as any well-heeled low-country gentleman. But the "fanaticism" of the abolitionists paled when compared to Hammond's; his was the faith of the converted. More simply, as one historian has noted, he was a "nation smasher." But inadvertently, in attempting to call attention to his own Southern patriotism, Hammond stirred up a storm of protest. He thereby helped to make abolitionism a national movement by giving it an impetus that Weld, Garrison, and the Tappans could have never matched.

For years, Garrison and Weld and Wright and the Tappans had struggled to transform their beliefs into a public crusade. Their efforts had won large numbers of converts to their cause, but they had not been able to dampen the power of the pro-slavery forces. The truth was, as all of them admitted at one time or another, that a family living in a free state, just thirty miles from a farm where men and women were held in bondage, might never give *one thought* to slavery, and might see nothing at all wrong with it. Slavery did not *concern* them. So Garrison, Weld, Wright, and the Tappans asked themselves the natural question: How could otherwise honorable and moral Americans be made to care about the issue? How could slavery be brought home, made real, palatable, *important* to people?

Now, in one fell swoop, James Henry Hammond and William Slade had transformed the debate over slavery into a debate over free speech. It would take a number of years for Garrison, Weld, and the rest of the abolitionist leadership fully to comprehend the implications of Hammond's attempt to curb the "inalienable right of petition," but then they would use it to great effect. Americans, they would conclude, might not care one whit about what happened to America's black population, but they cared a great deal about their own rights. Disappointed and even disenchanted though the antislavery leaders would be in the face of this realization, they would swallow their disgust at the North's lack of moral outrage and transform the crusade *against* slavery into a movement *for* free speech. If the Southerners had only kept their mouths shut, everything might well have been fine; but now, in late 1836—just as it seemed as if the abolitionist crusade were losing steam—Congressman James Hammond handed the antislavery movement its most potent political gift.

———

The Grimké sisters continued their New York agency into the first months of 1837. Every week, and sometimes two or three times a week, the sisters would walk quietly from their rooms at the home of the New York abolitionist minister Henry Ludlow to a nearby church to "lecture" on slavery's "evil" and "immorality." More often than not, the crowds that greeted them would spill out into the streets. Their appearances were so popular, and so effective, that hundreds of women who came to see them in January and February came back a second and even a third time. The result was that more than one half of all AAS members in the state of New York—a membership of more than twenty thousand in all—were women. A large portion of these had been recruited to the antislavery crusade by the Grimké sisters. When Angelina and Sarah were not lecturing, they were discussing their crusade and refining their arguments during private discussions with Theodore Weld. Soon the three were acting as a team, planning the sisters' lecture strategy and promoting their mission.

In March, in response to a letter published in the *New Haven Religious Intelligencer* and signed "Clarkson," the Grimkés embarked on a comprehensive antislavery program. The document they wrote in response to Clarkson, who had criticized abolitionists for targeting Northerners and not focusing their efforts on the South, was more detailed and politically sophisticated than anything yet published by the AAS. The Grimkés' position was eventually adopted by the society as a part of its "unofficial" organizing strategy in the North. Unlike their previous works, the Grimké sisters' Clarkson response focused on Northerners' complicity in slavery and the slave trade; in all, ten of their ten points emphasized ending Northern cooperation with Southern slavery. They charged that Northerners "are striving to perpetuate slavery in the District of Columbia"; "Northern votes in Congress have admitted seven new Slave States into the Union"; "Northern manufacturers, merchants and consumers, are constantly lending their aid to support the system of slavery;" "Northern ministers go to the South and close their lips on the subject of slavery"; "Northern men go to the South to make their fortunes; they frequently become slaveholders"; "Northern prejudice against color is grinding the colored man to the dust in our free states"; and "Northern men are themselves *slaveholders,* and in the city of New York alone, the merchants hold mortgages on the southern plantations and slaves to the amount of 10,000,000 dollars."

The Grimké sisters' response to "Clarkson" did not endear them to the leadership of the AAS (inevitably, some of the merchants targeted by them were friends of the Tappans'), but no one moved to silence them; they were too valuable. Nor could any of the AAS's leaders disagree with their conclusions, and many—the Garrisonians in particular—applauded them. Garrison noted that if "Northerners were to do all we have marked out, can any one doubt the powerful influence which it would produce on southern conscience and Southern interest? Could slavery live a single year under such an organized, disinterested, noble opposition to it? No!" Having given the Grimkés free rein, the AAS leadership could do little but stand aside and watch their power and influence grow, and with them, the power and influence of the entire antislavery movement. By May 1837, it had become clear that the Grimké sisters were transforming the antislavery movement into a social revolution. They were rewriting the AAS's national organizing slogan, changing it from "immediate emancipation, gradually obtained" to "immediate emancipation and full equality."

In this respect, at least, Sarah and Angelina's years of struggle with their religion, and their conversions from Episcopalians to Presbyterians to orthodox Quakers and finally to lapsed Quakers, served them well. No longer fearful of such changes, they now welcomed them. Nor were they intimidated, as they had once been, by the judgments of others; they were now willing to disagree openly with those whom they most admired. It had started with Catherine Morris and the elders of the Fourth and Arch Street Meeting, but their willingness to assert their independence—to lead the abolitionist movement instead of simply following its leaders' dictates—reached its zenith after Catherine Beecher (whom Angelina, especially, admired) published "An Essay on Slavery and Abolitionism with Reference to the Duty of American Females."

Beecher's essay, "Addressed to Miss A. D. [sic] Grimké," defended the policy of gradualism, endorsed the work of the American Colonization Society, and criticized women abolitionists for acting outside their moral and domestic "sphere." Its author adopted the tone of an older woman addressing a well-meaning but sadly misled daughter who needed to be taught how a woman should act. "Men are the proper persons to make appeals to the rulers whom they appoint," she wrote, "and if their female friends, by arguments and persuasions, can induce them to petition, all the good that can be done by such measures will be secured. But if females cannot influence their nearest friends, to urge forward a public measure in this way, they surely are out of their place in attempting to do it themselves."

Beecher, perhaps the most celebrated woman of her time, was a legend in the minds of many American women. They looked to her for advice and counsel on everything from child rearing, to being good and obedient wives. Most American women agreed with her view that the proper female role, in the proper "sphere" for a woman, was as a quiet voice of reason in the home—but never in public. Six months before the publication of "The Duty of American Females," Beecher penned an essay intended for a much wider audience. "Letters on the Difficulty of Religion" provided a prologue to Beecher's Grimké essay and left no doubt as to her views on the role of women in the "public sphere." She used Fanny Wright, the Scottish socialist reformer and political activist, as an example of what a woman should *not* do:

> Who can look without disgust and abhorrence upon such a one as Fanny Wright, with her great masculine person, her loud voice, her untasteful attire, going about unprotected, and feeling no need of protection, mingling with men in stormy debate, and standing up with bare-faced impudence, to lecture to a public assembly. . . . I cannot conceive any thing in the shape of a woman, more intolerably offensive and disgusting.

No one could have mistaken the Grimké sisters for Frances Wright. Nearly everything about them belied their outspokenness, their growing public identity, their controversial views. They did not see themselves as radicals, nor did they look like revolutionaries. Clad in simple gray dresses, with matching bonnets, both Grimké sisters might be (and were) described as "plain," "soft-spoken," "well-mannered," "deferential," and "modest"—all qualities that Catherine Beecher admired and urged on her faithful readers. They were neither "masculine" nor "loud" nor "untasteful." Sarah and Angelina Grimké were increasingly independent of any man's view, and at the ages of forty-five and thirty-two, respectively, they were self-assured enough to strike out on their own. But as Beecher warned, and as the leadership of the AAS feared, by their very appearance in public, the Grimké sisters raised an entirely new set of issues. They were no longer simply antislavery activists; they were feminists. The shift was profound.

Angelina's response to Beecher's essay, entitled "Letters to Catherine Beecher," appeared in consecutive issues of *The Liberator* from June to November of 1837. There were thirteen letters in all, covering every aspect of the sisters' abolitionist views. Although ostensibly written as a defense of the Grimkés' commitment to "immediate emancipation," the letters also presented ideas new to the antislavery crusade. At the heart of this new thinking was the notion that slavery was based on differences not in race but in skin color, a view first broached privately by William Lloyd Garrison. The Grimkés proposed that slavery was fueled by prejudice; once this was admitted, they argued, every other defense of the practice fell apart. If color and not race prejudice was at the heart of slavery, the sisters said, then the goal of the abolitionist movement must go well beyond emancipation: once freed, black Americans must be granted equal rights.

This argument was not only new, but so controversial that it threatened the very existence of the AAS, whose leaders carefully dodged questions about granting black Americans political rights. After reading Angelina's "Letters to Catherine Beecher," abolitionists knew that the Grimkés had gone further in their political program than the leadership of the AAS ever had—or could. It wasn't necessary, AAS leaders knew, for white America to love black people; that was expecting too much. It was necessary only that they act to free them. Angelina and Sarah disagreed, and "Letters to Catherine Beecher" put their views on display, reserving for the aims of the American Colonization Society a special scorn:

> Every true friend of the oppressed American has great cause to rejoice, that the cloak of benevolence has been torn off from the monster of Prejudice, which could love the colored man *after* he got to Africa, but seemed to delight to pour contumely upon him whilst he remained in the land of his birth. I confess it would be very hard for me to believe that any association of men and women loved me or my family, if, because we have become obnoxious to them, they were to meet together, and concentrate their energies and pour out their money for the purpose of transporting us back to France, whence our Huguenot father fled to this country to escape the storm of persecutions. Why not let us live in America, if you really *love* us? Surely you never want to *"get rid"* of people

whom you *love*. I like to have such near me; and it is because I love the colored Americans, that I want them to stay in this country; and in order to make it a happy home to them, I am trying to talk down, and write down, and love down this hor- rible prejudice.

There it was, the "heart of the matter" (as the Grimké sisters them- selves would say). The great problem that America faced was not slavery (horrible though it was) or racism (for it was clear that the Negro *race* was not inherently inferior, no matter what anyone claimed) but rather color prejudice—the enslavement of men and women not because they were from Africa but because they looked different.

"Letters to Catherine Beecher" went even further than that, for it contained the seeds of a feminist political philosophy that was emerging as the greatest threat to the unity of the antislavery crusade. The same ar- guments that Catherine Beecher had used in her essays on the correct be- havior of women were now used against *her* by Angelina. The same words that Angelina used to describe the condition of black Americans (and their "proper behavior") were, Angelina knew, *also used to keep women* in their place. "And so," wrote Angelina, "the colored people are to be taught to be 'very humble' and 'unassuming,' 'gentle,' and 'meek,' and then the 'pity and generosity' of their fellow citizens are to be ap- pealed to." So it was with women as well, Angelina implied. Black America's "sphere" was bondage, while a woman's "sphere" was silence. The profound conclusion drawn by Angelina was that silencing women was simply another way of ensuring the continuation of slavery. In a jab at her friend Catherine, she noted, "The truth always irritates the proud, impenitent sinner."

The next logical step was to speak to women bluntly and simply on the subject of *their* rights, which Angelina did in drafting "An Appeal to the Women of the Nominally Free States." She delivered the address during the first Anti-Slavery Convention of American Women, held in New York City in May 1837. In attendance were, besides the Grimké sisters, Lydia Maria Child, Maria Weston Chapman, Anne Warren Weston, Lucretia Mott, and Julia and Susan Tappan: the first generation of what can truly be called the American women's movement. Angelina Grimké made clear her views when she pointed out, in her address to the conven- tion, what every woman present knew to be true: "Women ought to feel a peculiar sympathy in the colored man's wrong, for, like him, she has been

accused of mental inferiority, and denied the privileges of a liberal education." The women in her audience did not politely applaud this statement, as they had been instructed to do in such situations by Catherine
Beecher; instead, a number of them did something very unladylike indeed: they cheered.

———

At the end of the same month, the American Anti-Slavery Society
dispatched the Grimké sisters to Massachusetts to continue the "aboli-
tionizing" of New England, already a hotbed of antislavery sentiment.
Angelina and Sarah looked forward to their new crusade. New England,
they believed, would welcome them in a way that New York never
had. This judgment proved accurate. The two were greeted with a sustained ovation at the meeting of the Boston Female Anti-Slavery Society,
which convened in the city's Washington Hall. More than four hundred
women attended, but none was better known than the Grimkés. The
meeting was a great success, and Sarah and Angelina felt more comfortable than they had at any time since their departure from Philadelphia.
Their only disappointment came when they met former president John
Quincy Adams, the leader of the petition campaign in the House of
Representatives.

Adams was in fine form, polite but brusque, irascible, and often argumentative, though he clearly admired the two women. Sarah and Angelina were neither intimidated by his manner nor awed by his
reputation. They pleaded with him to take a more public role in the anti-
slavery movement and to lend his voice to the crusade for immediate
abolition. He listened closely, then turned them down: "Upon this subject of antislavery my principles and my personality make it necessary for
me to be more circumspect in my conduct than belongs to my nature," he
explained. He nodded sagely at their arguments but would not alter his
position. After the meeting, he seemed taken aback when asked whether
he thought women should have a role in the antislavery movement. "If it
is abolished," he said, "they must do it."

The sisters spent the next eighteen months lecturing in New England,
mostly in Massachusetts. At first they confined their appearances to
"parlor meetings" like the ones they had held in New York, but they
agreed to speak at larger venues when more people wanted to hear them.
By the end of 1837, they had spoken to hundreds of listeners (the vast

majority of them women) in public meeting halls and churches in Rox-
bury, Boston, Lynn, Danvers, Salem, and New Mills. Their message in
Massachusetts was the same one they had championed in New York:
slavery was a sin that must be expunged from America's soul. Everywhere they went, they took petitions to be signed, recruited members for
the AAS, established female AAS "auxiliary" chapters, and gathered donations that they then forwarded to the AAS offices in New York. Everywhere they went, newspaper reporters came to hear and cover them as
they did what few women had done before: speak in public.

The force of their presentation was undeniable, and their message itself clear, precise, consistent, and sometimes overpowering. Years later,
when the most publicly prominent leaders of the abolitionist movement
recalled this time, they would testify that just as Theodore Weld had
"abolitionized" Ohio, the Grimké sisters had "abolitionized" New England. "I well remember evening after evening listening to eloquence
such as never then had been heard from a woman," Bostonian Wendell
Phillips would rhapsodize, speaking of Angelina. "She swept the chords
of the human heart with a power that has never been surpassed and rarely
equaled."

Sarah Grimké stayed close by as a helper to her sister Angelina; their
relationship had never been better. They continued to perfect their arguments and their presentations and shaped each message to fit the New
England community. Taking John Woolman and an entire generation of
Quakers as their inspiration, they made friends wherever they went,
building the first political network of women activists in the nation's history. But Sarah was fast moving beyond Angelina's already revolutionary
views. In late 1837, she began to study the writings of John Humphrey
Noyes, who argued against paying the clergy, rejected public worship
and the observance of the Sabbath, and questioned the need for civil government. An advocate of nonviolent resistance, Noyes believed that human institutions were obstacles to human growth, and that the human
spirit was "infinitely perfectible." Sarah included some of his thinking in
her lectures.

Also attracted to Noyes's "perfectionist" philosophy was William
Lloyd Garrison, who endorsed his views in the pages of The Liberator.
Garrison contended that in supporting slavery, the American government had betrayed the ideals of the American people, and that for this
reason, the American people should "come outta" the government. This

"come outerism" doctrine (as it came to be known) marked the abolitionist movement's most radical departure from political action. Sarah defended this "come outta" doctrine in a series of letters to Gerrit Smith, a
Utica, New York, native and philanthropist and the founder and president of the New York Anti-Slavery Society. Smith was entranced by
Sarah's simple message and her guileless belief in Noyes's "perfectionism," and he became one of her biggest supporters inside the AAS leadership. Sarah was particularly drawn to Noyes's argument that while all
political action required compromise, such compromise, by its very nature, undermined public morality. The only way to maintain morality,
Noyes believed, was to reject political life. Without government, he said,
simple citizens would be at liberty to follow their natural sentiments and
to construct a society free from institutional interference.

Just after completing her letters to Gerrit Smith, Sarah acceded to
Mary Parker's request that she set aside her reading of Noyes in order to
issue a defense of women's rights. Such a work, Parker said, would be of
inestimable value. As president of the Boston Female Anti-Slavery Society, Parker had heard Angelina and Sarah speak and was intent on making use of their name to broaden the appeal of the antislavery movement,
hoping to draw in women who were also interested in women's rights.
The result was the first feminist manifesto in American history, tinged
by Sarah's reading of Noyes's doctrines. Sarah Grimké's "Letters on the
Equality of the Sexes and the Condition of Woman" appeared in the
pages of both the *Boston Spectator* and *The Liberator* in late 1837.

Sarah Grimké relied, like her sister, on a closely argued position derived from Scripture. Her devotion to interpretation of the Bible was as
deep as Angelina's, as she took her viewpoints and positions from a text
that was commonly known and understood by nearly all women. But unlike Angelina, Sarah distilled her most compelling arguments from her
own experience, from what she had seen with her own eyes and heard
from the women she met as an antislavery agent, and from her belief in the
"perfectibility" of human relations. What she saw all around her, she wrote,
was the undeniable subservience of women to men. The existence of such
subservience in the face of evil—an evil such as slavery, for example—
made the fight for women's rights a moral imperative. She confided:

> I have sometimes been astonished and grieved at the servitude
> of women, and at the little idea many of them seem to have of

their own moral existence and responsibilities. A woman who is asked to sign a petition for the abolition of slavery in the District of Columbia, or to join a society for the purpose of carrying forward the annihilation of American slavery, or any other great reformation, not unfrequently replies, "My husband does not approve of it." She merges her rights and her duties in her husband, and thus virtually chooses him for a savior and a king, and rejects Christ as her Ruler and Redeemer.

The Grimkés' tour of Massachusetts ended abruptly in November of 1837, with both sisters exhausted and ill. They accepted an invitation from their fellow abolitionists Samuel and Eliza Philbrick to stay at their home in Brookline, outside Boston, and rest. The Philbricks had become close friends with the Grimkés over the previous months and now dedicated themselves to nursing the two women back to health. Angelina was in fact deathly ill with typhoid fever, while Sarah was beset by a case of bronchitis. By almost any measure, their work in Massachusetts had been a startling success, but it had exacted a steep physical toll on them. In their temporary home in Brookline, the sisters slowly began to recover, all the while monitoring the controversy their public crusade had sparked. While New England's establishment—that is to say, its churches—was in the forefront of public efforts to silence the Grimké sisters, their public appearances and increasing notoriety had also strained their relations with a former supporter, Theodore Weld.

The "thunderer of the West" was concerned that Garrison and his colleagues were turning the Grimké sisters into advocates for women's rights, at the expense of the abolitionist movement. Weld pointed as evidence to a letter printed in *The Liberator* from one of Garrison's most outspoken allies, Henry C. Wright of Newburyport, who was working for the AAS as a New England agent. Wright defended the sisters and added that other abolitionists would be well served by following their example in adopting the women's rights movement as a cause. His argument provoked such consternation in the top echelons of the American Anti-Slavery Society that the AAS executive committee transferred him to Philadelphia (where the ideas he was advocating would not reach such a wide audience), over Sarah and Angelina's objections. In all probability, Wright's aim had been not to defend the Grimkés by calling for a broadening of the abolitionist mandate, but merely to support them in the wake of sustained and bitter attacks by New England's powerful community of clergymen, which he deemed unfairly harsh.

Most disturbing to New England's ministers was Sarah Grimké's view that women could, and should, preach the Gospel (an opinion expressed in chapter 14, "Ministry of Women," of her "Letters on the Equality of the Sexes"). Direct criticism came from the pulpit after she not only refused to recant her views but pointedly repeated them, in a series of addresses on the topic to female audiences. In one such speech she even poked fun at the ministry, stating, "Surely, there is nothing either astonishing or novel in the gifts of the Spirit being bestowed on woman: nothing astonishing, because there is no respect of persons with God; the soul of the woman in his sight is as the soul of the man, and both are alike capable of the influence of the Holy Spirit." That was just about enough. The General Association of Massachusetts issued a pastoral letter "to the Churches Under Their Care," instructing ministers to warn their congregations of the "dangers which at present seem to threaten the female character with wide spread and permanent injury." Sarah Grimké was not mentioned by name in the mandate, but she was nonetheless its target.

Two other church letters followed, both condemning the public lecturing of "females" as "improper and unwise." The pastoral letters generally praised women for their devotions and prayers in the home but counseled them to avoid becoming involved in political questions. And what if they should ignore this advice? After due consideration, the Massachusetts Assembly decided that God Himself would intervene: "If the vine, whose strength and beauty is to lean upon the trellis and half conceal its clusters, thinks to assume the independence and the overshading nature of the elm, it will not only cease to bear fruit, but fall in shame and dishonor in the dust." These were subtle words for a questionable proscription, whether issued by God or by his earthly representatives: any woman who dared to speak out in public on political questions would have her womb blighted.

While the Grimkés did not respond publicly to any of this, the normally taciturn, understated, and sometimes sentimental New England poet John Greenleaf Whittier could hardly help himself. His ditty on the churches' condemnation of the Grimké sister was soon making the rounds:

So this is all—the utmost reach
Of priestly power the mind to fetter!
When laymen think—when women preach—
A war of words—a "Pastoral Letter"!

In November 1837, an abolitionist editor named Elijah Lovejoy was murdered by a mob in Alton, Illinois. Lovejoy and his reform-minded newspaper, *The Observer*, had been a target of antiabolitionist sentiment since the day he first called on his readers to help form an Illinois anti-slavery society. Alton's civic leaders had pressured him to shut down his newspaper, but he had refused. The growing public clamor had even brought Edward Beecher, Lyman Beecher's well-known brother and the president of Illinois College, to Alton in an attempt to mediate the conflict and keep Lovejoy's newspaper in business. Protestors had destroyed his printing press in October, but he had simply ordered another one. Then, on the evening of November 7, a mob marched on the warehouse that contained the new printing press and set it on fire. When Lovejoy ran out of the warehouse, he was shot.

The antislavery movement made the most of the murder. The power of slavery was everywhere, they said; it could reach even into the peaceful towns of the North. New converts flocked to the movement in the Midwest. Elijah Lovejoy's brother was overwhelmed by his loss, but he admitted that the cause of abolitionism had gained more through his brother's death than it ever had from the pages of his newspaper. Meeting in New York, the American Anti-Slavery Society declared the editor a martyr and issued AAS writing paper emblazoned with a new logo and motto: "LOVEJOY the first MARTYR to American LIBERTY. MURDERED for asserting FREEDOM of the PRESS. Alton Nov. 7, 1837." The word *slavery* was nowhere to be seen.

Sarah, a follower of her brother Thomas's beliefs and an avowed pacifist, was devastated by Lovejoy's death. Her remorse was obvious to all. "My heart sinks within me when I remember the fearful scenes of Alton," she wrote in a letter to Weld. "Will God continue to bless an enterprise which is baptized in blood?" She prophesized that the fight over slavery might yet consume the entire nation. "The blood spilt at Alton," Sarah wrote to Sarah Douglass, "will be the seed of future discord; those who were engaged in the mob, as well as the defenders of the press, will thirst for more and who can foresee the calamities that await us."

In January 1838, recovered finally from their illnesses, the Grimkés renewed their public campaign. They appeared at the Boston Lyceum to debate the question "Would the condition of woman and of society be improved by placing the two sexes on an equality in respect to civil rights and duties?" The debate brought hundreds of women to the Lyceum, but Angelina herself described the meeting as a "farce." In February, two events occurred that were to have a profound impact on the lives of Sarah and Angelina Grimké. At the beginning of the month, the state legislature of Massachusetts invited the sisters to present their views on slavery in a public forum. The invitation was unprecedented—no government body had ever before asked a woman to testify—and it caused a sensation. The Grimkés agreed to speak before the legislature on February 21.

Significant though this was, in many ways, the second event was even more important. For a number of months, Angelina and Theodore Dwight Weld had been exchanging letters about their lives, their views, and their hopes for the future. The correspondence had become increasingly personal, and on February 8, Weld penned the following message to Angelina: "I know it will surprise and even amaze you, Angelina," he wrote, "when I say to you as I now do, that for a long time, you have had my whole heart." But Angelina was *not* surprised: "I felt[,] my Theodore," she responded, "that we are the two halves of one whole, a twain one, two bodies animated by one soul and that the Lord has given us to each other." Angelina Grimké was in love.

EIGHT

"We Abolition Women are turning
the world upside down . . ."

Just after noon on February 21, 1838, Maria Weston Chapman and Angelina Grimké emerged from a carriage on Beacon Hill and walked the short distance to the Massachusetts State House, overlooking the Boston Common. It was a bright but cold day, typical for New England in winter. It is likely that the two women walked arm in arm, for Angelina needed Maria's support this day as never before. Sarah was ill and had decided not to come. When they turned in to the front of the building, they were greeted by the spectacle of a huge crowd pushing and shoving its way into the public gallery of the legislative chambers' hearing room. Some in the crowd noticed them; there were a few catcalls, some jeers, and a smattering of applause.

The two women walked through the front door of the State House and into the legislative chambers, where a special committee had been called to hear Angelina's testimony on the evils of slavery. The two women were forced to squeeze past the assembled legislators and the crowd of spectators. As soon as they entered, they were greeted by applause, scattered at first, and restrained, but then growing in strength. They took their seats near the front of the room as the onlookers strained to see them. A number of their friends were there to show their support and to celebrate the triumph of their cause. They were convinced that Angelina Grimké's appearance here, and her being asked to speak out against slavery in public—before an official committee of the government, no less—

marked a long-awaited formal recognition of their crusade. The abolitionist movement had come of age; it had entered the mainstream.

Angelina wore a simple gray dress, fittingly modest for the occasion. Behind her, the crowd continued to pour in, taking up every seat in the gallery, standing along the back wall, filling a staircase. The legislators were arrayed in the front of the room. The chairman of the committee called for order, but it took some time for the crowd to get settled. Angelina waited patiently, if nervously. She kept her eyes trained straight forward. "I never was so near fainting under the tremendous pressure of feeling," she would later admit. "My heart almost died within me. The novelty of the scene, the weight of responsibility, the ceaseless exercise of mind thro' which I had passed for more than a week—all together sunk me to earth [so] I well nigh despaired." As the gallery finally grew quiet, Mrs. Chapman leaned over to speak in Angelina's ear: "God strengthen you, my sister," she said.

The chairman of the committee called on Angelina to come up and give her remarks. She rose uncertainly and stepped forward. There was a commotion in the hall, and a hiss sounded from the back of the room. The chairman called for order. Angelina was alone. She turned to face the audience and began to speak, but there was another disturbance—some applause, some jeering—and the chairman asked her to suspend her remarks until the hall was quiet. When she began speaking again, she was interrupted for a third time. Finally, so that she could be heard, but also so that her testimony would silence her detractors, she was invited to stand in the chairman's place, facing the crowd. The platform was slightly elevated, and she stood quietly until the crowd grew silent. After a short introduction, she plunged into her text. She spoke forcefully, emotionally:

> I stand before you as a southerner, exiled from the land of my birth by the sound of the lash and the piteous cry of the slave. I stand before you as a repentant slaveholder. I stand before you as a moral being and as a moral being I feel that I owe it to the suffering slave and to the deluded master, to my country and to the world to do all that I can to overturn a system of complicated crimes, built upon the broken hearts and prostrate bodies of my countrymen in chains and cemented by [the] blood, sweat and tears of my sisters in bonds.

Behind Angelina, the secretary of the committee attempted to blink back the tears from his eyes. Before her, in the hall, there was silence. She spoke for two hours, and when she finished, there was thunderous applause. Her friends in the abolitionist movement were overwhelmed. "[Her] testimony was not only the testimony of one most competent to speak," Wendell Phillips later wrote, "but it was the profound religious experience of one who had broken out of the charmed circle, and whose intense earnestness melted all opposition." Angelina herself put it more simply: "We Abolition Women are turning the world upside down," she said.

———

Two days later, Angelina once again appeared before the committee. This time she was accompanied by her sister, who took a seat nearby. Her testimony again lasted for hours. The focus of her remarks, on both days, was slavery. But she was careful to present a unique message tailored for her Northern audience. Her intention was not to woo listeners to her side, or recruit them to her cause, but rather to speak the truth about an institution and a way of life that she had seen for herself and they could only begin to imagine.

At the heart of slavery, she said, was color prejudice; emancipation, once won, would not be the end of the battle. She larded her testimony with remarks on the importance of equality and provided biblical citations to prove her point. The fact of her appearance before the committee was far more important than what she actually said, but what she said nonetheless placed her in the forefront of the antislavery movement. Angelina was now not only its primary and most public organizer but also its chief social and political theorist. Nearly all who were in the audience on the two days of her testimony in Boston believed they were witnessing a historic event that would be remembered by succeeding generations. For them, Angelina Grimké's appearance before a committee of the Massachusetts legislature was, as one participant suggested, as significant as Washington's Farewell Address.

The *Boston Gazette* was less impressed: "She exhibited considerable talent for a female," the reporter editorialized, "and as an orator, appeared not at all abashed in exhibiting herself in a position so unsuitable to her sex, totally disregarding the doctrine of St. Paul who says, 'Is it not a shame for a woman to speak in public?' " Angelina ignored such comments. She was convinced that her appearance had been a triumph. She spent the next several weeks corresponding with her friends about her "adventure" and planning her spring crusade with Sarah. The two wanted to pick up where they had left off just months before, hoping to capitalize on Angelina's notoriety as a means to bring more New Englanders into the antislavery movement. But of course, Angelina could no longer devote all of her time to the antislavery issue; she had other things on her mind.

Over the previous month and a half, Angelina and Theodore Weld had been secretly exchanging love letters between Brookline and Manhattan. Both expressed their feelings openly, unabashedly, but both also worried that their commitment to each other would harm their dedication to the abolitionist cause. Still, neither could stop the relationship, or really wanted to, and they gleefully planned to meet in Brookline in mid-March. Theodore was gushingly sentimental about his feelings, even after Angelina admitted to her attachment to Edward Bettles. "My heart's desire," he wrote, "you have knitted me to you still closer if possible by the free disclosure of your deep and tender affection for that loved one who was snatched from you by death. I love you the more Angelina that you *loved* and *love him still.*" Both were timid, inexperienced in such relationships, and fearful of intimacy. One exchange found Weld pleading for understanding. His was an exercise in indirectness, ambiguity, and double meaning—what one historian has termed "an orgy of self-restraint":

> From your knowledge of my natural impulsiveness, I have forboded almost everything as to your natural inferences from the state of mind which I fear was manifest in that letter. I pray you not to infer from that letter that I have lost *self control* and am drifting, helmless, before the mighty gust. No. I feel the steady helm in my hand and God's strength in my arm to turn it withersoever he bids. . . . I had striven and resisted almost unto blood against my love for you. I had seized it and with violent hands had struggled to throttle it, and thus had violated the laws of my being and blindly resisted our Father, under whose ordering the absorbing feeling had taken possession of my soul and was doing there *His own* work.

So it went. The letters raced back and forth, with a feint here and a jab there until finally, consumed by their own passion, both took a step back.

Both confessed that they loved each other, surely, but (yes! they had to admit it to each other) they loved God more. With that detail out of the way, they continued their long-distance courting until Weld arrived at the Philbrick house in Brookline on March 17. It was immediately apparent that Angelina was in love with him and that they must be married. That should have been good news to everyone in the antislavery movement, but it was not. The AAS leadership, in particular, feared that a union between Angelina Grimké and Theodore Dwight Weld would further hobble Weld's ambition, which had been sharply curbed, it seemed, since the end of the New York agents' convention fifteen months earlier. From that time until his appearance in Brookline, Weld had not spoken in public, and he claimed he would never speak again.

Weld brushed aside the AAS leaders' concerns. He said he much preferred working on the movement from the society's offices in New York to being an agent anywhere else. It was there that he was needed most, he argued, to handle correspondence, edit publications, and help James Thome write a book on slavery. He was occupied every day with the business of the organization, he said, and he was an invaluable political strategist. The leadership was not convinced, fearing that Weld's failure at Troy had been his "Golgotha" and had persuaded him that his public agency was at an end. Weld's supporters disagreed. His defeat at Troy had had nothing to do with his decision to end his public career, they said, and reminded his detractors that he had hardly been able to speak above a whisper after the convention, that he had been mentally and physically spent, and that his health was not good.

If Weld was anxious about his own role, he did not show it. He was consumed by his relationship with Angelina. He was pleased to see her—overwhelmed, even. They chatted amicably, though uncomfortably, with the Philbricks before being given some time alone to say in person what they had until now said only in their letters. There were some embarrassing moments. At one point, with the Philbricks seated nearby, Weld had to rush from the room in order to keep his emotions (and presumably his desires) in check. In addition to spending time with Angelina, Weld worked with the two sisters on their antislavery message, taking great care in preparing them for a series of lectures at Boston's Odeon Hall. With Weld finally at her side, Angelina was at ease; she spoke first at these appearances, then deferred to Sarah.

Sarah's talks did not go well. At one point she criticized the governor of Massachusetts for promising to send militiamen to the South in case of a slave uprising. The controversy over her remarks did not deter her, however: she showed as much determination as Angelina had shown before the state legislature, and was more outspoken on the subject of women's rights than her sister. Even so, Sarah was not the polished speaker that Angelina had become, and some abolitionists felt certain that her continued public appearances would dampen enthusiasm for the cause. She was monotonous and heavy as an orator, they said. Fearful of hurting her feelings, they told her that her true gift lay in her ability to put the antislavery message into words—*written* words. She should stay away from public events, they contended. After the first of the Odeon lectures, the AAS's leadership consistently pushed Angelina into the public limelight and Sarah into the background. At last, seeing that Sarah was confused and hurt by this turn of events, Weld intervened and told her the truth. She had to work more diligently on her speaking style, he said; she was too erudite and too argumentative.

Once back in Manhattan, Weld expressed his views in a letter to Sarah. He did not spare her feelings. He began by saying that he had been told by a number of abolitionists that they would much rather hear Angelina speak at the remaining Odeon lectures than Sarah. But he added that "the lack of interest in your lectures was not at all for lack of excellent [subject] matter, but for lack of an interesting and happy manner of speaking." This was damning her with faint praise, but Weld was concerned that the dissent he was hearing inside the AAS might become public. He was also worried that Sarah might decide to appear at the Odeon *instead* of Angelina. He did not dare say that, of course. "Now my beloved sister," he wrote, "I am persuaded you will agree with me that the only question to be thought of for a moment in settling the question between you as to who should deliver the Odeon lectures is this: *which* of you will produce the *best* effect. Surely the object is to do not *good* merely, but the *greatest* amount of good." There was almost a palpable pause in the letter before he went on, "The crisis is momentous in Boston and demands the highest effect."

Sarah was hurt by Weld's words, but she said little and deferred to Angelina, as she had so many times before. The Odeon series concluded at the end of March, whereupon Angelina turned her attention to planning her wedding. To both of the sisters, it must have seemed that a very special time was ending. Neither Sarah nor Angelina Grimké would ever again be so well known, or so celebrated, as she was during the first months of 1838. But both women were changing. It was not simply that Angelina was about to be married, or that her relationship with Sarah would be transformed: Weld had written to Sarah that he expected all three of them to live together, adding that he admired Sarah and felt great affection for her. No, that was not the problem. The problem was in the antislavery movement itself.

———

The fame of the Grimké sisters and their insistence on linking the rights of women to the rights of American slaves were dividing the abolitionist movement. Within a year of their lectures in Boston, the American Anti-Slavery Society would itself snap and break under the pressure of its two warring factions: the New England Garrisonians and the New York reformers. The debate was furious and intense, not least because of the stern and stubborn personalities involved. The contest was as old as the New World, pitting New England Puritans against New York revivalists and Philadelphia Quakers, and it reflected the nation's short history, reprising the political battles that had once set New England antifederalists against mid-Atlantic nationalists. The issues were deeply felt and bitterly fought. Both sides believed they were absolutely and incontestably right. But to anyone who has ever been part of a large national movement, campaign, or organization, the fight that divided the American Anti-Slavery Society will sound familiar. This debate, in essence, was between political idealism and political realism (as the followers of the Tappan brothers might have stated it), or (as William Lloyd Garrison's supporters would have put it) between those who would compromise their ideals for political gain (the Tappan faction) and those who would not (the Garrisonians).

Garrison and his followers, representing the movement's "radical" wing, welcomed the Grimké sisters' call for a national recommitment to "equality" for all Americans. They believed that abolitionists should follow any cause that would transform the nation's spirit, whether it was "perfectionism," pacifism, or women's rights. This was not just some political fantasy or a dip into fashionable utopianism; Garrison was convinced that the nation actually *could,* and eventually *would,* be transformed through constant and diligent moral suasion. In fact, he said, true reform and real emancipation were possible only after a thoroughgoing change of heart, a purifying absolution of the soul. Garrison was uncompromising in his views. The stain of slavery was universal, he insisted, and touched every American. Those who could not see it were simply not looking. They were deluded.

Garrison had always been outspoken, but he became even more so during the Grimkés' tour of New England. As the principles they enunciated touched off a storm of controversy, and as the crowds that came to greet them grew ever greater in size, Garrison rhapsodized in the pages of *The Liberator* about the moral transformation that was just then, he said, infusing the American spirit. He imagined the triumph of the righteous and the washing away of America's sins, if only people would follow the banner of the abolitionists. "Be not afraid to look the monster *Slavery* boldly in the face," he urged his readers. "He is your implacable foe—the vampyre who is sucking your life blood—the ravager of a large portion of your country, and the enemy of God and man." Garrison's purpose was to kindle a moral renaissance, so that America, once cleansed, could lead the rest of the world to a new Eden. Such a renaissance, he said, must start in the souls of individual Americans; from there it would sweep the nation. He angrily dismissed calls for political action, charging that the American political system itself stood guilty of allowing slavery in the first place. There was nothing sacred or honorable about the American experiment. The Constitution was not some great, soul-inspiring document that had inaugurated a new era; rather, it was "the most bloody and heaven-daring arrangement ever made by men for the continuance and protection of a system of the most atrocious villainy ever exhibited on earth."

The New York reformers, led by Lewis and Arthur Tappan, were horrified by such words. As the movement's "conservative" wing, they saw it as their task to use the nation's instruments, its political and legal system, to reform the Republic's institutions. They scoffed at Garrison's vision for a new America, labeling his views "wild" and "absurd." The Grimkés were important, Weld had done a tremendous job, and the Lane Rebels had brought thousands into the crusade against human bondage. But the simple, awful, and unutterable truth about the antislavery movement was that two decades after first becoming a public topic, abolitionism was still viewed as a minor, a fringe, a marginal, cause. If Garrison was going to depend on "moral suasion" to free the slaves, the Tappans suggested, emancipation might never happen. Instead, they argued, the antislavery movement should transform itself from a church-based crusade into a political movement that would gain and use political power. Such a movement would compel the nation to fight slavery whether it wanted to or not.

James G. Birney, the rich and worldly Alabama slaveholder-turned-abolitionist, led the fight to shift the movement's focus away from Garrison's radicalism. "It is vain to think of succeeding in emancipation without the co-operation of the great mass of the intelligent minds of the nation," Birney wrote. "This can be attracted, only by the reasonableness, the *religion*, of our enterprise." *Reasonableness?* Garrison was enraged by such words. "Brethren, 'cease from man,' " he wrote, mimicking Isaiah, "beware of a worldly policy; do not compromise principle; fasten yourself to the throne of God; and lean upon the arm of Omnipotence." Put in its simplest terms, the division that split the abolitionist movement in 1838 was a fundamental one: Garrison wanted to change people's values, while the Tappans wanted to win their votes. Garrison wanted to establish a new Eden, and the Tappans a republic of laws. Garrison wanted people to be infused with the Holy Spirit; the Tappans wanted them to be inundated with AAS mailings.

The Grimkés and Weld were caught in the middle of this fight. In the weeks and months prior to their wedding, Weld and Angelina exchanged expansive and detailed letters on their beliefs and on their roles in the battle. But it was not simply discomfort over the sisters' appearance in public that bothered Weld (like so many others, he supported their activism but feared they would divert public attention from the abolitionist cause); it was also their adoption of some of Garrison's views (including his "no government" argument and his condemnation of "vain" and "corrupting" human institutions). He told Angelina as much, and bluntly. In response, the sisters (Angelina was almost always the one who wrote to him, appending a shorter note from her sister) replied that *they* disapproved of some of *his* political viewpoints, and thought him "not a peace man." Weld responded by reminding Angelina and Sarah of their own ties to Garrison. "Practically I have always been a 'peace man' in my sense of the word," he argued. "Not a 'no government' man—that doctrine fills me with shuddering and I pray [for] you and all who are bewildered in its mazes and stumbling on its dark mountains 'Father forgive them' and open their eyes!" Weld's criticism was pointed. He went on to imply that Sarah and Angelina's heads had been turned by their public notoriety. This was a dicey topic, no less apt to inspire indirectness than the subject of intimacy. Weld had a talent in that area, and he used it well.

Both Angelina and Theodore believed it was time to leave the abolitionist movement, but not simply because they were getting married or because they could not agree on the most fundamental debate in the antislavery crusade. Deep down, they knew that the focus of the movement was shifting, and that the inevitable split between New Englanders and New Yorkers would spell the end of the public crusade for abolition. Both of them, and Sarah as well, could see it as clearly as they could the "War which hangs round the horizon of our country." Weld welcomed this "irrepressible conflict," but Angelina despaired for the future and worried about her relatives in South Carolina. "Sometimes the hope gleams across my mind that as we have labored so publicly in the cause of the slave, our services will be remembered in the hour of darkness and death and their lives will be spared—at least our Mother's," she wrote. "Are those vain and foolish hopes?"

———

Angelina Grimké and Theodore Dwight Weld were married on May 14, 1838, in the home of Angelina's sister Anna Grimké Frost. Fewer than forty people attended the multiracial ceremony, which was conducted as a celebration of the unity of the two most outspoken antislavery voices in the nation. There was no minister present, for Weld and Grimké both believed that they could not "conscientiously consent" to be married by a clergyman; instead, they repeated those vows that occurred to them at the moment. Sarah memorialized the event in a letter to Catherine Beecher: "Theodore addressed Angelina in a solemn and tender manner. He alluded to the unrighteous power vested in an husband by the laws of the United States over the person and property of his wife, and he abjured all authority, all government, save the influence which love would give them over each other as moral and immortal beings. Angelina's address to him was brief but comprehensive, containing a promise to honor him, to prefer him above herself, to love him with a pure heart fervently."

The event was as political as it was social. The greatest lights of the abolitionist movement were in attendance, including William Lloyd Garrison, Henry B. Stanton, Abby Kelley, Jane Smith, Anne Warren Weston, John Greenleaf Whittier, Maria Weston Chapman, Gerrit Smith, Lewis Tappan, James Thome, and Weld's disciples from the Oneida Institute and the Lane Seminary. After the marriage, two former slaves who had been given to Anna by her mother (and subsequently freed by her) delivered a short discourse on the slave life and bore testimony "against the horrible prejudice which prevails against colored persons, and the equally awful prejudice against the poor." The wedding was unadorned, the ceremony simple; there was no drinking (of course) and no formal reception. Angelina knew that marrying Weld, who was not a Quaker, would get her barred from the Fourth and Arch Street Meeting; but she and Sarah had long since decided that they were lapsed Quakers, and over the last year they had openly criticized the Friends for their "quietist" stance on abolition. Angelina Grimké's marriage to Weld thus only made official what was already an accomplished fact: neither Angelina nor Sarah would ever return to the Society of Friends.

May 14 was auspicious for another reason as well. As Angelina and Theodore were exchanging their vows, a group of Philadelphia reformers, including a large contingent of abolitionists (those, that is, who were not in attendance at the Grimké-Weld wedding), were dedicating Pennsylvania Hall, in downtown Philadelphia. The hall had been built by subscription, by an association led by men and women frustrated by their inability to find a facility for their meetings. After collecting forty thousand dollars over a period of two years, the group had erected the hall to serve as a safe haven for their activities. It was large but simply decorated, with a substantial conference area and several meeting rooms. The president of the association, a local businessman named Daniel Neall, gave the opening address and then turned the floor over to the secretary, William Dorsey, a prominent Philadelphian. Dorsey read the hall's dedication statement: "A number of individuals of all sects, and those of no sect, of all parties, and those of no party, being desirous that the citizens of Philadelphia should possess a room wherein the principles of liberty and equality of civil rights could be freely discussed, and the evils of slavery fearlessly portrayed, have erected this building, which we are now about to dedicate to liberty and the rights of man." The secretary then read letters of support from well-known abolitionists, including Theodore Weld.

Two days later, on May 16, the Anti-Slavery Convention of American Women called a meeting to order in the new hall. The meeting had been well publicized, and the public invited to attend; as a further inducement, the convention had invited Angelina Grimké Weld and Maria Chapman to speak. Earlier that day, as placards had gone up around the city to announce the women's public appearance, other notices were posted urging all Philadelphians to close the meeting—"forcibly if necessary." The organizers ignored the threats. By the time the meeting began, late in the afternoon, the hall was jammed with more than three thousand people; hundreds of others had to be turned away. The organizers were overjoyed by the response.

The program opened with a short address by William Lloyd Garrison, whose thunderous voice overcame the scattered hissing and audible groans that punctuated his comments. When he had finished his speech, protestors attempted to end the meeting: catcalls and jeers came from the back of the hall, and there were disturbances in the aisles, with much pushing and shoving. A crowd of men endeavored to keep the speakers from reaching the platform. Maria Chapman finally made her way to the front of the room, where she tried to calm the crowd and continue the program. Just then, a shout from someone standing near one of the windows in back announced the arrival of an angry mob in the street in front of the hall. Stones flew, and then chairs, and the sound of windows breaking could be heard. In an effort to help Chapman, now besieged on the stage by an angry crowd, Angelina Grimké hurried up the center aisle and attempted to call the convention to order. The yelling subsided at the sight of her. She raised her voice to be heard and shouted above the boos; bricks came through the windows, but she went on with her address, undeterred. It was perhaps her finest moment. In spite of the din all around her, she held the crowd in the room, though many wanted to flee. She faced the mob, angrily raising her voice to ask, "What is a mob? What would the breaking of every window be? Any evidence that we are wrong, or that slavery is a good and wholesome institution? What if that mob should now burst in upon us, break up our meeting, and commit violence on our persons—would this be anything compared with what the slaves endure?"

Angelina next turned to the institution of slavery itself, linking the mob violence of Philadelphia to the violence she had witnessed growing up in South Carolina:

I have seen it! I have seen it! I know it has horrors that can never be described. I was brought up under its wing. I witnessed for many years its demoralizing influences and its destructiveness to human happiness. I have never seen a happy slave. I have seen him dance in his chains, it is true, but he was not happy. There is a wide difference between happiness and mirth. Man can not enjoy happiness while his manhood is destroyed. Slaves, however, may be and sometimes are mirthful. When hope is extinguished, they say "Let us eat and drink, for tomorrow we die."

The noise from the mob outside grew, but the meeting continued. Angelina Grimké was followed to the podium by reformer Abby Kelley, then becoming nationally known for her views on women's rights. After Kelley came Lucretia Mott, who gave an abbreviated speech. By then the crowd outside in the street had quieted, and most of the people in the meeting hall had taken their seats. The danger seemed to be over. Grimké's words, the refusal of large numbers of attendees to abandon the hall, and the arrival of the police (late, even though the meeting's organizers had asked for their protection) all combined to calm the protest. But the mob did not disperse. As the conventioneers filed out of Pennsylvania Hall, they were met by a cascade of jeers. The mob remained in the streets through the night, its leaders vowing to continue their protest into the next day.

———

May 17 dawned bright and clear. Early in the morning, a group of abolitionist women made their way to Pennsylvania Hall to continue the proceedings that had been suspended the night before. They fervently hoped that the mob would have disbanded by now, but when they arrived at the hall, they discovered that more than a thousand Philadelphians, many of them from the city docks, remained on the street outside. There were no policemen in sight. Undaunted, the antislavery women walked past the crowd, into the building, and began preparations for their meeting. Inexplicably, tensions eased throughout the day, and the proceedings were not interrupted. But toward evening, the protestors outside the hall were reinforced by a large group of workingmen. "The crowd around the building increased," biographer Catherine Birney would later write, "and the secret agents of slavery were busy inflaming the passions of the rabble against the abolitionists, and inciting it to outrage."

For the safety of the participants, the meeting scheduled for that evening was canceled, and the leaders of the association that owned the hall called on Philadelphia's mayor, John Swift, for protection. The mayor duly appeared and attempted to persuade the crowd to leave, announcing that the meeting had been canceled and that there was thus no reason for anyone to stay. His effort, however, was perfunctory: at times he bantered with members of the crowd whom he recognized, and when he was done speaking, he bid everyone to "have a good evening." The crowd gave him three cheers ("Hooray for the mayor") and then broke into the hall. The police did not intervene.

Looting began. The hall's "repository" of papers and books was ripped from its shelves and tables and thrown into the street. A gang climbed the interior stairs to the meeting rooms, piled papers and books on the podium, and lit the whole thing on fire. Within minutes, the main meeting room was ablaze, the flames visible through the windows. The mob below, now estimated at some ten to fifteen thousand people, cheered in triumph. The fire company appeared, but its attempts to extinguish the flames were halfhearted. Less than three hours later, before the clock struck midnight, all that was left of Pennsylvania Hall was its outer walls; flames had gutted its interior. It was a total loss.

After the Pennsylvania Hall riot, Philadelphia's abolitionist community went into self-imposed internal exile. The abolitionists feared for their lives. The fire unleashed the white community's rage at "amalgamation," which was then spurred on by wild rumors, including one spread by mob leaders who said they had seen a black man escorting a white woman in downtown Philadelphia. This rumor turned out to be true, at least in part: the black man was Robert Purvis, and the woman his light-skinned wife. William Lloyd Garrison did not linger in Philadelphia to learn the outcome of the subsequent investigation into the fire; he was spirited out of town, against his will, by an abolitionist committee for public safety. His life was repeatedly threatened, and no one took those threats lightly.

Several weeks after the fire, and the attacks that followed on the black community, a special investigatory committee blamed both the mob and the Philadelphia abolitionists for the troubles. The antislavery movement, the commission concluded, had been responsible for the violence because it promoted "doctrines repulsive to the moral sense of a large majority." The commission's report did not mention any abolitionist by name, but if it had done so, it might well have singled out Sarah Grimké. At a key moment in the convention's proceedings, Sarah had urged the antislavery women to adopt a resolution calling on all abolitionists to work for both emancipation and racial equality. They could do this, she said, if only they would choose to "identify themselves with these oppressed Americans, by sitting with them in places of worship, by appearing with them in our streets, by giving them our countenance in steamboats and stages, by visiting them at their homes and encouraging them to visit us, receiving them as we do our white fellow citizens."

Three weeks after the Pennsylvania Hall fire, Angelina, Sarah, and Theodore moved from Philadelphia to Fort Lee, New Jersey, where Weld had bought a small farm. They intended to continue their work in the abolitionist movement, but from a distance, and primarily through their writing. Weld still insisted that he would never speak in public again, that his voice was too impaired from years of lecturing. Sarah, who had never really mastered the art of public speaking anyway, now decided to follow a new vocation: she would become an essayist on women's rights. Angelina, for her part, was bent on being a good wife and mother and helping her husband in his writing. Together, the couple planned a book on slavery in America, a work that they hoped would be even more effective in recruiting Americans to the antislavery cause than any of their public appearances had been.

Angelina and Sarah's move with Theodore to Fort Lee marked as much of a shift in their lives as their journey from Charleston to Philadelphia. Just as the sisters' move north had foreshadowed their work in the antislavery movement (and in their new cause, equal rights for women), so now their decision to live wholly private lives signified the end of their public careers. In the years leading up to the Civil War, neither Angelina nor Sarah would ever again speak in public on the subject of slavery. From time to time over the next three decades, Sarah, Angelina, and Theodore would be urged to reignite and restoke the passions they had fired in the 1830s, but in each instance, they would turn down the invitation.

The Grimké sisters were now the Grimké family. The three—Sarah Grimké, Angelina Grimké Weld, and her husband, Theodore Weld—left Philadelphia to take up a life "in retirement" that would be a simple reflection of their beliefs in self-sustenance and intellectual and religious independence. Their Fort Lee farm was perfectly suited for such a life. The house was small but functional and placed well back from the bluffs overlooking the Hudson River. There was room for a large vegetable garden, and the farm's orchards were a constant source of fresh fruit. Sarah, now forty-six, helped her "dear Nina" with the chores and spent her free time reading and writing. Angelina, thirty-three, struggled for a while with her new responsibilities but took pride in her little accomplishments, writing friends that her situation proved that her public career had not "spoiled" her for "domestic life." Both sisters were happy, perhaps happier than they had ever been. But neither they nor Weld forgot who they all were and why they had met, and none wavered in his or her antislavery views. In the parlor, just inside the entrance to their home, they hung a picture of a kneeling slave. "It is just such a monument of suffering as we want in our parlor," Angelina wrote in a letter to a friend. "We want those who come into our house to see at a glance that we are on the side of the oppressed and the poor."

All three followed the diet then fashionable among the Eastern Seaboard's educated classes. The "Graham diet" was the brainchild of Sylvester Graham, a well-known Boston nutritionist and the first American to start a "health fad." The sisters had heard him lecture in Boston and had become convinced that adopting his diet would help them lead healthier lives. The Graham diet emphasized simple but nutritious foods such as apples, crackers, asparagus, potatoes, rice, stewed fruit, milk, beans, tomatoes, and the ever-present "Graham bread," which we now know as Graham crackers. Left out were all condiments, meat, alcohol, tea, and coffee. All three lost weight and increased their strength, as Weld continued his daily walks and jogs, an unusual form of exercise for the time (he was not one of America's first joggers, but nearly so). All three were poor: Angelina had brought her five-thousand-dollar inheritance to the marriage, and Weld was paid a thousand dollars a year by the American Anti-Slavery Society, but they had no other income; Sarah kept her own accounts and contributed to the household expenses by handing over a small monthly sum. They lived frugally but without want.

Angelina was intent on practicing good housekeeping. To this end, she kept William Andrus Alcott's *Young Housekeeper* close at hand, as it recommended the most efficient ways for a young wife to clean and cook, leaving her time for the more important duties of a woman: moral elevation, religious training, and self-reflection. Everything, according to Alcott, was to be closely monitored and scheduled; if done properly, he confided, the endless tasks of cooking, washing, and cleaning would consume only one quarter as much time as they took up in a normal (un-Alcottized) household. Angelina, Sarah, and Theodore were convinced

Graham and Alcott disciples, and the strict regimens they followed seemed to pay dividends, at least according to Sarah. "We believe it [the Graham-Alcott regimen] is the most conducive to health," she wrote, "and, besides, it is such an emancipation of woman from the toils of the kitchen and saves so much precious time for purposes more important than eating and drinking."

The three got along well. There was mutual respect among them, and a full and open relationship between Angelina and Theodore. If the new bride had any difficulty acclimating to married life, she never mentioned it in any of her writings. They worked together on Weld's numerous writing assignments for the AAS, and several times each week he went into New York to work at the society's offices. Having broken their ties with the Quakers of Philadelphia, the sisters seemed astonishingly unconcerned with religion, such an obsession for both of them just a few years earlier. They were comfortable in their Christian beliefs, in their dedication to leading a moral life, and in their conviction that no church, no minister, and no professed public belief was more important than their own unmediated relationship with an all-powerful and all-forgiving deity. There they let the matter rest.

By the end of the year, Weld had announced to Sarah and Angelina that he needed their help on his newest project, an exhaustive study of American slavery that would recount its actual horrors through the testimony of slaves, slave owners, and overseers, and through reliance on public records. He wanted it to be the most detailed account of slavery ever written. He and Angelina and Sarah spent weeks deciding how best to do the research for the book, then carefully composed extensive questionnaires to be mailed to Southern abolitionists, newspaper editors, newly freed slaves, public and religious officials, and members of Congress. The study they designed would, Weld hoped, result in the first comprehensive and empirical survey of the "peculiar institution."

The purpose of the project, Weld said, was not merely to condemn slavery. Rather, it was to provide a full overview of slavery's impact as related by those intimately engaged in it—to show its day-to-day practice, and to do so through "the testimony of slaveholders in all parts of the slave states, by slaveholding members of Congress and of state legislatures, by ambassadors to foreign courts, by judges, by doctors of divinity, and clergymen of all denominations, by merchants, mechanics, lawyers and physicians, by presidents and professors in college and professional seminaries, by planters, overseers and drivers." Weld also involved the leadership of the AAS in his project: not trusting the results of the questionnaires alone, he persuaded James Birney, Arthur and Lewis Tappan, and Henry Stanton to check every testimonial, every article, and every anecdote to make certain they were factual.

To aid his study, Weld purchased the newspaper files of the New York Commercial Reading Room for the period from 1837 to 1838 and turned them over to Sarah and Angelina. Every day for the next several months, nearly from dawn until dusk, the sisters cataloged articles about slave sales, punishments, court proceedings, and the passage of penal codes, as well as birth and marriage announcements, notices about runaway slaves, and anything else of value from newspapers in Charleston, Vicksburg, New Orleans, Montgomery, Mobile, Memphis, Richmond, and Raleigh. They compiled the most extensive picture of slavery then in existence. From the newspapers, the sisters gleaned a vivid overview of everyday life in the slave South, as well as details about the common and ruthless abuse of particular slaves. Southern newspapers apparently had no qualms about reporting the whipping, lashing, beating, mutilation, execution, and even murder of black slaves by their white slaveholders. The testimonials were vivid and horrifying.

What Weld intended to do—condemn slavery through the words of slaveholders and slaves—he accomplished. The finished book, *American Slavery as It Is*, was begun in late 1838 and published in the summer of 1839. It was a labor of love that contained the testimony of one thousand witnesses—including the two Grimké sisters, who in sparse but powerful prose told of their experience with slavery in South Carolina. Weld, who offered his own trenchant analyses on the public testimonies, wrote the introduction to the book, laying out the evidence that he and his wife and sister-in-law had gathered through their months of detailed work. His words painted a dark picture of the life of American slaves.

> [That] they are overworked, underfed, wretchedly clad and lodged, and have insufficient sleep; that they are often made to wear round their necks iron collars armed with prongs, to drag heavy chains and weights at their feet while working in the field, and to wear yokes, and bells, and iron horns; that they are often kept confined in the stocks day and night for weeks together, made to wear gags in their mouths for hours or days, have some of their front teeth removed or broken off, that they

may be easily detected when they run away . . . . that their ears
are often cut off, their eyes knocked out, their bones broken,
their flesh branded with red hot irons; that they are maimed,
mutilated and burned to death over slow fires. All these
things, and more, and worse, we shall *prove*.

American Slavery as It Is was ignored by the national press, went unre-
viewed in most of America's major publications, and was passed over
without comment by the nation's political and intellectual elite. Its grim
portraits, its "ghoulish" details, and its vivid sketches were decried in the
North, laughed at in the South, and summarily dismissed in the halls of
Congress. But in its first year of publication, *American Slavery as It Is*
sold one hundred thousand copies. Its success came almost solely by
word of mouth.

In faraway Cincinnati, Harriet Beecher Stowe—a daughter of Weld's
old nemesis and friend Lyman Beecher, and the wife of Calvin Stowe, a
professor at the Lane Seminary during the time of the Lane Rebellion—
read *American Slavery as It Is*, put it down, and then immediately picked
it up again and reread it. She was overwhelmed by the book. The depic-
tions of individual suffering that Weld and the Grimkés provided would
stay with her for years. Later she would incorporate what she had read
into a number of scenes in *Uncle Tom's Cabin*. When asked how she had
created such vivid incidents, Stowe would answer that they had been
supplied her by Theodore Dwight Weld. *American Slavery as It Is* and
Uncle Tom's Cabin would become, and remain, the twin Bibles of the
abolitionist crusades.

———

The Grimké sisters were attacked by their Southern relatives for their
testimony in *American Slavery as It Is*. By now this was hardly new to
them, but they were stung by the continuing claim that they had betrayed their family and friends, their state and region, and even the principles that their father had held dear. Angelina defended the work to her
sister Anna Frost, who was in Charleston looking after their ill mother,
by insisting Sarah's and her views could not be censored simply because
they made people in Charleston uncomfortable. "It cost us more *agony of
soul* to write those testimonies than any thing we ever did," she wrote,
"but the Lord required it and gave us strength to do it, leaving all
the consequences in HIS holy hands." Northern abolitionists praised

the book but added their own unique criticism, suggesting that if the Grimkés really wanted to do something useful for the antislavery movement, they could set off on a new speaking tour and leave Weld to his own designs.

Inevitably, a whispering campaign—charging that the Grimkés were now firmly ensconced in a way of life they had once rejected, that they had settled down to a conventional life-style for which they were ill suited, and that they luxuriated in their own comforts while their former colleagues in the movement toiled unceasingly in the fields of reform—made the rounds, scurrilously, accompanied by winks and knowing smiles (what were the three of them, two women and one man, doing up there on the New Jersey bluffs, anyway?). Eventually word of it reached the Weld home in Fort Lee. Taking up her pen, Lydia Maria Child did not ask quite so blunt a question, but still still chided Sarah and Angelina for the choice they had made: "I began to think it was with you as with a girl, who being met by a person with whom she had formerly lived at service, was asked, 'Where do you live now, Nancy?' 'Please ma'am, I don't live anywhere now; I'm married.' " An old abolitionist friend, Deborah Weston, put it even more boldly: "The Grimkés, I think, are extinct," she told a friend.

Weld reacted angrily to such whispers and criticisms. He viewed *American Slavery as It Is* as difficult and hard work that had been necessary for the cause and that could not be put aside in favor of public posturing. It was the same position he had taken years before in turning down invitations to speak at conventions and meetings. "Enough of that," he had said then. Now he played a variation on this old theme. "The great body of Abolitionists seem to be mere *passengers* on a pleasure sail," he wrote to his fellow New York abolitionist Gerrit Smith. "They are willing to take the helm, or handle the speaking trumpet or *go up aloft* to see and *be seen,* but to bone down to *ship work* as a common sailor, especially in the *hold,* is a sort of business that cometh not with observation, and they are off."

What Weld did not say was that he and Angelina and Sarah also had other responsibilities to meet just now. The battles of the abolitionist movement seemed far away and much less important than they had a year before. After the publication of *American Slavery as It Is,* Mary Smith Grimké had fallen ill in Charleston. She was old and tired and missed her husband and children. In August 1839, she died. Anna Frost wrote from Charleston to inform her sisters, and noted that their mother had died without knowing of the appearance of *American Slavery as It Is* (Anna had kept it from her in her last days); she had thus been "spared," in Anna's words, the "bitter cup" of this "last infamous publication."

The sorrow that the sisters felt at their mother's passing was mitigated by the birth, that December, of Angelina and Theodore's first child, Charles Stuart Faucheraud Weld, named for his father's closest friend. Charley, as they would sometimes call him in the years to come, was raised according the principles laid down in Andrew Combes's *Physiological and Moral Management of Infancy*, one of the standard child-rearing texts of the era. He was fed, laid in his crib, and bathed by the clock. But the infant was not healthy and suffered from colic until Sarah intervened. She ignored Combes's advice that infants be fed only five spoonfuls of formula at each feeding and allowed the child to eat his fill, whereupon he grew fat and happy. Sarah was horrified by the baby's "gluttony" but could think of no reason that he should not eat, so she kept feeding him as Angelina fretted over her inability to nurse him. These minor (and hardly unusual) problems aside, the sisters were overjoyed by Charley's arrival. Angelina looked on him as a "little teacher sent from God," and Sarah took much the same view, though for her the infant also provided a respite from her loneliness. "Oh, the ecstasy and the gratitude!" she exclaimed in her diary. "How I opened the little blanket and peeped in to gaze, with swimming eyes, at my treasure, and looked upon that face forever so dear!"

In April 1840, a national nominating convention of antislavery delegates (officially named the National Convention of Friends of Immediate Emancipation) met in Albany, New York, to form a political party opposed to slavery. The convention, organized by upstate reformers, members of politically active AAS chapters, and Tappan allies, crafted a strong immediate-emancipation party platform and then nominated James G. Birney to run for president. Thomas Earle of Pennsylvania, a well-known abolitionist, was chosen as his running mate. The new political movement was dubbed the Liberty party by New Yorker Gerrit Smith. The party's formation was a watershed for the abolitionist movement, for it drew an uncrossable line between the Tappans and their Garrisonian adversaries. Garrison had counseled abolitionists against polluting themselves with political work, but his words went unheeded in New York, where the Tappans braced for the predicted Garrison backlash. Garrison, they knew, wanted to either take over the AAS or dissolve it, so that its two wings could go their separate ways.

The long-anticipated showdown between Tappan's New York reformers and Garrison's New England "ultras" took place on a bright Tuesday afternoon in May 1840, at the annual convention of the American Anti-Slavery Society. The meeting was held in the large Fourth Free Church at the corner of Madison and Catherine streets in Manhattan. The nearly one thousand people who crowded into the church (and the many observers and allies of Garrison and the Tappans who stood outside in the street, jostling for the best spot to hear about the proceedings) expected the clash to be short but bloody. Each side drew up strategies to defeat the other. Looking out over the crowd, Lewis Tappan realized that Garrison had successfully packed the church; Tappan's reformers were outnumbered. The Garrison faction included trainloads of pro-labor activists from the textile mills of Lynn, Massachusetts, a group of prominent radical women, and more than the usual handful of black males. Garrison surveyed the same scene and was exultant, seeing a veritable "Gideon's Army" ready to do battle with "the slave power."

The stage for the great battle had been set a year before, at the 1839 national meeting, when the convention defied the Tappans and gave women the right to vote in AAS proceedings. To add luster to that victory for Garrison, James Birney's resolution condemning the "no government" and "nonresistance" strains of the AAS had ignominiously failed by a wide margin of votes. At that moment, the Tappans had realized that they no longer controlled the movement they had founded. They had maneuvered to win more support in the intervening year, but their efforts had been unsuccessful. Now, in 1840, the two questions before the convention were much the same ones that had been raised the year before: Should the AAS give women the right to vote in its proceedings? And more important, would the AAS endorse the nonpolitical strategy of "moral suasion" to gain new adherents, or would it turn its attention to building a political movement?

The meeting opened with a raucous call for order, the seating of the delegates, and preparation for the arrival of the convention's chair, Arthur Tappan, who was scheduled to open the meeting. But the two o'clock deadline for opening the convention came and went, and still

Tappan did not appear. The crowd was restive but then fell silent in anticipation of a full boycott of the meeting by the AAS's most important supporter and his followers. Nothing happened for many minutes, though each camp eyed the other warily. A few delegates believed that William Garrison himself (editor of *The Lie-berator*, as Tappan's followers had taken to calling his paper) would take the chair and order the organization dissolved. But word eventually came that Arthur Tappan would not attend the meeting and had decided instead to resign the presidency of the AAS. The rumor flew through the church before the news was announced peremptorily from the pulpit. Tappan's resignation began a stampede. A Garrison ally seized the podium, and within a few short minutes, New Englander Francis Jackson (a Garrison partisan) had been elected as the new AAS president. In one moment, it seemed, power over the society had passed from the Tappans to the Garrisonians.

But the Tappans were not yet defeated and, as Garrison's followers carefully noted, had not left the meeting. In fact, while Garrison and his followers had had the votes to elect a new AAS president, it was not at all clear that they had enough to unseat the Tappans or any of their followers, much less denounce the brothers and Birney for their attempts to shift the organization's goals. From the rostrum, Jackson moved to quell an embarrassment for the Garrison forces by announcing that the first order of business was to approve the nomination of the AAS "business committee." A slate of nominees was offered that included Lewis Tappan (Arthur's brother was still present, waiting to see what would happen) as well as the "sober, serious and prayerful" Amos Phelps, a New Englander but a Tappan ally. Jackson quickly proposed that two others be added to the committee: Abby Kelley and Charles Burleigh, both outspoken Garrisonians.

The problem, of course, was over the seating of the Quaker Abby Kelley, a courageous and articulate former Worcester, Massachusetts, schoolteacher who had followed the same path as the Grimkés in lecturing to "mixed audiences" on the slavery question. She had become almost as famous as Angelina and insisted on journeying into the most dangerous parts of New England to spread the AAS message. Like the Grimkés, however, Kelley had begun mixing her call for black emancipation with other reformist impulses, including women's equality. Her most stirring message sparked the bitterest of responses: when she shouted at the women who attended one meeting, "We are manacled ourselves," newspapers called her a harlot, an Amazon, a sorcerer, and a temptress. Angelina Grimké might be outspoken, Lucretia Mott tough-minded, and Maria Chapman, Prudence Crandall, and Lydia Maria Child well known (and respected), but Kelley was a true radical. She helped Garrison organize the nonresistance wing of the AAS and was even the subject of a Garrison editorial on courage.

The Kelley test vote came after the convention approved, without objection, the seating of Tappan and Phelps on the business committee. At first it seemed that her nomination had been overwhelmingly carried, for when the voice vote was called for, the crowd gave a thunderous "aye." But then someone in the back of the church (undoubtedly a Tappan ally) asked for a full and recorded count of every vote. Jackson acceded to the request, though he certainly knew it would divide the membership, pitting the Garrisonians on one side against the Tappans on the other. He had no choice. He asked those in favor of Kelley's nomination to stand. The church was so full that the clerks had difficulty making their count and had to go over and over their numbers to make sure they had counted everyone in every pew as well as all those standing along the church walls, but after a quarter of an hour, Jackson announced that there were 571 in favor. He then asked for those opposed to stand, and as one half of the hall sat, the other stood. There was then an open question from the floor: Could women vote on this point? Amos Phelps maintained that they could not, a remark that was greeted with hisses from Garrison's allies. It would not have mattered anyway: 571 delegates had voted in favor of seating Kelley, and 451 against. The Garrisonians had prevailed.

The process had taken most of the afternoon. Jackson, anxious to keep the AAS from splintering, attempted to gain control of the meeting as thunderous applause greeted Kelley's victory. Garrison called for order from the back of the church and endeavored to mollify the Tappan forces, but then Lewis Tappan rose from his seat and shouted, loud enough for everyone to hear, that he would never serve on a "promiscuous" committee "in defiance of Scriptures." His allies stood up one by one to support him. Kelley had her own view: "In Congress the masters speak while the slaves are denied a voice," she proclaimed. "I rise because I am not a slave." She glared across the church at Tappan, who ignored her. Jackson finally regained control of the floor, gaveled the convention to silence, and quickly announced that the meeting was adjourned until the next morning. The crowd filed from the church, voices still raised in argument. But for all intents, the American Anti-Slavery

Society had been, in Whittier's word, "exploded," and Abby Kelley had been the bombshell.

That evening, at his home, Lewis Tappan met with three dozen of his friends to announce his plans for a new organization. Its first meeting, he said, would take place the next day, in the room below the hall where the AAS was holding its convention. The new American & Foreign Anti-Slavery Society consisted of Arthur and Lewis Tappan's political friends and organizers and a core group of Birney supporters from the new anti-slavery Liberty party. Its greatest support came from New York reformers and from Christian moderates wedded to the idea of political action shorn of the controversy that Garrison, the "nonresisters," and women had brought to the AAS. Upstairs, the American Anti-Slavery Society, now fully under Garrison's control, elected a new executive board comprising three women, one free black, and three New England Garrisonians, including Garrison himself. His triumph was complete. "We have made a clear work of everything," he wrote to his wife.

Just across the Hudson River, Angelina and Sarah Grimké and Angelina's husband, Theodore Weld, could hardly bring themselves to read about the convention. They viewed its proceedings with distaste, not simply because the antagonists had split the movement, but because they understood that abolitionism as they had known it was dead. When William Lloyd Garrison and his followers captured the American Anti-Slavery Society, they conquered a shell. The great crusade of the 1830s was over, and its leaders (the Grimkés, Weld, the Lane Rebels, the Tappans, even Garrison himself) were in eclipse. The movement was entering a new phase. The future of abolitionism was being placed in the hands of political activists who were interested less in shifting public opinion than in forcing a confrontation with the South.

The old abolitionist societies would live on, but their work of building a movement was over. Their epitaph would be written, three years after the AAS's schism, by an Illinois politician who served as Benjamin Lundy's editorial assistant: "The Societies have done a good work in their day," he would note, "and we can cherish them still, for the love of old associations, if we choose, without any detriment to the work they have so successfully built up.—But the advanced state of the cause, the political aspect which it has taken, require a different organization, as one which has not the stiffness and sluggishness of age upon it."

NINE

"... that great earthquake ..."

In March 1840, the Welds and Sarah Grimké moved to a fifty-acre farm near Belleville, New Jersey. While the sisters were able to maintain a modest life-style on their inheritance, the addition of an infant son meant that Theodore had to concentrate on farming to supplement their income. The family was also dependent on the modest fees Theodore's friends forwarded as a result of his antislavery writing. The farm was in poor repair, but it included a house, a barn, a corncrib, a stable, one hundred feet of river frontage, and fifty acres of rich bottomland dotted with vegetable gardens and orchards. The family planted sweet corn, summer beans, potatoes, beets, onions, tomatoes, squash, and pumpkins.

The land needed work. Weld labored to rebuild a long stone wall that fronted the river, and bought neighboring parcels for seventy-five dollars an acre, a price well beyond both market value and the family's means. He readily admitted that he was not a businessman (he often turned to the Tappan brothers for help in negotiating land purchases) and joked about his attempts to "play the yankee." Soon after they settled in, the family agreed to care for an old Grimké slave named Stephen, though it meant another mouth to feed. And by late spring, Angelina had discovered she was pregnant again.

Theodore Grimké Weld was born on January 3, 1841. This time Angelina had no trouble nursing, and she recovered more quickly from her pregnancy and labor. The Welds and Sarah continued to welcome a steady stream of guests from the antislavery movement; their home was always crowded. But all was not well in the household. Having deliber-ately put aside their public duties in favor of building a family, Angelina and Theodore suddenly realized how much they missed their old life-style. Raising children and making a living weighed especially heavily on Theodore, who was often short-tempered, even discourteous. He found escape from his responsibilities in his daily chores on the farm, where he worked for four months, twelve hours a day, hoeing, weeding, splitting rails, felling trees, cultivating, planting, repairing, and digging and haul-ing rocks.

Angelina's second pregnancy had helped to relieve the fears that arose after her first, when she was upset by her inability to nurse Charley. But after the successful and seemingly easy birth of her second child, she be-gan to experience increasing pain, which she and Sarah would ever after say was the result of an "accident." As Grimké biographer Gerda Lerner points out in her book on the sisters, the word *accident* was used by women in the nineteenth century as a euphemism for gynecological problems—most often treatable now, but untreatable (and unmention-able) then. Angelina's husband wrote of her "invalidism" in the follow-ing terms: "Early in her married life, she was twice severely injured. These injuries, though wholly unlike, were in their effect a unit, one causing, the other intensifying a life-long weakness. Together they shat-tered incurably her nervous system. The one was wholly internal; the other caused a deep wound which never healed."

Lerner explains these "accidents" by citing the "woman problems" mentioned by Sarah in her personal letters:

> In correspondence with her friend Harriot Hunt, the first fe-male medical practitioner in the United States, Sarah referred to [Angelina's] condition as a prolapsed uterus, so severe that at times it protruded externally, causing great pain. This con-dition, which with modern medical knowledge is easily cor-rected, was incurable during Angelina's lifetime. The second "injury" referred to by Weld may have been a miscarriage be-tween the second and the third baby; or, possibly, Weld was referring to a hernia condition which developed later.

In any event, Angelina's health progressively deteriorated after the birth of her second child. "She shared the fate of countless nineteenth-century women who were doomed by medical ignorance, inadequate obstetrical care and too frequent pregnancies to suffer chronic disabilities and pain with patient resignation as God-given—the normal 'trials' of a woman's life," Lerner notes.

For a brief period from late 1841 into 1842, Weld was in Washington to help Congressmen Joshua Giddings and John Quincy Adams in their fight against the "gag rule," which barred the presentation of antislavery petitions in the House of Representatives. The fight over the gag rule was the brainchild of Joshua Levitt, the editor of the Washington-based *Emancipator*, a well-known antislavery newspaper supported by the Tappan brothers. Levitt and the Tappans used the newspaper to promote the antislavery movement's newest slogan, "No union with slave-holders." The slogan marked a decisive departure from the immediate-emancipation stand of the Garrisonians and allowed the Tappans to draw a purposeful distinction between the free-labor North and the "slave South."

Weld's departure left Angelina and Sarah alone to raise the children, to plant, weed, and harvest, and to keep the farm in repair. Angelina, now in constant pain, was pregnant once more (she would eventually suffer a miscarriage), with her husband nowhere in sight. Still, she was gratified that Theodore was again engaged in abolition work, and he, too, was pleased. The prospect of once again working directly for the antislavery cause energized him; his health improved, and almost miraculously, his voice returned to its normal, booming timbre. Before leaving Belleville, he had promised Angelina that he would write her every Monday. She promised to write back each Thursday.

Weld went to Washington convinced that he could do more good in Congress than he had done in all of his years as an antislavery crusader in Ohio, New York, and Pennsylvania. Southerners could muzzle him by simply refusing to circulate or read his work, by barring him from traveling in the South, or by threatening his life. But they could not silence John Quincy Adams. When Adams and his congressional allies spoke, people in the North listened. "These men are in a position to do for the Anti-Slavery cause by a single speech more than our best lecturers can do in a year," Weld noted. He also knew that every time Congress's South-

ern members protested abolitionism by attempting to gag slavery's critics, the antislavery movement gained new adherents.

Weld was looking forward to learning about politics at the knee of
John Quincy Adams, who was widely acknowledged to be Washington's
foremost political strategist. Weld would not be disappointed. When the
two men met, Adams paid him a high compliment: "I know you well sir
by your writings," he said, extending his hand. Adams inquired about
Angelina and Sarah and asked Weld to send them his best wishes. From
that moment on, Weld was one of Adams's chief admirers, referring to
him as "the Old Nest[o]r" in his letters to Angelina. The two got along
well, and Adams came to rely on Weld's counsel. If Weld knew little of
politics, Adams did not know much more about the realities of slavery.
And in a debate with slaveholders, such knowledge would be essential.

Adams gave Weld no instructions as to his precise role in the upcoming battle over the gag rule. He said only that he was to provide the research for the debate, so that Adams would have every fact about slavery
at his fingertips. Adams, Levitt, and the Tappans had already recruited a
core group of Northern congressmen—a "Select Committee on Slavery"—
to carry the fight onto the floor of the House. Included among this unofficial caucus were William Slade and John Mattocks of Vermont, Sherlock
Andrews and Joshua Giddings of Ohio, Francis James of Pennsylvania,
Nathaniel Borden of Massachusetts, and Seth Gates of New York. Weld
plotted the strategy of this antislavery vanguard from his room "at Mrs.
Spriggs' boardinghouse" (or Abolition House, as it would come to be
called), just across from the Capitol. But it was Adams who led the way,
tutoring Weld in parliamentary tactics and leavening his all-or-nothing
crusading methods.

Adams knew the American public better, perhaps, than any other
member of Congress. He recognized that despite the abolitionists' decades of effort, most Americans simply did not care about the plight of
black Americans. To capture the public's attention, the issue of slavery
had to be brought into stark relief; the message must be, Adams believed,
that slavery affected not only black Americans, but *all* Americans. The
only way to make that point was to transform the question from whether
slavery was right or wrong into whether or not the issue could be discussed at all. That was what the petition campaign was all about: freedom of speech. It was unlikely that white Americans would defend black
Americans, but Adams had no doubt that they would stand up for their
own freedoms. He had led a similar fight in the late 1830s, but the debate

had been sidetracked by Southerners, depriving him of the decisive victory he wanted. Back then, he felt, the time had not been ripe; now, in 1842, he believed it was.

Adams was convinced that sooner or later the Southern members of the House of Representatives would overplay their hand and undercut their own position. To hurry that eventuality along, he intended to "bait" the Southerners by purposely violating the gag rule and inviting their censure. In this way, the House's Southern pro-slavery bloc would inadvertently provide him with a forum in which to discuss slavery—the very issue that they did not want to have discussed. They would then be held up to ridicule. In early January 1842, therefore, Adams made public a citizens' petition that had been circulated in Georgia, which demanded that he be relieved of his duties as chairman of the House Foreign Affairs Committee because of his abolitionist views.

While the anti-Adams petition had been originally sent out at their behest, the Southern House members now moved quickly to have it tabled, to act consistently with their position that antislavery petitions should not be heard. But Adams pressed the attack, pointing out that the tabled petition represented the sentiments of the Southern members of his own committee. He believed, he said, that *all* such petitions should be heard, even those at odds with his personal convictions. Every citizen, he said, had a right to his own views. It was a fact: petitions had been circulated in the South calling for Adams to resign his chairmanship of the committee. Should those petitions be tabled? he asked. Should Southerners be denied the right to a hearing on the issue? Let everyone speak, Adams urged. Let every petition be considered—even this one questioning his leadership of an important House committee.

On the day Adams responded to the Georgia petition on the House floor, Theodore Weld was seated in the gallery. He witnessed the uproar that followed. Adams argued then, as he had before, that no petition was so controversial that it should be quashed. *He* was willing to let his views be questioned; why weren't the "honorable members" from the Southern states? Weld wrote to Angelina about the debate:

> Wise of Va., Raynor of N.C., W. C. Johnson of Md., and scores more of slaveholders, striving constantly to stop him by starting questions of order and by every now and then screaming at the top of their voices "That is false," "I demand Mr.

Speaker that you put him down," "What are we to sit here and endure such insults," "I demand that you shut the mouth of that old harlequin." A perfect uproar like Babel would burst forth every two or three minutes as Mr. A, with his bold surety would smite his cleaver into the very bones. At least half of the slaveholding members of the house left their seats and gathered in the quarter of the Hall where Mr. A. stood. Whenever any of them broke out upon him, Mr. A. would say "I see where the shoe pinches, Mr. Speaker, [but] it will pinch more yet."

And pinch it did. After the floor debate, it was decided that the Georgia petition should be put before the House Committee on Foreign Affairs. When the committee met, Adams put the petition on the table and asked that either his chairmanship be confirmed or he be removed. He knew that his opponents did not have the votes either to remove him or to table the petition, and that was his trick—to lure them into a vote that would reveal their weakness. But the Southern members of the committee had foreseen the trap and had been working tirelessly on their own strategy, believing that they could embarrass Adams and force his resignation. They were so confident of their strength that they had already worked out a political deal with other members of the committee, whereby Adams would be replaced as chair by another Northerner, albeit one more sympathetic to their cause. The mastermind of the plot was none other than Robert Barnwell Rhett, the Grimké sisters' now-famous cousin and one of the House of Representatives' leading Southern nationalists. Rhett was struttingly certain that his strategy would work.

But Adams had been doing his own strategizing, and had contacted all of the Northern committee members polled by Rhett. His own numbers reflected his power among Northerners. Feeling safe enough to call Rhett's bluff, he asked for a committee vote on his chairmanship. Stunned by Adams's tactics, Rhett and his allies recalculated their committee strength, saw that they were weak, and attempted to delay the vote. It was clear that Rhett had gambled badly. Adams succeeded in turning the political tables on the South; in the end, it was not he who resigned, but Rhett, along with four other Southern members of the House Foreign Affairs Committee.

But the fight over Adams's committee chairmanship was only the prologue to the far nastier fight to come. The debate over the gag rule now turned into a political brawl, one of the ugliest and most bitterly contested debates in congressional history. Enraged by Adams's political sleight-of-hand during the chairmanship fight, Southern House members conspired to censure him and remove him from Congress. Once again, however, Adams outsmarted his enemies. Soon after retaining his chairmanship, Adams presented a petition from Haverhill, Massachusetts, demanding that the Republic be dissolved because "a vast proportion of the resources of one section of the Union is annually drained to sustain the views and course of another section." This was red meat: Southern House members rose in shock at the proposal. Congressman Henry A. Wise of Virginia thought Adams had blundered; here, finally, Wise believed, he had overstepped, by actually going so far as to propose "disunion," which could be construed as treason.

> MR. WISE: Is it in order to move to censure any member presenting such a petition, and to move that the House do now proceed to inquire whether a member has offered such a petition to this body, and to proceed accordingly?

> MR. ADAMS: Good!

Fearful that Wise's censure motion might pass, Northerners banded together to table it, at least until tempers cooled. But Adams himself *wanted* a censure vote—after an appropriately long trial. While the Southerners knew that Adams would use such a trial to condemn slavery, they believed they had the votes to dismiss him from the House in humiliation. They were willing to give him his forum, if that was what it would take to be rid of him. Once again, as in the fight over his committee chairmanship, Adams was counting on commanding all of the Northern votes, as well as some from the Southern delegation, in the fight over his censure. Weld checked and rechecked the pro- and anti-Adams votes and, after dinners at Abolition House, gathered materials on slavery that Adams could use in defending himself during his House trial.

The trial of John Quincy Adams commenced on January 25, 1842. After the reading of the motion of censure, Adams began his defense by asking that the House clerk read the Declaration of Independence. Many

Southern members groaned, and some protested, but the reading went forward. Adams then rose from his seat to face his accusers. If the founders of the nation, he said, had dissolved their union with Britain on the basis of its having denied them the right of a petition for a redress of grievances—as noted in the Declaration—then certainly the people of Haverhill had the same right, and he, as a member of the House, had a perfect right to present such a petition. Did the Southerners in the House disagree with this? Were they willing to deny American citizens a right that had once been denied them by royalty, and for the sake of which they had shed blood in a great revolution? The House members listened silently. "If the right of habeas corpus, and the right of trial by jury are to be taken away by this coalition of Southern slaveholders and Northern Democracy," Adams continued, "it is time for the Northern people to see if they cannot shake it off, and it is time to present petitions such as this. I can say it is not yet time to do this—that is, actually proceed to the disunion the Haverhill people proposed. But almost. In any case, one could certainly present the petition of those who believe it *was* time."

At the end of the first week of the Adams trial, the Southerners realized that they had once again miscalculated. Thousands of petitions demanding that the censure motion be dropped began to arrive on the House floor, and thousands more protesting the gag rule. A group of Southern House leaders approached Adams with an offer: they would drop the censure motion if he would withdraw the Haverhill petition. He refused and took to the House floor. "If I withdraw the petition," he said, "I would consider myself as having sacrificed the right of petition; as having sacrificed the right of habeas corpus; as having sacrificed trial by jury; as having sacrificed the sacred confidence of the post office; as having sacrificed freedom of the press; as having sacrificed every element of liberty that was enjoyed by my fellow citizens."

On February 25, at the end of the trial, Adams uttered the word *slavery,* in clear violation of the gag rule. Southern House leaders filed an objection, moving that the word be stricken from the trial record. The motion was overwhelmingly defeated. With Weld feeding him materials from the gallery, Adams extended his defense into a second week. The trial now brought hundreds of petitions every day. But Adams was never allowed to finish his defense, as the Southerners, spooked by Adams's continuing offensive, moved quickly to end the trial and succeeded in tabling the censure motion by a vote of 97 to 25. When the motion to table passed, the House gallery broke into sustained cheers. Weld was ecstatic. "Slave holding, slave trading and slave breeding absolutely quailed and howled under his dissecting knife," he wrote to Angelina. "The triumph of Mr. Adams is complete. This is the first defeat of the slaveholders in a body ever yet achieved since the foundation of the government, and from this time their downfall takes its date."

———

In March 1844, Angelina gave birth to Sarah Grimké Weld, her third and last child. Within the year, Weld's aging parents and his invalid brother and sister moved into a home nearby. All were dependent on him for their care. With their arrival, Angelina, Sarah, and Theodore became more concerned about their finances: their responsibilities had increased, but their income had not. The Belleville farm produced everything they needed, but they were unable to earn the extra money that would have allowed them to live more comfortable lives. The work was constant and backbreaking. Angelina's health continued to deteriorate, and Theodore was constantly tired and worried. When asked Weld's whereabouts by John Greenleaf Whittier, Lewis Tappan penned the following reply: "He is in the ditch opposite his house, doing the work any Irishman could do for 75 cents a day."

Angelina relied more and more on Sarah to carry out the daily chores in the household and on the farm. Their roles reverted to those they had once filled in South Carolina, only now Sarah was not merely an older sister to Angelina but also a nursemaid to her children. She referred to Angelina and Theodore's two sons and one daughter as "my children" and reveled in her involvement in their lives, confiding to a friend, "They have saved me from I knew not what horrible despair, or rushing into some new and untried and unsanctified effort to let off the fire that consumed me, and furnished me with objects of interest which drew me from myself. I feel that they were the gift of a pitying Father, and that to love and cherish them is my highest manifestation of love to the Giver." At the age of fifty-two, Sarah was the virtual head of the Grimké-Weld household.

Angelina and Theodore continued to look for new ways to support their family. In October 1848, they took in two children as boarders, having contracted with their parents to provide them with a full-time education. The number soon expanded to six. When their friends learned what they were doing, they sent their own children to Belleville. Eventually, Weld and the Grimkés decided to make their tutoring and boarding official and open a private boarding school. Among the students in attendance were the offspring of some of the best-known abolitionists in the country, including Henry and Elizabeth Cady Stanton, James Birney, and Gerrit Smith. The "Belleville School" would ultimately enroll twenty students. Sarah and Angelina made the meals and helped with the mending, while Theodore looked after the school's administration; Angelina taught history, Sarah French, and Weld all the rest of the courses in a curriculum that included composition, mathematics, and drawing.

The Belleville School was one of the first American academies to institute a liberalized curriculum that rewarded independent thinking and allowed students to learn in an "open" environment. The children had the run of the house and the nearby woods, where they collected snakes and frogs for their science class. Classes were conducted either outdoors or on the flat, open roof of the Weld home, whichever better suited the teacher. Theodore Weld was deeply impressed by the theories of the nineteenth century's leading educational reformers, and he put them into practice at Belleville. He believed that educational instruction provided the most appropriate means of inculcating morality, and thought the classroom the ideal locale for the careful cultivation of "Christian ideals." The school was coeducational—in itself a "radical experiment."

But while Belleville's students loved their teachers and would write, years later, of the wonderful education they had received there, the school was not a financial success, and by 1853, the Welds and Sarah were looking for other opportunities. The most promising of these appeared in the form of the Raritan Bay Union, a New Jersey cooperative community run by Marcus Spring, a wealthy reformer and follower of the French utopian Charles Fourier. Spring had left the Fourierist North American phalanx—Fourier's name for his utopian, "planned" communities—after a nine-year experiment, due to a disagreement over finances. He and thirty of his followers had then established a new colony near Perth Amboy. Spring contacted Weld and offered him a job as headmaster of the community school, pledging to him the use of the colony's new schoolhouse and complete freedom in the selection and teaching of courses. Weld accepted, and in early 1854, he, Angelina, their children, and Sarah all moved to Eagleswood, New Jersey, where the community had purchased 270 acres of land.

The Grimké-Welds enjoyed the new surroundings, trusted the community's leaders, and were attracted by its goals, which included establishing "branches of agriculture and mechanics whereby industry, education and social life may in principle and practice be arranged in conformity to the Christian religion," and wherein "all ties conjugal, parental, filial, fraternal and communal which are sanctified by the will of God, the laws of nature and the highest experience of mankind, may be purified and perfected." Angelina in particular was overjoyed by the move, since their new position promised to alleviate their financial woes. "Our location here is enchanting [and] far far superior to our Belleville home," she wrote to a friend soon after their arrival.

But within a few years, the school at Raritan Bay (just twenty-five miles from New York) would turn out to be yet another disappointment. Spring's promise of full and constant financing was ephemeral. Their first winter there was bitterly cold, and Theodore, Angelina, and Sarah, in turn, all became ill. To make matters worse, the Raritan Bay Union was soon beset by the same bickering that had divided the original Fourier community. By 1856, the group was breaking up, and the Welds and Sarah were disenchanted with Fourier's followers. But they were intent on keeping the school open, and Spring finally agreed to help them renovate the schoolhouse and build a new gymnasium in the hope of attracting more students. After Weld and the Grimké sisters took control of the finances, the school—now renamed Eagleswood, for the town— actually prospered. It drew students from nearby communities, along with a liberal sprinkling of children from abolitionist circles, and earned an excellent reputation. Weld and the Grimkés proved adept teachers and administrators. For the first time in many years, the family was both happy and financially secure.

———

By 1857, the Eagleswood School was the centerpiece of a thriving reform community, and Weld, his wife, and Sarah Grimké were the masters of their own lives. Late that year, Weld expanded the school's faculty, with the most notable addition being Elizabeth Peabody, a nationally known educational reformer and disciple of Bronson Alcott, America's leading educator. At the heart of the Eagleswood philosophy was a belief in the value of coeducational instruction, a principle that was prominently featured in the school brochure: "The education of the sexes together, under a wise supervision," it explained, "gives symmetry to mental and moral development, excites attention to personal habits, quickens the perception of those nameless proprieties which adorn mutual relations, adds refinement to feelings, gentleness, grace and courtesy to manners, simplicity, modesty, purity, and general elevation and equilibrium to character."

The Eagleswood School was a model of progressive education in the nineteenth century, and through it the Welds were able to maintain strong ties to their abolitionist colleagues. Many of the children of noted antislavery activists were educated at Eagleswood, and their parents and other old friends of the Welds' resided nearby. Theodore's brother and sister lived within walking distance of the Weld home (having moved from Belleville), as did James G. Birney, who had retired from politics and the antislavery movement after two unsuccessful Liberty party campaigns for the presidency. The Welds and Sarah also stayed in close touch with Henry and Elizabeth Cady Stanton and with their old friend Gerrit Smith. One person with whom Weld rarely communicated, however, was Lewis Tappan, who was angered by the former orator's self-imposed exile.

Eagleswood became a meeting ground for the graying generation of abolitionists, reformers, and intellectuals. Throughout the late 1850s, dozens of Weld and Grimké friends made a kind of pilgrimage to Raritan Bay to visit with the old "great lights" of the antislavery movement. William H. Channing, Henry Bellow, William Furness, William Cullen Bryant, Joshua Giddings, Horace Greeley, Henry David Thoreau (who lectured to Eagleswood's students), Ralph Waldo Emerson, A. Bronson Alcott, and a number of former Lane Rebels all came to see Theodore, Angelina, and Sarah. Such visitors inevitably stayed over to hear Weld give his usual Sunday "layman's service" for the students, which unerringly touched on slavery, reform, education, and the nature of God. On Sunday afternoons, the Welds and Grimké hosted one of America's first intellectual salons, adding luster to their reputation as reformers and educators.

Eagleswood's small cemetery would soon fill with the names of the era's leading crusaders. James Birney—former slaveholder, abolitionist, and presidential candidate—was laid to rest there in 1857. Six years later his son, James G. Birney, a general of volunteers, would lead his division into the woods near Gettysburg against the corps of Confederate general James Longstreet; a year after that, the younger Birney would die in Philadelphia. His last words were "Keep your eyes on the flag, boys."

James Birney's grandson Fitzhugh Birney was educated at Eagleswood. As his grandfather lay dying, Fitzhugh trod the boards of the Eagleswood School stage as Starveling in the play *Pyramus and Thisbe*, along with Theodore and Angelina's son Charles Stuart. Afterward there was a school dance, which irked Thoreau. That irritable New England intellectual and secret misanthropist was a grudging participant in such occasions, complaining that Theodore, Angelina, and Sarah "take it for granted that you *want* society."

Weld organized these evenings and, with his gray eminence and long beard, presided over nearly all of the school's activities. He was teacher, counselor, and minister to the students. Like his wife and her sister, Weld now shunned the rituals of organized religion, having replaced them with a deep belief in moral principles followed for their own sake. Even Weld's closest friend, the English reformer Charles Stuart (for whom he and Angelina had named their firstborn son), condemned the "Bible-less" education Weld offered at Eagleswood, and broke off their relationship after nearly four decades. Weld himself was indifferent to such criticism. Although he was still nominally a New England Puritan, his marriage, the birth of his children, the bouts of illness in his family, and his alienation from politics had all diluted his strict religious observance. After years of isolation, he welcomed the easy and liberal culture provided by Eagleswood and urged his students to take part in the "promiscuous," or mixed, society of equals that so many of his reform-minded colleagues had once condemned.

Weld's newfound liberalism was due in part to the religious speculations of Angelina and Sarah. In the early 1840s, the sisters had been attracted to the prophecies of William Miller, a preacher from upstate New York who predicted that the world would end at precisely three o'clock in the morning on October 12, 1843. But that day had come and gone, with America and the world (and sin) still intact. Angelina was disappointed. In 1849, she had met the spiritualist Andrew Jackson Davis (known as the "Poughkeepsie Seer") at a spa in South Orange, New Jersey, where she was taking the "water cure" to alleviate her uterine pain. Davis and Angelina had become good friends, and Angelina had written to her husband about Davis's magnetic personality (a critic noted that he seemed "especially attracted to women") and his strangely compelling, if appropriately ambiguous, philosophy:

A. J. Davis believes and teaches that the time will come when mankind can say, Each is as the whole, and the whole are one. Whose temple is the experience and wisdom of every age and nation—Whose book is nature, whose master is Reason, whose language is all forms and kingdoms, whose creed is love to man—Whose religion is Justice, and whose light is Truth; whose oneness is Association—whose path is Progression; whose works are Development; whose motto is Excelsior, whose home is Heaven, whose Heaven is Harmony, and whose God is the Universal Father.

While Angelina and Sarah's interest in the Poughkeepsie Seer had eventually waned, their appetite for other, even more exotic (and popular) religious experiences had only deepened. On March 31, 1848, fifteen-year-old Maggie Fox and her sister Kate (of Hydesville, in upstate New York) had told their parents that they were communicating with the dead. They said they had worked out a code, a series of "rappings" on their bedroom wall, whereby they could exchange messages with a man who had been murdered in their house many years before. Indeed, as their parents discovered, distinct rappings could be heard in their daughters' room.

News of the rappings spread throughout upstate New York and then the rest of the nation. Thousands of people made the pilgrimage to Hydesville to speak with the sisters, who, in response to the throngs, fell into suitable trances before communicating with the dead fathers, sisters, brothers, mothers, aunts, uncles, and children of their visitors. The Fox sisters spawned an industry of "spiritualists" who toured the nation giving lectures on the afterlife ("the other side") and the new "telegraph line with the dead." Soon rappings could be heard everywhere, as the dead came alive, having discovered (or so the Fox sisters said) a way of reaching out to the living. Thousands followed the new religion, and spiritualist "camps" traveled from city to city spreading the word of the Fox sisters.

Angelina and Sarah were entranced by spiritualism, which they felt furnished proof of their own belief in a benevolent and all-seeing God who transported the souls of good Christians to an afterlife of rest and spiritual renewal. Spiritualism's appeal was strongest in upstate New York, where the Great Revival was (by 1848) nearly burned out. The new religion took root first among the region's abolitionist Quakers and then spread into the state's religious heartland, where it was adopted by anti-slavery Congregationalists and Presbyterians. Even William Lloyd Garrison believed that an "unbroken chain of communication exists between the Infinite and all beings." For millions of American women, the Fox sisters' "discovery" offered hope that they might finally be able to communicate with their lost infants. It was a great comfort for them to know, especially in an era when infant death was common, that their children were not consigned to the fires of hell but lived on and loved and even, from "the other side," knew their families.

The hotbed of spiritualism was the Rochester area, where the rappings the Fox sisters had first heard were rife. A favored gathering place was the Waterloo Congregational Friends Meeting House, where Quaker believers often came together to discuss the new "spiritualist telegraph." There, in the late spring of 1848, five women who had been brought together by their views on spiritualism, political reform, and slavery met to consider the plight of women. Three of the five—Lucretia Mott, Martha Coffin Wright, and Elizabeth Cady Stanton—were already well known in the antislavery movement; they were joined by Mary Ann McClintock and Jane Hunt, two Quakers dedicated to social reform. Led by a frustrated and outspoken Stanton, the five agreed that it was time to begin working for equal rights for all Americans, and that the best way to do that would be to hold a convention to "discuss the social, civil, and religious condition and rights of women."

Determined to transform the group's ideas into a political declaration of principles, Stanton laid a paper on the "spirit table" of the Waterloo meeting house and began to copy out the Declaration of Independence, making some key changes as she went: "We hold these truths to be self-evident," she wrote, "that all men *and women* are created equal. . . ." The five then agreed to call a convention in Seneca Falls, to be held on July 19 and 20 of that year. The invitations went out to the most prominent women leaders in the nation, including the Grimké sisters. Sarah and Angelina were unable to attend, but they understood clearly what the Seneca Falls convention meant and were overjoyed when they learned that those present had approved Stanton's most controversial resolution: "That it is the duty of the women of this country to secure to themselves their sacred right to the elective franchise."

Seneca Falls was a turning point for women reformers. The convention was attended by women who had built the antislavery movement and who in its midst had made a connection between the rights of enslaved black Americans and their own rights. But it was Angelina Grimké who had seen that link: "The investigation of the rights of the slave has led me to a better understanding of my own," she had written nearly fifteen years earlier. And as the years passed, it would be increasingly recognized that the intellectual progenitor of the women's rights movement had been not Elizabeth Cady Stanton (nor her colleague Susan B. Anthony) but Sarah Moore Grimké, whose "Letters on the Equality of the Sexes and the Condition of Woman" predated the Seneca Falls Convention by ten years. Following the Seneca Falls meeting, Sarah Grimké's groundbreaking essay would become the Bible of the women's movement.

In the 1850s, Sarah would add to her prodigious intellectual contributions to the women's movement, pushing the matter well beyond the already revolutionary call for the franchise expressed in Stanton's Seneca Falls resolution. In a letter published in the *Christian Inquirer* in early 1852, Sarah Grimké argued that marriage represented an unequal economic exchange, a dependence conceded by women simply because it ensured their survival. Women got married, Grimké maintained, because they had no choice:

> Thousands are thus sacrificed, either by their parents or themselves, who, had they been educated in honorable independence, and been able to earn a livelihood by their own exertions, would have scorned so to violate the sacredness of those feelings which God has given as a safeguard to domestic happiness. Too much importance cannot be attached to the independence of woman. Her present dependent condition is fraught with every evil, for to act consciously, uprightly, unswervingly true to God and ourselves, while dependent for daily bread upon those who differ from us in opinion, and use all their influence to induce us to surrender our judgment to theirs, is one of the highest and rarest of human achievements.

A coherent line of intellectual development may be traced in Sarah Grimké's thinking, from her childhood frustration at being barred from reading Latin ("To me, learning was a passion . . ."), through her conversion at the hands of the Reverend Kollock ("a providential sign") and her nursing of her dying father ("I regard this as the greatest blessing next to my conversion that I have ever received from God"), to the mystical experiences that led her north ("I communed with spirits, I heard voices"). But her feminist essays of the 1850s are so out of character with her other appeals, and so progressive, so matter-of-fact, and so *powerful,* that they could have sprung only from personal experience—that is, from what she herself saw. Her views on marriage, and on women's dependence on men, derived not from some intellectual feat but from firsthand knowledge of her sister Angelina's marriage to Theodore Weld.

———

Theodore Weld's journey to Washington at the end of 1841, to participate in John Quincy Adams's fight against the gag rule, had been supported by Angelina, who had urged him to get involved again in the antislavery movement. While he was in Washington, she had encouraged him in letter after letter, at the same time providing a detailed account of the growth and achievements of their children. Proud mother though she was, there were tensions between her and her husband resulting from her realization that while he might reenter the public arena, she herself could not. She was now firmly required to inhabit the "private sphere" of childbearing and child rearing, and she chafed under the obligation. Soon enough, like many women of her time, Angelina had come to resent her husband's independence and been angered by his long-distance instructions on how to raise their children.

Angelina and Theodore had disagreed over the proper way to discipline Charley, their first son, whose temper was ferocious. On one occasion, exasperated by his constant manipulations ("Ma kiss Ma kiss—naughty boy naughty boy—done—done—Ma kiss—Ma kiss," he would plead after his tantrums), she had locked the child in a closet. "Now is the time [to subdue his temper]," Angelina wrote to her husband, "or it will sweep like a whirlwind over our little family, destroying our peace and *his soul.*" These were strong sentiments, but Theodore wondered why she had lost her temper, and gave her some advice: "Effectually to soften and subdue those impulses must be the work of every hour and moment, by the cultivation of gentle forbearing, benevolent affections, and by exhibiting them in our example, thus filling the soil with springing wheat which, in its sure growth, will root out the tares." Angelina had no idea what he was talking about. He was not there.

Theodore had listed the steps Angelina must take in raising the children, ideas whose exact origin remains unknown: "Thousands of minds have been dwarfed in childhood by [being] crammed with stuff from which their *elemental* powers could digest no nutriment," he wrote. But Angelina knew that raising Charley, Theodore, and now Sarah (their third child, happier in infancy than the other two, she thought) was a much more difficult proposition than suggested by her husband. One pressing problem was that little Charley was "handling himself," a habit that Theodore, in a letter, insisted must be ended "immediately" because it was "filthy and dangerous." Angelina's solution was to sew up the flap in the front of the boy's pants. "I thought nothing else would be effectual," she wrote to her husband, "for I dreaded his refraining in our presence for fear of punishment. This would have driven him to do it secretly and the habit would then become inveterate."

Beset by chronic ill health, and in the absence of her husband, Angelina had left the raising of the children to Sarah, who doted on them and, inevitably, clashed with their mother over how best to raise them. The tensions mounted until, in 1853, Angelina and Sarah separated. The ostensible reason for the break was Angelina's sensitivity over Sarah's need to contribute her inheritance to the household income. When Angelina suggested that they keep their accounts separate, Sarah was offended and threatened to move out and live on her own. Angelina did not protest. All the next year, Sarah attempted to reenter the antislavery ranks, traveling first to Washington and then to New York, but the movement had passed her by. "There is plenty of work to be done, but I see nothing in the wide world that I can do," she wrote to her best friend at the time, Dr. Harriot Hunt.

After a year, Angelina and Sarah reconciled, never to be apart again. Both compromised and spoke honestly about the tension produced by the reversal of roles in their lives. For decades, Sarah had been "Mother" to her "dear Nina," and over the past few years, she had wanted to be a "mother" once again, this time to "Theodore's" children. Even in her writings and correspondence, Sarah always referred to them either as her own children or as Theodore's—seldom as Angelina's. Now she had to concede that they were *also* Angelina's, and could never really be hers. Angelina, too, had to reach an accommodation, but with her own frustrations. She was a wife and a mother in a century that rarely rewarded either role, and she lived in a culture that provided few outlets for ambitious women. Angelina wrote of this, bluntly but simply, in a letter she sent to Sarah in mid-1854:

> There are times I feel humbled in the dust, because I never have been willing to share my blessings with you equally. Often, very often, when I look at all the sorrow and disappointment you have met with in life and all that you have done for me I feel ashamed and confounded at my ingratitude and selfishness. Then again, it seems unnatural that a wife and Mother should ever thus be willing to share of the affection of her dearest ones with any human being and my heart refuses its assent and struggles on in darkness and death for I know these feelings wither and blight and keep me from growth and yet it seems impossible for me to overcome them. . . .

Having admitted this, Angelina invited Sarah to return to the Weld home. Sarah agreed. "Separation from these darling children, who have brightened a few years of my lonely and sorrowful life, overwhelmed me," she confessed to her sister. "Without them existence would have no charm."

With Sarah's return, the Weld household went on as before. Sarah and Angelina tended to the children and the cleaning and taught classes at Raritan Bay, and then at Eagleswood, to a new generation of abolitionist offspring. Until at least 1857, the two sisters expressed their political views by wearing bloomers, a uniform officially described as "a tunic, short skirt and pantaloons fastened at the ankles," named after Amelia Bloomer, the feminist editor of *The Lily*, a temperance magazine. The term was meant to ridicule the style of dress, but the sisters wore their bloomers as a symbol of their pride and independence—in spite of the fact that they were distinctly uncomfortable in them. Sarah and Angelina gave up the practice after Elizabeth Cady Stanton wrote to advise them (with a note of exasperation), "It is not wise . . . to use up so much energy and feeling that way." The sisters agreed and changed back into their modest gray Quaker garb. "We put the dress on for greater freedom, but what is physical freedom compared with mental bondage?" Angelina reflected.

A new family crisis loomed in 1859, when Theodore and Angelina's second son, Theodore—nicknamed Sody—became dangerously ill. He had spent a happy and full childhood, but at the age of eighteen, on the eve of the Civil War, he left home to work, only to return after several months in perilous health. It was obvious to his parents that he was suffering from some debilitating disease that made him listless and apathetic, and they consulted a number of doctors. When no medical reason could be found for his condition, Theodore and Angelina turned to soothsayers and mediums. One reported that Sody was experiencing a "fatalistic period of speculation," while another attributed his poor health to a build-up of "seminal fluids"—in other words, the young man was masturbating too much, a habit that could lead to "insanity or idiocy." His parents and aunt were horrified.

Sody was sent to Boston for physical conditioning in the hope that his nightly "emissions" would cease, but still his health failed to improve. The Welds next contacted a spiritualist, a certain "Mrs. Coleman," who disagreed with the previous diagnosis, at least in part. She suggested that Sody was not a masturbator, but rather the victim of an age of "lymphatic tendencies" that was causing a "drainage" on his strength. What Sody needed, Mrs. Coleman said, was the "healthful love of woman" to keep him from becoming "starved and flabby." She prescribed a full course of treatment—which she herself could provide. Lest the Welds think she was interested in something other than a purely scientific program, she couched her remedy in empirical terms:

> It is only necessary to lay upon the small of the back the hand often, and at other times, it is simply necessary for the hand to be placed upon the ovarium. In this manner can the brain be affected to such a degree that the love element immediately commences passing down into the testicles, filling them, when again the brain acts upon the interior organs, and they transmute to the basilar portion a liquid which forms the proper fluid by which the whole system is clear from the otherwise thickened mass of secretions.

We can only imagine what effect this statement may have had on Sarah Grimké, but such was the social environment of America in those years, when good citizens routinely heard distant voices or rapped with the dead. It was a time when abolitionist husbands might be conveniently absent while their wives gave birth (as was Henry Stanton, whose wife, Elizabeth, took care of their seven children) and nowhere to be seen during their children's rearing (returning only long enough to impregnate their wives again), or, alternatively, might lovingly take on the responsibility of teaching others' children while ignoring the education of their own—as was the case with that famous abolitionist, that "thunderer of the West," that indifferent father Theodore Dwight Weld. As Sody dissolved into mental illness, Sarah's cry symbolized the dreadful shriek of an entire family that had sought to cure a nation yet could not cure itself: "What can I say," she wrote in a particularly personal letter to Theodore. "I am blind and know not how to help you." There was no help. No one knew what was wrong with Sody, and no one would ever know. Although physically he seemed fine, he would grow progressively weaker, his voice barely above a whisper, until he was confined to a wheelchair. There he would stay.

Apart from the scandal over the sisters' wearing of bloomers and the progressive illness of Angelina and Theodore's second son, the late 1850s was a comparatively quiet time for the family. Although Sarah and Angelina were deeply interested in the increasingly violent debate over slavery, neither of them spoke out publicly on the issue. Both women knew that not only had their public lives ended, but the movement they had helped to establish was now being transformed beyond their wildest imaginings. Slavery was no longer the exclusive province of the abolitionists; it had finally become the concern of all Americans. The only political issue of consequence in those years, it was debated endlessly in the halls of Congress, became the subject of countless state resolutions, and could by itself elect or defeat anyone running for any political office. The topic of slavery consumed the nation. Sarah and Angelina watched with almost morbid fascination as crisis after crisis pushed the North and the South further apart.

Perhaps the greatest of these crises was fostered by the Compromise of 1850, which, among other things, opened up new Western territories to slavery, so long as the citizens of those lands voted in favor of it. The most heinous aspect of the compromise was a provision calling for the forced return of escaped slaves to the South. Intended to appease Southerners, the Fugitive Slave Act instead sparked riots in Detroit, Boston, Cincinnati, Philadelphia, New York, and dozens of other Northern cities, as mobs descended on slave catchers who were pursuing Southern "property." Although relatively few slaves were actually captured and returned to the South, the law nonetheless enraged Northerners, who complained that the most fundamental guarantee of the Constitution, that an American could be safe in his or her own home, was being undermined. Northerners now listened more closely when abolitionists talked about "the slave power."

Just how explosive the situation had become was made apparent on October 16, 1859, when John Brown led a band of twenty-one raiders into Harper's Ferry, Virginia, where they captured the federal arsenal and issued a call for a slave uprising. After a two-day siege, Brown's men were overwhelmed by federal soldiers, who killed several of them and took the rest prisoner. John Brown's raid struck close to home in the antislavery movement. A number of well-known abolitionists had contributed funds to his cause, including a committee of supporters who called themselves the secret six: Samuel Gridley Howe, a doctor and educator; Theodore Parker, a Unitarian minister of national renown; Franklin B. Sanborn, a Concord, Massachusetts, schoolteacher; George Luther Stearns, the chairman of the Massachusetts Kansas Committee (which had backed Brown in his fight against slaveholders in Kansas); Gerrit Smith; and Thomas Wentworth Higginson, a Worcester, Massachusetts, minister who once asserted, "The worst trait of the American race seems to me this infernal color-phobia." Another of Brown's supporters was Frederick Douglass, the best known and most influential African American of his generation, who did not, however, endorse the Harper's Ferry raid. He thought the action crazy.

In the aftermath of the Harper's Ferry bloodletting, most members of the "secret six" worried that they might be indicted for their role in the raid. Franklin Sanborn hurriedly burned all of his correspondence with Brown, and Dr. Howe paced back and forth in Sanborn's home for three days before fleeing to Canada. Gerrit Smith was so overwhelmed by anxiety about his financial participation in the episode that he went temporarily insane, provoking his friends to commit him, for a short time, to the state mental institution in Utica, New York (he recovered his reason after realizing that he would not be prosecuted). Thomas Wentworth Higginson, meanwhile, was elated by Brown's exploits in Harper's Ferry. He refused to destroy his correspondence with Brown, plotted his rescue, and suggested that he be defended by the Massachusetts lawyer John A. Andrew. He was embarrassed by what he viewed as his colleagues' cowardice: "Sanborn," he asked, "is there no such thing as honor among confederates?" In December, Brown and a number of other raiders were hanged for treason. The bodies of two of these men, Aaron Stevens and Albert Hazlett, were brought by the abolitionist community to the small cemetery at Eagleswood for an honorable burial.

Sarah and Angelina, pacifists and "nonresisters" both, celebrated Brown's raid and revered its leader as a saint. They grieved, along with a large crowd of other abolitionist mourners, during the burials of Stevens and Hazlett, then turned back to Eagleswood to continue their teaching. But they must have realized that now, with Brown's raid, the war they feared had become inevitable. Twenty-four years earlier, in a letter to William Lloyd Garrison—the same letter that had inaugurated her career—Angelina Grimké had foretold the controversy, division, and eventual bloodletting that the abolitionist crusade would bring. She had turned the implications of her public testimony on the horrors of slavery over and over in her mind and decided that even if it should separate sons from their families and send them off to America's green fields to die, the cause would be worth the heartache. War? "Let it come," she had written to Garrison.

Now her prediction had come true.

TEN

"... go on! go on! ..."

When Abraham Lincoln was elected president, on November 6, 1860, Charleston became a city possessed. Its people were "in the utmost state of excitement," all rallying to the cause of Southern independence. There were torchlight parades, spontaneous speeches, political meetings, and a call for volunteers to defend the state. On December 20, South Carolina seceded from the Union, to be followed soon after by the other states of the Deep South. In February 1861, the Confederate States of America was formed by a delegation of secessionist representatives meeting in Montgomery, Alabama, and the newly appointed Confederate general P. G. T. Beauregard was dispatched to Charleston to command the city's defenses and seize the federal installation at Fort Sumter. Beauregard was greeted by great fanfare. He had not yet fought a battle, but he was already a hero in the South.

Charleston's boys rallied to their new flag, spoiling for a fight; any one Rebel could whip ten Yankees, they said. Near the docks, the South Carolina Militia drilled daily to the swooning admiration of the city's fairest. In early March, caissons of artillery rolled through the streets and into Battery Park, a movement that was a mere show of force, though proudly undertaken, for the shells could not effectively target Fort Sumter and its federal garrison, in the harbor's far distance. Instead, the task of taking the fort was left to Beauregard's artillerists at three major positions—Fort

Moultrie, Sullivan's Island, and James Island—and nearly half a dozen other vantage points on spits of land jutting into the harbor.

The federal commander of the fort, Major Robert Anderson, refused to evacuate Sumter and prepared for the final bombardment. At 3:20 A.M. on April 12, he received a note from Beauregard's aide-de-camp: "Sir: By authority of Brigadier-General Beauregard commanding the Provisional Force of the Confederate States, we have the honor to notify you that he will open the fire with his batteries on Fort Sumter [in] one hour from this time." It was all very polite, this first hostile exchange of the war, but it would not be long before both sides discarded the formalities and got down to the business of spilling blood. At 4:30 A.M., Beauregard gave his gunners the order to reduce the fort. At Fort Johnson, on James Island, the honor of firing the first shot was bestowed on Virginian Roger Pryor, who declined it: "I could not fire the first gun of the war," he would later declare. The radical secessionist Edmund Ruffin showed no such hesitation; he pulled the lanyard and sent a shell arcing out across the harbor to burst over the fort, its detonation rumbling through the city.

The shelling began from all the Confederate batteries simultaneously, waking the people of Charleston to the sound of war. Soon the residents of the city (and many others who had started out from the countryside the previous evening in anticipation of just such an eventuality) were crowded on rooftops to witness the battle. One hour after the first shell was fired, the sun rose crimson over Sumter as Beauregard's forty-seven howitzers and mortars continued their deafening barrage. From atop houses along the waterfront, Charleston's elite watched. Anderson's response to the shelling was measured and deliberate; he did not have the ammunition to engage in a long-distance duel with trained Confederate gunners, so he just hung on, hoping for naval support. The bombardment continued through a second day and on into a third, lasting for forty hours in all. It ended when the two commanders negotiated a Union evacuation, leaving the fort to be occupied by Rebel troops.

The war that was to follow this first contest would take the lives of more than six hundred thousand American men fighting in more than forty major battles, hundreds of engagements, and thousands of skirmishes. Before the final surrender, the lands of South Carolina would come under the occupation of troops commanded by William T. Sherman, who had already "made Georgia howl" and laid waste to the Carolinas. Sherman's army would reserve special treatment for South Carolina, however, because it was the "cradle of secession" and home to the most outspoken Southern nationalists. Sherman and his men, like most Northerners, would blame South Carolina for causing the war by leading the South out of the Union. In this they would not be far wrong. There was no question as to why the war was fought, especially for South Carolinians. The state's delegates to the secession convention had not only drafted a statement of independence, but also signed a declaration addressed to "the people of the Slaveholding States of the United States." The war was about slavery; there was never any doubt about that.

There *were* dissenters in the South, but they were almost silent. "South Carolina is too small to be a Republic," pronounced a political moderate named James L. Petigru, "but too large to be an insane asylum." Robert Barnwell Rhett, Angelina and Sarah's famous cousin, was of a different mind. He had done perhaps more than any other South Carolinian to bring his state out of the Union, but after the formation of the Confederate States, his radicalism did not sit well with the South's new leaders. "For God's sake, and the sake of our beloved state," Judge David L. Wardlaw of South Carolina had written to a friend on the eve of secession, "don't let Rhett be elected Governor." Wardlaw's fear proved unfounded: Rhett instead took the helm of the *Charleston Mercury*, the South's leading newspaper. From that lofty perch, he did much to undermine the authority of the new government in Richmond, spewing invective at Confederate President Jefferson Davis, opposing the Southern draft, and regularly criticizing Confederate military leadership.

South Carolina's response to the call for a war of defense far outstripped that of any other Southern state, with a higher proportion of white males volunteering to serve in her regiments than in any of their counterparts. The sixty thousand Palmetto State volunteers would pay a heavy price: by war's end, in April 1865, more than twenty-one thousand would be dead, fully 35 percent of the volunteer force. Columbia, the capital city that John Faucheraud Grimké had helped to plan, would lie in ruins, the victim of a fire started by Sherman's troops. In 1860, Governor Francis W. Pickens had told South Carolinians that he would "be willing to appeal to the god of battles—if need be, cover the state with ruin, conflagration and blood rather than submit." He would get his wish. Charleston would finally submit on February 17, 1865, after nearly every great family in the state had been bankrupted, its plantations destroyed, its slaves scattered, its way of life changed forever.

Angelina and Sarah welcomed the war. Lincoln was not perfect, they agreed after Sumter, but at least he was a fighter. They decided to withhold judgment on him, even as they publicly pushed him to declare the slaves free. Angelina's writings on the war were prophetic, foreshadowing the descent of the South and its eventual and bloody demise: "The South are dissolving the Union in order to prevent the abolition of Slavery and yet they are too blind to see that this dissolution will only hasten instead of prevent its overthrow," she wrote in one letter. "Things look very dark and gloomy and . . . I have given up all hope of its abolition except thro' blood and insurrection. I feel willing it should come in my day, for the longer it is put off the worse it will be." Like his wife and sister-in-law, Theodore Weld believed he saw in the war not only the defeat of the slave power but a spiritual regeneration for Americans. "The elements of a vast moral revolution are all aglow in the surging mass," he announced in a letter to his fellow abolitionist Ellie Wright (later to be the wife of William Lloyd Garrison's son) at the war's outset. It was, he added, a "nationalist religious revival better deserving the name, than anything that preceded it."

Keeping one eye on the war and the other on their family, the Welds and Sarah ended their long and successful association with the Eagleswood School in early 1862 and moved to Perth Amboy. They felt they had little choice. Not only was Eagleswood dying a natural death (its popularity had waned, and its last class had just graduated), but Angelina, Theodore, and Sarah were in a perpetual state of anxiety over Sody's deteriorating health. They believed that by taking some time off from their continuous work and paying more attention to his disease, they might aid in his recovery. (When several months of their constant care failed to make a difference in Sody's health, he would be sent north to an asylum, where he could be looked after full-time.) The change of scene also marked a shift in the lives of the family. For Sarah, the decision to leave Eagleswood came as something of a relief. Unlike her sister, who was a natural teacher (of history), Sarah struggled as an instructor (of French), though she applied herself tenaciously to the task. She was, as always, lacking in confidence, tentative in her presentation, and vividly aware of her own failings. "I am driven to [teaching]," she wrote at the time, "by a stern sense of duty. I feel its responsibilities and my own insufficiency so deeply, that I never hear the school bell with pleasure, and seldom enter the schoolroom without a sinking of the heart, a dread as of some approaching catastrophe."

The departure from Eagleswood was welcomed by all of them, not just Sarah. Given the nomadic lives they had previously lived, the length of their tenure at the school was in itself an achievement. While teaching was a great joy for both Angelina and Theodore, running Eagleswood required more of them than just teaching. "We had indulged a delightful hope that Theodore would have no cares outside of the schoolroom, and Angelina would have leisure to pursue her studies and aid in the cause of woman," Sarah wrote. "Her heart is in it, and her talents qualify her for enlarged usefulness. She was no more designed to serve tables than Theodore to dig potatoes." But the truth was that being in charge of Eagleswood more often meant serving tables and digging potatoes than it did teaching. Each of them was ready for a new beginning, and each wanted to reenter public life, though all realized that considering their advanced age—Sarah would turn seventy this year, Theodore fifty-nine, and Angelina fifty-seven—whatever activity they undertook must be short-lived.

When Lincoln issued the Emancipation Proclamation in September 1862, in the wake of the Battle of Antietam, the three rejoiced, though none marked the event as the end of their collective life as political activists. Racism was still an evil to be conquered, a new and fertile ground for their continuing crusade. Abolitionism demanded not just an end to slavery but the full integration of black Americans into the nation's life. And so the struggle would go on. On November 9, 1862, Theodore gave a speech before a crowd of abolitionists at Boston's Music Hall, entitled "The Conspirators—Their False Issues and Lying Pretenses." Angelina and Sarah supported his coming-out: "If Theodore finds that he can use his voice as a lecturer," Sarah wrote to one of her friends, "and any field of usefulness opens to him, Nina and myself will joyfully and gratefully resign him."

It was the first time in many years that Weld had appeared in public, and he was fearful not only that his voice would fail him, but that his crusading style would appear quaint and out-of-step. In fact, he was a great success and would follow up his appearance with a tour of Massachusetts and New Hampshire (where he campaigned for the Republican candidate in a tough congressional contest). He lectured on the evils of slavery, the challenges brought on by the war, and the goals that had yet to be reached by abolitionist activists. The end of 1862 found Weld in the West, where, in a reprise of his antislavery mission more than twenty-five years earlier, he made an extended tour of eighteen weeks. He seemed revitalized and spoke as a prophet vindicated by the sweep of events. His audiences responded in kind, recognizing that his crusade had helped to bring about the conflict, which was now transformed, by Lincoln, from a "war for the Union" into a "war to free the slaves." On May 12, 1863, Weld mounted the dais as an honored official at the American Anti-Slavery Society's convention in New York. He was seated next to William Lloyd Garrison and was greeted with a sustained standing ovation.

Angelina also reentered public life. In March 1863, she and Sarah issued "An Appeal to the Women of the Republic," which appeared in the *New York Tribune*. This short essay was also signed by Elizabeth Cady Stanton and Susan B. Anthony, who were now nearly as well known, and as controversial, as the Grimké sisters had been at the height of their own public mission a quarter century before. The appeal summoned American women to support the war and called for a meeting of women to determine how they could best do so. The convention was held on May 14, 1863, in New York, with Angelina listed as a vice president. As she had done so many years before, she raised her voice against slavery and tied emancipation to the conquest of her home state of South Carolina. She fairly shouted out her message from the lectern, her voice now thunderous in anticipation of a Union victory: "My country is bleeding, my people are perishing around me. But I feel as a South Carolinian. I am bound to tell the North, go on! go on! Never falter, never abandon the principles which you have adopted."

At the end of the convention, Angelina drafted an "Address to the Soldiers of our Second Revolution." In many ways, it was as popular as her earlier "Letters" had been at the height of the abolitionist crusade. As a political document, however, it went further than any other public appeal of its day, touching on social, cultural, and economic problems that were only then emerging as national issues. For the first time in American history, a public document linked the plight of black Americans to that of women and "workingmen" of all colors, in terms that would not gain wide currency until the end of the century. Once again, Angelina Grimké positioned herself at the forefront of her era's most progressive causes.

This war is not, as the South falsely pretends, a war of races, nor of sections, nor of political parties, but a war of *Principles;* a war upon the working classes, whether white or black; a war against *Man,* the world over. In this war, the black man was the first victim, the workingman of whatever color the next; and now all who contend for the rights of labor, for free speech, free schools, free suffrage, and a free government are . . . driven to do battle in defense of these or fall with them, victims of the same violence that for two centuries has held the black man a prisoner of war. While the South has waged this war against human rights, the North has stood by holding the garments of those who were stoning liberty to death. . . .

The nation is in a death-struggle. It must either become one vast slaveocracy of petty tyrants, or wholly the land of the free. . . .

Soldiers of this revolution, to your hands is committed the sacred duty of carrying out in these latter days the ideal of your fathers, which was to secure to ALL "life, liberty and the pursuit of happiness."

———

Such sentiments, progressive or not, would not have been welcome on the fields of southern Pennsylvania, where, outside a small town called Gettysburg, young Union soldiers (the sons of those who, according to Angelina, held the garments of the slave drivers) died by the thousands in a bloody three-day battle. Within days, the lists of the dead were posted on courthouses and printed in long, black-bordered columns in newspapers throughout the nation. Reports of the battle shattered the South's morale. Months later, Mathew Brady's exhibition of photographs of the Union and Confederate dead in the Wheat Field, in the Devils' Den, and at Little Round Top—"bodies gathered for burial"—would shock the nation. But still the war went on. Lincoln called for more and more troops, then appointed Ulysses S. Grant to lead the Union armies. Sarah had a dream one night in which she saw the war as a "human ball" made up of "human bones and heads and shattered limbs and mutilated trunks of men," rolling ever onward and consuming all it touched. It was a vivid and horrific nightmare that would stay with her for years.

Sarah and Angelina's sisters Eliza and Mary (as well as John Faucheraud Grimké's remaining Charleston son, Dr. John Grimké) knew the war from firsthand experience. From the moment General Beauregard's guns opened on Sumter, two years before, the city's militia had been preparing its defenses. By late 1863, Charleston would be a veritable fortress, protected by redoubts on land and a string of defensive works (with Sumter at the center) by sea. The defenses were more than adequate: an attack from the south along Stono Inlet had been repulsed in June 1862, and nine new ironclad vessels had failed in their attempt to reduce the fort in April 1863. That May, the War Department had made Charleston one of its key targets and assigned Major General Quincy Gillmore to capture it.

In Charleston, the abundance of Confederate scrip caused havoc among shop owners. A soldier named David Harris wrote:

> I am called into service. One of my hands is demanded by the Government. A tenth of all I make is taken by the Government. I am taxed up all I sell, or have to sell, and still have to buy at these extravagant prices while the Government only gives me eleven dollars per month. But money is very plenty, by far too plenty. Every man, woman, child & negro has their pocket full. It is hard upon those who have nothing to sell, hard upon the Soldiers' wive [sic] & widow who have nothing but children & they do not seem to bring much of a price at present.

The state government responded to such complaints by establishing a number of aid associations and issuing a public appeal that excess flour, salt, butter, and pork be immediately distributed to the poor. It was a halfhearted measure that did little to check the escalating poverty.

In the summer of 1863, Charleston braced for Gillmore's assault, which was launched with an attack on the southern end of Morris Island on July 9. The attack was a success, carrying the Union forces (some sixty-five hundred men in all) up the length of the island to within sight of the Confederacy's main line of defense, anchored by Battery Wagner, a reinforced artillery redoubt that covered the island's northern end. If Battery Wagner could be taken, then Charleston Harbor itself might be opened, and Fort Sumter, the key to the city's defenses, placed in jeopardy. The Union forces' first attempt to storm Battery Wagner, undertaken on July 11, was repulsed with heavy losses. A second attack was planned, but Gillmore knew it would be costly. "Against us," he would later write, "the fort presented an armed front about 800 feet in length reaching entirely across the island, while our advance must be made over a strip of low shifting sand only about 80 feet wide, and two feet above the range of ordinary tides."

The second assault on Battery Wagner took place on the evening of July 18. The orders Gillmore gave his troops were simple: they were to proceed in battle order along the beach leading to the battery, mount its works, kill or capture its defenders, and then await further instructions. They would be supported by naval guns, which would cease firing as soon as the Union troops reached the battery's parapets. What Gillmore did not anticipate was that as the assaulting column charged along the beach, it would come under the fire of converging Confederate batteries from Fort Sumter and from defensive artillery positions on Sullivan's Island and James Island. The mission, in retrospect, must have seemed suicidal to those who were lucky enough to survive. Years later, Gillmore would issue his own modest but forlorn summary of the action: "Although the troops went gallantly forward," he wrote, "and gained the south-east bastion of the work and held it for more than two hours, the advantages which local knowledge and the deepening darkness gave the enemy forced a withdrawal."

Among those killed on this day was Colonel Robert Gould Shaw, the son of a prominent New York abolitionist and commander of an all-black regiment. His unit was destroyed at Battery Wagner (which, despite further attacks, would never be taken), with more than fifteen hundred of its men being killed, wounded, or captured. Behind Union lines, along the Sea Islands of South Carolina (which had come under Union control in 1862), Northern nurses treated the wounded of Shaw's command. One of those performing such duties was Charlotte Forten, a member of a prominent black Philadelphia family that supported the Grimké sisters' work and knew them well. Forten, destined to become one of America's foremost poets and essayists, was stunned by Shaw's death and memorialized his life in her famous journal, which would be published and repeatedly reprinted in the years to come. "Our noble, beautiful young Colonel is killed, and the regt. cut to pieces!" she wrote.

Alone and horrified by the carnage that surrounded her, Forten divided her time between caring for the wounded and introducing herself to the owners of nearby plantations, whose lands now lay fallow and whose former slaves had enlisted in the Union army. She was distressed and confused by the strangeness of the blacks she met here, who spoke gullah, a dialect so foreign to her as to be beyond her understanding.

Much more comfortable for her was the strong relationship she developed with Dr. Seth Rogers, a married and older white man to whom she was deeply attracted and whom she described as "one of the best and noblest types of manhood I ever saw." She hoped their bond might blossom into something more than a friendship, but Dr. Rogers was proper and warned her against such intimacy. Nor could her loneliness be assuaged by her revolutionary assignment, which was to recruit the first group of teachers for the freed blacks of the Sea Islands, a project that became known as the Port Royal Experiment. She chronicled her experiences in South Carolina in a series of pieces written for *The Liberator*.

The Port Royal Experiment represented the nation's first attempt to deal with the fact of slavery—or rather, its first attempt to address the needs of the newly freed slaves. It was also a test for the abolitionists, who had talked of freedom and worked for freedom and claimed again and again—at least the most radical among them had—that black Americans were equal, in every way, to white Americans. Now it was time to prove that claim. The Port Royal project would be a testing ground for the massive social programs that would be required during Reconstruction, the national effort to acclimate former slaves to free American life. The test was a formidable one: most slaves were illiterate, and many of those who *were* educated were filled with an anger so deep that their role in the new society of the future was cast into doubt. Lincoln's secretary of the Treasury, Salmon P. Chase, thought about all of this and inaugurated in South Carolina a program so comprehensive and so exhaustive that it would become the model for the Freedman's Bureau, the Republican administration's attempt to create black American citizens (and Republicans, as Southerners would bitterly add). The abolitionist community responded by sending teachers south to Port Royal, and then following those teachers up with money for South Carolina's schools.

At the heart of the Port Royal Experiment (begun even before the war's end—on land occupied by Union troops) was a national commitment to educating the freed slaves as quickly and as comprehensively as possible. The old American Anti-Slavery Society and other abolitionist organizations and churches now banded together to found the American Missionary Association, which hired and trained hundreds of "Yankee schoolmarms" to send south—as soon as the war was over. Their job would be to build integrated schools in which black children would learn not only how to read and write but also how to be good citizens. "Gideon bands" of abolitionists, intent on seeing through the revolution they had begun, were formed all over the North, fired with a missionary zeal to accomplish in America what ministers of the faith, armed with Bibles and good intentions, tried to do with the world's heathens. The great American experiment, they said, would continue, but on American soil; the nation, once stained by slavery, would transform the blood that had been shed in the Civil War into a new democratic covenant. Charlotte Forten was one of these new Gideons. Ironically, while she taught newly free blacks the fundamentals of literacy, she was teaching *herself* about black Americans. The freed slaves, she discovered, were quite different from the blacks she had met in Philadelphia, New York, and Boston. She concluded that it would be many years, perhaps decades, before the experiment initiated at Port Royal would result in equality. But at least the work had begun.

After nine months in South Carolina, exhausted by her experiences and nearly overwhelmed by the tasks that she now knew faced the black community, Charlotte Forten decided to return to Philadelphia. She missed her family and friends and the culture offered by the free black community of the North, but she could hardly bring herself to explain what she had seen. Her time in the Deep South had provided her with a view of the nation that few others like her experienced. She felt alienated and overcome by what lay ahead. But most of all, she yearned for someone with whom to share it all. She wrote longingly in her journal of "one earnest sympathizing soul to be in close communion with my own. I long for the pressure of a loving hand in mine, the touch of loving lips upon my aching brow."

Charlotte Forten could not have known it then, but the man who would be her companion in life was at that moment just a few short miles away, in the Charleston workhouse. Within weeks, he would be sold as a slave to a Confederate soldier. Coincidentally, his father came from a family that the Philadelphia Fortens thought of as friends. His last name, famous in the North and controversial in the South, was Grimké.

In late 1863, Theodore, Angelina, and Sarah moved first to West Newton, outside Boston, and then to Fairmount (soon to be Hyde Park), where they purchased a home. All three joined the faculty of a private school in Lexington. Angelina taught history, as she had done at Eagleswood, and was an excellent instructor: "I am not satisfied to teach only what is in the text books," she wrote to a friend of her new job. "I read a great deal of the larger works, so as to be a *live* teacher and lift the pupils' minds above the glitter and pomp of war and conquest." She monitored the war news closely and in the evenings wrote to her sisters in Charleston, hoping that somehow they would receive the letters. By May 1864, the people of Charleston, including the Grimkés, were subsisting on crackers, water, the odd ear of corn, and scraps of pork boiled in water. Sherman was still many miles away, in northern Georgia, but he was coming. That same month, Grant turned to face Lee in northern Virginia, inaugurating the bloodiest campaign of conquest in American history. The "forty days" of bloodshed that followed would leave the nation deeply demoralized, but by the end of that period, the Confederate forces would be besieged in Richmond, and the war's eventual outcome would no longer be in doubt.

Sody, of course, was not with Grant, or anywhere else in the Union armies, being too infirm to serve. Nor was Charley in uniform: Angelina and Theodore's first son insisted that the war was unjust and had informed his parents that he would refuse to serve if drafted. Theodore offered to pay for a "substitute" (an arrangement whereby someone else, for an agreed-upon sum, would take a draftee's place—a common but controversial practice at the time), but Charley angrily declined, saying that his refusal to serve was based on principle and that he would rather go to jail than fight. That neither of their sons was serving, even as thousands of others were losing their lives, was a source of acute embarrassment for Theodore and Angelina, but there was little they could do to change the situation. Charles Stuart Weld stayed at Harvard, graduated, and maintained his principles.

In Charleston, meanwhile, the situation was deteriorating even further. Although the Union forces had failed in their attempt to capture Fort Sumter, and repeated attacks were unable to reduce Battery Wagner, the city was a shell of what it had been three years before. The stores were empty, and the citizenry was surviving on what few remnants of the harvest came in from the countryside. Food was hoarded, and because Confederate scrip was being printed to meet the demands of rising prices (or perhaps, as Charlestonians guessed, the other way around), it was nearly useless. When looting began in late 1864, citizens were forced to establish local vigilante committees. Eliza and Mary Grimké and their brother John were better off than most: they had some food, and their morale remained high. They defiantly announced to Angelina and Sarah that they would defend their homes to the last.

The Union army of General William Tecumseh Sherman entered South Carolina on February 1, 1865, made a feint toward Charleston, and then struck out northwest, toward Columbia. Sherman's men left a swath of destruction in their wake. The towns of Robertville, Hardeeville, Gillisonville, Orangeburg, Springfield, Hickory Hill, Barnwell, and McPherson were looted and burned. Any plantation unlucky enough to be in the path of the army was destroyed. Behind Sherman's forces, a separate corps of "bummers"—criminals, prostitutes, and stevedores—snatched up what was left, and behind *them* came a veritable army of newly freed black Americans in search of their relatives, new homes, and a new way of life.

In the spring of 1865, Sherman and his men marched to Bentonville, North Carolina, where they accepted the surrender of the remaining Confederate forces east of the Mississippi River; one week earlier, Lee had surrendered to Grant at Appomattox. In Hyde Park, the Welds and Sarah celebrated the end of the war by pledging to rededicate themselves to the cause of the newly freed slaves—the "freedmen." All three supported radical Reconstruction policies that would give black Americans equal rights. Weld spoke out on the need to maintain a federal military presence in the South: "The Nation is its *citizens*," he told one audience, "[and] the Nation's right and duty to protect and defend its citizens, all of them, [are] absolute and paramount." The soldiers came home from Appomattox and Bentonville, America buried its assassinated president, and Washington marked the occasion with a Grand Review. Andrew Johnson took office.

In 1867, at the age of seventy-five, Sarah Grimké finished a project she had been working on for three years: a translation of Lamartine's *Joan of Arc*, which was then, to her great satisfaction, privately published. That same year, the Lexington school where all three had been teaching burned down, never to be rebuilt. The Grimké-Welds were now officially in retirement, and if they were not exactly affluent, their income from years of teaching and lecturing, added to the remnants of Angelina and Sarah's inheritance from the Grimké lands in South Carolina, at least made their lives comfortable. The Welds were both in their sixties now, and their children were grown: Sody was in a New York asylum, Charles Stuart was living at home and writing, and Sarah (or "Sissy," as they called her) was pursuing her studies.

In mid-1867, Eliza Grimké came north from Charleston for a visit. Although deeply embittered by the war's outcome, she was pleasant enough toward Sarah and Angelina and wide-eyed at being in Boston. The family lands were gone, she reported—confiscated by the Union army—and all the Grimké slaves had been freed. Most of them had left Charleston, but some had stayed on to begin new lives. The family, too, she said, had changed forever. Angelina and Sarah's sisters and brothers were slowly, one by one, dying. Frederick Grimké of Ohio (a believer in states' rights and a defender of the South) had died during the war, after a respectable career as a jurist. Anna Grimké Frost had returned to Charleston after the war and died soon thereafter. After a short stay in Boston, Eliza herself went back to Charleston, intent on starting a new life. She and Mary, the other Charleston sister, would remain unreconstructed supporters of Southern nationalism to the very end.

The only solace that might have been left for Angelina and Sarah was their brother Henry, whom they had both admired. But in 1852, in the middle of a successful career as a lawyer and planter, Henry had died. Angelina and Sarah had been particularly close to him and had known him to be a kind master. "His slaves will feel his loss deeply," Sarah had commented at the time. "They haunt me day and night. Sleeplessness is my portion, thinking what will become of them."

———

We can paint a vivid if gentle picture of Theodore, Angelina, and Sarah in retirement. They are in their home in Hyde Park, living frugal but full lives. People of ideas who write and read constantly, they continue to discuss the events of the day even as they age and their memories grow dimmer. They are still, in the late 1860s, lionized by their peers and celebrated by the generation that changed the nation. They likely believe (indeed, they say as much themselves) that their work will live on after them, even as the nation enters a "gilded age" of breathless expansion. Ulysses S. Grant is in the White House, a great railroad is beginning to stretch from one coast to another, and Mark Twain has started writing *Huckleberry Finn*. Scandals are brewing. Even in 1867, just two years after the end of the war, the great victory of the Union, the sacrifice of its young soldiers, and the murder of its savior, Lincoln, are but fading memories.

Still, Weld and the Grimké sisters had accomplished much more than they would have believed possible, and in ways they could not then have begun to explain. Their work as abolitionists had awakened the nation to its greatest sorrow. Simply by summoning the courage to appear and speak out in public on the issue, Sarah and Angelina Grimké had established a foundation for the feminist revolution to follow. Both movements—the crusade to free the slave and the campaign to win full rights for women—reverberate into the present. That we are aware of these issues, that we recognize the need to fight continually for race and gender equality, that we choose to give a voice to those who do not have one—all of these things are directly attributable to the sisters' work. We look back at the nineteenth century and see Andrew Jackson, Abraham Lincoln, and Robert E. Lee. Those men were giants. But other giants stood with them, men and women who were in every sense as great and as good and as committed to their cause. They walk with us now not simply because of the work they did but because of the way in which they did it.

Sarah Grimké, Angelina Grimké Weld, and Theodore Weld shaped the way reform would be carried out in America. They came up with the idea of political action and forged the implements of the modern political enterprise. All of the tools that we use today in our political and social re-form efforts were first employed by the Grimké sisters and Weld. The abolitionist movement was not born of circumstance; it was thought through. The question faced by the sisters in the nineteenth century was the same one that confronts any political organizer in modern America: How can the American people be made to care about something that does not directly affect them? For the Grimkés, the challenge was to bring the horror of slavery into American homes, to make it real to those who had never seen it.

At a key moment in the abolitionist enterprise, just when it seemed that the movement would never gain the public attention or support it needed to succeed, Theodore Weld traveled to Washington to help John Quincy Adams (the century's other giant) transform the fight *against* slavery into a battle *for* free speech. It was one thing for Southerners to hold slaves, and quite another for them to silence their critics with a gag rule. When the abolitionists realized that the lesson they learned at Adams's knee could turn their movement from a crusade into a political cause, they flooded Congress with petitions. The terrible irony for America's abolitionists, and the basis of their ultimate triumph, was that while their outrage at the notion of human bondage was shared by only some Americans, retaining the rights of free speech, the right to petition, and the right to be safe and secure in one's own home (from slave catchers or anyone else) was a concern common to all. A hard lesson was thereby learned, for no political movement can succeed simply by being right. In a democracy, in *our* democracy, a cause must be translated into votes. Lincoln knew this better than any other nineteenth-century leader, but the Grimkés and Weld understood it first, and so made him possible.

The tools of modern political organizing were first crafted by the abolitionists. Today we use "direct-mail appeals" to raise money for social and political causes; they invented the approach. Today we circulate petitions and call for millions of signatures to bring good causes to public attention; they did those things first. Today activists preach in churches and view churchgoers as the most potent weapon of any political cause; abolitionism was organized first in America's churches. Today we translate the public mood into political equity, transforming the work of the neighborhood into votes in Congress; in this, too, we follow their lead. Single-issue conventions, rallies, published broadsides, manifestos, political polling, campaign funding, direct nonviolent action, and focus groups, the currency of the modern political trade, all had their precedents in work done by the abolitionists.

In a fundamental way, Angelina Grimké loaded the charge and lit the spark that fired the gun that sent the shell arcing over Fort Sumter. She might have walked from that place just outside Charleston with her sister Sarah, up the road and past the plantations to their father's home on Front Street. By 1867, the plantations were gone, but so were the slave pens that the Grimkés had, as children, passed nearly every Sunday on their way to church. But the sisters' most important contribution had nothing to do with slavery. Instead, it was this: from the moment in 1838 when Angelina Grimké testified before the state legislature in Boston, women could no longer be counted on to remain silent. Although they still could not vote, and would not win that right for another half century, political candidates and political organizers could never again take their assent for granted. Women thus became the most potent force in American political life, and remain so today. The Grimkés, and hundreds of others like them in the leadership of the abolitionist movement, had erased the stain of slavery from the resewn cloth of the Union. They had changed the nation.

While Angelina and Sarah Grimké were aware of their importance in the movement, they did not believe they had changed America; rather, they felt they had merely defended what was right. They saw themselves not as major political figures, or celebrities, but as simple women dedicated to a profound cause. At the same time, they realized that the mission they had been involved with almost since its inception, the mission they had promoted and seen through to its natural end—freeing slaves from bondage—was not yet completed. The end was not an end at all. For in 1867, though abolition was a reality, political and social equality was not. At the heart of slavery, Angelina and Sarah knew, lay the issue of race, or rather, as they had insisted again and again (much to the chagrin of many of their abolitionist colleagues), not *race* at all, but color prejudice. They preached this message at every opportunity. But in early 1868, the Grimké sisters were to meet the test of color prejudice in their own lives, and in a form they could never have foreseen.

On a February evening in 1868, Angelina Grimké's interest was caught by a brief notice in the *National Anti-Slavery Standard.* Although others now believed that the work of the abolitionist movement was finished, Angelina continued to pore over every article on slavery and black equality that she found. Carefully reading the *Standard,* and every other antislavery newspaper she could get, was a habit she had developed over many years; she did not intend to give it up simply because the Civil War was over. But on this evening, what she read in the *Standard* sent her to the seclusion of her room, where she stayed, thinking quietly to herself, for three hours. The article that had so disturbed her, a reprint of a news item that had first appeared in the *Boston Commonwealth,* was entitled "Negroes and Higher Studies." Its author, Professor Edwin S. Bower, wrote that he could disprove the notion that blacks were inferior by pointing to examples from his own experience as a teacher at Lincoln University. The scholarship of black students at that school, including two named Grimké (who had come to Lincoln, he noted, "just out of slavery"), shattered the myth of black inferiority.

Angelina was stunned by the article. She knew of no other Grimké family besides hers in America. She could conclude only that these two young men must be the sons of her dead brother Henry, the same slaves over whom Sarah had fretted in 1852, writing, "They haunt me day and night." After the shock of this discovery—for Angelina knew exactly what it meant—she recovered and spoke of the matter to her sister and husband. She told them that they must right the wrong done by Henry, by first contacting and then helping the young Grimké brothers. Angelina displayed an outward calm through all of this, but inside she was in turmoil: the news had far-reaching implications, for she doubted that any provision had been made by the Grimké family for these former slaves. Sarah agreed that Angelina should immediately write to one of the young men, Francis Grimké, and Angelina did so, introducing herself as a Grimké from Charleston, the sister of "Dr. John Grimké." She asked whether Francis and his brother Archibald were the slave sons of her brother Henry. She formed her words carefully, almost gingerly, then folded the paper over and the next morning—a wintry Saturday in Boston—posted it to Philadelphia.

The reply came to Angelina in Hyde Park, from Philadelphia, on February 20, just one week later. The letter was signed Archibald Grimké.

Dear Madam, I am very happy to hear from Miss Angelina Grimké of Anti-Slavery celebrity. I am the son of Henry Grimké, your brother. Of course you know more about my father than I do, suffice it to say he was a lawyer and was married to a Miss Simons. She died, leaving three children viz. Henrietta, Montague, and Thomas. After her death he took my mother, who was his slave and his children's nurse; her name is Nancy Weston. I don't think you know her. By my mother he had three children also. Archibald, which is my name, and Francis and John. He died about fifteen years ago, leaving my mother, with two children and in a pregnant state, for John was born two mos. after he died, in the care of his son, Mr. E. M. [Montague] Grimké in his own words, as I heard "I leave Nancy and her two children to be treated as members of the family."

I am the eldest of the bros., was born 17th Aug. 1849. Therefore, my poor mother a defenceless woman, crippled in one arm, with no one to care for her in the world, for Mr. G. did not do as his father commanded, and three small children to provide for, was thrown upon the uncharitable world. . . .

He [Montague] informed my mother [in 1860] that he wanted me and that she should send me to his house. His mandate was irresistible; it was a severe shock to my mother. . . . But this was only the beginning of her sorrows, thus he kept on until she was rendered childless. . . .

I hope dear Madam you will excuse this badly written epistle. . . . Perhaps you would like to see our pictures, they are enclosed. I shall hope to hear from you soon. Most respectfully yours, Archibald Henry Grimké.

There were three brothers, then: Archibald, Francis, and John. Two of them, Archibald and Francis, were enrolled as students at Lincoln University, near Philadelphia; the third was still in Charleston. After sharing the letter with Sarah and Theodore, Angelina announced that she would write to Archibald and Francis again and then go to Philadelphia to visit them. Sarah and Theodore at once approved her intentions, but still, she did not know what she would do after she met the boys, or how she would feel. She believed, however, she had little choice but to go ahead with her plan. Other Southerners might ignore the ties that bound them to their slaves, but not she. Her daughter, Sarah Weld, would later summarize this family discussion: "Her brother had wronged these children; his sisters must right them." On February 29, 1868, Angelina responded to Archibald's letter:

> Dear young friends, I cannot express the mingled emotions with which I perused your deeply interesting and touching letter. The facts disclosed were *no* surprise to me. Indeed had I not suspected that you might be my nephews, I should probably not have addressed you. . . . I will not dwell on the past—let that all go—it cannot be altered—our work is in the present. I am glad you have taken the name of Grimké—it was *once*, one of the noblest names of Carolina—a purer patriot never lived than my brother Thomas S. Grimké.
>
> You my young friends now bear this once honored name—I charge you most solemnly by your upright conduct, and your life-long devotion to the eternal principles of justice and humanity and religion[,] to lift this name out of the dust, where it now lies, and set it once more among the princes of our land.

That June, Angelina and her son Charles Stuart Weld traveled to Philadelphia to attend Lincoln University's commencement exercises and to meet Francis and Archibald, then finishing their second year at the school. Angelina worried about the visit and what it would bring to light. She knew some of the details of the young men's life, but she did not know how to begin a relationship with them. The future seemed clouded, and so the trip itself became a deep emotional and physical strain. She met first with Lincoln's president, and then Archibald and Francis entered the room. It was an uncomfortable moment, but Angelina immediately liked them both. They looked so much like Grimkés, and they acted just as she expected Grimkés to act: they were intelligent, articulate, polite, and kind, as her brother Henry had once been. They were his sons, her nephews, and they could not be rejected, disavowed, or ignored. No, Angelina decided; they must be embraced. They were Grimkés. They were family.

The two brothers repaid Angelina's visit several months later, appearing at Hyde Park wearing formal suits. They were embarrassed to see their aunts in their usual plain dresses. Archibald's daughter would later write of their discomfort: "To the boys this was a great occasion, the greatest in all their lives and, cost what it might, they were determined to live up to it. They were virtually penniless, but each carried a cane, wore a high silk hat which had been made to order, and boots that were custom-made." They were greeted by Angelina, Theodore, and Sarah, three modest people, modestly dressed, for whom being unassuming was almost a religion. "The simplicity here," Archibald's daughter would note, "taught them their lesson."

Whatever unease Archibald and Francis Grimké felt was quickly put aside as a new Grimké family bond was cemented. Sarah in particular focused on her nephews' education and promised to support them as best she could. Theodore was pleased by the meeting. He viewed the discovery of Archibald and Francis as the completion of the fateful union he had entered into so many years before with Angelina, coupling the destiny of the Weld family forever with that of the Grimkés—the *black* Grimkés—of Charleston. Here was a chance, finally, to put into practice what they had all been preaching for so long. Archibald, Francis, and John could carry on the fight for black equality to which Theodore, Angelina, and Sarah had dedicated their lives. The road ahead might be difficult for these "new" Grimkés, but it could be no worse than that already traversed by the "old" ones. Indeed, the very existence of Henry's three slave sons seemed a natural progression in the family history. The work of the Grimké sisters, and then of the Grimké family, would be carried on—by the Grimké brothers.

PART THREE

The Grimké Brothers

ELEVEN

"Everyone was for himself..."

As an adult, Henry Grimké had looked like his father—tall, with kind features and a strong profile. He was an upright man, soft-spoken, intelligent, and gentle, who rarely lost his temper and was well liked and admired by all of Charleston. The Grimké family home in the city and the family cotton plantation in the Union District, as well as his father's smaller holdings along the coast, had fallen to Henry by default. His brothers were all gone—either dead or in the North—except for John, a well-respected and successful doctor who had no interest in managing a plantation. Henry Grimké took his responsibility seriously, overseeing the work of planting and harvesting with a rare diligence. He was a kind master who gave out special gifts to favored servants and field hands. He married well and loved his wife and their three children. When he was not looking after the Grimké holdings, he could be seen nearly every day in Charleston, walking to and from his law offices.

While Henry Grimké was perhaps the best choice to carry on the family's Southern legacy, that had not always been the case. As a young man, he had been unfocused, unmotivated, and uncertain, an indifferent student who had the reputation of being an untamed boy, a rogue. His parents had worried about him, and his sisters had commented on his cruelty and lack of compassion. Angelina knew about those traits better than any of her other siblings: as a child, she had often witnessed Henry beating his slaves. On one occasion, little Angelina had heard her brother giving his manservant, John, a whipping, and had confronted him. By her account,

> He very openly acknowledged that he meant to give John such a whipping as would cure him of ever doing the same thing again, and that he deserved to be whipped until he could not stand. I said that would be treating him worse than he would treat his horse. He now became excited, and replied that he considered his horse no comparison better than John, and would not treat it so. By this time my heart was full, and I felt so much overcome as to be compelling to seat myself, or rather to fall into a chair before him, but I don't think he observed this. I pleaded the cause of humanity. He grew very angry and said I had no business meddling with him, that he never did so with me. . . . I had much better go and live at the North. I told him that as soon as I felt released from Carolina I would go. . . . To my surprise he readily acknowledged that he felt something within him which fully met all I asserted, and that I had harrowed his feelings and made him wretched. Much more passed. . . .

In those days, however, Henry never seemed to feel wretched for long. He was continually angry and acted distant and detached, an embittered youth who was not yet a man. A racist and a white supremacist, he had a wicked temper and believed that the family slaves were inferior and deserved their slavery. He was mean-spirited and sharp-tongued. But then, in the late 1830s, suddenly, shockingly, he changed. Although he was still prone to striking out at those nearest him when angry over the slightest indiscretion, there were long periods in which he was surprisingly warm, even empathetic. Some in Charleston said he had simply matured; others put it down to the influence of his new wife, Selina, a kind and intelligent woman. Whatever the reason, he seemed to grab hold of himself. He set aside his wild habits and entered the community as one of "the young Grimkés," dedicated to carrying on his father's reputation and the family name. He became a "good master" and was known for caring for his slaves.

By the early 1840s, Henry Grimké had made his mark on the world, much as John Faucheraud Grimké had done before him. He was involved in South Carolina politics, had become a partner in his late brother Thomas's already successful law practice, and enjoyed a reputation as one of the best lawyers in the city, if not in the state. Like his father, he was listened to and admired; unlike the judge, however, Henry Grimké would lead a life filled with tragedy. His wife died in 1843, leaving him with the task of raising their three children, a teenaged girl and two young sons. In 1847, he ran for a seat on the state supreme court but lost the election. Lonely and alone, he decided to abandon politics. He bought a large rice plantation staffed by thirty slaves, Cane Acre, in Saint Paul's Parish in the Colleton District, just twenty-five miles from Charleston. Surrounded by other great homes owned by some of the city's most prominent families, the plantation was located in the heart of South Carolina's low country, where rice planting and harvesting thrived. Henry Grimké moved there with some of his Charleston slaves in 1847.

Henry lived at Cane Acre for most of the year, traveling to Charleston only to conduct necessary business. He concentrated on the work of the plantation and kept a proper Southern home, entertaining visitors and often partaking of leisurely dinners with neighbors. At night he tended to the plantation's books or wrote letters to friends and relatives. He cared for his children and even sent one son north to be educated by his sisters and Theodore Weld. As far as Charlestonians were concerned, Henry Grimké was living the life of a proper widower, still grieving for his lost wife. The reality of the situation, however, was quite different: after Selina's death, Henry Grimké had taken Nancy Weston, a slave woman, as his mistress. If there was ever any talk about this among the whites of Charleston, no record of it has survived. But Henry did little to hide his relationship with Nancy, for though she lived in a separate house, she became the virtual head of his home and managed the plantation. Henry's Charleston sisters, Eliza and Mary, knew of the relationship, but they never mentioned it to anyone.

We do not know, and cannot know, whether Henry Grimké was in love with Nancy Weston, or she with him. But the evidence we do have (including Nancy's own words, recorded by her sons) strongly suggests that Nancy Weston was neither raped nor coerced by Henry Grimké, nor was she an unwilling participant in their relationship. To the contrary—controversial though it may be—all available evidence (including Archibald and Francis's views on the relationship) indicates that Nancy Weston and Henry Grimké were in love. A number of historians have argued that love between a master and a slave was simply not possible, that the coercive nature of slavery itself rendered such a relationship, by definition, "forced." The same might be said, of course, of *any* sexual relationship in the nineteenth century, free or slave. A great many such relationships, perhaps even most, were indeed coercive, as the Grimké sisters, Elizabeth Cady Stanton, and Susan B. Anthony observed. (When the Grimké sisters insisted that they understood the plight of slaves because they themselves felt the onerous prejudice that attended women's restriction to the "private sphere," they were not speaking merely of their status as mothers or sisters or daughters.)

There can be no doubt that the vast majority of master-slave sexual relations were, in fact, coerced; white Southern women knew of such abominations and occasionally wrote about them. But to say that all master-slave sexual unions came about through rape or coercion is simply wrong. It contradicts almost everything we know about slavery and about the peculiar intimacy of the Southern master-slave relationship. It was that intimacy that gave American slavery its most tragic and horrifying face. For while black Americans were the ones who were enslaved and abused, the unutterable and unalterable truth of Southern slaveholders is that (despite their protests to the contrary) many of them *knew* that what they were doing was wrong. There were likely hundreds and perhaps even thousands of Henrys with "harrowed feelings" and "wretched" emotions. They understood that slavery was a stain on their soul, and they practiced it anyway. To defend slavery, to defend this wrong, white Americans invented a unique form of prejudice that they claimed was based on race (though in fact it was based on color); when in doubt, they retreated to their Bibles to seek justification.

If there was anything worse, in South Carolina, than fathering children with a black woman whom you had raped, it was falling in love with a black woman and sharing your life with her. To do so was to imply that she was intelligent, attractive, worthy, interesting—in a word, *equal*. And by the very laws of the state of South Carolina, that simply could not be. Blacks were viewed as ignorant, ugly, unworthy, barbarian—in short, inferior. Rape, coercion, a master's "visit to the slave cabins," the examples of "all those mulatto children" (as Mary Chesnut so indelicately phrased it)—all of these things were discussed by the wives of slaveholders, quietly and privately, for decades. But falling in love with a black woman was never mentioned, not once. It was the greatest stigma of all. If we know one thing about the South before the Civil War, it must be this:

Southern society was so twisted by slavery that the rape of a black woman by a white man could be and was defended and tolerated, while the love of a white man for a black woman was seen as the ultimate betrayal of the white race. It was a mortal sin.

We may suppose, then, if we wish, that Nancy Weston was coerced. But she herself denied it, and so did her sons. At a time when nearly every other male slave child at Cane Acre was called James by Henry Grimké, he named his own children Archibald and Francis and nicknamed them Archie and Frank. Nancy and Henry's third son, John— born after Henry died—was named by his mother for Henry's brother Dr. John Grimké. Nancy Weston took Henry's name and made it her own; she died Nancy Weston Grimké. She told her sons about their father. She said she had "faith" in him and "believed" in him. She told them that Henry Grimké sent them to school because he wanted them to learn how to read and write. Finally, given the timing of his purchase of Cane Acre, it seems likely that Henry Grimké moved to Saint Paul's Parish precisely because he wanted to continue his relationship with Nancy Weston far from the prying eyes of Charleston's white community. There they lived as man and wife, or as near to that ideal as they could manage.

———

Nancy Weston was a woman of enormous intellectual capacity, physical strength, and religious conviction. She was thin but tough and carried out her duties despite being "crippled in one arm." She was a serious woman with piercing eyes. Her son Archibald, who would later pen a famous portrait of her entitled "A Madonna of the South," viewed her as the presence of God incarnate, a figure much loved, if also feared, by her children. She was feared, too, by Henry Grimké. One day, she later told her sons, Henry lost his temper and raised his hand to her. She stopped him in midswing, and threw him to the ground, then stood over him. He got up, looked at her sheepishly, and never did it again. Piety and strength, her two strongest characteristics, combined to animate this woman who was ambitious on behalf of her children and insisted on teaching them right and wrong. "Profanity was a terrible sin and obscenity was in her mind like handling filth," Archibald would recall. She attended the Zion Colored Church on Anson Street in Charleston, and was close to its minister. Prayer, she felt, was a person's most powerful weapon, and accordingly, she prayed often and sincerely and taught her sons to pray. She watched over them, sternly, as they knelt beside their beds at night.

God was important to her, the center of her life, but her sons—hers and Henry Grimké's—always came first. They came before anything else. Nancy Weston believed that education was the one means by which they would ultimately gain their freedom, the thing that could prepare them for their lives as free men. And she knew something about freedom, for she saw it every day, even in her own community. She was well known within the free black community of Charleston and mixed easily with its members. She was related to the city's large Weston clan and to the O'Hears, a prominent free black family. Her mother was dark-skinned, but Weston herself was referred to by her peers (and by Henry) as a mulatto. Her father may well have been white; the records of her paternity are lost. She worked hard and, after the death of Henry's wife, became the mistress in all but name of the Grimké home in Charleston, and later of Cane Acre. Henry treated their children affectionately, but the law strictly forbade his "recognizing" them as his heirs.

Henry Grimké died on the 28th of September, 1852, when the typhoid fever that swept through the low country struck Cane Acre. His remains were buried in a small plot on an island "amidst the rice ponds" of his plantation home, everything he had owned was sold at auction, including the land, the house, and the Cane Acre slaves. Nancy and her sons would undoubtedly also have been sold were it not for the special provision made for them in Henry's will: they were now (and "forever") the property of Montague Grimké. He took them to Charleston, where they would all stay for a time at the home of Mary and Eliza Grimké, Henry's sisters. Nancy Weston was then pregnant with her third child, John, who would be born two months after Henry's death. It was during this same year, 1852, that Harriet Beecher Stowe's novel *Uncle Tom's Cabin* was published in the North.

That Nancy Weston and Henry Grimké had lived as man and wife did not come as a shock to his Charleston sisters, who had known of the relationship and now used the proceeds from the sale of Cane Acre to acquire a three-room home for Nancy and her children. The small house was located on Coming Street, not far from Henry's old town house. It is hard to imagine that Henry and Nancy's relationship could really have been kept from Angelina and Sarah, for though the two would express surprise on learning of the three children in 1868, Sarah's worries about Henry's slaves after his death must have been founded on at least a suspicion of a more personal bond. They had corresponded with their brother often and known him well.

Life in the Grimké household in Charleston was nothing like the existence that Nancy and her sons had grown accustomed to at Cane Acre. Eliza and Mary Grimké were cut from the same cloth as their mother and like her believed deeply in the rectitude of Southern customs. They were religious women, they were proper and polite, they mixed well with Charleston's other aristocratic families, and they cared a great deal about appearances. They loved South Carolina and never questioned its slave system. Montague was much like them. He was also quick-tempered, narrow-minded, and sometimes violent—as his father had been in his younger days. But Montague Grimké was nothing like Henry Grimké the man. They shared only a name.

———

Montague allowed Nancy Weston and her sons the small house on Coming Street in Charleston, but little else. He employed Nancy as a seamstress and recommended her to a number of other families. She worked constantly to support her children and lived in fear that they would get in trouble, or get hurt, for they lived in "a part of the city," as Archibald later wrote, "where there was a great deal of coarseness, of moral and social degradation. The atmosphere of this quarter, indeed of the whole city, was very unfavorable to the maintenance of the purity of [Nancy's] domestic life and to the growth of virtue in the breasts of her little ones." Although she had to struggle to make ends meet, she earned a reputation as an excellent worker. Archie, Frank, and later John all helped her wash and mend shirts, socks, and pants, and then delivered them to the doorsteps of Charleston's most affluent citizens.

All three sons participated in the work of the home. Archie and Frank carried water from a nearby well, split wood, and spent hours in front of the washbasin, before starting in on their own chores. The boys also helped their mother prepare the day's main meal at noon; the family diet consisted of rice and fish, sweet corn, tomatoes, and ham bits or pork bones. Supper was predictable: just bread and water. The dishes they ate were traditionally Southern, with names intended to cover their meagerness: hopping John, okra soup (boiled water seasoned with leftover vegetables), chicken gumbo. There was never enough. Sometimes in the afternoons, after finishing their chores, Archie and Frank would visit a former slave woman who knew how to read. She taught them the alphabet and numbers. On other occasions, Nancy's sons attended unofficial "home schools" for free blacks, though this was a violation of South Carolina's strict slave code. Nancy paid a teacher a dollar a month to teach her sons to read and write.

The black community of Charleston was tight-knit, interrelated, and devoted to the shared goal of eventual freedom for all. The Grimké boys made friendships here that would last a lifetime. Tom Miller, who would later join them at Lincoln University, lived only a few short blocks away during these years, and near and distant relatives of Nancy's—especially the Westons, O'Hears, and Owens—kept an eye on the children and reported their activities to their mother when necessary. There was a thin but discernible line between Charleston's population of black slaves and its population of free blacks. Although the two communities were not interdependent, networks of families and friends, both free and slave, insulated their members from the worst excesses of slavery. There were thirty-four hundred free blacks in Charleston in 1850, a considerable number for a city of its size. During the Civil War, they would play a critical role in helping the slave population make the transition to freedom.

Although she herself was a Baptist, Nancy Weston sent her children to the Second Presbyterian Church of Charleston because it afforded them greater opportunities. The white minister there was dedicated to black education; he made the Grimké boys memorize verses from the Bible and led them in their weekly devotions. The childhood of the three boys might have been comparatively uneventful if their half-brother Montague had not reentered their lives in 1857 and insisted that Archie come to his home to be the slave of his new wife. Nancy objected so strenuously that she was thrown into Charleston's workhouse for a week. Frank was taken next, and then John. All of the brothers were forced to wear livery (black pressed suits with brass buttons), like most of Charleston's other houseboys, and all eventually rebelled, openly defying Montague and his wife. Frank was the worst offender, at least in his master's eyes, and was whipped mercilessly several times by Montague and his wife; whenever he ran away, Montague would catch him and lock him in the attic. Fearing that her sons would be sold at auction, Nancy always returned the runaway to Montague, protesting that he was just a child and did not know any better.

Frank continued to outwit his captor at every turn. After confinement in the attic failed to break his spirit, Montague locked him in an airless room in the stable, with no apparent means of escape. But there *was* a fireplace, and the boy managed to shinny up the chimney, jump onto the roof of an adjoining shed, and then climb over a nearby fence. Archie, standing in the yard, saw his brother leap from the fence into the street, take a quick look around, and disappear. The exasperated Montague responded by apprenticing Frank to a local workman known for his brutality, and for most of the next year, as Charleston prepared for war, the child was regularly beaten and starved by his new master. The morning of General Beauregard's shelling of Fort Sumter found him half clothed and half starved, attempting to protect himself from that day's beating.

With Frank out of the way, meanwhile, Montague focused on Archie, whom he viewed as a surly, callow, ungracious, and insulting servant. At one point, he sent the boy to the Charleston workhouse for thirty lashes. Like his brother before him, Archie decided to escape. In early 1862, just as the Eagleswood School was about to graduate its last class, twelve-year-old Archibald Grimké left his owner's home and vanished.

———

The Civil War brought changes to Charleston that its people could not have imagined just years or even months before. In mid-1861, Union forces had occupied Port Royal and thereby slipped a noose around the city. On December 11 of the same year, a fire had swept through, destroying block after block of homes in a half-mile-long swath stretching from the Cooper to the Ashley River. The fire seemed like fate's retribution to the city's residents, who had not lived through such a crisis since the Revolution. The Union troops' presence on Morris Island sent expectations of freedom rippling through Charleston's slave population, and with most of South Carolina's white men either serving in General Lee's Army of Northern Virginia or manning the city's defenses, the free blacks became openly defiant. The ties between the two groups grew even stronger. When Archie ran away from Montague Grimké's home in early 1862, it was to the black community of Charleston that he turned for help.

Believing that all the roads leading out of Charleston would be policed, Archie planned to hide with a family named Cole on Line Street until he could make his escape to the Union lines. But his opportunity never came. For two years, from mid-1862 until Union forces finally occupied the city in 1864, Archie stayed with the Coles. He never dared to go out during the day, and when he had to go out at night, he disguised himself as a girl. The Coles devised a sophisticated series of signals with which to warn Archie when he was in danger, including the use of the code name Morgan (after a Confederate cavalry commander who was "always in retreat"). Archie made good use of his forced isolation, spending his days reading and writing and expanding on the rudimentary education he had received at the home schools of the free black community. Within months, he was mastering Harriet Beecher Stowe's best-selling novel *Uncle Tom's Cabin* and Hinton Rowan Helper's pre–Civil War classic on slavery, *The Impending Crisis* (both of which were banned in South Carolina). He followed the war closely in the newspapers, praying for a Union victory.

Francis Grimké was not nearly as fortunate during this period as his elder brother. Unlike Archie, Frank decided to take his chances outside the city. Having freed himself from the grip of his brutal workman master, he spent a few nights hiding in Charleston and then took to the roads, hoping to make it to the Union lines. A worker on the Charleston-Savannah railroad, probably a free black laborer, found him half starved and half naked in a culvert and delivered him to Saint Andrew's Parish, well away from the city. Mistaking the boy for a free black, some Confederate soldiers offered him food in exchange for his service as a laborer. Frank himself had other ideas: he pressed Lieutenant Moore Rhett, a young officer in Preston's Light Artillery and most likely a distant relative of the Grimkés', to take him on as his valet. When Rhett agreed, the boy was overjoyed, for it meant he would be regularly fed.

Frank washed the officer's clothes, shined his shoes, brushed his uniform, and groomed his horse—all the things a normal "body servant" in the Confederate service was expected to do. Freedom seemed close at hand, and the war itself an adventure. Frank wanted to stay on with Rhett, who treated him kindly, but another young lieutenant named Francis Miller requested that the boy accompany him and his unit to Castle Pinckney, a fortress protecting Charleston. While posted with Miller at Pinckney, Frank took the opportunity repeatedly to sneak into the city to visit his mother, whom he missed terribly. He knew that what he was doing was dangerous: he might be recognized, caught, and thrown into the workhouse or, worse, sold to some new master far away. Still, he persisted in his visits, only to learn on one such sojourn that Montague was looking for him and had placed a notice in the *Charleston Mercury*:

FIFTY DOLLARS REWARD

FRANCIS (a brown boy) about 15
years old, 4 feet 9 inches high;
he ran away from the Charleston
Hotel in July.

Two months after this ad appeared, Frank's worst fears were realized when he was spotted in the street and seized. For the first months of 1864, he was kept in the workhouse, where he was beaten, starved, and exposed to the elements. His mother was barred from seeing him. That even many years later he could so matter-of-factly recount his experiences as a forgotten child of Henry Grimké, without showing any interest in exacting revenge, may seem difficult to believe; but the truth is that while he hated Montague, he rarely gave him a thought: in his estimation, Montague was beneath contempt. If, however, Francis Grimké could forget his half-brother and former master, the same would never be true of his time in the Charleston workhouse.

> There I remained for several months, and there I was taken dangerously ill from exposure and bad treatment, and came very near losing my life. It was only by being finally removed to my mother's house, and by the most skillful treatment that I recovered.
>
> I had thus fallen into the hands of my half-brother Montague and guardian; he, fearing that I would go away again, sold me, before I was well enough to go out, to an officer, and again I went back into the Army, where I remained until the close of the war.

The officer who bought him was the same Lieutenant Miller with whom he had served at Castle Pinckney. But the fact of his sale (that is, the fact that he was no longer taken for a free black, and could be sold) changed his status: he was now officially chattel property. While Miller was a decided improvement over Montague Grimké, he treated Frank like the chattel he was and revoked the trust he had earlier placed in him. The boy was not beaten or mistreated, but he was carefully watched lest he make his way to the Union lines and freedom. He was now a slave who belonged to a Confederate soldier.

In mid-February 1865, General Beauregard advised Confederate States President Jefferson Davis that Charleston should be abandoned. On February 17, Mayor Charles Macbeth informed the Union commanders on James Island that the city was no longer under Confederate control. The next afternoon, black troops in blue uniforms occupied the city, and Archie Grimké emerged from his prison in the Cole household. Miles away, his brother Frank ended his service with Lieutenant Miller and made his way home. Charleston was in a state of bedlam, its white citizens cowering behind their doors while outside, in the streets, black men and women danced and sang and fawned over the black soldiers who had liberated them. The guns that pointed out toward Fort Sumter from Battery Park were silent.

Reunited at last, Archie and Frank and two of their cousins, Art O'Hear and Francis Weston, struck out for the Union lines and fell in with two officers whose units were pressing the retreating Confederates. The "Day of Jubilee" had arrived, and many of Charleston's slaves were celebrating in the one way they knew would assure their freedom: they were helping to defeat the Confederacy. For Frank, Archie, Art, and Francis, attaching themselves to the Union army and doggedly pursuing the scattered and defeated remnants of Charleston's defenders made for the greatest adventure they had ever had. They were free and could not be bothered to think about the future.

In addition to its men in blue, the Union army brought to the South thieves, murderers, vagabonds, and a host of others with loftier motives. Along the roads of the region, the army's "contraband," former slaves who were now free, searched for friends, relatives, and loved ones as well as a new way of life. Teachers and workers arrived, bent on transforming Southern society. A Union colonel named Stewart Woodford took control of Charleston, occupied its government buildings, and turned over its schools to an army of Northern educators who wanted to prove that black men and women were not inferior, that they could learn and become a part of American society. To head up the reorganization of the city's school system, Woodford chose James Redpath, a nationally known reporter for the *New York Tribune* who had made his name as a journalist by writing about an obscure abolitionist by the name of John Brown. His only requirement was that he educate both white and black children, without discrimination. Redpath, a born crusader and tireless worker, would do just that. A mere month after Union forces occupied Charleston, Redpath opened seven schools and hired eighty-three teachers to instruct the city's three thousand school-age children. The schools were so crowded that students had to attend classes in shifts, but for the first time in American history, black and white children learned side by side.

Archie, Frank, and John Grimké were enrolled at the Morris Street School, which was under the direction of the Massachusetts abolitionist Frances Pillsbury. Coaxed by Redpath from her post at Port Royal, where she had been teaching former slaves, Pillsbury was the perfect choice for the job. She had acquired her abolitionist views from Parker Pillsbury, her brother-in-law and the strategist behind William Lloyd Garrison's takeover of the American Anti-Slavery Society, and as soon as she was offered the position in Charleston, she began recruiting a group of abolitionist teachers. They were instructed to identify the best black students and prepare them for college, a formidable task. Soon enough, Pillsbury heard that three of her charges were named Grimké. While she understood who these young men were, she did not mention their existence to either Angelina or Sarah, both of whom she knew. It was undoubtedly because of their family ties to the celebrated sisters that Pillsbury gave Archie, Frank, and John special attention, but it was the elder boys' intellectual gifts, their ability to do academic work far in advance of their years, that truly won her over. She wrote about them in letters to her friends back home during the summer of 1865.

Archie and Frank were the most literate of all Pillsbury's students. Unfortunately, the same could not be said of John, who was unaffected by the educator's efforts and would remain, for many years to come, the most deeply embittered of Nancy's sons. At the end of the summer of 1865, Frances Pillsbury told Archie and Frank that she had secured positions for them in the North. Archie, she said, would be apprenticed to Samuel Sewall, a Boston lawyer and prominent abolitionist (who was also an old friend of Angelina and Sarah Grimké's, though Pillsbury did not reveal that fact). Frank, meanwhile, was to travel to Stoneham, Massachusetts, to work with a Dr. Brown, a former surgeon of the Fifty-fifth Colored Regiment.

A month later, after saying good-bye to their mother (who approved of the move, seeing in it the culmination of her greatest wish), and newly outfitted with suitable clothes, Archie and Frank made the journey north aboard the *McClellan*, a government transport. They were accompanied by Major Martin Delany, a black Union officer and Pillsbury family friend. In New York, they boarded a train bound for Springfield, Massachusetts, and their new lives. After one night in Springfield (in the course of which they were taken to the theater to see the eminent American actor Edwin Forrest in the title role of *King Lear*), they made their way to the Boston offices of the Freemen's Aid Society. There, the twenty-eight-year-old Charlotte Forten introduced herself and told the brothers what they could expect in their new jobs. Archie left, unaccompanied, to begin his career as a "reader" in the law, while Frank departed for Stoneham.

It must have seemed to the Grimkés that their futures were now assured. They were in the North; they were free; they were to be educated. But if slavery was finally behind them, poverty and ill fortune were not. Although Archie ultimately fared well under the guiding hand of Samuel Sewall, he did not actually stay with the lawyer or his family, nor did he read the law. Instead, he was sent to another family close to the Sewalls, in Peacedale, Rhode Island, because Sewall thought it best that he learn a trade. It was not what Archie had hoped for, but at least he seemed welcome in Peacedale. Frank, by contrast, was clearly *not* welcome in Stoneham; the family there either was not expecting him or had not planned for his arrival. Dr. Brown had no intention of making young Grimké his assistant and would not even allow him into his home. "During my whole stay with them I was forced to sleep in the barn, in the hay-loft, with no other mattress than the hay, and no other bedstead than the floor," Frank would later write. "My treatment while with them was so different from what I had been led to expect that I would receive. . . ." The family paid little attention to him, and he came and went as he pleased.

Chastened by this experience, Frank hired himself out to Lyman Dyke, the owner of a Lynn, Massachusetts, shoe factory, who paid him well and looked after him. Nancy Weston learned what had happened and suggested to Frances Pillsbury that other arrangements be made for her sons. Embarrassed by their treatment, Pillsbury immediately wrote about the Grimké brothers to a number of her friends, asking their advice. Several weeks later, she was told about a small university for black students, near Philadelphia, that had recently been renamed for Abraham Lincoln. Dr. Isaac Rendall, the school's president, agreed to interview Archie and Frank to determine whether they were qualified to attend. Reunited, the two brothers arrived in Philadelphia and, after meeting with Rendall, were admitted to Lincoln. In retrospect, it seems surprising that Rendall should have offered places to the two prospective students, for he judged both unimpressive, slight for their ages, and ill prepared for the university's academic rigor. But Lincoln was a small and struggling school that was dependent on the largesse of white philanthropists; it desperately needed students just to survive. Frank and Archie were admitted for the 1866–1867 school year and spent the spring of 1866 in the preparatory department, hoping to acquire in a few short months a foundation that would carry them through the work that lay ahead. They were still only sixteen and seventeen years old.

Lincoln University was a unique institution set among the rolling oak-and-maple-filled hills just west of Philadelphia. There were a few modest buildings, a group of teachers, and enough firewood to make the winters warm, but little else. Chartered by the state legislature in 1856, the school had originally been founded to prepare black "Christian leaders" for "missionary and Colonization work in Africa." In line with the strictly uncontroversial position of northern Presbyterians on the issue of slavery, the Ashmun Institute (as it was then called) was designed to be the cradle of a new kind of missionary—free, black, and millennial. Its founders believed that the Bible would "convert Central Africa into a garden of the Lord." But in the wake of the war at home, Ashmun's administrators decided to take advantage of the government's willingness to expend funds on the freedmen's education: they appointed a new board of directors (which included General Oliver O. Howard, the new head of the powerful Freedmen's Bureau), changed the institution's name to Lincoln University, and revised its charter to reflect its newly discovered mission—which mirrored the abolitionist impulse to go south as part of the exciting program to educate freed slaves. Lincoln University trumpeted its newfound goal in 1866:

The late wonderful providences of God towards the colored race in this country have opened new and large fields of usefulness, and now the calls are urgent for men of talents and education to serve their race in new relations and positions. It is in view of the history of the last few years that the Trustees, through the Legislature, have given the Institution a new name and have greatly enlarged its plans. The present year has been one of experiment with these new aims, but it has been full of promise.

Despite its new political crusade, Lincoln University remained a religious school. Each day began and ended with prayer, each class took the Bible as its major text, and attendance at chapel services was obligatory (though none of the more devout students would ever have considered skipping chapel). At first, Frank was unimpressed by Lincoln's religious ethos and argued about it with his brother. He was even less interested in the revival that swept the school soon after their arrival. Archie tried to convert him, but it was no use; at one point, the two nearly came to blows. "I thought," Archie would later write, "if you couldn't convert people by love then they must be converted by force." Frank vowed that he would never become a "holy roller." But during that first summer, he spent some time with a family of free blacks in Philadelphia and went to the Central Presbyterian Church with them every Sunday. The church's minister, John B. Reeve, had better luck than Archie in converting Frank: "I never heard him preach a poor sermon, I never heard him when I was not benefited," Frank would later say of him. Reeve had a profound effect on Francis Grimké and was largely responsible for his later commitment to the ministry.

When the fall semester began, in September, Archie and Frank each had a full load of courses in the school's upper department. They studied Bible history, geography, Latin and English grammar, arithmetic, U.S. history, and religious training. The curriculum was accelerated to prepare students for the regular university. Within weeks, it was clear to the well-educated faculty (most of whom had graduated from the Princeton Theological Seminary) that the Grimké brothers were exceptional students; indeed, both would finish at the top of their class the following June. Their achievement was duly reported by the university to their sponsors—in Frank's case, a wealthy Eastern philanthropist, and in Archie's, "Dr. Spring's Church in New York City." Both Frank and Archie entered the university program the next autumn. The study of Greek was added to their schedules, along with world history and algebra. Friday evenings found them in attendance first at the Garnet Literary Association and then at meetings of the Philosophian Society; these clubs taught them "debating, declamation, and composition." It was during a presentation at the Philosophian Society, in the fall of 1867, that the Grimké brothers were noticed by Professor Edwin S. Bower, who wrote of them in the *Boston Commonwealth*. The article was reprinted in February 1868 in the *National Anti-Slavery Standard*, where it came to the attention of Angelina Grimké.

———

Having made their acquaintance, Angelina, Sarah, and Theodore gave Archie and Frank what financial help they could—which was not much. Thrift was always a necessity in the Weld home. But one thing the sisters and Theodore did have plenty of was advice, and they gave that freely. Sarah was filled with ideas about Frank's, Archie's, and John's educations (the third brother joined the other two at Lincoln for a year before returning to Charleston and then moving to central Florida), while Angelina commented on the shaping of their character. The advice came in a torrent of letters and included recommendations on spelling, emphasis on the need for "punctuality and promptness in action," and, of course, exhortations to exercise "frugality," "modesty," "moderation," and "prudence." Angelina was particularly intent on making certain that none of her nephews was lacking in "independence of spirit," which she believed was "a great defect in Southern character." Surprisingly, perhaps, Frank and Archie did not chafe at such counsel or show any impatience with their aunts, but rather attempted to put their advice into practice. They dressed simply, saved their money, and dedicated themselves to their studies.

The summer of 1869 found Frank in Saint Leonard's, Maryland, where he taught recently freed black students as part of Lincoln University's plan to dispatch an army of educated freedmen back to the South. Archie was similarly employed. As their graduation approached, in 1870, their aunts began to investigate universities where they could continue their education. Both had excelled at Lincoln in an accelerated curriculum that demanded their utmost efforts. Their senior year was taken up with advanced Latin and Greek, a section on trigonometry (and practical instruction in navigating and surveying), a course in astronomy (demonstrating that "the heavens declare the glory of God"), and another section on geology. Their favorite, however, was a class in mental and moral philosophy, intended to "acquaint the student with the operation of his own mind . . . and to fortify him against the insidious and destructive influence of skepticism."

Throughout their last year at Lincoln, Archie and Frank continued to receive advice from their two aunts, as well as financial assistance when the family could afford it. A letter from Angelina might include twenty dollars along with a set-piece paragraph, a virtual monologue, urging the brothers to look for examples of right conduct and clean living to the Grimkés who were their forebears. Angelina and Sarah constantly put forward their brother Thomas as the incarnation of what they hoped their nephews might one day become, and sent them his books and writings for inspiration. In his name, they championed manual labor as a great soul cleanser, and they cited his life as one of intellectual and moral growth. But both aunts were disappointed when some of their advice was ignored. At one point, Sarah wrote:

> It seems a long time since I sent you the pamphlets about Cornell University but as you have nine months to deliberate as to the course you are to pursue after graduating there is no necessity for making up your minds suddenly. The best way is to keep your eyes and ears open to anything that might happen to turn up in the meantime. I have no doubt that we shall see the right thing to do as the time approaches. Have you thought of the Howard College? I was very much surprised to hear that there were as many white students as colored. This is good, for there is nothing so effectual [in] overcoming prejudice as daily contact.

Despite this endorsement, neither brother decided to attend Cornell, or Howard, as both Angelina and Sarah hoped. Instead, Archibald and Francis planned to enter Lincoln University's new law school in the autumn of 1870. It was the first semester that law courses were offered at Lincoln, and the curriculum was supplemented by a practical course of study in various law offices and courts in Chester County. The sisters doubted it would satisfy the academic needs of their nephews, but they put aside their uncertainties and continued their financial and moral support.

———

Archie lasted only a year at the Lincoln University Law School. The curriculum and faculty simply did not meet his needs, and there was only one other student besides him and Frank in his classes. Frank soldiered on for two more years at Lincoln, but he found the course of study no more satisfying than his brother had, and in 1873, he transferred to the Howard University Law School. He stayed there for another two years but felt increasingly unhappy at the prospect of becoming a lawyer, and so began to look for new challenges. In 1875, after much reflection, he entered the Princeton Theological Seminary (not a part of Princeton University), intent on becoming a Presbyterian minister. He had decided to walk the path first shown him in 1866 by the Philadelphia minister John B. Reeve. Frank's brother Archie had meanwhile chosen his own course: in 1874, on the advice of Angelina and with her full financial support, he had entered the Harvard Law School. He was one of its first black students.

Archibald and Francis Grimké had been together their entire lives, except during the war, and were as close as two brothers could be; they were as devoted to each other as Sarah and Angelina had been in their younger years. But while Archie and Frank would always maintain that bond, and would work together often over the next four decades, their interests and their ways of looking at the world reflected two very different personalities. Frank was quiet, unemotional, serious, and focused. During his time at Howard, he began to learn about the city that he would one day shape and be shaped by. Washington, D.C., would be his home for much of the rest of his life, and its trials and frustrations would mark him more even than his time as a slave child in Charleston had done.

In the 1870s, Washington was a city in search of an identity. Essentially Southern in character and attitude, it boasted a large and proud black community that produced a sophisticated, educated, and progressive African American elite. But it was also beginning to suffer the repercussions of Reconstruction and of the Southern backlash that would eventually destroy the hopes of the freedmen. At the heart of the black community in Washington were its enormously powerful black churches. For four decades, save for a single interlude of four years, Francis Grimké would be the most influential minister in the city.

Archibald Grimké was as much unlike his brother Frank as Angelina was unlike Sarah. He was adventurous, outspoken, and willing to experiment. Whereas Frank's voice was so soft that it nearly kept him out of the Princeton Theological Seminary (the admissions board doubted he would be able to deliver an effective sermon), Archie's fairly boomed. Nancy Weston's oldest son was an orator who admired other orators. He, too, would be shaped by the community in which he lived. For while Washington was beset by frustration and anxiety, Boston was a city that nurtured black hopes. Its community views on black America were based, at least in the 1870s, on the abolitionist legacy that was such a proud part of its history. Boston would change, and Archie would see it change, but its transformation into a bastion of prejudice, where some of the bitterest battles of school integration would later be fought (ten years short of one century later), would be much more gradual than Washington's.

Different though they were, Francis and Archibald Grimké also had much in common. Both were scholars, and both would dedicate their lives to the cause of equal rights. That they would both carry on, in very different environments and using very different means in the name of the same cause to which their aunts had been devoted before them, was a tribute to their ambition and inner strength—and to their family legacy. For while both cited their mother as their greatest influence (which she was), both were also profoundly affected by their Grimké relatives. They were, of course, more like Thomas and Henry and Angelina and Sarah (and John Faucheraud Grimké) than like Montague or Eliza or Mary. But still, there are both irony and paradox in such a comparison. Most like his aunt Sarah Moore Grimké, Frank was a quiet but influential thinker whose contributions would not seem, over the years, to be nearly as dominant as those of his more public sibling. But like Sarah's, Frank Grimké's quiet asceticism, search for faith, love of books and learning, constant attention to personal moral standing, agony over sin, and celebration of the spirit (his "gravity") would eventually be recognized as the more progressive, revolutionary, and effective approach. As it had been with Sarah and Angelina, so it was now with Francis and Archibald. As Sarah had once lived in her sister's shadow, so Frank lived in his brother's, though only for a time.

Frank Grimké gave up his study of the law and embarked on a new career on the advice of John B. Reeve and Lorenzo Westcott, a former professor at Lincoln. Both men had joined the Howard faculty in the early 1870s, and during Frank's time there they urged him to devote his life to the ministry. To this end, he was admitted by Reeve as a member of Philadelphia's Lombard Street Central Presbyterian Church in the summer of 1875. He was then presented, again by Reeve, to the Presbytery of Philadelphia, to stand for an entrance examination for the Princeton Theological Seminary. While Frank acquitted himself adequately before the examining board of the Presbytery, it was Reeve who convinced its members that the young, soft-spoken (he was barely audible during his presentation) Southern man would make a dedicated minister.

The training at Princeton was both lengthy and competitive, and the course of studies demanding: classes in Greek, Hebrew, "Jewish and Christian antiquities," Oriental and biblical literature, composition, communication, "ecclesiastical discipline," church discipline and administration, and the application of "methods of natural, polemic, and casuistic theology" were required. The program turned out foot soldiers in a Christian army deployed as "defenders of the Christian faith." Frank Grimké thrived at the seminary, where, amid the "seclusion and quiet of a rural village," he could finally be alone with his books.

Archibald Grimké, meanwhile, had entered the Harvard Law School in 1874, in the midst of a crisis. In response to a series of internal criticisms in the late 1860s, the university had appointed a new law dean, Christopher C. Langdell, and revamped and tightened its curriculum. As a result of that change, and based on recommendations from Lincoln, Archie was one of two students—the only two who could actually boast of having college degrees—admitted without having to take an entrance examination. Among his classmates was Henry Cabot Lodge, who would become his lifelong friend and political competitor, and a force in the Massachusetts Republican party. Archie excelled at Harvard, taking courses in real property and civil and constitutional law. In his last year, he was awarded one of four special scholarships given to "meritorious students . . . in need of such assistance." He graduated at the head of his class, though no transcript of his grades or record of his standing survives. Unlike his brother Frank, who was happiest in seclusion, Archie Grimké was a social being, and he celebrated his time in Boston by attending a series of dinners and receptions with the city's most prominent abolitionists. Over the course of his two years of study, Archie met and became friends with Lucy Stone, Wendell Phillips, Parker and Gilbert Pillsbury (with whom, because of his association with Frances Pillsbury, he felt a particular bond), William Lloyd Garrison, and the era's most famous voice of black America, Frederick Douglass.

Sarah and Angelina Grimké were proud of their nephews and sacrificed their own financial security to ensure their education. But by the early 1870s, it had become clear to both sisters, and to Theodore Weld (now aging gracefully, gray-bearded and much in demand), that the young men must follow their own paths. Abolitionism was a fading movement, its leaders now old and dying, but the fight for equal rights beckoned. Sarah and Angelina knew that Archie and Frank would have to wage this new battle in a nation that had, in the name of political expediency, turned its back on the freedmen. The great crusade that had sent hundreds of abolitionists into the South on behalf of the newly freed slaves was being opposed, at every turn, by a resurgent Southern Democratic party.

The Grimké sisters, for their part, were still agitating on behalf of America's women. In 1870, when the Massachusetts Woman Suffrage Association was established, both Angelina and Sarah agreed to serve on its board. When Lucy Stone appeared to speak before an audience in Hyde Park, the sisters were in attendance. And on March 7, 1870, they marched with forty other women to a Hyde Park polling place, past a crowd of men shouting taunts, and deposited ballots in a special voting box. It was a symbolic gesture of protest and an expression of hope that eventually women would triumph and be granted the right to cast votes that were actually counted. But it was not enough for Sarah Grimké. In 1871, at the age of seventy-nine, she would trudge through the Hyde Park winter carrying 150 copies of John Stuart Mill's monograph *On the Subjection of Women* (written in 1861 and published in 1869), which she handed out on the street to friends, colleagues, neighbors, and strangers. "Please read this," she would say kindly, her voice wispy with age. Then she would make her way home again, to Angelina and Theodore, through the snow.

Two years later, at eighty-one, Sarah would die at her home in Hyde Park with her beloved Nina at her side. Nearly every living former abolitionist would attend the funeral, in obeisance toward and recognition of Sarah Grimké. They would march arm in arm, two at a time, led by Angelina to the gravesite—blacks and whites, linking arms in a gesture of solidarity with Sarah's life and beliefs. Sarah Moore Grimké had borne no children, but she was nonetheless the mother of the abolitionist movement.

TWELVE

". . . through the lonely dark . . ."

I n 1874, a new era dawned in America. That year, Mark Twain and Charles Dudley Warner published *The Gilded Age*, whose major character, Colonel Sellers, the fast-buck grandfather of all American boosters, dreamed of unlimited wealth while living in a poverty-stricken, whiskey soaked, rough-and-tumble frontier. The Greenback party was formed, its sworn mission being to inflate the currency and thereby pay off the debts of Western farmers bankrupted by the panic of the year before. Henry Ward Beecher continued his torrid love affair with the wife of Theodore Tilton, which would make national headlines in 1875 (he would be sued but would win the case, to remain the nation's most influential moral voice). The Chautauqua Movement, an encampment dedicated to training Sunday-school teachers, was founded in upstate New York. In the West, Joseph F. Glidden invented barbed wire, a godsend for Great Plains farmers lacking wood for fences. The first public zoo was built in Philadelphia, rugby was introduced in colleges (eventually to lead to the development of the sport of football), and the elephant became the symbol of the Republican party.

On most mornings in 1874, Archibald Grimké, "rather slender, erect, and I should say of medium height, with a clear direct look of great intelligence" (as a friend remembered him), could be seen walking through Boston's business district on his way to work in the law offices of his fellow Harvard Law School graduate William Bowditch. Archie was well known in Boston as the nephew of the famous Grimkés, a good friend of William Lloyd Garrison, Parker Pillsbury, and Wendell Phillips, and an articulate and soon-to-be-successful young lawyer. Most evenings found him escorting the elderly Phillips home from the Welds' Hyde Park house, after hours of talk about Phillips's crusading days as an outspoken abolitionist. On other occasions, however, Archie's walk with Phillips was set aside in favor of more interesting pursuits, including stepping out with Lillie Buffum Chace Wyman, the daughter of renowned abolitionist parents, or Ellen ("Nelly") Bradford, a descendant of *Mayflower* passengers. Both women were very intelligent and very pretty.

Archie had been taken into Bowditch's firm to help the older attorney fight for pensions for black Civil War veterans. The work served as a good introduction to the law, though it provided little in the way of financial comforts. In 1875, after being admitted to the Suffolk County Bar, Archie agreed to open a firm with his law-school friend James Wolff; they rented an office on Washington Street in Boston and began to search for clients. Archie had rooms in Hyde Park, where he was joined by his mother, Nancy Weston Grimké. They were within walking distance of Theodore and Angelina's, and the families visited each other often. Theodore was in good health, but Angelina was weak, often ill, and she had lost the fire that had once burned in her. At seventy-one, she suffered a paralytic stroke, which threw her on the mercy of her family, since she and Theodore could not afford a nurse. She clung to life but regretted troubling her loving husband, who spent nearly every waking minute attending to her needs. With Sarah gone and Theodore aging, Angelina felt that the end was in sight. Her one remaining wish was to ensure the success of her nephews, who, she was now certain, would lift the Grimké name out of the mire of the family's slaveholding past. She hoped that Archie would one day return to South Carolina as a lawyer and do just that, but she did not oppose his decision to stay in Boston.

Archie had fallen in love with Nelly Bradford, and the two were now inseparable. They spent Sundays in the country, went together to political meetings and lectures on temperance and suffrage, and toured Boston's museums and historic sites. Archie shared the details of his early life with Nelly, valued her opinions, and looked to her for advice. She was a constant visitor in the Weld home, where Theodore and Angelina welcomed her warmly; they were convinced that she and Archie were a perfect match. And indeed, that seemed to be the case: they "laughed a great deal together on slight provocation," admired the same writers, and held the same beliefs. Nelly took an interest in Archie's work and often stopped in to see him at his Washington Street offices. That he was black and she was white appeared to matter not at all to her or to her family; she would later recall that Archie had "manners so exactly right there was nothing to remark about them."

Archie might well have married Nelly had her father not taken a job outside Boston and moved the family. They corresponded often, and for the rest of their lives would remain good friends, but their budding romance did not survive the separation. In 1877, Archie met Sarah Stanley, a student at Boston University and the daughter of a prominent Episcopal minister in Michigan. Sarah's family had been active in the abolitionist movement in the Midwest, and her attraction to the young lawyer and former slave was immediate. Archie courted her for two years before finally, in early 1879, asking her to marry him. In a letter dated February 9, Archie met the requirements of his station and upbringing by asking Sarah's father for his blessing: "I cannot do what I now intend without first seeking to secure your approval," he wrote. "Such approval sir would give me great pleasure." He talked about Sarah in glowing terms but made it clear that his intentions were honorable, promising that he would make a loyal husband and adding that Sarah herself had accepted his proposal.

The Reverend Stanley's response was not what Archie had anticipated. Although he addressed his prospective son-in-law politely enough, he said that Archie's letter had filled him and his wife with "misgivings." Such a marriage would cause difficulties for his family, he noted, and most especially for his daughter. In a separate letter to Sarah, he was more explicit and angrier, and accused her of falling "under the influence" of "Boston's Unitarians." He implied that in agreeing to marry Archie, she had betrayed her family. He did not specifically forbid the marriage, but she knew that if she went ahead with it, it would be over his objections. "We look upon it as a sad day when you went to Boston," he wrote to her, "and especially when you associated yourself with the deniers of Christ and the insane theorizers of that infidel city." Stanley had nothing personal against Archibald Grimké; it was simply that he was black, and Sarah was white. Progressive, tolerant, and open though he claimed to be, the reverend could not abide the idea of his daughter's marrying a black man. But Sarah Stanley had made up her mind, and on April 19, 1879, in a simple ceremony at a friend's home on Boston's Beacon Hill, she and Archibald Grimké were wed.

———

Upon his graduation from the Princeton Theological Seminary, in 1877, Francis Grimké had taken his vows as a Presbyterian minister: "I accept, and accept without reservation, the Scriptures of the Old and New Testaments as God's word, sent to Adam's sinful race and pointing out the only way by which it can be saved. . . . Without the Holy Scriptures and what they reveal, there is no hope for humanity. To build on anything else is to build on sand." He was prepared for his life's work. Not only had he excelled as a seminarian, but he had spent the summer prior to his graduation working as a guest of Washington's prestigious Fifteenth Street Presbyterian Church. Because he was not yet ordained, he had been unable to preach to the congregation, but he had received training in nearly every other aspect of a minister's work, including conducting prayer meetings, teaching Sunday school, and visiting the sick. He had even been called upon to hear the testimony of a member charged with "causing scandal to herself and the church by violation of the seventh commandment." The female congregant had ultimately been expelled.

His summer at the church had served a test run for a possible ministry there after his graduation, and he had done well enough to be interviewed for the post by a committee of churchmen who visited him at Princeton. They offered him the assistant pastorship of the church, and he accepted the appointment and the promise of a one-thousand-dollar yearly salary. Frank Grimké may well have been the most educated and best-prepared minister in the history of the Fifteenth Street Presbyterian Church. His three years at the Princeton Theological Seminary had coincided with a "golden age" during which the school was highly regarded, nationally known, and possessed of, in the words of Grimké biographer Henry Justi Ferry, "a well-deserved reputation as the bastion of scholastic Reformed orthodoxy." Frank Grimké's career as a minister in Washington would reflect what he had learned at the seminary, with its emphasis on biblical readings, liturgical teachings, and the unshakable power of the pulpit.

Throughout his nearly forty-year career, Francis Grimké would follow the seminary's tradition. He believed in the power of a minister to influence his congregation through the words of his sermon. In this, he was immensely affected by the example of Charles Hodge, his instructor in the Old and New Testaments at Princeton. Hodge began his daily instruction with a prayer, but after that, according to Henry Ferry, "he scarcely again glanced at the Testament during the hour, the text was evidently before his mind, verbally, and the matter of his exposition thoroughly at his command. In an unbroken stream it flowed from subject to subject, simple, clear, cogent, unfailingly reverent. . . . Nothing could surpass the clearness with which he set forth the general argument and the main connections of thought."

Almost immediately after taking on his pastorate, Frank once again encountered Charlotte Forten, whom he had first met at the office of the Massachusetts Freemen's Aid Society on his arrival from Charleston. The two may well have maintained some contact over the years, but it was only after she petitioned for membership in his church that they became good friends. They soon developed a close bond and were often seen engaging in deep conversation. Still, it came as a surprise to many when they decided to marry, given that she was forty-one to his twenty-eight. Frank would be happy in the marriage—happier than he had ever been. He was devoted to "Lottie," as he called her, and very proud of her celebrity.

A member of a respected and affluent Philadelphia family, Charlotte was best known to the public for her poetry and her articles recounting her experiences during the Civil War, in the Sea Islands of South Carolina. She was an expert essayist, extremely learned, with an abiding interest in black literature. Diminutive, strong-willed, opinionated, and deeply moral, Charlotte was a perfect match for Frank. She would become his alter ego and his most loyal defender, helping to shape his ideas and urging him toward more and more outspoken views. The marriage would not only bring Francis Grimké and Charlotte Forten together, but also link two of the most storied families of the abolitionist movement. Harriet Forten Purvis, Charlotte's aunt, was as well known in Philadelphia antislavery circles as Angelina and Sarah, and had been, like her mother, Charlotte (for whom Lottie was named), one of the founding members of the Female Anti-Slavery Society. The elder Charlotte's husband, James Forten, Sr. (Lottie's grandfather), was a prominent Philadelphia sailmaker, abolitionist, and temperance activist, and a founder of the American Anti-Slavery Society. And Lottie's uncle Robert Purvis, Harriet's husband, was mentioned in the same breath as Frederick Douglass, the acknowledged leader of the black community.

Francis Grimké married Charlotte Forten in December 1879. Sadly, Angelina Grimké Weld, Frank's last surviving aunt—and his last link to the Grimké past in South Carolina—had joined her sister Sarah in death just two months before. It is unlikely that Angelina could have attended the wedding even if she had lived; the victim of a series of debilitating strokes, she had been unable, in her last years, to lead the active life that she preferred. Her funeral brought together the remnants of the abolitionist community and a large contingent of their successors. Lucy Stone, Wendell Phillips, and Elizur Wright spoke eloquently of Angelina's life, her commitment to her sister, her pride in her nephews, her hatred of slavery and inequality, and her love of South Carolina. The two Southern sisters, with their prim bonnets and outlandish opinions, were now gone. So, too, was William Lloyd Garrison, who had died the previous May, unbowed and hawk-faced to the end. Of the great lights of the abolitionist movement, only one nationally known figure, Theodore Dwight Weld, remained. Now alone, he would dedicate his remaining years to his family and could often be seen walking slowly, on the arm of Sarah Stanley Grimké, through the streets of Hyde Park, where he had once jogged.

I hope that the time is not far distant when . . . liberty in its true sense will prevail in this country—when equal and exact justice shall be meted out to all; when the American people shall have forgotten their prejudices; when the lapse of ages shall have washed out forever the virus of slavery from our hearts; when the genius of liberty with all its glowing beauty shall extend its sway over this nation; when there shall be no white, no black, no East, no West, no North, no South, but one common brotherhood and one united people, going forward forever in the progress of nations.

So wrote South Carolina congressman R. H. Cain in the first heady decade of black emancipation, when it indeed looked as if slavery might forever be dismissed as a dark chapter in the nation's history, and not seen for what it was: a prologue to the continuing struggle against racial prejudice. That such prejudice existed nearly everywhere in the nation was apparent after Appomattox, but the first ten years following the South's defeat seemed like a golden age for black Americans. With freedom came limitless possibilities. Thousands of former slaves settled on new land, built families, and started to educate their children. Some, like the Grimké brothers, excelled, obtaining an advanced education and moving north, where they were welcomed in the vibrant free black communities of Philadelphia, New York, Baltimore, Washington, and Boston.

But for every success story, there were thousands of other former slaves languishing on run-down farms, living in the midst of a hostile and impoverished Southern white population. Acts of violence against freedmen were common. The South lay prostrate, its infrastructure destroyed, its political institutions in disarray, its most talented generation of young men dead on the nation's battlefields; Southerners blamed their former slaves for all of that, and resented their newfound freedom. Still, the presence of a strong federal establishment dedicated to protecting the rights of the freedmen, even to the point of disenfranchising the white Rebels, gave great hope for the future. There was in this policy an implicit promise of equal rights that brooked no opposition. For many Americans, the Civil War had settled the matter: the slaves were free, the Union one, the South humbled.

The Compromise of 1877 changed all that. The November 1876 election led to a constitutional crisis when neither Republican Rutherford B. Hayes nor Democrat Samuel Tilden received the necessary majority of 185 electoral votes to become president. In January 1877, the Senate appointed a special commission to determine the disposition of twenty contested electoral votes, nineteen of them from the South. New Yorker Tilden was the clear favorite going in, since he was within one electoral vote (at 184) of claiming the White House. But the special commission awarded Hayes all of the disputed twenty votes. The Senate concurred on March 2, and on March 4, President Hayes was inaugurated.

Within months, the details of the special commission's proceedings were made public, and the Compromise of 1877 came to be known as "the great betrayal." In exchange for the support of the Southern members of the commission, Hayes had agreed, once he became president, to withdraw the remaining federal troops from the South—that is, from Louisiana, South Carolina, and Florida. He had also promised to appoint a Southerner to his cabinet and to provide federal aid to the Texas and Pacific Railroad. Modest though all these sacrifices might have seemed at the time, the withdrawal of federal troops from the old Confederacy would in fact mark the end of Reconstruction and the virtual abandonment of federal policies ensuring fair treatment for the freedmen. In his inaugural address, Hayes had pledged to restore "wise, honest, and peaceful local self-government" to the South, but when the last federal troops in the region were withdrawn from Louisiana in April 1877, the nation's commitment to the freedmen was revoked, and the nearly century-long battle for equal rights began.

The black community was slow to recognize the danger inherent in Hayes's concession. In the immediate aftermath of Appomattox, the truest expression of African American political hopes had come in the form of the Convention movement, a state-by-state effort to organize black political power. Unfortunately, the movement had failed to take hold, largely because a surprising number of leading African Americans believed that the federal government's promise to protect black rights rendered political organizing unnecessary. The debate over black activism had emerged most forcefully at the 1869 meeting of the National Equal Rights League Convention, held in Washington, D.C. In that forum, a number of black delegates had contended that the establishment of black organizations actually provided ammunition for white racists, who could point to them as evidence that black Americans really wanted to be separate.

The most persistent and influential champion of black rights in the post–Civil War period, Frederick Douglass, disagreed with this view and took the lead in arguing in favor of establishing African American organizations. Douglass's stature was unquestioned: respected in the black community and known for his activist views, he was a man of storied patience and uncanny political prescience. Now he squared off against the black leaders who opposed his call for a black political movement, wagging his finger at them while repeating the words "Beware, beware." To Archie and Frank Grimké, who would meet him in Washington in the mid-1870s, and to thousands of other black Americans like them, Douglass was a mythic figure: an author, poet, organizer, and orator who confronted white America with the blunt facts of black life. He could not be silenced. Many years later, in the most sorrowful and violent days of segregation, when hundreds of African Americans were being lynched, the poet Paul Laurence Dunbar would pen an incantation, a wearying howl, to call Douglass back from the dead:

> *Oh, for thy voice high-sounding o'er the storm,*
> *For thy strong arm to guide the shivering bark,*
> *The blast-defying power of thy form,*
> *To give us comfort through the lonely dark.*

As Douglass was the leader of the national black community, so he guided its most important and most politically aware contingent, in Washington. He attended Frank Grimké's wedding in December 1879 and often dined with him. Douglass explained his views on black leadership to both Archie and Frank and encouraged them to take a public stance on the critical questions facing the black community. Although he was clearly the senior partner in the relationship, Douglass viewed the Grimkés as friends and colleagues and took them as his model for a new generation of black leaders. He urged them on in their careers and implored them to dedicate their lives to building a community of ambitious and successful black entrepreneurs and scholars. They would be, he predicted, among the leaders of an elite that would see through the slow, incremental, but sure process of winning equal rights.

Douglass's message was essentially conservative and thus eventually controversial, even among those who viewed him as the leader of their community. Although Douglass was seen as black America's moral leader, some of his statements seemed contrived and designed less to sharpen the emerging differences between white and black political goals than to curry favor with white audiences. "Neither we, nor any other people," he said in one speech, "will ever be respected till we respect ourselves, and we will never respect ourselves till we have the means to live respectably. . . . If the time shall ever come when we shall possess in the colored people of the United States, a class of men noted for enterprise, industry, economy and success, we shall no longer have any trouble in the matter of civil and political rights." While such statements had rung true in the immediate aftermath of the Civil War, they seemed hopelessly naive by the late 1870s, when resurgent Southern nationalism was stripping the meaning from the Fourteenth and Fifteenth amendments, and "Southern Bourbons" were restoring the power of racist "self-government."

Frank Grimké was not always under Douglass's sway, but in the first years of his pastorate in Washington, he emphasized many of his themes. In his sermons, he focused continually on the importance of "self improvement," "self-respect," "self-reliance," and "high moral values"— all qualities that he associated with Douglass. Like Douglass's orations, Frank Grimké's sermons seem almost quaint now, but in those early years, they struck a deep chord with the congregation and were noted for their "clearness and depth of thought," their "grandeur and weight." Frank was well aware that his audience ("the most intellectual and cultured group of colored people to be found anywhere in the country at that time," as he noted) comprised the elite of Washington's African American society. He shaped his remarks specifically to reach them.

———

On the evening of January 24, 1884, Francis Grimké presided over the marriage of Frederick Douglass and Helen Pitts. Pitts was Douglass's second wife, a trusted friend and his secretary—and a white woman. The ceremony was simple and matter-of-fact. Frank knew the marriage would be controversial—not least because Douglass, a widower, had been rumored to be interested in any number of eligible local black women—but he had no reason to predict the deep and bitter scandal-mongering it would engender among some of Douglass's black colleagues. Within days of the wedding, a whispering campaign was launched, its central tenet being that Douglass had married his secretary because he did not think any black woman was "good enough" for him. Douglass was shocked by the reaction and expressed surprise that anything so simple as his marrying a white woman could elicit such outrage.

Francis Grimké took a different view. Although he brusquely dismissed the group of reporters who appeared at his door in the middle of the night, just hours after the ceremony, he was neither shocked nor surprised by the avalanche of public criticism directed at his friend. He responded to these attacks on Douglass by issuing a firm and outspoken defense of his friend's rights—mindful that his own brother, in Boston, had likewise married a white woman. Unstated, but certainly prominent in Frank's thoughts, was the experience of his mother, who as a slave had been barred not only from marrying a white man but from living in his house. If emancipation meant anything, Frank believed, it was that every man had the right to choose his own social relations—even the leader of black America. Grimké's only quibble with Douglass, expressed many years later, was that he should have anticipated that such a marriage would invite controversy: "Why he decided in his second marriage, to select a white woman as his help mate was a matter which concerned him only," Francis would confide in his diary. "If he wanted to marry a white woman and she wanted to marry him, it was a matter between them only. It was nobody else's business. The intermarriage of the races may not be a wise thing, in this country, in view of present conditions, but the right to marry if they want is inherited, God-given. No one may rightfully forbid it."

In Boston, Archibald Grimké read of the attacks on Douglass and formed his own opinion: to him, Douglass's marriage to a white woman seemed an act of consummate courage. But like his brother Frank, Archie knew that courage was often not enough in the face of racial prejudice. His own marriage, to Sarah Stanley, was a case in point. From the first, he had been deeply committed to the marriage; he and Sarah had set up house near his offices in downtown Boston, and he had walked to work every day and hurried home every night, anxious to show that he was a devoted husband. He attended to Sarah's every need and built a strong relationship with his new father-in-law, who not only reconciled himself to the marriage but became Archie's steadfast defender (he called him "my dear son") and one of his many admirers. Just a month after their wedding, Sarah became pregnant, and the couple joyfully planned for the arrival of their first child. Sarah Stanley's love for her new husband was boundless: "I no longer have a separate being," she wrote to him during one of his trips away from Boston. "My soul has gone and only a dull machine moves about these rooms on the streets and Commons of Boston, all is unmeaning haze until my prince return and revivify with his breath and magic touch." When their daughter was born, on February 27, 1880, they named her Angelina Weld Grimké, after Archie's admired aunt.

But there was tension in the marriage, a worrisome and deep-seated anxiety that Archie believed was the result of the "unusual circumstance of our union." There were, of course, the predictable whispers, looks, and veiled criticisms, even within the relatively safe environment in which the Grimkés moved. But Archie wondered whether they took a toll on his wife, whether "perhaps she regretted our marriage." That their union had been opposed at the outset by her father, and no doubt by his community of believers in Michigan as well, also caused problems, despite the fact that Archie and the Reverend Stanley had since made amends. There is also a hint, though indirect and uncertain, that Sarah believed her husband had taken up with another woman; at times she seemed inordinately jealous, accusing him of seeing "one that you call your good fairly." There is no evidence that she was right, however, and it is hard to believe, from Archie's own writings, that he would ever be unfaithful.

After the new family moved back to Hyde Park from Boston, Sarah took her newborn "Nana" and traveled west for an extended stay with her parents. She returned briefly, only to leave again for Michigan. By early 1883, it was apparent to all of their friends that the marriage was failing. Archie was plunged into the depths of despair and turned to his uncle Theodore for help, asking him to check the tone of his letters to Sarah, in faraway Michigan, to make certain it was "just right." The Reverend Stanley attempted to patch things up between the couple, but none of his efforts succeeded. In mid-1883, Sarah wrote to inform Archie that she wanted a divorce, provided she could retain custody of Angelina. Still hoping that somehow the marriage might be salvaged, Archie agreed. Magnanimously, he suggested that perhaps now that their separation was official, they could somehow, together, begin again. He pleaded with his wife to come back to him, but she did not answer his letter.

Archibald Grimké would never remarry, and for as long as Sarah remained a part of his life, he would hope for her return. His daughter, Angelina, would later write that her mother's decision to leave Boston and return to her parents was "a terrible blow" that had a profound effect on Archie's life, touching everything from his personal relationships with his family to his political beliefs. It took him many years to recover, she said. It seems almost certain that the issue of color was at the root of Archie and Sarah's marital problems, for she later wrote him worrying letters about their daughter's reaction to racism. Nana, she said at one point, "is getting old enough to see and feel the *thoughts* of others, which the difference of race and color naturally engender regarding her."

There is one other, much simpler explanation for the couple's troubles. For many years prior to their marriage, Sarah had been in poor health. At times, she focused on her own physical condition to the exclusion of almost everything else; thinking about her health and about potential ailments became the bedrock of her life. In the spring of 1887, she would put seven-year-old Nana on a train to Boston and leave for California, where she would write on the relationship between physical illness and personal problems. She would become well known for linking alchemy, astrology, and mysticism with physical well-being, and would travel widely lecturing on such topics. She would write to her former husband and her daughter often, telling them of her travels, which were extensive: after lecturing in California, she journeyed to New Zealand (where she suffered a heart attack), then returned to Michigan to visit her family, and finally lived for a time in San Diego. She would never reconcile with Archie and, after 1887, never again see her daughter. She would commit suicide, by poison, in 1898.

In August 1883, Archibald Grimké became the editor of the *Hub*, a Boston Republican newspaper serving the black community. His acceptance of the editorship, arranged for him through a friendship he had developed with the well-known Boston Republican Solomon Stebbins and a Boston University student named Butler Wilson, plunged him into the middle of one of the most raucous and hard-fought governor's races in post–Civil War Massachusetts politics. The 1883 election pitted Democrat and former Civil War general Benjamin Butler against Republican George Robinson. Butler was a national figure. As the postwar military commander in Louisiana, he had been outspoken in his defense of Reconstruction, and he was known for his radical advocacy of black rights. But the Democratic resurgence threatened the Republican's Reconstruction policies, and Butler was, after all, a Democrat. With violence against freedmen increasing throughout the South, almost always with the support of the Democratic "Bourbon Restoration" (whose leaders won Southern votes by preaching white supremacy), Butler's defeat would send a message and mark a rollback in Democratic power, even if it did cost the nation one of its most outspoken equal rights activists. The Republicans therefore worked desperately for his defeat.

For Grimké, the election was a test of his interest in politics as well as a talisman of his status in the black community. A convinced Republican, he wanted to persuade black Bostonians to vote with the party despite Butler's vaunted support of black rights. Butler was admired by a number of leading black politicians in Massachusetts, and he hoped to use them to divide the black Republican vote. Three of these leaders—James Monroe Trotter, Edwin Walker, and George Temple Downing—formed his core support. Butler had also recruited a number of well-known figures from the abolitionist community, including Grimké's good friend and mentor Wendell Phillips. Grimké's task—to bring in the overwhelmingly Republican black vote for Robinson by making the *Hub* a respected political voice in the black community—was going to be difficult, but he attacked it with the fervor for which he would soon become known.

In his first issue as editor, Grimké promised to report the truth "without fear or favor," then weighed in against Butler and the Democrats in tones reminiscent of Garrison's columns in *The Liberator*. A Garrison admirer, he leveled a torrent of invective at Butler, calling him a tool of the party that was "the protector of the Ku Klux Klan and the parent of lawlessness." And that was only the beginning. Focusing on Butler's corruption and questionable reputation as a rabble-rouser, hard-drinker, and womanizer, Grimké announced that he could never vote for a man who received most of his support "from the bar-room." He concluded by noting acerbically that Independents who voted for Democrats were infected with "negrophobia." Garrison would have been proud.

Butler worked hard for the black vote. To court the black community, he "waved the bloody red shirt" of his Civil War career and reminded black Bostonians that he had stood "almost single-handedly" against Southern rebels in New Orleans during Reconstruction. As voting day approached, Grimké stepped up his attacks, telling his readers that it was the Democrats who now led the South, and the Democratic party that had first divided the nation back in 1860. In Bostonian James Monroe Trotter, however, Archibald Grimké met his match. Trotter, seven years Grimké's senior, was a native of Grand Gulf, Mississippi, on the river just south of Vicksburg. His family had escaped slavery in the late 1840s and settled in Cincinnati. When Massachusetts abolitionist James Andrews received permission to recruit black troops, Trotter had made his way to Boston, where he enlisted in the Fifty-fifth Massachusetts regiment. Quickly promoted, he had struck up a correspondence with William Lloyd Garrison's son (a leading Massachusetts abolitionist in his own right) over the question of equal pay for black troops—lodging a protest that, through sheer tenacity, he won. After the war, he had married Virginia Isaacs, reputedly a great-granddaughter of Thomas Jefferson (the Trotter family claimed that her grandfather was Jefferson's son), moved to Hyde Park, and become a Democrat.

James Monroe Trotter was an adept political organizer. While Archibald Grimké was issuing scathing critiques of Butler, Trotter was working the black community. With his years of experience in Boston and his ties to its storied black regiment, Trotter had the greater influence. He mistrusted the Republicans, believing that Hayes had purposely betrayed the black vote in order to win the White House. Despite their party differences, Trotter and Grimké had much in common: both believed that black Americans should "pull themselves up," both had entered the black community from the outside (the relatively affluent Hyde Park), and both were skilled at using the characteristically strident language of late-nineteenth-century politics. Both looked at the political world through the prism of their own pain: Trotter as the son of a woman who, against enormous odds, had brought her family North from bondage, and Grimké as the son of a woman whose regal bearing and moral standing made her, in her children's eyes, a "madonna."

In the end, Butler triumphed, and Trotter celebrated. "Although it cannot be fairly claimed that the colored break from the so-called Republican party has been general," he reflected, "yet it has been of proportions so large as to occasion surprise and delight, and to be without a parallel in any of the states." His next statement was aimed at Grimké: "The writer (while not claiming for himself superior goodness) would appeal now to our men as he has often done in the past, to cease from this degrading practice of annually hiring themselves out for political work. . . . Our race is yet so far 'in the woods' that it cannot afford to imitate these Caucasian vices. Let us not contaminate our holy cause by baseness of any kind." So was initiated a three-decade competition, sometimes friendly but as often bitter, between the Grimkés, Archibald and Francis, on the one side, and James Monroe Trotter and his even more outspoken son William—the "Guardian of Boston"—on the other.

Archibald Grimké's masterful handling of the *Hub* during the election helped propel him into the vanguard of Boston's black leadership. Over the next decade, he would be called on repeatedly to give speeches and write articles on black issues, and would be viewed, with Trotter, as Boston's leading voice in the black community. Just two weeks after Butler's election, Archie was an honored guest at the eightieth-birthday celebration of Theodore Dwight Weld, in the company of such luminaries as John Greenleaf Whittier, Samuel Sewall, Thomas Wentworth Higginson, Lucy Stone, and Julia Ward Howe, the poet and writer who had penned "The Battle Hymn of the Republic." February of 1884 found him in Washington, at his brother's church, giving a surprisingly even-handed lecture on the life of John Calhoun. Archibald Grimké, just thirty-five years old, was making a name for himself and was counted among the group that included Bostonians James Wolff, George Ruffin, and James Monroe Trotter; T. Thomas Fortune (editor and publisher of the *Age*) and T. McCants Stewart of New York; W. Calvin Chase (editor of the *Bee*) of Washington; Robert Purvis of Philadelphia; lawyer and politician C. H. J. Taylor of Kansas City; Peter H. Clark of Cincinnati; George T. Downing of Rhode Island; and Booker T. Washington, founder of the Tuskegee Institute in Alabama, the newest and most forceful voice of all. But none of them was yet mentioned in the same breath as Frederick Douglass.

Douglass's leadership was sorely missing in the mid- and late 1880s, however, when the promise of Reconstruction had faded and attacks on freedmen continued to mount throughout the South. Douglass, sixty-seven years old in 1885, was now noticeably aging and increasingly infirm. He continued to focus on the message expressed in his books, emphasizing self-reliance and hard work (tiresome advice for a community that was, in Fortune's words, "being pushed to the wall"). He was retiring from public life, leaving politics to others. His last plea, on behalf of the Republican party, had come during a black leadership convention in Louisville in 1883, when he attempted to defend himself against charges that he had continued to support Hayes even after the betrayal of 1877. His words were met with derision. He quickly backtracked, first calling himself an "uneasy Republican" and then, though sensing the dissatisfaction among his own supporters and most loyal admirers, going even further, telling the delegates, "If the Republican party cannot stand a demand for justice and fair play, it ought to go down." It was nearly his last hurrah.

With Douglass aging and no recognized national leader waiting in the wings to take his place, the black community was deeply divided between "uneasy Republicans" and newly minted "Independent" Democrats. Throughout the mid- and late 1880s, the Republicans remained a dominant force in the black community, but Hayes's betrayal, combined with the refusal of Republican party leaders to reward black activists with political jobs and the party's indifference to the very black rights it had worked to institutionalize in the Thirteenth and Fourteenth amendments, inexorably cut into their support and eventually (and in spite of the virulent racism that accompanied the resurgence of the Democratic party in the South) destroyed it totally.

The division in the black community was unmistakable in 1884, when the Republicans dumped Chester A. Arthur as their standard-bearer and nominated Senator James G. Blaine of Maine for president. Grimké attended the Chicago nominating convention as an alternate delegate from Massachusetts, with responsibility for keeping black Southern delegates in line for President Arthur. He did his job well but, as it turned out, not well enough. When Blaine was nominated, Massachusetts reformers (called Mugwumps, from the Algonquin word meaning "big chief"—that is, those who thought themselves above petty party politics) bolted the party, shifting their support to Democratic nominee Grover Cleveland. Grimké, for his part, held fast, using the *Hub* as a mouthpiece for Republican indignation. Although the "bolters" included his lifelong friends Thomas Wentworth Higginson, Charles R. Codman, and former abolitionist John F. Andrews, Grimké grimly soldiered on, predicting a massive Blaine win—"the Adams family, the kid glove aristocracy, and the blue blood money bags and reformers to the contrary notwithstanding." After one reform rally for Cleveland, he set pen to paper for the *Hub* and described the speeches made by his friends Higginson and Codman as "eloquent cant and twaddle." Grimké never veered from his support for Blaine, though he realized that the Maine senator was facing an uphill battle. Finally, one month before the election, the tide ran out on Blaine when he refused to disavow the remarks of a supporter who had called the Democrats the party of "Rum, Romanism and Rebellion" (thereby losing the Roman Catholic vote in New York), and as his own involvement in Republican financial scandals ("Blaine, Blaine, James G. Blaine, the continental liar from the state of Maine," Cleveland supporters chanted) gained wide circulation. Grimké was disappointed and humbled by the defeat, but even more so by his increasing isolation, as a staunch Republican party defender, from the black community.

For Archie Grimké, loyalty to the Republican party was paramount, even in the face of the Hayes betrayal and the failure of successive Republican administrations to defend black rights. He could not forget the work the Republicans had done in enfranchising and promoting black rights in the South, nor the fact that abolitionists had once formed the bedrock of their support, nor that it was the Republicans who had organized the armies that came to South Carolina to set him and his brothers free. Neither could he forget the family ties that bound him to the fading generation of abolitionists, the majority of them still, and forever, radical "equal rights" Republicans. But even he knew, in the wake of Blaine's defeat, that he could not long ignore the words of his colleagues, whose bitter attacks on Republican corruption mounted as the decade waned.

Like almost every other black leader of his time, Archibald Grimké realized that he was becoming a man without a party. His dilemma was the one faced by every black American: Should he maintain his loyalty to Lincoln's party, even though it had so blithely abandoned the freedmen in the hope of political gain? Or should he shift his support to the higher bidder, knowing that that bidder would never turn its back on its Southern wing, any more than it had done in 1860, when the choice was between Union and slavery? The black journalist T. Thomas Fortune spoke bluntly of this dilemma in the pages of the *New York Age*, castigating the Republicans for their "base ingratitude, subterfuge and hypocrisy." But then, in the same breath, he urged his readers to act on the motto "Race first; then party." Which would it be? Or should it be neither? By the end of Cleveland's first term in office, it was becoming clear that there was no answer to the question. African Americans would inevitably be forced to defend themselves without help from any political party. They were alone.

THIRTEEN

"A cowardly and sinful silence . . ."

rchibald Grimké officially left the Republican party in 1886,
but his abandonment of the "party of emancipation" had actually begun two years earlier, just after the 1884 presidential
campaign. The shift in his political allegiance was inevitable: many of his
friends and much of the leadership of Boston's black community had already gone over to the Democratic party. By early 1886, Grimké was politically isolated. But his was a blunt political calculus, faintly tinged by
personal necessity: he was willing to make sacrifices for the Republicans,
but he refused to work in an environment of broken promises. For almost
a year, the most important part of it during the Blaine campaign, the *Hub*
had survived solely because of Grimké's own financial support. Monies
promised by the Republicans, and pledged by his old Harvard Law
School friend Henry Cabot Lodge, had never arrived. He felt deceived.

Shifting his political base was no easy task, however. Lest he be accused of betraying his ideals to serve his pocketbook, Grimké set the
stage for his defection during a series of public speeches carefully crafted
to show that he was slowly rethinking his views. The process began even
before Cleveland's election, when he noted in a public speech that while
the Republicans had "dropped" their commitment to the freedmen in
1876, the Democrats had moved to "cultivate Africa." Next, during a
speech before the National Woman Suffrage Association, he tied the crusade for racial equality to the suffrage movement. He said that black

Americans, like women, should be willing to give their support to any party that supported their views, regardless of that party's history. He also agreed to chair the Massachusetts Woman Suffrage Association, a black organization that was filled with Democrats. A further shift was marked by his new emphasis on the economic basis of inequality, a favorite Democratic theme. "Corporate wealth has become the motive force behind government," he said in one address. "Monopoly and money are constantly growing to be the power behind elections, behind legislatures, behind the multifarious forces of our American democracy." That was the same position the Democratic party took.

By the middle of 1886, Grimké's disenchantment with the Republicans was widely known. He successfully revived his friendship with prominent Independents and Mugwumps, including Higginson and the increasingly important Charles Codman. A friend of Grover Cleveland's and an important dispenser of Democratic largesse in Massachusetts, Codman was the key to Grimké's political future. The two men were seen together so often that they became linked in people's minds as political comrades; they served side by side on a number of boards and in local and state black organizations. Codman was also Grimké's link to James Monroe Trotter, arguably the best-known and most outspoken advocate for equal rights in Massachusetts, and his ever more influential son William. Grimké got along well with the elder Trotter and admired his pugnacious attacks on segregation and his outspoken defense of Southern blacks. They also shared a unique and emotional history, since Trotter had served in a Union unit just outside Charleston while Grimké was hidden in the city as a boy.

By late 1886, Grimké's association with the "bolters" was public knowledge, if not yet official. After the *Hub* stopped publication due to financial difficulties, he worked with the Independents on the campaign to elect John F. Andrews as governor of Massachusetts and helped former abolitionist Thomas Wentworth Higginson plan his run for the state's Fifth Congressional District seat. This latter must have been a somewhat distasteful task for Grimké, for Higginson, like many other abolitionists, trimmed his political sails to remain palatable to the Democratic party and even refused to criticize Southerners for their treatment of the freedmen. To assuage Southern Democrats, Higginson publicly argued that the black community in the South would do well to refrain from all participation in politics—and this from a man who had been a member of John Brown's "secret six," and whose courage, therefore, was not in question. Even Frederick Douglass's criticism of Higginson did not change Grimké's mind. Instead, Grimké discounted Douglass, noting during one speech that Higginson had been working as an abolitionist when Douglass was still a slave. Grimké's break with the Republican party became official when he wrote a letter to the *Boston Herald*, a Mugwump newspaper, urging black voters to support Andrews's run for the statehouse. He also wrote a lengthy letter defending his shift and sent it to a number of African American newspapers.

While Grimké's break with the Republicans was a result partly of his anger over their unkept financial pledges, and partly, too, of his need to shore up his own support in the black community, there were also strong reasons of principle behind his decision. African Americans, he said, were bound to support the party that defended their rights, regardless of which party that might be. Although the Republicans had once been "the party of emancipation," that was in the past. The "great betrayal of 1877," the Republicans' willingness to turn their backs on black supporters in the name of national unity, and their party's unmet promises to the freedmen all required the black community to secure its future elsewhere. Ultimately, however, the argument that had the greatest influence on Grimké was stated simply, in the pages of the *New York Age*, by T. Thomas Fortune, who asserted that no matter what the political question, race must always come first. This motto—"Race first; then party"—made sense to Grimké from the moment he read it.

Archibald Grimké's transformation from a stalwart Republican into a loyal Democrat (though he insisted on calling himself an Independent, thereby keeping his options open), took two years of work, but by the time the next national campaign began, the shift was complete. On October 19, 1888, Grimké spoke as a Democrat in support of the candidacy of Grover Cleveland at a gathering held by the Harvard Tariff Reform Club, at Boston's Tremont Temple. He felt politically at home for the first time since the Blaine campaign. A number of prominent black Bostonians attended, along with the state's upper-crust Democratic leadership: William Lloyd Garrison, Jr., John F. Andrews, William James, Harvard's Charles Eliot Norton, the historian Francis Parkman, and Democratic kingmaker Leveritt Saltonstall. Grimké made an impassioned speech against the tariff, the major national issue then confronting the political parties. As a free-trader, he pleaded with the black community to "take hold of this tariff question" and support "the Democrats and that noble man, Grover Cleveland." The audience listened closely for any hint of uncertainty in his words, but there was none. Archibald Grimké was now an antitariff Democrat.

———

In the up-country of the Carolinas, in the backcountry of Alabama, Georgia, and Mississippi, and in the swamps and groves of Florida and Louisiana, the last thing on the minds of black Americans was the tariff. In Mississippi, in March 1886, thirteen black men were shot down in cold blood in one of the ugliest racial incidents of the post-Reconstruction era. In Jackson, Tennessee, a black woman accused of poisoning a white woman was dragged from a jail cell, tied to a tree, and shot, her body riddled with bullets. The season of lynching that would dominate the next forty years of African American life reached its crescendo in the mid-1880s, just as Archibald Grimké was telling black Americans to "take hold of this tariff question." The Ku Klux Klan was on the loose throughout the Southern heartland, enforcing segregationist policies, intimidating the free black population, and murdering the black community's most outspoken local leaders. The Klan was the arm of the South's white Democratic regimes.

By the mid-1880s, the dream of creating a prosperous and independent black agricultural class in the South had become a fading reality. The vast majority of black Southern farmers were sharecroppers, leasing equipment, livestock, and seed from white entrepreneurs in exchange for the profits from the sale of the harvests they produced. Slavery was dead, but its ramifications endured. Sharecropping impoverished hundreds of thousands of Southern blacks, forcing them to depend on white society for their livelihoods. The same was true for black entrepreneurs, whose hopes for economic independence were smashed by the reality of "Southern redemption"—that is, the reelection of white Democratic state governments that promoted policies of racial discrimination and white supremacy. History was being quickly rewritten. The bloody sectional conflict was now the "Lost Cause." Robert E. Lee had been a great and honorable American, and the Civil War had not really been about slavery at all—it had been about "Southern rights." Having lost the argument over slavery, Southerners were now intent on winning the one over racial equality. If black Americans could actually compete, and successfully so, then everything the South had fought for was wrong. If black Americans were *not* inferior, then their Lost Cause had not been just.

Archibald Grimké was out of touch with this crisis. Although he was aware of the mounting violence against African Americans in the South, the reality of it was not reflected in either his writings or his public speeches. Grimké's views on how best to win equal rights for African Americans would evolve dramatically over the next ten years, but in 1888 he remained under the influence of the old abolitionist community of New England, many of whose members believed that their crusade had succeeded: black Americans were emancipated, and all that needed to be done now was to see to it that the federal government enforced Reconstruction laws. Many of the old-line abolitionists truly thought that black Americans were being educated, that farmland was being redistributed, and that the sound of the whip was no longer to be heard. Grimké did not agree, but he did believe that political action held out the best hope for building a society dedicated to defending racial equality.

The impact of increasingly segregationist "separate but equal" laws, the economic disaster of sharecropping, the unwillingness of political institutions to defend the freedmen after the end of Reconstruction, the rising tide of lynching in the South, and the failure of abolitionists to transform their movement into a new crusade for equal rights—none of these had "radicalized" the African American elite as exemplified by Archibald Grimké. Rather, the transformation in such leaders' thinking was glacial. In 1888, Grimké still believed that the fight for economic rights for all Americans represented the one means of ensuring equal rights for African Americans. In spite of his experiences as a slave in Charleston, the pain of his failed marriage, and the daily slights he faced as a black man in Boston, Archibald Grimké did not yet understand the depth of the racial hatreds that were alive in the nation. Much like his aunt Angelina in 1835, he was awaiting "the call" that would spark him to "do something."

He was not alone in his views. Most Northern black Americans, especially those descended from the free black families of Boston, New York, Philadelphia, and Baltimore, took it as a given that the slow march toward equal rights would proceed on course. The gains that had been made over the previous two decades, since the Emancipation Proclamation of 1863, seemed to them irreversible. Although race prejudice (which Grimké, following his aunts' lead, would pointedly call "color prejudice") was an everyday reality, black leaders in the North were persuaded that an assiduous focus on building racial pride and on taking advantage of what opportunities were available to black Americans would enable the dream of black equality to be realized. In this environment, participation in party politics was a necessity, as the most meaningful way for influential black leaders to make an impact on a white-dominated society.

There was some disagreement on this point, however, and a growing awareness that the crisis faced by black Americans in the South might be more than just a regional problem, or even a "temporary" obstacle along the inevitable path to black participation in all aspects of American life. While a convinced Democrat, and a full participant in the political process (as well as an ally of Archibald Grimké's), T. Thomas Fortune was one of those who felt uncomfortable with the black elite's focus on party politics. He maintained a diligent silence when it came to publicizing his own doubts, but he liberally sprinkled dissent throughout the pages of his New York newspaper. One of Fortune's trusted contributors was Ida B. Wells, a black Memphis woman who was just beginning to make her mark as a journalist. She came to the attention of men such as Grimké, Codman, Douglass, and Trotter through her vocal criticism of the black elite, whose ambition, she said, was to "get all they can for their own use." Her views were discomfiting to those she targeted, but she forced them to listen to her anyway. As Grimké was struggling to transform himself into a Democrat, Wells had been transforming herself into a black militant. She took both parties to task in the pages of Fortune's *New York Freeman:*

> I am not a Democrat, because the Democrats considered me chattel and possibly might have always considered me [so], because their record from the beginning has been inimical to my interests; because they have become notorious in their hatred of the Negro as a man, have refused him the ballot; have murdered, beaten and outraged him and refused him his rights. I am not a Republican, because after they—as a party measure and an inevitable result of the war—had "given the Negro his freedom" and the ballot hoax following, all through their reign—while advocating the doctrine of the Federal Government's right of protecting her citizens—they suffered the crimes against the Negro, that have made the South notorious, to go unpunished and almost unnoticed, and turned them over to the tender mercies of the South entirely, as a matter of barter in '76, to secure the Presidency.

The reality was that by the beginning of the 1890s, the hopes that men such as Archibald or his brother Francis Grimké, or any other African American man or woman, could actually become a part of the political process, that color would not be a barrier to full participation in American life, and that the work of Reconstruction would go on—these hopes had been extinguished altogether. "But why speak of our drawing the color-line?" the journalist Josephine Turpin Washington asked bitterly. "It is drawn and most persistently by the whites. For us to attempt to ignore the fact would be like trying to walk through a stone wall by simply making up your mind it is not there. The wall stands and you have only a broken head for your pains."

———

A sense of isolation and hope deferred was beginning to dawn on the American black community. It was felt first in the South, where prejudice was a reality and violence an everyday possibility. It was felt next among the well-organized urban black population. Finally, belatedly, it was felt among the black Northern elite. Certainly the full breadth of the coming crisis was not yet obvious to Archibald Grimké, consumed as he was by Massachusetts party politics and by the necessity of making himself heard within Boston's black community. But the crisis in the South and the growing isolation of black America were being felt by his brother Francis in Washington. Francis Grimké was much like his aunt Sarah, and he served the same purpose for Archibald that Sarah had served for Angelina. Like Sarah, Francis understood the intractability of race prejudice and was humbled by the obstacles it presented. Although he continued to preach his message of personal salvation and self-pride, the fact of prejudice was obvious to him every day on the streets of Washington in a way that it was not to his brother in Boston.

His biographer Henry Justi Ferry has suggested that this sense of isolation from the American mainstream was perceived by Francis Grimké from the moment he began his ministry. In Washington, Grimké encountered a black community that was deeply divided: one part was "optimistic, open, glowing with promise for the Negro," while the other was "cynical, restrictive, sullied by the compromise of Negro dreams." Bringing the two together, especially in the face of mounting racism and official apathy, would be a lifelong challenge. After an auspicious start in his ministry, Frank Grimké saw his hopes for racial equality gradually wither. While other members of the black community reacted to the same despair by turning inward, abandoning all trust in the American political process, Francis Grimké reverted to his faith in God and in his own ability to influence public opinion from the pulpit. The spoken word, he believed, was his most potent weapon. He returned to this conviction again and again in the pages of his diary:

> The pulpit, the sacred desk is no place for the man who wants to boom himself, to center attention upon himself instead of the Lord Jesus Christ and the truth of God. The aim of the sermon is not to show one's skill in the production of a literary work that will win for the writer or speaker admiration . . . ; but rather, in fact, its aim always should be to reach the mind and heart and to influence the will in the direction of what is just, pure, lovely, and of good report.

Francis Grimké never lost his confidence in the importance and power of a minister's word, but by the beginning of 1885, after just seven years as a minister, he was mentally and physically exhausted, and disappointed by Washington's reaction to his message. He preached to a racially mixed audience and attracted some of the city's leading political figures to his services (including, notably, members of Congress and the Supreme Court), but none of what he said took root. Francis responded to this by losing himself in his work and devoting all his time to ministering, advising, working with his congregation and in the black community, building local organizations, and raising money to support good causes.

In 1885, Francis was embroiled in a bitter controversy with Howard University's theological department. The dispute was complicated by the fact that the Presbyterian Church had partial control over the department: in exchange for its support, the church had been given the right to approve prospective faculty members and have qualified students trained at the school. It was with this in mind that Francis Grimké recommended four black students from Howard's preparatory department for enrollment in the theology program. All were rejected, however, after they received a negative recommendation from the department dean, who accused them of a "defect in piety." Grimké maintained his support of the students, pointed out that their failure to be admitted had not been communicated to the church (as was required under the department's agreement with the Presbytery), and suggested that the theological department had been "remiss in its duties."

After a series of board meetings, communications with the university, and vocal protests by Grimké, the students were finally admitted, but the relationship between the university and the church, and especially the church in Washington, was strained. As a member of the special committee appointed to investigate the church's relations with the university, Grimké voted to end the connection—a decision he reached only after an agonizing internal debate, for he also sat on Howard's board of trustees and was a strong supporter of the institution's commitment to black education. His vote put him in a minority of one on the special committee, whose resolution to maintain the church's relationship to the university struck Grimké as a personal affront. His disappointment at the vote, coupled with the controversy over Frederick Douglass's marriage and his own deteriorating health, led him to accept the offer of a pastorate at the Laura Street Presbyterian Church in Jacksonville, Florida. Frank Grimké's congregation was shocked by the announcement that he was leaving, but reassured him that he would be welcomed back at any time.

On the evening of November 1, 1885, the members of the Monday Night Club expressed their dismay over his leave-taking in a written valedictory that was presented to him after being read aloud:

> Our loss is great, but we have some sustaining thoughts; one of which is that though you may carry from us the light and benefit that would surely be our portion should you remain, yet there must be some overturning, some opposing force dispensing its unhallowed influence with tremendous energy before the light of your Washington career be dimmed, or the onward march of your example be checked. And again, we have another gratifying conviction; it is that wherever you may make your abode, humanity must still be the gainer.

The next evening, just days before his departure, the church held a reception for Grimké. The congregation's gratitude for his service was obvious: "We sincerely commend him to those to whom he goes, in the land of the flowers and sweet perfumes, of generous and hospitable people. May he find warm hearts, devoted friends, and helping hands, to remind him of those to whom he now says 'Good friends, for a while, farewell.' "

Many of Frank Grimké's parishioners believed that he would find the South much less hospitable than he assumed, and that after a season of battling the demons of Southern hatred, he would return to his real church in Washington.

———

Frank and Charlotte Grimké looked forward to their new life in Jacksonville. Frank saw his assignment as a special challenge because he would be facing issues in Florida that he had not faced in Washington. He was moving to a parish that he could build, in a part of the country where the question of race was a violent reality, where prejudice was meted out by white supremacists and the defense of equality issued by Washington's elite was never heard. He viewed the move as providing him with an opportunity to do missionary work—that is, to be a Presbyterian in a land of Baptists and Southern Methodists. His new parish in Jacksonville, then a comparatively small city, needed a pastor to spend time ministering and building community support. Attendance at the Laura Street Presbyterian Church was falling (there were only thirty parishioners and fifty Sunday-school students), and the building was in need of repairs. The church welcomed its new minister as a savior. Grimké plunged into his work, but he also started to focus on refining his thinking on racial issues. It was a time of reflection that allowed him to build the intellectual ground for his later activism. (Francis was so consumed by his meditations and by looking after his parishioners in his first weeks in Florida that he did not even take time to visit his brother John, whom he would rarely see in the years that followed.)

Grimké understood immediately that Florida's black population was facing a major crisis. Overawed by segregation and by the lack of economic opportunity, his congregants had been cast out of the larger community, and poverty, vice, criminality, and alcoholism were taking a heavy toll. Within weeks of his arrival, Grimké launched a temperance campaign, which he believed was essential to forging a sense of black solidarity. Only by building strong communities, Grimké felt, could black Americans hope to compete with white society, and only *then* could they exert the leadership to overcome prejudice's legacy. He told his congregation:

> When I think of the sad inheritance which slavery has entailed upon the race, of the low moral plane upon which it left it, and

then think of what the saloon is doing to sink it lower, do you
wonder when I tell you, that, as a race-loving Negro, I hate it
with perfect hatred because it is making criminals and vagabonds of many of my race, I hate it because it is undermining
the foundation upon which alone you can make a strong, self-
respecting race; because it is a debasing, character-destroying,
institution.

When not ministering in Jacksonville, Grimké spoke before large congregations in Atlanta, Montgomery, Mobile, and Savannah. He toured
black universities and colleges and participated in innumerable African
American economic, cultural, and religious conferences. Nowhere in all
of his travels, however, was Grimké more affected than he was by his
tour of Booker T. Washington's Tuskegee Institute, which had been
founded by Alabama's state legislature in 1881 as a Normal School for
black students. Washington gave the institute its impetus and driving
force: a philosophy of teaching practical agricultural and industrial working skills that stood as a counterbalance to the Northern elite's insistence
on higher education.

Grimké had been impressed by Washington when he first met him,
though he did not agree with his educational philosophy. For Francis
Grimké, a formal education was a necessary foundation for spiritual
growth; he mistrusted "the Tuskegee way." But after the two men met
during a religious convention, Grimké accepted Washington's invitation
to visit the Alabama school and see for himself whether Tuskegee offered
any hope of alleviating the plight of Southern African Americans. He
was particularly interested in learning what kind of religious training
Washington was providing to the students. Grimké spent three days at
Tuskegee and was overwhelmed by what he saw. As he wrote in a letter to
the *New York Age*, Tuskegee's emphasis on community, self-help, self-
respect, modesty, and hard work made it a model for black education. In
Tuskegee, Grimké discovered a school where the moral imperatives that
he insisted on in his sermons were put into practice:

It is not only training the young men and women to think, and
to be industrious, but to be virtuous. The emphasis which it
lays on character—the pains which it takes to inspire them
with a love for the things that are true and just and good and
lovely and of good report is one of the most delightful features

about it, and one of the things which most strongly commend it. It is working in the line of true development. Its influence is being felt, not only in giving skill to the hand and culture to the brain, but in the more important work of character-building, without which all else is as nothing.

Booker T. Washington was the force behind Tuskegee, its soul and brain, its primary philosopher and chief advocate. Francis Grimké found him to be a man of immense self-confidence and intelligence. Born in West Virginia to a slave mother and a white father whom he never knew (he assumed the man was his mother's master), Washington felt the sting of poverty more than he did the burden of racial oppression. As he wrote in his famous autobiography *Up from Slavery*, "It was a piece of bread here and a scrap of meat there. It was a cup of milk at one time and some potatoes at another." He made his living as a young boy in the coal and salt mines, before enrolling at the Hampton Institute, a Virginia school for black students.

Hampton's head and founder, General Samuel Chapman Armstrong, had had an enormous influence on Washington. Armstrong believed that black Americans should be taught to compete with the rising tide of immigrants by learning trades. The historian August Meier notes that while Armstrong was shaped by his own questionable racial views (the "colored races," he said, were "slothful, backward, lascivious, and inferior" and would remain so until they "assimilated the values and skills" of white civilization), his presidency of the Hampton Institute was part of a growing American educational movement that emphasized the acquisition of industrial and agricultural skills as a means of gaining financial independence. In a nation that at that time placed less value on higher education, Armstrong's views were decidedly mainstream and widely endorsed by African American leaders. The black community was, it was true, in desperate need of skilled black labor.

In 1881, Armstrong had recommended that the state of Alabama hire Washington to head its new school for black students, and he had been named to the position soon thereafter. Tuskegee was a poor school when Washington arrived; though backed by state funds, it was in need of new supporters and better facilities. Washington single-handedly took control of Tuskegee and vowed that he would make it one of the richest and most successful black schools in the nation. His timing was perfect. In the early 1880s, the idea of providing black Americans with an industrial and agricultural education was beginning to command the attention of philanthropists, including abolitionist activists, who funneled money into black education through a Northern organization, the American Missionary Association. Still, Washington's success was not guaranteed. The Tuskegee Institute was competing for funds with schools in Mississippi (Alcorn College), South Carolina (Claflin College), Georgia (Atlanta University), and Mississippi (Tugaloo College).

Francis Grimké accepted Washington's challenge to speak as often as possible at Southern industrial colleges. This, along with his commitment to attend as many Southern black conventions as possible, and his efforts to help build a new Presbyterian church in Jacksonville, consumed much of his time. Unfortunately, Francis's wife, Charlotte Forten Grimké, had not thrived in Florida, and illness forced her to spend many months with friends in Boston. Pleased though her husband was with his new parish, he soon tired of the scant attention his sermons received in the small church in Jacksonville. He needed a larger audience. Then, too, he was disappointed to discover just how little religious whites in the South had learned from their experiences during the Civil War: prejudice was rife everywhere, even among committed white Christians. Grimké fought a running battle with the premier white minister of the day, Dwight L. Moody, who deferred to Southern segregationist policies and ministered separately to the races. And even in the face of such open discrimination, Northern supporters of equality remained silent. Grimké was outraged by that and confided to his diary his dismay at the abolitionists' abandonment of the equal rights campaign: "Only a few hours' ride from one section of our country to another has the most surprising effect. People who once thought that they were friendly to the Negro, and who were not slow to express their sympathy with him in the North, wake up suddenly, under the influence of a Southern sky, to discover that they had been laboring under a delusion."

It was under this cloud of apprehension that, when his old church in Washington asked him to return, in December 1888, Francis Grimké willingly accepted. He searched for a new minister to take his place in Jacksonville, then packed his bags once again and departed for Washington. His four-year interlude in the South was over, but it had given him an opportunity to see, with his own eyes, the crisis that black America faced.

Soon after Francis Grimké's return to Washington, his brother Archibald began to think about changing his own life. Like Frank, Archie was exhausted after the battles of the previous decade. He needed a change of scene, a new job—a new challenge. Accordingly, just prior to Harrison's inauguration, Archie's friend and political ally Charles Codman had written a letter to the outgoing president, Grover Cleveland, suggesting him for the post of consul to Santo Domingo, in the Dominican Republic. After reminding Cleveland of Grimké's support for him during the election and recounting his friend's journey from slavery to freedom, Codman added that James Trotter supported the nomination. Cleveland agreed to the idea, and on January 23, 1889, he sent the nomination to the Senate, where everyone believed Grimké would be confirmed. The *Boston Transcript* endorsed the appointment, saying, "The country needs a man of sterling character and level head as its representative at the Dominican capital, and should the present nomination be confirmed, its requirements will be fully and thoroughly met."

Grimké looked forward to his new assignment. He was concerned about the welfare of his nine-year-old daughter, but his brother agreed to care for her while he was in the Dominican Republic. The job was just too good to pass up, holding as it did the promise of a long public career, and with the demise of the *Hub*, there was little to keep Archibald in Boston. Sadly, however, the Senate allowed his nomination to die, even though other Cleveland appointments were approved. Grimké's abandonment of the Republican party was partly responsible for this outcome, for he had made enemies of many former supporters, including Massachusetts Senator George F. Hoar, when he switched his party allegiance. Hoar wanted to make it clear that such independence, and the support Grimké had earlier shown for Republican reformers, would not go unpunished. As one commentator noted at the time, "Mr. Grimké is a scholarly gentleman, of rare refinement and purity of character also. This makes the case all the worse. He is all the more dangerous [an] example to set before the people."

Disappointed, Grimké recommitted himself to political work. In the 1890 election, he worked with Codman for the Democrats, speaking against the Republicans for their stand on the tariff and criticizing his former Harvard classmate Henry Cabot Lodge for his support of the Force Bill, which was meant to protect black voting rights in the South. Believing that political work and party loyalty were the keys to winning equal rights, Grimké knew that his stand on the Force Bill would be controversial within the black community, but he saw it as a simple matter of partisan politics: as he quickly argued, the bill's real purpose was not to protect black voting rights but to regain a Republican majority in the South. He would maintain this position, though in fact he would do little to publicize his opposition to Lodge either in the press or in public speeches.

With his law practice now all but abandoned and his future political career uncertain, Grimké set out on a new course. In 1890, he engaged in a debate with the paleontologist Edward D. Cope, who argued that certain racial characteristics made African Americans particularly immune to the "civilizing" aspects of American culture: they would thus always, he said, be on the outside of that culture, looking in. Grimké angrily rejected Cope's assertion in the pages of *Open Court*, an intellectual journal, noting the thrift and industriousness of black Americans and citing their contribution to American economic growth. His response was part condemnation, part defense. His most telling denunciation was of Cope's claim that the "Indo-European races" should actually take pride in their prejudice, since it reflected the reality of nature's design. Grimké dismissed this view as preposterous and called it "the worst exploitation imaginable."

In the early years of the new decade, Archibald Grimké's reputation as a leading spokesman for African Americans was enhanced by his increased public profile. Always a popular speaker, he now focused much of his effort on the writing of essays and monographs on a variety of political issues. In May 1890, he delivered an address at Boston's Tremont Temple entitled "The Opening Up of Africa," in which he extolled the industrial and agricultural potential of that continent and its people. In 1891, he published a well-received essay on anti-Semitism, which branded the pogroms then under way in Russia a "crime of international proportions." That same year, he came out with a biography of William Lloyd Garrison, to be followed the next year by one of the Massachusetts senator and abolitionist firebrand Charles Sumner. The books were published as part of Funk & Wagnalls' American Reformer Series, to much praise and widespread popularity.

In his two biographies, Grimké developed the activist ideas that would mark his later years. At the center of his thinking was his view that for all of Garrison's and Sumner's efforts, equal rights had not yet been won. The battle those men had fought, he wrote, must be continued, but from now on by black Americans. In writing of Garrison, he noted the disappointment of that crusader's last years:

> He watched with stern and vigilant eye, and bleeding heart the new rebellion at the South whose purpose was the nullification of the civil and political rights of the blacks, and the overthrow of military rule of the National Government in the Southern states. . . . The last written words of his, addressed to the public, were words in defence of the race to whose freedom he had devoted his life—words which, trumpet-tongued raised anew the rally-cry of "Liberty and equal rights for each, for all, and for ever, wherever the lot of man is cast within our broad domains."

In June 1892, Archibald Grimké announced his support for Grover Cleveland, who, after a four-year absence, had once again become the standard-bearer of the Democratic party, this time in its fight against Benjamin Harrison. Grimké worked vigorously in the black community for Cleveland's election, arguing that his tariff policies represented the best hope for black advancement. When Cleveland was elected in November, Grimké was overjoyed, since it meant that his appointment as consul in Santo Domingo would be revived. Charles Codman was once again instrumental in putting Grimké's name before Cleveland. Cleveland hesitated for two years, concerned that Grimké was too controversial among Republicans to gain their assent, but finally, in July 1894, he passed the nomination on to the Senate. Grimké's appointment was approved, without undue debate, on June 30. He was at last to join the distinguished ranks of black diplomats who had served the United States, among them Frederick Douglass, once the American representative in Haiti.

Archibald Grimké's appointment as consul in Santo Domingo, along with his authorship of biographies of Garrison and Sumner, provided a fitting coda to his first years as a political force in the black community. During this period, he had been influenced by the views of his two famous aunts and by those of the old-line abolitionists of the Northeast, most of whom were adherents of William Lloyd Garrison's radical "moralistic" form of abolitionism. But unlike Garrison, and unlike his own brother Francis (who always regarded political efforts to gain equal rights with skepticism), Archibald Grimké believed in the political process—in large part because he had learned that it *worked*. Of his two biographical subjects, Grimké believed that Sumner had actually been the more effective: he had overcome enormous political odds, Grimké argued, in establishing the foundation for Reconstruction. Now Garrison and Sumner were both gone, leaving Theodore Dwight Weld as Grimké's only real link to the past. And then, on February 3, 1895, Weld died at his home in Hyde Park. William Lloyd Garrison, Jr., gave his eulogy, remembering him as a man with a "spiritual nature, a logical mind, a sensitive conscience, moral courage," and an "eloquent tongue."

At his memorial, Weld was celebrated as a great abolitionist, but he had also been a great leader in the fight for equal rights. His passing formalized a change of leadership in that movement that had already been under way for a generation. The leadership of the crusade for equal rights now belonged to black Americans. While African American leaders would acknowledge their debt to the abolitionists over the next generation, the challenges they faced were far different from those posed in the decades leading up to the Civil War. For many, race prejudice seemed more pernicious than even slavery itself, for slavery was only its most obvious manifestation. But as the Grimké sisters used to say, it was not slavery or even race prejudice but *color* prejudice that was a pillar of American social relations. The evidence for this was embarrassingly clear to Archibald and Francis Grimké, for even those who had once spoken out most forcefully against slavery now counted themselves among the defenders of segregation. Elizabeth Cady Stanton was no exception.

Stanton was appalled that black males should be enfranchised by the Fifteenth Amendment while women were ignored. She had a right to be angry, but her reaction to the language of the amendment was vicious, narrow-minded, and racist. "The best interests of the nation demand that we outweigh this incoming pauperism, ignorance, and degradation, with the wealth, education, and refinement of the women of the republic," she had said in the aftermath of the Civil War. While Stanton would one day atone for those bitter words, the leaders of the women's movement nonetheless spent three decades debating whether in tying their fortunes to the rights of black Americans, they risked dampening public support for women's rights. By the end of the century, they would resolve that question: in order to gain Southern backing for the woman suffrage movement, the women's movement would put aside the crusade for equal rights and turn its back on black America.

With the death of Theodore Weld, Archibald Grimké resolved to strike out on his own. He paid tribute to the past, but he now began to focus more closely on uniquely black problems. Economic questions continued to interest him, but like most black leaders, he was compelled to spend most of his time responding to the "philosophy" of black inferiority. Events conspired to push him further and further away from his old identity as a black moderate at ease in a white society; slowly, like his brother Francis, he was being transformed into an agitator. He was well positioned for his new role: his name was well known to black Americans, and at the age of forty-five, he was viewed as one of his community's most respected leaders.

Archibald Grimké's new sense of himself was highlighted by his appointment as consul in Santo Domingo. He was breaking his ties to his past. As if to emphasize that, three weeks after the death of Theodore Dwight Weld, Archibald's mother, Nancy Weston Grimké, died in Washington. He and his brother, weighed down by grief, buried her and packed up her few belongings. They saved a picture of her seated in a rocker, silver-eyed, staring back at the camera. She looks, in the photo, just as she was said to be all of her life: dedicated and serious, strong and vital. It was hard for Archibald and Francis to believe that she was dead. The week after her death, they received a letter from their brother John, in Florida. He was sorry their mother had died, he said, but he would not be coming north for the funeral.

In October 1895, Archibald Grimké closed up his home in Hyde Park and traveled to Washington, where he was confirmed as America's new consul in Santo Domingo. As usual, he stayed in Washington with his brother Francis and Francis's wife, Charlotte, and ascertained that the arrangements he had made with them for the care of his daughter—his "Nana"—were to everyone's liking. He visited Francis's church and heard two of his sermons. Shortly thereafter, he boarded a ship for Santo Domingo and his new life. He arrived on November 16, 1895, and took up residence in a large home owned by an American planter. He was now the most important American in the Dominican Republic, a nation settled and dominated by people of African descent—and a nation in which there seemed to be not one hint of racial antagonism. Archibald Grimké was excited by his new challenge, though he was uneasy about leaving America at a time when the black community most needed strong leadership. He held to his principles and followed his political course: economic advancement offered the best hope for black progress, he had always said. As he took up his new position in Santo Domingo, he still believed that was true. But he was beginning to have doubts. Perhaps racial hatreds were simply too deep to be healed by such simple nostrums as economic progress; perhaps, after all, African Americans, no matter how willing they might be to participate in American society, would simply not be allowed to do so.

Across America, other black leaders were also debating how best to respond to the race hate that seemed to be affecting America. Frustrated and angry, many Americans blamed the violence on a lack of leadership in the black community. African Americans yearned for a new champion, someone who was articulate and strong. They could no longer count on Frederick Douglass, whose era had passed and who had only three years to live. In Tuskegee, Alabama, Booker T. Washington believed that he could point the way to the future. What he proposed was that white America and black America forge a common strategy—a "compromise." Blacks would forget about equal rights, accept their politically inferior position in the South, bend to Jim Crow, and remain, in Francis Grimké's words, "sinfully silent"—if only whites would stop murdering them. Washington knew his idea was controversial, but he thought it would work. At the very least, he felt, it would unite black America behind a common purpose.

He would never be more wrong.

FOURTEEN

"... the means which God uses to arouse the sleeping conscience"

The crowd that gathered inside the huge pavilion to witness Booker T. Washington open the Cotton States International Exhibition in Atlanta, on May 18, 1895, did not realize that the speech it was about to hear would make history. Washington was well known as a black educator, but the invitation that the sponsoring committee had issued was unusual: in an age of expositions—the massive Chicago Columbian Exposition of 1892 had drawn millions of visitors—speakers were never invited to hold forth at such ceremonies. Washington was the first. After a short but polite introduction, he began his address. As with the Grimké sisters nearly six decades before, most of those who had come to listen to Washington were motivated by simple curiosity. Many in the crowd had never heard a black man speak in public.

Washington opened his remarks by thanking the organizers for their invitation and praising the exposition for its recognition of the labors of Southern blacks. Then his address took an unexpected turn as he bluntly alluded to the topic of race relations in the South. Washington's listeners undoubtedly feared that he would condemn white Southerners for their bitter reaction to the Civil War and Reconstruction, but if so, they were pleasantly surprised: he had nothing but praise for the South. "It is well to bear in mind," he said in clear and even tones, "that whatever other sins the South may be called to bear, when it comes to business, pure and simple, it is in the South that the Negro is given a man's chance in the commercial world, and in nothing is this exposition more eloquent than in emphasizing this chance."

That statement alone would have been enough to bring down criticism on Washington from the black community, for the facts of Southern business showed that of all the peoples in the South, black Americans were the last to get "a man's chance." Washington went on to issue a special plea, wrapped inside a folktale about a ship's captain who, desperate for water for his crew, does not realize that all he needs to do is lower a bucket over the side—for while he believes his ship is marooned in the middle of an unforgiving ocean, it is actually drifting just outside the mouth of the Amazon River, where fresh water is plentiful. So, too, Washington said, white Southerners should look to their black neighbors for new markets, cheap and efficient labor, industriousness, and loyalty. This was especially important in the midst of an economic crisis. "Cast down your bucket where you are," Washington implored his white listeners.

> Cast it down among the eight millions of Negroes whose habits you know, whose fidelity and love you have tested in days when to have proved treacherous meant the ruin of your firesides. Cast down your bucket among these people who have, without strikes and labour wars, tilled your fields, cleared your forests, builded your railroads and cities, and brought forth treasures from the bowels of the earth, and helped make possible this magnificent representation of the progress of the South. Casting down your bucket among my people, helping and encouraging them as you are doing on these grounds, and to education of head, hand, and heart, you will find that they will buy your surplus land, make blossom the waste places in your fields, and run your factories. While doing this, you can be sure in the future, as in the past, that you and your families will be surrounded by the most patient, faithful, law-abiding, and unresentful people that the world has yet seen.

Many black Americans agreed with Washington; they loved the South and could think of living nowhere else. It was their home. But in Atlanta, Washington went well beyond such an expression of love for his region, in an attempt to ameliorate the deep racial biases infecting the nation. If black Americans were to live in the South, Washington believed, they had to live in security and, by his reasoning, at peace with Southern customs. In the next section of his speech, Washington proposed an accommodation that was to remain a subject of controversy until the end of his life. It is still so today.

> As we have proved our loyalty to you in the past, in nursing your children, watching by the sick-bed of your mothers and fathers, and often following them with tear-dimmed eyes to their graves, so in the future, in our humble way, we shall stand by you with a devotion that no foreigner can approach, ready to lay down our lives, if need be, in defense of yours, interlacing our industrial, commercial, civil, and religious life with yours in a way that shall make the interests of both races one. In all things that are purely social we can be as separate as fingers, yet one as the hand in all things essential to mutual progress.

This last remark, that blacks and whites could "be as separate as fingers" and yet act "one as the hand," would be repeated again and again over the next two decades and cited as a virtual acceptance not only of segregation but of white supremacy. Washington explicitly rejected political action as a means of achieving equal rights. He called instead for a retreat: if equal rights were realized, he said, it would be as a natural outgrowth of economic progress, not through the enforcement of federal law. "The wisest among my race," he said, looking out at the hushed crowd, "understand that the agitation of questions of social equality is the extremist folly, and that progress in the enjoyment of all the privileges that will come to us must be the result of severe and constant struggle rather than of artificial forcing. No race that has anything to contribute to the markets of the world is long in any degree ostracized. It is important and right that all privileges of the law be ours, but it is vastly more important that we be prepared for the exercise of these privileges."

Washington finished his address by once again extolling the South, then took his seat to sustained applause, which grew and grew until it reached enormous proportions. The crowd stood in awe of his address and marveled at the eloquence of his presentation. From the back of the room came a rustle and then a stormy rush, and out of the standing crowd appeared Howell Clark, the editor of the *Atlanta Constitution*, who climbed up onto the platform next to Washington, pointed dramatically at him, and triumphantly stated, "That man's speech is the beginning of a moral revolution in America." Two days later, President Grover Cleveland grasped Washington's hand upon meeting him and congratulated him on his well-chosen words. From all over the nation, praise for Washington poured into his office at Tuskegee.

Washington was proposing nothing less than a great racial compromise engineered between blacks and whites. In the words of W. E. B. Du Bois, the brilliant black educator and writer who was then teaching at Wilberforce University in Ohio, "Here might be the basis of a real settlement between whites and blacks in the South, if the South opened to the Negroes the doors of economic opportunity and the Negroes cooperated with the white South in political sympathy." Du Bois knew that Washington's "Atlanta Compromise" might backfire, that "nigger-hating America" (as Du Bois would later put it) might take his offer as a license to continue enforcing the violent separation of blacks and whites. But Du Bois believed that black America, now "pushed to the wall," had no choice.

Francis Grimké added his own voice to the chorus of praise for Washington, writing the "Wizard of Tuskegee" a note of congratulations. For the next two years, Grimké would maintain his support for Washington's proposal. Speaking at a series of yearly conferences on black issues held at the Hampton Institute, Grimké expanded on the philosophy by repeating his assertion that black Americans could best become full participants in the nation's life by building strong families based on firm religious principles. "Here is the key to the future," he wrote, "and that key will respond to no touch but our own. White men cannot help us except in an indirect way. We have got to work out our own salvation." Grimké's endorsement of Washington, couched in moral terms, was strongly seconded by other black leaders.

But by 1898, the praise for Washington would cease, and two of his major supporters and public defenders, W. E. B. Du Bois and Francis Grimké, would turn against him. The criticism of Du Bois and Grimké emerged from their experience and background as members of the black community's intellectual elite, a group that came to be called the talented tenth. It was not so much Washington's words that caused problems (for many black leaders still supported his views) as the fact that he used his notoriety to cast aspersions on black intellectuals—those, that is, who had not been educated at Tuskegee Institute or the other black industrial

schools. Anger and irritation now greeted many of Washington's pronouncements on education, for it seemed at times as if he were poking
fun at his own race, and most especially at men such as Du Bois and the
Grimké brothers. The "proud fop with his beaver hat, kid gloves, and
walking cane," said Washington, hurt black Americans more than any
racial bias. Nor was he above making jokes about the "darkies," words
that brought laughs from appreciative white audiences.

Washington and his "Tuskegee Machine" were thus pitted against the
talented tenth, an elite group that counted among its members Du Bois,
Paul Laurence Dunbar, Howard University philosophy professor Kelly
Miller, Cleveland author Charles Chesnutt, William Monroe Trotter,
Archibald and Francis Grimké, and many others. The bitter struggle
over who should lead the black community and what strategy should be
followed to secure equal rights began just three years after Washington
offered his "Atlanta Compromise." That struggle would be resolved only
two decades later, with the establishment of the National Association for
the Advancement of Colored People, the first truly united, national black
political organization. The Grimké brothers were at the center of the debate that swirled around Washington and his views for the next twenty
years.

Archibald Grimké proved to be a surprisingly good diplomat and an
adept negotiator. After arriving in Santo Domingo, he met frequently
with General Ulises Heureaux, the country's president, who had made a
name for himself as a military commander. Heureaux kept an iron grip
on the country, navigating a delicate course toward full independence
from American influence even as he sought out American investments.
Grimké served as an intermediary in Heureaux's dealings with investors,
attempting to gain the best financial position for U.S. businesses while at
the same time promoting contacts that could provide economic benefits
and opportunities for Dominican citizens. He successfully negotiated a
number of such economic agreements, in the process building a strong
working relationship with Heureaux that he believed would serve as a
model for future relations between the United States and the multiracial
countries of the Caribbean, with their mix of African, Indian, and Spanish peoples.

Grimké had no illusions about Heureaux. He knew that the general
had fought his way up the country's political ladder through the force

of his military experience and his willingness to eliminate any opposition to his rule. He was ruthless, cold, and single-minded. But Grimké liked Heureaux personally and believed that his hold on his office offered the best hope of alleviating the country's crushing poverty. The two men became friends and collaborated closely in shaping the Dominican Republic's foreign policy. Grimké agreed with Heureaux that American expansion in the Caribbean could signal a setback for the region's economic and political growth, which had to be self-determined. The president depended on the American consul to help him stop the trend, for he knew he would have little recourse if the United States decided to make his country a protectorate: his government was too weak and his country too poor to defend themselves.

Grimké supported Heureaux's views and felt it was particularly important that multiracial nations be held up as examples of what America could become. If the United States dominated the life of Heureaux's republic, then all hope for racial peace would be lost. To Grimké's mind, while the U.S. would bring political stability to Santo Domingo, it would also bring "colorphobia." He wrote, "There will appear for the first time there also cruel caste distinction, race contempt and insolence and plenty of them, race rule, inequality and oppression and no end of them, such as curse to-day the colored people of the United States." Grimké's experience in the Dominican Republic convinced him that it was possible for blacks and whites to live peacefully together in the same society. In many ways, he believed, the Dominican Republic could serve as a useful model for racially obsessed Americans.

Archibald Grimké commented on the possibility of racial peace in a letter he wrote to his brother after attending an official state ball in Santo Domingo. "There is not the slightest hint on such an occasion of the existence of such a thing as prejudice against color, not even among the Americans," he noted. "You will hardly credit it that after they live here a while they (the Americans) seem to lose their diabolic ability of detecting the presence of a drop of black blood in one of us. The gift seems to be reversed for they seem to have a marvelous faculty for finding in one of us a drop of white blood. And a few drops of this blood have a wonderfully whitening effect."

Grimké's tenure as consul in Santo Domingo passed without incident, but his personal life was troubled during this period. His daughter, Angelina, fourteen when he left, argued with Francis and Charlotte, who complained in letters to Archibald that she was unruly. Angelina's father was disappointed but not surprised by this report, as she had shown such "willfulness" before. He responded to this crisis by writing her long letters urging her to focus on her education and to show more respect for other members of her family. Concerned about her having to spend some of the most important years of her life without her father, Archibald considered sending for her but quickly decided it was out of the question: Santo Domingo was simply too dangerous for a teenage girl. And, too, he decided against returning to the United States to straighten things out, instead hoping that the differences between his daughter and her uncle and aunt would somehow resolve themselves. That hope was shattered, however, in June 1895, when Charlotte wrote that she and Francis could not keep Angelina another year. Her presence in the Grimké household in Washington, she said, was unbearable. Archibald was embarrassed. "I had hoped against hope that you would disappoint this dread of mine & prove your self in every respect worthy to live in such a city as Washington," he told Angelina in a letter, "[and] that you would try to be a comfort & joy in the home of your uncle & aunt. I know now that you have been neither, my dear child."

In successive letters, he tried to heal the wounds between his brother and sister-in-law and his daughter. He reminded Angelina of her proud legacy, expressing his hopes for her future in tones reminiscent of those used by earlier generations of Grimkés who had thought of themselves in noble terms: "You don't want to be like every Tom, Dick & Harry of a shopgirl of the mentally weak & empty pated simpletons of the feminine world, I know well." He was thinking here of the examples set by his aunts Angelina and Sarah, by Charlotte Forten, and by his own mother, Nancy Weston Grimké, all women of prodigious ambition and accomplishment. But his long, moralizing letters did little good. Finally, with no other choice, and wanting to spare his brother and his brother's wife an embarrassing confrontation with his daughter, he sent Angelina to the Northfield Academy in Minnesota, where she was enrolled in 1896.

Archibald was concerned about his daughter, but not so much so that he intended to give up his position as the American representative in Santo Domingo. Indeed, he began working for his reappointment well before he was due to return to Washington. But the election of Republican William McKinley, in 1896, made the extension of Grimké's consulship seem less likely. In May 1897, Francis wrote to President McKinley's secretary of the Navy, John Long, seeking his brother's reappointment; the following January, Archibald received word from Washington that McKinley thought he had done a good job in Santo Domingo and that his loyalty to the Democratic party would not hurt his chances of retaining his post under the Republican administration. But then, in March, McKinley changed course and appointed a Republican stalwart, Campbell G. Maxwell, as the new consul. In July, Archie turned over his duties to Maxwell and sailed for Washington. Although he would be known as the Honorable Archibald Grimké for the rest of his life, his days as a diplomat were over.

———

After Archibald Grimké returned to the United States, he divided his time equally between Washington and Boston, living with Francis and Charlotte in Washington for months at a time and then moving to Boston, where he spent weeks boarding in the house of a colleague. Grimké had both feet in two different worlds: the all-black community of segregated Washington and the still racially mixed elite society of Boston. One of his first acts was to join the American Negro Academy (founded by his brother Francis, among others), a forum for black intellectuals "devoted to literary, statistical, ethnographical, folk-lore investigation, pertaining wholly and entirely to Africa and to the world-wide Negro race." In time, the American Negro Academy would become a nexus of discontent for those disenchanted with Washington's accommodationist philosophy, as well as a meeting ground for those who feared the growing power of the Tuskegee Machine.

By joining the academy, Archibald Grimké immersed himself in the world of black politics. His diplomatic experience, his political background, and his increasingly militant views made him a popular speaker. Gone were the days when he had focused on the tariff; now he spoke bluntly about the crisis facing black America in the form of lynching, race riots, color prejudice, and segregation. He quickly became known for his strident and unbending criticism of white America's tolerance of antiblack violence. Soon after his arrival from the Dominican Republic, he gave an address at Boston's People's Temple in which he argued that it was up to white Northerners to police their white-supremacist cousins: "If thou dost not soon kill the mob," he said, "the mob will ultimately make an end in the North as it has already done in the South of all the good [that] men value highest in American character, institutions and civilization."

Francis Grimké, meanwhile, took the same harsh tone in defending black rights. While he continued to talk about the need to build strong families and reiterated his oft-stated hatred of alcohol, his sermons became increasingly political and outspoken. Like his brother, he found himself reacting to white attacks on black America by adopting the language of a militant. Francis Grimké's transformation from a black moderate who counseled patience and self-improvement had begun during a national meeting of Presbyterian ministers, called in an effort to heal the North-South division in the church. Grimké sharply criticized the church's leadership for its "cringing spirit" and willingness to overlook the mistreatment of black Americans in the South. "They are so anxious for union," he said of the Presbyterian leader, "that they are willing to purchase it at any sacrifice of their colored brethren which will gratify the prejudice of the South." He bitterly told friends that support of segregation in the name of church peace was simply a disguise for white supremacy. He paraphrased William Lloyd Garrison in defending his own position: "Let the right be done," he exclaimed, "though the heavens should fall."

Francis Grimké was the first black leader to question Booker T. Washington's views, and the first to map out a credible black response to white supremacy. In early 1898, after consulting with his brother Archibald, Francis wrote out a series of sermons on the "Atlanta Compromise," then began a campaign in the black community to have them circulated. Grimké's four sermons on Washington and the Tuskegee Machine were ground-breaking for him, containing words he had never before uttered in public. He delivered the first of them at the end of November 1898. Although never mentioning Washington by name, Grimké nonetheless made his views on Washington's accommodationist philosophy unambiguous. He denounced any compromise with racists and, in the last sermon of the four, called on the black community to adopt measures of self-defense. But his most combative and pointed remarks were aimed directly at Washington:

> Hundreds of the men of our race have laid their lives down on Southern soil in vindication of their rights as American citizens. And shall we be told, and by black men, too, that the sacred cause for which they poured out their life's blood is to be relinquished, that the white ruffians who shot them down were justified, that it was just what was to have been expected, and therefore we have no reasonable ground for complaint?

Away with such treasonable utterances—treason to God, treason to man, treason to free institutions, treason to the spirit of
an enlightened and Christian sentiment.

Grimké closed in on his target, signaling his congregants that just as
he himself had transformed his own views, so must they change theirs.
Black leaders who glibly issued apologies for their race, referred to other
blacks as "darkies," or sought to capture the respect of white America
through a shuffling acquiescence to racist policies, Grimké said, were be-
trayers of black rights and enemies of liberty. What was needed was a
new response to racism. Just as Sarah and Angelina Grimké had once defended John Brown, Francis Grimké now said that violence was a natural
and understandable reaction to oppression. "I am not counseling violence," he explained. "I am not saying that it is a wise thing for the Negro
to resort to violence; but I am saying that sometimes violence is the
means which God uses to arouse the sleeping conscience. I trust that it
may not be necessary, but if it must come, then I for one say, let it come,
and the sooner it comes, the better."

Warming to his subject, Grimké went on to accuse those who supported
Washington of advocating a "pernicious doctrine" of self-effacement. "A
race that permits itself to be trampled upon will be trampled upon. A
race that goes around with hat in hand, in a cringing attitude[,] is sure to
be an object of contempt. Let us here, today, one and all of us, before
God—in this sacred place [—] pledge ourselves to eternal hostility to any
teaching that would put the Negro in such an attitude. Be assured that
nothing is to be gained by compromising with evil."

———

The black community's response to Francis Grimké's criticism was immediate and overwhelming. Black leaders who had remained silent for
the three years following Washington's Atlanta speech now flocked to
endorse Grimké's views. Slowly, a core group of Washington antagonists
was formed around Grimké, who was now seen, along with his brother
Archibald, as providing an alternative to Washington's leadership. Even
as Francis was speaking out against the policy of accommodation in the
black community of Washington, Archibald Grimké was speaking out
on the lynching crisis in Boston, in a deliberate attempt to expand on his
brother's new strategy of confrontation. Archibald called on black
Americans to use every means at their disposal to end racial injustice

and, like his brother, targeted Booker T. Washington for special criticism. Like Francis, Archibald avoided mentioning Washington by name,
though his pointed words left no doubt as to his sentiments. "Let me not
be understood by what I am about to say as in any way countenancing
even by implication the new folly which has been launched as the cure-
all of our woes," he wrote in a commentary entitled "Lessons of the
Hour," "namely our voluntary political self-effacement in the South.
Palsied by the parricidal hand of one of us, that lifts a pen at this moment
of our deepest agony to utter one treacherous word against his race. May
the blood in its veins turn to the color of ink, and the ink to the tint of
blood before it commit so unnatural, so foul a deed."

Washington reciprocated. Ignoring Francis Grimké's public attacks
on him, Washington wrote to Archibald to compliment him on his anti-
lynching remarks in Boston. The letter made it clear that like the
Grimkés, Washington opposed mob violence. Like the Grimkés, he said,
he was searching for a creative black response to the "crisis." At first,
Archibald was puzzled by Washington's overture, but then he inter-
preted it as the Tuskegeean's way of protecting his hold on the black leadership. Washington, he believed, was willing to overlook the Grimké
brothers' condemnation of him for the sake of black solidarity. It was
in all of their interests to prevent an outright break, or at least to paper
over their differences. Neither Archibald nor Francis had the political
strength to win a pitched battle against the Tuskegee Machine and
Washington, for his part, could not afford a break with the talented
tenth, however much he criticized its members' "foppery."

The exchange between Archibald Grimké and Booker T. Washington
continued for two years after Francis Grimké's condemnation of Washington in his 1898 sermons. The correspondence reflected the complex
relationship between the two increasingly divergent camps—the talented
tenth and the Tuskegee Machine—as each side criticized the other in
public, sometimes harshly, while maintaining amiable relations with it in
private. It was a delicate, highly charged political dance, shot through
with feelings of vulnerability and isolation and the realization that the
white community would almost certainly use the divisions in the black
leadership to its own ends.

Modern historians agree that Washington's views were far more complex than his Atlanta Exposition address suggested. While he was ac-
commodating and moderate in public, they point out, he also worked
diligently behind the scenes to mitigate the worst excesses of white

racism. This is not simply historical hindsight, adopted to explain away an embarrassing policy: the Grimké brothers, W. E. B. Du Bois, William Monroe Trotter, and many others believed that Washington was far less a "white man's black man" than he was a political realist. Washington was no coward. He was convinced that African Americans would be best served by adopting a long-term strategy designed to foster their identity and ensure their continuation as a community. In 1900, it was not black America's credibility that was at stake, but its very survival. Francis and Archibald Grimké carefully acknowledged this reality, but they wanted Washington to move toward a more radical position. They believed it was possible for black America to advance on all fronts at once, to appear accommodationist in principle while being confrontational in practice. The strategy was nuanced: without an aggressive push for equal rights, the Grimké brothers felt, any enhancement of black identity and black economic opportunity was impossible.

The Grimkés themselves best symbolized this middle road, a philosophy falling somewhere between Washington's accommodationist views and the opinions of the Boston "radicals" led by the increasingly shrill William Monroe Trotter. In their hearts, the Grimkés sympathized with Washington's approach. Like him, and unlike either Trotter or W. E. B. Du Bois, the Grimkés were themselves former slaves and understood the reality of black life in America in a way that many other members of the talented tenth never could: dressed in livery as young boys in Charleston, they nursed their hatred and prepared for their day of freedom. That was essentially what Washington was doing now, and like him, the Grimkés knew that for many black Americans, even in 1898, the choice was between acquiescence and the workhouse. It would take time to build up the black community, establish a unique black identity, and solidify black political power.

It was that bond, then, that led Archibald and Francis Grimké to maintain close personal ties to Washington, and though both disagreed with him in public, and even exchanged harsh words with him in private, neither sought a complete break with him. He was one of them, and more like them than either Trotter or Du Bois. In 1901, Archibald Grimké detailed his opinions about the Wizard of Tuskegee in a public paper, a sophisticated and dramatic recounting of the Denmark Vesey Conspiracy. Entitled "Right on the Scaffold; or the Martyrs of 1822," it was the first published account of Vesey's plan to incite a slave insurrection in Charleston. The narrative was larded with anecdotes Archibald had heard from his aunts and their friends, and its research backed by records he had had sent from Charleston.

The real importance of Archibald Grimké's paper on Vesey lay in its description of Vesey's attitude toward white Charlestonians. Vesey, Grimké wrote, knew that he had to be careful in hatching his plot because "his oppressors were strong" and "he was weak." The more obedient he appeared to be, and the more comfortable in Charleston's white-dominated community, the more likely it was that his conspiracy would succeed. He needed to exercise "discretion and self-control," Grimké pointedly noted. Vesey was a man, Grimké said, who had a habit of "smiling and fawning on unjust and cruel power" until the moment came to strike: he nearly fooled white Charleston by seeming to be the shuffling "Cuffey" of Southern lore, even as he raged and plotted against white oppression and harbored a "passionate hope for freedom." That same tactic, Grimké believed, could be used in 1901. But it was one thing to understand or even approve of Vesey's strategy, and quite another to accept Washington as the right man to execute it. Grimké did not believe Washington was that man.

Beginning at the turn of the century, therefore, Archibald Grimké launched a program aimed at undermining the power of the Tuskegee Machine. It was a bald bid for black leadership. In what would come to be known within the African American community as the great debate—between the forces of Booker T. Washington and the talented tenth—Grimké fired the first salvo. During an appearance at Washington's alma mater, the Hampton Institute, Grimké gave a paper entitled "Modern Industrialism and the Negroes of the United States." His argument attacked the centerpiece of Washington's philosophy: the notion that black Americans could gain respectability through industrial training and win equal rights by providing labor for white America. The problem with that view, Grimké argued, was that it overlooked the "inveterate hostility" of white America toward blacks. Grimké's language was militant and uncompromising. Expanding on the same theme in "The Negroes' Case Against the Republic," he characterized white attitudes as condemning black Americans to be "forever an alien race, an inferior race, a servile race, allowed to live here in strict subordination and subjection of the white race."

In these essays, Grimké provided a telling, point-by-point refutation of Washington's views, especially those detailed in his Atlanta Exposition speech and during his May 1900 appearance before Francis Grimké's Bethel Literary and Historical Association. "Blood proves thicker than water," Archibald wrote. "In any contest between the white race and the black race in this country, you will find all white men like birds of a feather, flocking together regardless of all standards of right and ethics or religion." He developed this theme even further on January 1, 1901, before a racially mixed crowd of prominent Bostonians gathered to commemorate the signing of Lincoln's Emancipation Proclamation. His address traced the historical development of post–Civil War racism, highlighted the great betrayal of 1877, and dramatically recounted the rise of mob rule in the South. And then Grimké, the well-dressed and articulate good Democrat, shocked the audience with his conclusion, which seemed less a celebration of Lincoln than a condemnation of white America. "On the race question," he said, his voice rising, "on the race question, a white man is a white man. Scratch the skin of a Republican or a Democrat and you will find close to the surface race prejudice."

Washington did not respond directly to Grimké, but he paid special heed to his public utterances. Fearful of a full-scale and irretrievable break with Grimké and the rest of the talented tenth, Washington took every opportunity to promote his views, while never deigning to suggest that a major segment of black America disagreed with him. In truth, the Washington-Grimké exchange was far less a debate than a long-distance presentation of competing monologues, but by 1903, it was clear that the two leaders were set on a collision course that threatened to split America's black leadership. It was not so much that Washington disagreed with Grimké's views (though he surely did), as that he resented the other man's purposeful attempt to offer an institutional alternative to the Tuskegee Machine. It was bad enough that Grimké's public profile cut into Washington's own prestige, but his efforts to establish another public forum for the exchange of ideas on the future of black-white relations—whether in Washington or in Boston—threatened the prominent position held by the Tuskegee Institute. And *that* Washington could not tolerate.

Archibald Grimké understood that Washington's vulnerability consisted in his desire not only to maintain his own public standing but also to assure the continuation of the Tuskegee Institute's role as the premier

arbiter of black political views. With that in mind, and mimicking his
brother Francis's founding of a forum for black educators and intellectuals in Washington, Archibald Grimké and a group of prominent black
Bostonians in early 1901 issued an invitation to their city's leading black
intellectuals to establish a local "literary" committee. Pointedly, the invitations were presented exclusively to black Bostonians known to be critics of Booker T. Washington, including William Monroe Trotter, Pauline
Hopkins, Granville Martin, Clement Morgan, William H. Scott, and
George W. Forbes, each a formidable and vocal presence in the black
community. In forming the Boston Literary and Historical Association,
Grimké wanted to ensure that his allies could also influence the larger
black community outside Boston. He therefore worked particularly hard
to court Trotter, whose *Guardian* newspaper had acquired a national
following.

It was only after the formation of the Boston group that Washington
publicly criticized Grimké's views and castigated him at rallies protesting black disenfranchisement. Grimké responded privately, asking
Washington in a letter to abandon his defense of Southern literacy and
property laws that marked a reversal of black political rights. He pointed
to a Washington speech that had praised Southern legislators for drafting
new state constitutions dictating that black rights were to be dependent
on blacks' possession of "property, intelligence, character, and thrift."
Washington dismissed the letter, but fearing that a break between him
and the Grimkés might become too conspicuous, he shifted his strategy
and invited Archibald and Francis to visit him at Tuskegee. The invitation, and Washington's hope for a quiet settlement of the dispute, were
ignored by both Grimké brothers. It was just as the Grimké-Washington
feud was reaching its apogee, in mid-1903, that W. E. B. Du Bois, the nation's newest voice for black rights, published *The Souls of Black Folk*,
which electrified the black community and highlighted the increasingly
public falling-out between Archibald Grimké and Washington. The
book contained a scathing attack on Washington's philosophy:

> The plain result of the attitude of mind of those who, in their
> advocacy of industrial schools, the unimportance of suffrage
> and civil rights and conciliation, have been significantly silent
> or evasive as to high training and the great principle of free
> self-respecting manhood for black folk—the plain result of
> this propaganda has been to help the cutting down of educa-

tional opportunity for Negro children, the legal disenfranchisement of nearly 5,000,000 Negroes, and a state of public
opinion which apologizes for lynching, listens complacently
to any insult or detraction directed against an eighth of the
population of the land, and silently allows a new slavery to rise
and clutch the South and paralyze the moral sense of a great
nation. . . .

This criticism was so provocative, so simply stated, and so powerfully
argued that its author was immediately propelled into a major leadership position in the black community and accorded a stature and reputation that could, if paralleled by the formation of a credible national
black organization, threaten Washington's ascendancy. From the moment *The Souls of Black Folk* was published, the division deepened between the Tuskegee Machine and the black intellectual elite represented
by the moniker "the talented tenth," with both sides vying more fiercely
than ever for the leadership of black America. The debate and the political struggle that Archibald Grimké had started would become so bitter
that their effects would be felt until Washington's death.

Washington's response to this threat was immediate. Although he affected the pose of an educated and sophisticated man, given to modesty
and great humility, he could be narrow-minded and vengeful in his personal relations. He had little moral compunction, therefore, about using
every stratagem he could devise to isolate both Grimké brothers, Trotter,
Du Bois, and others in the black community. A network of prestigious
local black economic groups, controlled by Washington and his supporters, made it clear that such naysayers were unwelcome at their meetings. Archibald and Francis Grimké were inclined to overlook such
slights, but the same could not be said of the volcanic William Monroe
Trotter, whose militant tone had established him as one of the leaders of
the anti-Washington camp.

Trotter, with Archibald Grimké's acquiescence, now attempted to in-
filtrate a number of pro-Washington African American organizations,
including the prestigious Afro-American Council, founded by T. Thomas
Fortune in 1890. The first attempt at stripping Washington of his leadership role had actually predated the publication of *The Souls of Black Folk*.
In 1902, when the Afro-American Council held its national meeting in
St. Paul, rumors circulated that a Grimké-Trotter slate of candidates for
the organization's leadership would stage a revolt. Washington was told

of the conspiracy and rallied his supporters. As it turned out, word of the plot had been exaggerated: neither Grimké nor Trotter yet had the power to launch a coup, and when it became apparent that they could not succeed, they called off the effort. But that did not keep Washington's close colleague Emmett Scott from crowing about the "victory" of the Wizard's political forces. "It was wonderful to see how completely your personality dominated everything at St. Paul," Scott wrote to Washington. On hearing reports of Washington's satisfaction at his victory, Trotter criticized him in the pages of the *Guardian*, pointing out that the Afro-American Council had been founded to defend black political rights—something that, as the editor gleefully noted, was not on the agenda of Booker T. Washington.

The stage was thus set for a second confrontation, during the organization's meeting in Louisville in 1903. In April, William Lewis, a trusted Washington lieutenant from Boston, traveled to Louisville with a delegation comprising Trotter, George W. Forbes, and William H. Ferris. In the course of the trip, Lewis learned of the others' intention to undermine Washington's leadership in the council. Informed of the plan, Washington again rallied his machine. Trouble began between Washington and Trotter on the first night of the meeting, when Trotter proposed that the council pass a resolution declaring that "agitation is the best means to secure our civil and political rights." The Tuskegee Machine rolled right over Trotter, and the resolution was defeated. From the podium, T. Thomas Fortune (a firm supporter of Washington's, in spite of his own earlier radicalism) gaveled the Boston delegation to silence. Beneath a portrait of Booker T. Washington overlooking the convention hall, Trotter and his Boston contingent made one last attempt to undermine the Tuskegeean's authority by objecting to the appearance of a pamphlet extolling his career. They were ignored by Fortune, who at one point publicly called Trotter a liar. Fortune was quickly reelected president, with few dissenting votes. Ecstatic over his easy victory, he told Washington, "The Boston gang, at least, know that I know how to boss their sort where brains and nerves are needed."

Most of the nation's black newspapers—the *Guardian*, of course, excepted—stood with Washington. Their views reflected those of Nashville businessman J. C. Napier, a well-known Washington supporter. "These young men who come from Boston," he wrote in a public commentary, "with their high notions of life, with their blood-thirsty speeches, would make it better by visiting the South, knowing something of the conditions of their people and preaching to them a gospel of peace." Washington, however, set a conciliatory tone. He appeared at the end of the Louisville convention and purposely tried to dampen the controversy. He called for "positive, constructive action" and "patience, self-control, and courage." Unmollified, Trotter, Grimké, and Du Bois pressed their attack. When it was announced that Washington would be appearing at a July 30 meeting of the Boston branch of the National Negro Business League, Trotter and the *Guardian* editorial board, including Grimké, published nine questions that they demanded that he answer during his appearance. The questions detailed pointed criticisms of Washington's views, and included: "Are you not actually upholding oppressing our race as a good thing for us, advocating peonage?," "Do you not know that the ballot is the only self-protection for any class of people in this country?," and "Don't you know you would help the race more by exposing the new form of slavery just outside the gates of Tuskegee than by preaching submission?"

A confrontation was inevitable. Trotter and Grimké carefully choreographed the first night of the meeting, which was to be held at a black church in Boston. They planned to pack the room with Washington antagonists, disrupt the proceedings, and demand that the speaker answer their questions. Unfortunately for them, the politically savvy T. Thomas Fortune was scheduled to chair the meeting and was prepared for the confrontation; he even invited it. He gaveled the meeting to order, stood solemnly during the opening prayer, and then deliberately (as the first order of business) noted that Booker T. Washington was due to give the opening keynote address. His announcement brought hisses from the audience. William Lewis, standing near Grimké in the front of the hall, spoke up, his voice ringing out over the crowd: "If there are any geese in the audience, they are privileged to retire." He then announced that if any "radicals" attempted to disrupt the meeting, they would be arrested. Finally, there was silence, but several minutes later, Granville Martin interrupted Fortune's remarks to demand that Washington answer the questions posed to him in the *Guardian*. Policemen, arrayed in a line at the back of the church, moved forward to arrest Martin. As pandemonium broke out, a Trotter ally, Bernard Charles, made his way to the podium and spread pepper near the speaker's lectern, which induced a coughing and spitting fit among Washington's lieutenants.

Martin was escorted from the hall by the police, and order was restored, but Trotter was enraged. When Washington was introduced, Trotter led the crowd in a chorus of boos. Standing on a chair, he waved a copy of the *Guardian*, insisting that Washington answer the "nine questions" it had put to him. At this point, Martin ran back into the hall and demanded to be heard. It took five policemen several minutes to subdue him and drag him from the church again. In the confusion, a fistfight broke out near the speaker's platform between supporters of the radicals and Washington's phalanx of supporters. One man was stabbed. Through all of this, William Monroe Trotter remained atop his chair, above the crowd, waving and shouting at Washington, who stood stone-faced at the front of the church. Washington allies began to chant, "Throw Trotter out the window, throw Trotter out the window," but they were unable to reach him, so they grabbed a number of his supporters instead to make good on their threats. They were stopped by a line of Boston policemen, who were desperately trying to get the crowd under control. At last, a group of Boston's finest arrested Trotter and handcuffed him, then escorted him from the church, loaded him into a carriage, and took him to a nearby police station, where he was booked on charges of disrupting a public meeting.

Washington's immediate reaction to the riot was to serve up his favorite speech, on self-respect and self-improvement, and issue a call for understanding and patience among black Americans. He seemed almost unconcerned with the growing controversy over his views, and winsomely surprised at any suggestion that his leadership was being questioned. He lightly waved off reporters' questions, sternly shook the hands of his supporters, and then went on his way, apparently unruffled by the tumult his presence had caused. In private, however, Washington was by turns deeply angered by and triumphant over what would come to be called the Boston Riot. He said in a letter to one supporter, "You will be glad to know that Trotter, Forbes, Grimké and two or three others, by their actions completely killed themselves among all classes, both white and colored, in Boston. Trotter was taken out of the church, in handcuffs, yelling like a baby."

Washington was right about the harm his detractors had done to their cause, but only as far as white America was concerned. The nation's newspapers were aghast at the reception accorded Washington in the black community. "If the Boston negro is not capable of understanding so able a representative of his race," the *St. Louis Post-Dispatch* editorialized, "what is to be expected of other Afro-Americans?" A Buffalo paper likened the riot to an "atavism suggestive of the Congo forests," while the *Boston Evening Transcript* pronounced its own judgment on the status of black America: "In no case is the old text, that a prophet is not without honor save in his own country, better exemplified than in the case of Booker T. Washington, whose work is appreciated and applauded even by the Negroes' hereditary oppressors, and whose person is persecuted only by his own race."

The trial of Trotter, Martin, and Bernard Charles was held on August 4, 1903. Among those testifying on Trotter's behalf was Archibald Grimké, who also led his defense team. The prosecution was aided in its efforts by some of Washington's closest protégés, including the black Bostonian William H. Lewis. Lewis's testimony focused on Trotter's ill will toward Washington and on his plans to disrupt the Boston meeting. The *Guardian* responded with a vicious personal attack on Lewis, charging that he was "colored for leadership and revenue only." After hearing the evidence, the court fined Charles twenty-five dollars and sentenced Trotter and Martin to thirty days in jail apiece. When Trotter and Martin appealed, Washington considered dropping his case against them, but the prospect of seeing the Boston radicals humbled, and Trotter in particular behind bars, proved too great a temptation for the Tuskegeean to resist. He had kept his own counsel and his temper for five years during "the great debate," but now his patience was at an end.

A second trial, this one of Trotter and Martin alone, began on October 2. Archibald Grimké was the most prominent witness for the defense. The only question at issue was whether or not the defendants had planned to disrupt the meeting beforehand—a claim the defendants denied. On October 8, the judge in the case upheld the sentence of thirty days in jail for the defendants, then advised them that their actions had been disgraceful, especially in a city where "we try to give them [black people] their rights." Back in Tuskegee, Washington privately celebrated Trotter's and Martin's incarceration, seeing it as a vindication of his beliefs. But within the black community, the points raised by the Boston radicals were gaining credibility. Slowly, as attacks on black Americans worsened, as race riots proliferated and lynchings continued unabated, black opinion turned against compromise and accommodation. Sensing, belatedly, that his unchallenged leadership of black America was in jeopardy, Washington lashed out in anger, blaming Archibald Grimké for starting the trouble with his series of speeches—his "great debate"—

Washington's program. Grimké, he now said, "represents a noisy, turbulent, and unscrupulous set of men."

———

At the age of fifty-four, Archibald Grimké was at the height of his powers: highly respected and known for his erudition and strong opinions, he was also articulate, a clear and forceful writer. In a little less than eight years, he had emerged as the head of the anti-Washington forces in the black community. Yet once again, his personal life was in shambles. After two years in Minnesota, his daughter, Angelina, had decided to continue her education at Wellesley College, which gave her father great pleasure; he had attended her graduation and celebrated her entrance into professional life. She lived with Archibald, Francis, and Charlotte in Washington, and pursued a career as a teacher in the city's schools. But in 1903, Angelina and her father nearly broke off their relationship for good after she announced that she was in love.

The news provoked an angry response from Archibald, who said he loathed her lover and pronounced him "a consummate ass." He gave his daughter a choice: she could choose her lover or she could choose him. For Angelina, there was no choice. The closest person to her in her life, and the person whom she admired above everyone else, was her father. She confided in him, advised him, listened to him, and considered him the source of all of her accomplishments. On his fifty-fifth birthday, she wrote him a poem that expressed all of that, as well as her deeper, more complex feelings about the mother who had abandoned her. There was no mistaking her affections and her commitment to Archibald, or her wish that they continue as father and daughter and as the best of friends. She promised him that she would devote herself to their relationship forever, even at the cost of her personal life.

> As bright as is this day, dear father, be thy life
> Henceforth. This day on which a new-made mother watched
> You lying in her arms, your little head against
> Her breast; and as you lay there, tiny wriggling mass,
> Her eyes adored you, softly bright with a great hope.
> Her trembling lips smiled ever, as she gazed upon
> Your form, and at the first long kiss, the great
> Sweet World of Motherhood was opened to her eyes,
> A World so beautiful and so divine, the breath

Forsook her lips, and God's grand face lit up the room
All dark before, and wrapped the mother and the babe
In haloed glory fair. Ah, gift of Motherhood!

In 1903, still just twenty-three, Angelina Weld Grimké was an accomplished poet and writer. Although she had had great difficulty in school, excelling only in her final years at Wellesley (then called the Boston Normal School of Gymnastics), her poetry was already being recognized for its depth and elegance. But Archibald Grimké, ever critical and demanding, did not appreciate his daughter's talent. While he was proud of her writing, he was too pragmatic—and too political—to believe that her creativity would ever garner the honors that he envisioned for her. He was undoubtedly also displeased by her choice of sexual partners, for it had been long apparent (the first evidence we have is from letters written when she was fourteen) that Angelina Weld Grimké was a lesbian or bisexual. The argument of 1903, in fact, may not have concerned a man at all, but may rather have been over Angelina's expression of affection for another woman. (As she grew older, Angelina's lesbianism would become more explicit in her poetry, and her attempts to cover up her feelings less contrived.)

At the age of sixteen, Angelina had written to Mamie Burrile, a close friend, "I know you are too young now to become my wife, but I hope, darling, that in a few years you will come to me and be my love, my wife! How my brain whirls how my pulse leaps with joy and madness when I think of these two words, 'my wife.' " Archibald knew of his daughter's preference at that point, and disapproved of it, but he quickly put it out of his mind. He had other concerns and believed that Angelina's education was far more important than any social or love life she might later seek. Accordingly, he pushed her first into teaching and then, slowly, as it at last dawned on him that she had real talent as a writer, into the public eye. But he would never retract the hurtful criticism he had leveled at her in 1899, so blunt and disappointed as to be downright cruel:

All you care about is self, and all the things which interest you in life are full of self, self, self. Although a woman you neglect the good, and earnest, and useful things of life, and are given up to thoughtlessness, pleasure, idleness, allowing all the golden opportunities for self-improvement, for fitting yourself for a life of usefulness to slip away. I supposed once that you had talents for intellectual pursuits, but I think so no longer.

For the first thirty years of her life, and beyond, Angelina Weld Grimké would live her life for her father. She wrote and taught, but her first commitment was (as she said in her poem commemorating his birthday) to Archibald Grimké, and to no one else.

> *Whose voice the last I heard before I close my eyes*
> *In sleep, and whose the first I heard when I awoke?*
> *It should have been my mother, but it was not so*
> *And, father dear, the sweetest tribute, that my hand*
> *Can find to lay before your feet this day, is this,*
> *That you have been a gentle mother to your child.*

Their angry exchange of 1903 was eventually forgotten, but only because Angelina herself did the only thing she thought possible: forced to choose between her own life and her father's, she chose his. In the years ahead, until he took his final breath, she would be at his side, often advising him and escorting him from meeting to meeting. It is likely that she served as his unofficial editor, red-lining his papers and addresses and here and there strengthening his language or, when necessary, tempering his militant vocabulary. She would prove an adept and gifted aide-de-camp. In the controversies and bitter debates that Archibald Grimké would face over the next fifteen years, his daughter's support would be desperately needed. His first challenge came almost immediately after the Boston Riot.

———

Anxious lest his grip on the leadership of the black community be too widely questioned, Booker T. Washington called for a national conference of black leaders, to be held in New York City in January 1904. The purpose of the meeting, Washington said, was to find common ground between his critics and his supporters. In public, Washington was magnanimous, maintaining that it was important for the black community not to be divided, and for all disputes to be aired. But in private, he showed another, vindictive face. He drew up an enemies list, in his own hand, that included the names of his most prominent opponents: William Monroe Trotter, W. E. B. Du Bois, and Archibald and Francis

Grimké. When he made up the roster of prospective invitees to the New York conference, however, Du Bois and Francis Grimké were on it. In truth, Washington thought he could still reason with those two, whereas Trotter and Francis's brother Archibald were now beneath his contempt.

Although Du Bois was suspicious of Washington's motives, he planned to attend, viewing the conference as offering him a chance to have a "heart to heart talk with Mr. Washington." Francis Grimké, meanwhile, tried politely to decline the invitation by forwarding Washington a list of other potential invitees, including his brother. Washington responded that Archibald would not be needed in New York, since other representatives from Boston would be there, as would other Democrats. Francis responded by saying that it had not been his understanding that the conference was to have only a certain number of delegates from each city, and that as to party allegiance, Archibald was not a Democrat but an Independent (a claim that was not exactly true). Washington held his ground: he was angry with Archibald, not only because of the Boston Riot and his subsequent defense of Trotter, but also because of Grimké's decision, in late December 1903, to assume the presidency of the American Negro Academy. Washington was irritated by Grimké's election in large part because he knew that his sophisticated organizing skills could make the ANA a national powerhouse—and thus a rival to the Tuskegee Machine.

The jockeying for position and power in the days leading up to the New York conference finally ended when Francis Grimké firmly turned down Washington's invitation. Since the conference could not go forward without *some* Grimké representation (given that its stated purpose was to resolve conflicts between the two camps), and given Francis Grimké's suggestion that any conference at which his brother was not present was bound to be controversial, Washington at last relented and asked Archibald to appear in New York on January 6, though he told associates that he had issued the invitation "strongly against my own will." Washington also sent his rival a message by letting friends know that Grimké was not wanted, most especially if he "attempts to have the same kind of 'nigger meeting' [referring to the meeting at which Grimké had been elected head of the American Negro Academy] that was had in Washington a few days ago."

FIFTEEN

"You hang him to a tree . . ."

The Carnegie Hall Conference was held in New York City on January 6, 7, and 8, 1904. The explicit purpose of the meeting was to iron out differences between the Tuskegee Machine and its critics and establish common ground for the future. In attendance were many of the nation's most important black leaders, including Booker T. Washington, W. E. B. Du Bois, Archibald Grimké, T. Thomas Fortune, Emmett Scott, William H. Morris (a Chicago attorney who had once labeled Washington a "racial sellout"), Clement Morgan (from Du Bois's class at Harvard), and Hugh Browne (thought to be a Washington enemy). Although Du Bois remained deeply skeptical about Washington's reason for calling the meeting, a flurry of letters between the two had persuaded him that he had little choice but to attend, if for no other reason than to keep an eye on the "Wizard."

For Washington, the meeting in New York held the key to his continued success. Grimké's power in Boston now rivaled that of William Monroe Trotter (who was not invited to the convention), and Du Bois's *The Souls of Black Folk* had stolen the Tuskegeean's thunder and made its author his most outspoken and most widely respected critic. Grimké and Du Bois arrived at Carnegie Hall in agreement: over the previous nine years, since Washington's remarkable concession in Atlanta, both had carefully calculated the cost of the "Atlanta Compromise" and found the philosophy of accommodation wanting. The tide of violence against black Americans had not yet crested, and in nearly every aspect of American life, black men and women were treated as second-class citizens—or worse. The problem had actually been magnified since 1900, as millions of white European workers had crowded into America's cities and made it more difficult for black men to obtain jobs.

Whereas Archibald Grimké's distaste for Washington was evident even from the expression on his face when his rival's name was mentioned, Du Bois was almost perceptibly afraid of facing him. The Wizard's power was so all-encompassing, his access to money so unquestioned, and his patronage so far-reaching that Du Bois, Grimké, and their allies could hope only to confront him, never defeat him. Du Bois had laid out an anti-Washington strategy, counting himself, Grimké, Morris, and Frederick L. McGhee, an attorney, as the only Carnegie delegates definitively in the anti-Washington camp. He wrote each of the others a letter of warning: refuse to be seduced by Washington's warm public personality, he advised them, and beware his power. "The main issue of this meeting is Washington," he insisted. Du Bois wanted to make Carnegie Hall Washington's Waterloo by getting the conference attendees to debate his leadership. Even with only four delegates firmly on his side, he believed he could win.

Washington was slated to give the conference's first address, but out of courtesy, he deferred to his host, the powerful industrialist and multimillionaire Andrew Carnegie. Carnegie solemnly ascended the speaker's platform and looked out over the crowd of almost sixty black men. A Washington partisan, he was disturbed that such a meeting was even necessary; there was no question in his mind that Booker T. Washington was America's greatest black leader, something that should be obvious, he believed, to everyone. So he praised Washington effusively. He was followed by a number of other white leaders who gave shorter addresses and then, like Carnegie, left the hall. Near the front, Grimké and Du Bois sat in silent rage: this was no way to start a supposedly bipartisan meeting, and they did not enjoy being lectured to by rich white men. Then Washington arose, and the hall became silent. Given Carnegie's opening remarks, many in the crowd expected Washington to gloat, but he surprised them by appearing modest and soft-spoken, and remarking only that hard work lay ahead of each of them. He concluded by saying that he was willing to compromise. Then he took his seat to polite applause. Du Bois spoke next and gave a typically intellectual presentation, joining in the spirit of the day by also pledging his willingness to compromise.

What followed over the next three days, however, would contradict those opening remarks. The exchanges were harsh, bitter, and filled with accusations. Washington tried to justify the strategy embedded in his "Atlanta Compromise" by arguing that it was the only means by which black America could hope to defend itself. Du Bois countered by criticizing him and his allies for betraying the cause of equal rights. Positions hardened on both sides during the meeting's first sessions, until Washington, Du Bois, and Grimké decided to focus on those principles that both camps could agree on. Grimké soon found himself in a difficult situation: after openly and publicly castigating him in the days leading up to the conference, Washington had then deliberately cultivated his friendship during the meeting's first session, shaking hands with him, exchanging pleasantries, and suggesting that the two of them had more in common than not. In spite of Du Bois's warning, Grimké was soon won over. As the meeting went into its second and third days, the relationship deepened, and Grimké became the unofficial mediator between the Tuskegeean and his critics. Although it made him uncomfortable, Grimké acted on Washington's opening, using his considerable intellectual skills to temper and moderate the positions held by both camps. By the end of the third day, he had successfully fashioned a national program uniting the two sides.

Under Grimké's guidance, Washington's supporters and his critics together hammered out a policy outlining how black America could best respond to attacks on black society. Both sides agreed to stand firm on the issue of suffrage, to support the filing of lawsuits against the most pernicious segregationist practices (something Washington had always advocated doing), to condemn lynching loudly, to recognize the validity of both industrial and higher education, and to endorse a statement calling for the Northern white and "the Southern white man and the Negro" all to work together to solve the nation's racial problems. While all of this was fine on paper, and a tribute to the work of Archibald Grimké, the most pressing criticisms of Washington had not yet been fully aired. As the delegates filed into the main hall to hear the Wizard close the conference, pockets of deep mistrust and suspicion of Washington and his Tuskegee Machine still existed. Du Bois, in particular, was not mollified by the Carnegie agreement and did not believe Washington would uphold it.

In his final address, though, Washington turned the tables on his accusers by seeming contrite and humbled, just as he had done on the first day. He all but apologized for his remarks nine years before, in Atlanta. He told the gathering that he was genuinely hurt and dismayed by the accusations that had been made against him; it had never been his intention, he said, to divide or disparage or to cause discord within the ranks of the black community. All he sought, he said, was unanimity and friendship. At one point, Washington wept openly at the bitter feelings his leadership had engendered and repeated his desire to ensure that everyone would stand together in crafting a response to the crisis faced by black America. He nearly pleaded for forgiveness and pledged that he would work to achieve harmony with other black leaders. Archibald Grimké, seated prominently in the audience, thought Washington's final address one of the greatest speeches he had ever heard, and commented to a friend that he was "completely overcome." Washington's points, he said, were "unanswerable." That was a sentiment, however, with which Du Bois did not agree.

The most profound achievement of the Carnegie Hall Conference was the agreement reached between pro- and anti-Washington camps to form a "Committee of Safety" to assure a unified response to antiblack actions. Washington, Du Bois, and Washington ally Dr. Charles Bentley, as the committee's first appointees, were given the task of appointing the remaining nine members. With Washington and Bentley in charge, the twelve-member Committee of Safety (which would later change its name to the Committee of Twelve for the Advancement of the Negro Race) was solidly in the hands of Washington's supporters. Archibald Grimké was one of the first to be named to the committee and was made its secretary, a reflection of Washington's newfound trust in him. Inevitably, however, Du Bois and Washington fought over the committee's membership, as well as over whether or not Du Bois had actually been invited to its first meeting. Washington acted hurt, then angry. Du Bois was not satisfied. Just one month after the Carnegie meeting, he resigned his position on the Committee of Twelve in disgust, repudiated the Carnegie Conference, and acidly announced that he would soon be forming an organization of his own to counter Washington's power—"a body of fearless people," he said, dedicated to battling for black rights outside the purview of the Tuskegee Machine.

As far as Du Bois was concerned, his fight with Washington was a fight to the finish. For him, it was not simply Washington's ideas that were suspect, but the man himself—"a terribly suspicious man" (Du Bois would say later), twisted inside and corrupt ("Now what is your racket?

What are you out for?" Du Bois said, mimicking him) and wholly the lapdog of white kingmakers and power brokers, spreading the butter of Tuskegee to buy the loyalty of his critics. Two such, Du Bois now thought, were Archibald Grimké and his Boston friend Kelly Miller, whom he now viewed as being in Washington's thrall. He wrote to them both, bluntly:

> I count it a clear misfortune to the Negro race when two clear-headed and honest men like you can see their way to put themselves under the dictation of a man with the record of Mr. Washington. I am sorry, very sorry to see it. Yet it will not alter my determination one jot or tittle. I refuse to wear Mr. Washington's livery or put on his collar. I have worked this long without having my work countersigned by Booker Washington or laid out by Robert Ogden [Washington's close colleague and secretary], and I think I'll peg along to the end in the same way.

On July 10, 1905, twenty-nine black men convened at the Erie Beach Hotel in Ontario, just across the Niagara River from Buffalo. The purpose of their meeting was to form an organization that could counter the Tuskegee Machine, complete with a national directorate and local chapters. Fifty-nine men in all had been invited to the conference, but many could not afford to make the trip. The previous month, all fifty-nine had signed a "call" written by Du Bois endorsing the need for an organization that would stand in the vanguard of the black race and provide "organized determination and aggressive action on the part of men who believe in Negro freedom and growth." Du Bois was at the forefront of the movement, its motivating personality; those he gathered were among the brightest young stars of the talented tenth. Archibald and Francis Grimké and Kelly Miller had not been invited.

Included among the conferees was William Monroe Trotter, the pale rider of Boston's *Guardian*, a man so vocal that many thought Du Bois would be unable to control him. But Du Bois had to court Trotter if his movement was to work, for his was one of the most outspoken and widely read newspapers in the African American community. Du Bois's greatest ally was Edwin Jourdain, a Boston University–educated lawyer and Massachusetts radical who may well have been the most brilliant thinker present. Slow of speech but careful with his words, Jourdain could fix a man with his eyes and convince him with the sheer power of his reasoning. There were others, too, who could claim the mantle of intelligence: Byron Gunner, a Rhode Island pastor who mistrusted Trotter; Alonzo F. Herndon, an Atlanta businessman destined to become one of America's wealthiest citizens; Clement Morgan, a Du Bois partisan and his good and longtime friend; Lafayette Hershaw, an Interior Department employee possessed of a cynical wit; Henry Lewis Bailey, a Howard University law professor and friend of Francis Grimké's; and Calvin Chase, the editor of the *Washington Bee* (who had recently branded Archibald Grimké a "hireling of Tuskegee").

After three days of meetings intended to formulate a set of common views, Du Bois and Trotter sat down to draft a manifesto for the new "Niagara Movement." Both knew what they wanted: a document that would live in history and distinguish their leadership from that provided by Booker Washington; reaffirm their commitment to equal rights and endorse a program of constant agitation; and be uncompromising while at the same time calling public attention to the problems of African Americans. The resulting "Declaration of Principles" was unanimously endorsed by Niagara's delegates:

> The Negro race in America, stolen, ravished and degraded, struggling up through difficulties and oppression, needs sympathy and receives criticism; needs help and is given hindrance, needs protection and is given mob-violence, needs justice and is given charity, needs leadership and is given cowardice and apology, needs bread and is given stone. This nation will never stand justified before God until these things are changed.

The challenge for Du Bois and Trotter was to transform these words into a practical program, to create a civil rights organization that could compete with Washington's Tuskegee Machine for the confidence of the African American community. To do this, Du Bois knew he would have to establish not only a working headquarters and extensive chapters, but also a national voice. The *Guardian* was not enough; it was too closely tied to Boston, and its editor too unpredictable. Over the next few months, therefore, Du Bois struggled to raise the financing to buy his own press. He located a suitable press, in Memphis, and poured his savings into it. In December 1905, he printed the first issue of the *Moon Illustrated Weekly*, a militant newspaper with a decidedly anti-Washington bent. It attracted few readers at first, but over time it would become known as an outspoken anti-Washington vehicle and be widely admired inside the African American intellectual community. It was smart and well written, and it spoke to the deep mistrust of the Tuskegee mafia.

The Niagara Movement maintained its unity of purpose throughout the year following its establishment, even after Trotter objected to Du Bois's proposal that women be permitted to enter its ranks. In truth, Trotter was not opposed to African American women becoming a part of the Niagara Movement so much as he wanted to derail the candidacy of Charlotte Forten Grimké, who had applied for membership. Intent on punishing the Grimké brothers for their abandonment of his colleague after the Carnegie Hall Conference, Trotter fairly screamed his dissent at Du Bois, who counseled him to calm down and show some forgiveness. Trotter did not win his point (Charlotte Grimké did become a member), but women were kept out of the Niagara Movement's second conference, held in Harper's Ferry on August 15, 1906.

———

Francis Grimké watched all this from afar, convinced that the contentiousness of America's black leaders would serve only to divide their cause. He himself had better work to do, though he knew that he must one day get caught up in the fight, just as his brother had done. There was no way around it. He was frequently asked for his opinion of Du Bois, of his brother, of Washington. He could not ignore the questions forever. He had read with mixed feelings (of anger and shrugging agreement) Du Bois's criticism of "the Grimké brothers" in *The Souls of Black Folk*, but he would not be baited to join any movement. Still, Du Bois's criticism hurt, for it hit its mark:

> They deprecate the sight of scattered counsels, of internal disagreement; and especially they dislike making their just criticism of a useful and earnest man [Washington] an excuse for a general discharge of venom from small-minded opponents. Nevertheless, the questions involved are so fundamental and

serious that it is difficult to see how men like the Grimkés can much longer be silent.

Francis Grimké was anything but silent, and he decided that he certainly did not need to be told what to do by men such as W. E. B. Du Bois, who had never set foot in a workhouse in his life, or Booker Washington, who seemed to be more interested in accruing power than he was in effecting real change. While Du Bois was out writing manifestos and contending with Washington for black leadership, Frank Grimké was making his views known where they most counted (as he believed): among his congregation of black "folks" in the District of Columbia. Where was Du Bois when they were insulted on the streets of the nation's capital? But in the end, it was not Du Bois's indirect condemnation that irritated Grimké so much as his disheartening and increasingly personal conflicts with Booker Washington. As for the criticisms of him and his brother, Grimké believed Du Bois had simply not been listening. He himself had always made his opinions about Washington clear, as in his series of sermons on the subject of compromise, which had made headlines. When Du Bois was being feted by Washington in a string of weekends arranged for him at Tuskegee, it was Grimké who had continued to work to convince black Americans to reject Washington's views.

Much as Francis Grimké might deplore factionalism and look askance at the bitter infighting between pro- and anti-Washington forces, there was really no doubt as to where he stood, and he had indicated as much in previous sermons condemning Washington. Grimké was a "militant" and an outspoken defender of black rights and would always remain so. In March 1905, in the run-up to the Carnegie Hall Conference, he had made his views explicit in a pamphlet entitled "The Negro and His Citizenship," which was published and circulated by the American Negro Academy. In it he asserted:

> We are citizens, clothed with citizenship rights; and there is no thought or intention on our part of ever surrendering a single one of them. Whatever others may think of it, or desire in regard to it, we do not propose to retreat a single inch, to give up for one moment the struggle. I say we, and in this, I believe I speak for those who represent the sentiment that is taking more and more firmly hold of the heart of this race. I belong to

what may be called the radical wing of the race, on the race question: I do not believe in compromises, in surrendering, or acquiescing, even temporarily, in the depravation of a single right, out of deference to an unrighteous public sentiment.

With that, Francis Grimké believed he had put his views on record; he could now give more of his attention to his congregation and to some nettlesome church business. He vigorously opposed a scheme of denominational reunion between Northern Presbyterians and the Cumberland General Assembly, which had backed the establishment of "separate but equal" (that is, segregated black and white) Southern Presbyterian churches. Grimké was enraged by the notion of reunion, since it would expressly endorse the racist policies of the white Southern church. Grimké led the fight against it, employing words reminiscent of those used by Martin Luther at the outset of the Reformation: "Union? Yes," Grimké wrote, "but never at the sacrifice of a great principle, never by sanctioning the spirit of caste, or by putting the stamp of inferiority upon any class or race within the Church. Here is where I stand; and here is where the Church ought to stand; where it will stand; if it is true to Jesus Christ."

Francis Grimké's disillusionment with Presbyterianism, though deeply felt, was perhaps surpassed by the disgust with which he viewed Howard University's administration and the actions of its white president, John Gordon. Gordon, as Grimké's biographer Henry Justi Ferry notes, was "one of the most insensitive figures ever to direct the school," a racist who appointed his cronies as administrators and talked down to black students. His attitude caused him continually to be pelted by rotten eggs while walking on his own campus. In response, he called in the all-white Washington, D.C., police, an act that almost drove the students into open rebellion. Francis Grimké's brother Archibald weighed in on the matter in a five-part series written for the *New York Age* (at which he had been hired as a columnist, by editor T. Thomas Fortune, in the wake of the Carnegie Hall Conference). Archibald accused Gordon of discriminating against black employees and even of "raiding the financial resources of other departments for his own benefit."

Gordon finally resigned, but only after a public meeting and a petition drive questioning his leadership made it clear that he could not continue in his post. He was charged by Archibald Grimké with "failure as an educator, administrator and financier, and with lack of sympathy with the race he professes to serve." His resignation was accepted on December 27, 1905, and just one week later, Francis Grimké was prominently mentioned as a possible successor. But Grimké urged his supporters to withdraw his name from consideration, insisting that he would not leave his church. As a member of Howard's board of trustees, he believed he could best serve the university by helping to find it a president who would make it among the best schools in the nation. In this task, he would perform admirably, recommending and then securing the appointment of William Patterson Thirkield, a white Methodist minister.

———

In the summer of 1906, Archibald Grimké published a paper on race that he had first written in 1904. It stands as his most important intellectual contribution to the problem of racism in America. When "The Heart of the Race Problem" appeared in *Arena* magazine, published by Grimké's friend and defender B. O. Fowler, it marked a departure from its author's earlier focus on the economic basis of racism. Now, he wrote, it had become evident that the "seed principles of wrong" lay in human sexuality, and most explicitly in the white race's apparent need—its compulsion, even—to undermine the racial integrity (though he did not use those exact words) of Africans imported as slaves to the New World. While the assertion was controversial and highly debatable, it struck a deep chord in the black community, much as it reflected Grimké's complex views of his own paternity. We do not know what either Archibald or Francis thought of Henry Grimké, beyond a few anecdotes about him remembered from childhood. But it is quite likely that they saw him as having taken advantage of their mother and of her vulnerable status as his slave—despite the fact that Nancy Weston, as far as we know, never criticized Henry Grimké and apparently never showed any embarrassment or regret about her liaison with him.

The result of the actual institution of slavery, Grimké noted in his essay, had been not, as was then argued by white supremacists, the degradation of blood—of "white blood"—but rather the "moral deterioration of the masters" and the "moral degradation of the slaves." Grimké was well aware of the Southern white man's practice, so pernicious that it can be characterized only as evil, of selling male slaves away from their wives in order to gain access to the females—a maneuver commented on by the wives of slaveholders, such as Mary Chesnut and Harriet Martineau, nearly a century before. The practice had led, Grimké noted, to the "evolution of a double moral standard" that undermined the claims of white supremacists bent on carrying out their philosophy of "racial purity." The real hypocrisy was that "the master or superior race will have one standard to regulate the conduct of individuals belonging to it in respect to one another, and another standard to regulate the conduct of those selfsame individuals in respect to individuals of the slave or inferior race." White men had thus been able to "live in licit intercourse with a woman of the other race" (as Henry Grimké had done with Archibald's mother) without condemnation (of the kind he himself and Frederick Douglass had suffered for marrying white women).

This policy of legalized sexual attack, Grimké argued, lay "at the heart of the race problem." Not only did it reflect the hypocrisy of white men; it also had enormous implications for the role of black males, for they were given to understand that while certain women were "off limits" to their own desires, black women were not similarly proscribed to white men. Instead, they were assaulted by them constantly, without fear of retribution. This in turn made the crime of lynching even more heinous, for whites regularly blamed black males for "causing" their own lynching by allegedly assaulting white women—a "crime" that was a lie. (Even Theodore Roosevelt endorsed this view in a State of the Union message, so angering Grimké that he broke with him, despite have supported his election.) What such cases of lynching actually amounted to, Grimké implied, was nothing less than an extended sexual attack on a race for the purpose of destroying it (he might have called this "sexual genocide," for that is what he meant, but the word *genocide* was not yet in use): white men were wiping out black men in order to have access to black women. Compounding the crime was the fact that though white women knew it was happening (they "are not fools," Grimké wrote, for they saw, every day, "black mothers with white colored children"), they did nothing to stop it. They thus virtually sanctioned it.

There are levels of complexity in Grimké's argument that he surely intended, but other, more ambiguous elements seem to belong to his understanding of his own experiences as a black man. Ironically (and surely he must have meant it so), his mother herself had been the product (or the "issue," as was said at the time) of a black-white liaison, as so, too, was he, and as was his daughter. If his mother had been half white, then he was three quarters white, and if he was three quarters white, then Angelina Weld Grimké, his daughter, was seven eighths white. The irony of such a lineage is suggested throughout Grimké's manuscript, which was composed carefully to imply, without anywhere stating explicitly, that the "question of race" was really one of color. White supremacists suffered not so much from racism, then, as from "colorphobia"—an idea that picked up on Angelina and Sarah Grimké's comments of the 1830s. This was not some niggling or small point undergirded by a semanticist's logic; it went to the heart of the matter, for if African Americans were inferior by dint of their racial background, then any prejudice against Grimké was ill founded, for he had more white blood than black, and Angelina, his daughter, had even more than he. No, Grimké said, the problem with white racism (or, rather, "colorphobia") was that it was based on unreasoning hatred, and unreasoning hatred must not and could not be "accommodated." It had to be fought. It had to be defeated.

Grimké's paper also served as a response to questions that were then quietly, almost surreptitiously, making the rounds of the African American community. It was just the kind of whispering campaign that Archibald and Francis Grimké despised: some of Du Bois's followers supposed that the nephews of the great Grimké sisters were too entranced by their abolitionist background to make clearheaded decisions about the future of black America. They were, it was said, too influenced by the old abolitionist crowd in Boston (meaning the old *white* abolitionist crowd in Boston) to stand courageously against Booker Washington, preferring to "lay on their bellies and lick the dust in admiration of the big 'White folks Negro' " whose purpose in life was to "keep the Negro down." Perhaps the comparatively light-skinned Archibald Grimké, his detractors seemed to suggest, did not fully understand what it meant to be black, and so found it easier to side with Washington, that white man (as his most vicious detractors claimed) inside a black man's skin.

Of course, what Grimké did *not* reveal in his article was that his life and his family—the entire, extended Grimké family—were a reflection of "the heart of the race problem." It was white hatred that had enslaved him, the son of Henry Grimké, and white hatred that had driven away his wife, Sarah Stanley. It was white hatred that had turned Du Bois and Trotter against Washington; only black unity could win black rights. Grimké's paper did not make headlines, and few black leaders or scholars seem to have commented on it at the time, but it would nonetheless have a great impact on black intellectuals. It would be passed from hand to hand through the next decades, even into the 1930s, when James Weldon

Johnson, the poet, author, scholar, essayist, and national black leader, would read it and be stunned by its simple truth: "In the core of the heart of the American race problem the sex factor is rooted," he would aver.

At the heart of Archibald Grimké's disquisition, in turn, lay the true history of the Grimké family, for each of its most progressive members (from Sarah and Angelina, to Archibald and Francis) had at one time or another been tarred with the same brush. All were either "amalgamationists" (it was black men that white abolitionist women wanted, pro-slavery voices had proclaimed, because they could not have white men) or "race mixers" who wanted to pollute white females with their "seed." Denmark Vesey and Booker Washington may well have shuffled along to keep from being sent to the workhouse, this line of reasoning went, but after a time, such silent protest turned into willing acquiescence, threatening all African Americans with permanent shuffling.

Grimké responded to such charges in kind, but without lashing out at either Du Bois or Trotter. He told friends that he was particularly disturbed by Du Bois's creation of a philosophy of "black distinctiveness," which he feared might lead to a new political movement that would only reinforce black separateness. For him, such separateness, such "black nationalism," constituted a surrender to the white supremacist ideal, a confirmation of the white racist's belief that black people were somehow different simply because of the color of their skin. Archibald Grimké, himself a thorough integrationist, believed that Du Bois's talk of the "black ideal," and his elevation of black America over white America precisely because it did not practice racism, would only institutionalize the hatreds on both sides. But Grimké trod lightly when it came to such subjects, primarily because he wanted to hold his steady middle course between Washington and Du Bois; he wrote as a militant anti-Washingtonian even as he maintained his presence in the Washington camp. By 1907, as the time approached for the third conference of the Niagara Movement, Grimké's position as a militant who could actually talk to Washington was so firmly established that Du Bois could no longer keep him out. And so, much to the consternation of William Monroe Trotter (whose dislike of Grimké had turned into an almost blind hatred), Grimké attended the Niagara Movement's conference as head of the delegation of Boston militants, as Trotter seethed on the sidelines.

The Niagara Movement had prospered since its founding, but by the summer of 1907, the vast national machinery that Du Bois had established was starting to break up. African American leaders were beginning to realize that the disagreements between Du Bois and Washington could prove fatal to their cause. Three separate incidents finally combined to persuade Du Bois, Grimké, Trotter, and Washington to put aside their differences, try to find a common ground, and work to establish a common equal rights organization. Each of the three events, as well as Washington's advancing age, had an enormous impact on the men's thinking, and eventually served to bind America's black leadership together.

The first incident took place in a military backwater of Brownsville, Texas, where the Twenty-fifth Infantry Regiment (Colored) had been assigned after serving in three campaigns and one barracks deployment—in the war with the Sioux tribes of the Dakotas, in Cuba during the Spanish American War, in the Philippines (where the troops had engaged in firefights with the Philippine insurgency), and on garrison duty in Nebraska. On a hot August night in 1905, a group of black soldiers from the First Battalion allegedly shot up the town of Brownsville, killing a white bartender and a policeman. President Theodore Roosevelt acted swiftly and politically, dismissing 167 of the battalion's 170 soldiers—every one of them black—and severing their pensions, all without the benefit of an investigation.

Booker T. Washington was called to the White House by Roosevelt and informed of his decision. He thought the president had made a blunder: black votes might have won him the election in 1904, he said, and if so, this was painful repayment for that support. Washington urged Roosevelt to reconsider, but he refused. His decision, he said, would stand. It was announced, to Washington's consternation, publicly—though only after Roosevelt had been assured of getting the black vote in the off-year elections. Black America felt betrayed, and even more so as it became apparent that not only had the account of the Brownsville "raid" (as the white community called it) been wildly exaggerated, but the charges against all of the men had been trumped up by a resentful white community whose income was dependent on the provision of services to a black regiment. Roosevelt was scorned: "Once enshrined in our hearts as Moses," Harlem's Baptist minister Adam Clayton Powell, Sr., thundered, "the president is now enshrouded in our scorn as Judas." Washington's reputation—for he was known as a personal friend of the president's, and practically an icon to an administration that openly courted black votes—was nearly destroyed. Even T. Thomas Fortune's *New York Age* now questioned the Tuskegeean's judgment. "Neither Mr. Washington nor the colored people can risk the hazard to be moved as mere pawns on this chess board of the President," Fortune editorialized. Within a year, Washington would have him dismissed as editor.

No less enraged than Fortune and others was Archibald Grimké, who had been informed that Washington knew of Roosevelt's decision soon after it was made but maintained his silence in order to keep alive his friendship with the president. Grimké decried this betrayal, spitting invective at Washington in the pages of the *New York Age* (prior to Fortune's dismissal): "There are some qualities, mental and moral, which the colored people of America need to acquire or develop in order to get what belongs to them as American citizens," he wrote. "And one of the chief of these qualities is courage—the courage to take a manly position on the race question and to stand by such [a] position in the face of the frowns of power and the teeth of hostile public sentiment, and under the falling axe of persecution, loss and even death itself." Black officeholders appointed by Roosevelt, and those African Americans closest to him, Grimké concluded, could not "serve God and Mammon, party and their race, at one and the same time."

Just one month after Brownsville, in the early-morning hours of September 22, 1906, the second incident occurred. It began with a confrontation between a white man and a black man in downtown Atlanta. A crowd of whites gathered, reportedly chased the black man into a black neighborhood, and commenced attacking and looting residences there. The police refused to intervene, even after a fire started. As the mob raged out of control, thousands of black families fled their homes, many never to return. When, after three days of rioting—white rioting, with many black residents, fearful of being murdered in cold blood, taking up arms in their own defense—the conflict at last came to an end, twenty-two Atlantans would be dead, slain in the streets of their city. Eighteen of them would be black. It was the worst race riot in American history up to that time.

But the Atlanta Riot, as it was called, was much more than just a black-white confrontation or even a "race riot." It was a white riot that targeted the black community, a riot fueled by white racial hatreds deliberately stirred up by white politicians seeking to win white Atlanta's votes in the upcoming gubernatorial election. Spurred on by local newspapers, which reported on alleged black crimes against white women ("Extra! Bold Negro Kisses White Girl's Hand," one headline screamed), white mobs hunted down black workmen who dared to walk the streets. On the first full night of rioting, September 22, a black drayman was beaten to death with iron bars; another was mutilated by a knife-wielding crowd, his toes and fingers taken as souvenirs. "A mob of poor white crackers caught our friend Frank Smith and stoned him to death," workman J. L. Black, would lament in a letter published in the *Atlanta Independent*. "It was said in one of the white papers that he was a self-important 'colored gentleman' meaning he thought more of himself than anyone thought of him, but it was only a mistake. . . . We do not know a single person who would or could say Frank ever did them harm." On the steps of Atlanta University, where he taught, W. E. B. Du Bois sat calmly with a shotgun, ready if the white mob should pour onto his campus and attempt to kill his wife and daughter. Order was finally restored when the Georgia Militia marched into the city and dispersed the white mob.

The third incident happened nearly two years later, in Springfield, Illinois, "in the shadow of Lincoln's tomb." It was a virtual replay of the Atlanta debacle. In August 1908, a a report circulated that a black railwayman had assaulted and raped a white woman. Although the charge was preposterous, the accused man was arrested and held. When a white mob began to form outside the jail, Springfield's sheriff (evidently aware that the man was innocent) tried, but failed, to spirit his prisoner out. A large white woman named Kate Howard egged on the crowd, crying to the men as they gathered in front of the jail, "What are you fellas afraid of? Women want protection!" The rioting that followed resulted in two lynchings, six shootings, and dozens of injuries, as well as countless black businesses and homes burned (the black railwayman was not one of those murdered). Some in the mob shouted, "Curse the day that Lincoln freed the niggers!" Later, the *Illinois State Journal* charged that Springfield's African American community was to blame for the riot. It was, the newspaper said, "the negroes' own misconduct, general inferiority or unfitness for free institutions that were at fault."

As Du Bois and Washington argued, as Tuskegee faced off against Niagara, as the Grimkés were sidelined by bitterness and frustration, the crisis deepened.

One of the witnesses to the horror in Springfield was a thirty-one-year-old former Southerner, a reformer and world traveler named William English Walling, who rushed to the scene in a vain attempt to stop the violence. A socialist and scholar who had left the University of Chicago to dedicate his life to political work—and whose family had once been Kentucky slaveholders—Walling decided that something needed to be done to break the endless cycle of racial hatred. He wrote articles about the riot and called on white Americans to do something to rein in white racism. "Either the spirit of the abolitionists, of Lincoln and of Lovejoy, must be revived and we must come to treat the negro on a plane of political and social equality, or [Southern racists James K.] Vadaman and [Ben] Tillman will soon have transferred the race war to the North. Yet, who realizes the seriousness of the situation, and what large and powerful body of citizens is ready to come to their aid?" In New York, the social activist and stern moralist Maria Ovington answered Walling's call and enlisted the aid of the socialist Charles Russell and a social worker named Henry Moskowitz. Walling, Ovington, and Moskowitz (Russell was unable to attend) met in Walling's New York apartment in January 1909 and resolved to form an organization dedicated to working against racism. It was to be composed of white liberals (they called themselves the new abolitionists) and prominent and progressive African Americans.

The charter members of the group, who now counted among their number Oswald Garrison Villard (a grandson of William Lloyd Garrison, and the publisher of *The Nation*), issued a "call" for the new organization. The call (written by Villard, whose words showed some of his grandfather's old spark) was published on the centennial of Lincoln's birth, in February 1909. Villard's manifesto urged black and white leaders to convene on May 31 of that year to found an organization to fight racism. Among the call's signers was Francis Grimké. The first meeting of the new entity, initially named the National Negro Conference, was held at the headquarters of the Charity Organization Society and featured the most prominent white progressives in the nation: Walling, Russell, Villard, Ovington, William Dean Howells, Jane Addams, and John Dewey. Du Bois was also in attendance, as was Archibald (though not Francis) Grimké.

The best minds of the black community, aware that their cause could not survive any more organizational fights, and for once aided in their efforts by the remnants of the abolitionist movement (all but silent these many years), were also well represented: Ida B. Wells-Barnett, William

Monroe Trotter, Kelly Miller, and Clement Morgan appeared, among many others. Booker T. Washington was invited, but with his star now in steep decline, he decided not to attend. He said it was not his kind of meeting. There were some one thousand delegates there on May 31, the vast majority white, and one third women. Walling, Villard, and Du Bois quickly emerged as the leaders of the movement.

On June 1, after the usual speeches and resolutions, as well as a number of behind-the-scenes caucuses among important white and black delegates, the convention established the National Committee for the Advancement of the Negro, which was to be run by an interim governing body called the Committee of Forty. Villard and Walling were stunned by the sometimes acrimonious debate among the African American attendees, who seemed unable to agree on anything. The deep animosity between pro- and anti-Washington forces took them by surprise, for they had never imagined that the disagreements between the factions could be so bitter, so unforgiving. At the end of the conference, especially in light of those disagreements, the white leaders were thankful that they had come away from the meeting with anything approaching unanimity. Villard and Walling were convinced that their new organization, unlike previous efforts such as Du Bois's Niagara Movement, could actually *do* something about racism, since it represented the collective wisdom of a third generation of abolitionists, combined with a sprinkling of socialists, labor activists, and suffragettes.

The conference's black leaders were less certain about the meeting's outcome. It seemed to them that the white progressives were a little too self-congratulatory and believed that blacks could win equal rights only with white help. The real challenge, many of them felt, would lie in keeping Garrison's egocentric grandson in line. Many white delegates agreed: Villard, self-effacing in public but outspoken and self-centered in private, thought of himself as the preeminent leader of the Committee of Forty, and he molded it to suit his own purposes—which were decidedly moderate. The new organization, he said, was "not to be a Washington movement, or a Du Bois movement." What it was to be instead, however, he did not exactly say.

After much debate, Archibald Grimké's name was added to the Committee of Forty, along with the names of Ida Wells-Barnett, Du Bois, educator Leslie Pinckney Hill, and half a dozen others. Whites dominated the committee, whose members served without pay and, according to Villard's plan, were there merely to rubber-stamp his selection of a national director, office, and staff. Villard himself, wispily unaware that his grating personality rankled black and white members of the committee alike, expected deference, considered himself an expert judge of writing, and acted as though the black members of the Committee of Forty owed him a debt of gratitude for establishing a new interracial equal rights organization. Grimké ignored him as best he could and set to work trying to make the organization effective. Unlike Washington's Tuskegee Machine or Du Bois's Niagara Movement, the Committee of Forty and the organization it steered might, Grimké felt, actually succeed. At first, however, that scenario seemed unlikely: the organization barely limped along until 1911, with Villard and Du Bois arguing incessantly while Archibald and Francis watched impatiently from the wings.

At a New York meeting in 1911 (called primarily to iron out these differences), the debate between Villard and Du Bois was resolved by the formation of a stronger governing body—a "Committee of One Hundred" that was to serve as a directorate. Moorfield Storey, an eminent Boston lawyer, was named head of the organization, which was now called the National Association for the Advancement of Colored People (NAACP). Du Bois was made director of publicity and research, with a salary of $2,500 per year. From his new position on Vesey Street in Philadelphia, Du Bois launched a monthly magazine for the NAACP, the *Crisis*, which would become the most powerful voice for black rights in the early twentieth century.

There was still no real place in the organization for Archibald Grimké, though he was promoted to membership in the Committee of One Hundred. He was satisfied with that limited role, having grown tired of the Du Bois–Washington and the Du Bois–Villard debates. By 1911, at the age of sixty-two, he was nearing the end of his professional life. While still in good health, he chose to spend more and more time on his writing and with his daughter, even as he continued to conduct the business of the thriving American Negro Academy. In 1913, however, he set aside time to help the new and powerful D.C. chapter of the NAACP oppose congressional legislation outlawing intermarriage—an issue that Archibald Grimké knew something about. Segregation had become the most important racial question in the nation, and it began to take up much of Grimké's energy. He still spent his summers in Boston, but he now focused more intently on Washington, keeping an eye on national legislation, helping his brother and his ailing sister-in-law, observing his daughter's teaching career, and monitoring the progress of the NAACP's local chapter. He found himself becoming increasingly involved in the chapter's efforts and came to see in the NAACP what he had never seen in either Booker T. Washington's or W. E. B. Du Bois's national organizations. Here, finally, was a professional group with an agreed-upon agenda. At last, he believed, the sniping of past years had been put aside.

In 1913, the D.C. chapter—the largest such group in the NAACP constellation—was led by J. Milton Waldron, a Baptist minister and reformer. Although soft-spoken, Waldron was a good leader. He was also a well-known Democrat and Woodrow Wilson partisan. Wilson, who had been elected president the year before, was not known as a friend of black America; his administration unashamedly endorsed segregationist policies in order to retain Southern votes for the party. None of that bothered Waldron, who attempted to land a job in the new administration, at one point even publicly supporting Southern segregationist practices in the hope of winning Wilson's backing. When it became apparent that Waldron had also purposely misused branch monies, however, a grassroots campaign was undertaken to strip him of his leadership position in the D.C. chapter of the NAACP. Waldron was his own worst enemy; in the middle of the fight, he attacked the city's assistant superintendent of black schools, Roscoe Conkling Bruce, a hardworking and dedicated public employee with connections to the once-powerful Tuskegee Machine.

Grimké stayed in the background during all of this, telling the national NAACP headquarters that he was disgusted with the D.C. branch and would never be a full participant in its activities as long as "self-seekers like Dr. Waldron" were its leaders. Oswald Garrison Villard watched the Waldron controversy closely, not simply because he disliked the man and thought him corrupt, but also because he believed that Grimké would make an able replacement for him, and a good addition to the NAACP board. Grimké was a perfect choice: he had strong ties to Washington, was well known and respected in the community, and had proven to be an adept organizer. In June 1913, Waldron was finally removed as the head of the D.C. branch by a vote of its executive committee, and Grimké was officially asked to take over the chapter's leadership role—at least on an interim basis. Grimké agreed and immediately set about stabilizing the membership, raising money for the national office, and appointing a "Committee of Fifty" to run the chapter and extend its power into the black community. The committee's membership represented a political cross section of the national capital's black elite and working-class populations and included a roster of its most nationally prominent black leaders. John Bruce (a friend of Grimké's from the American Negro Academy), Alain Locke (a philosophy professor at Howard University), Angelina Weld Grimké, and the brilliant historian and gifted writer Carter Woodson were all drafted to serve.

Grimké decided that the best way to put the chapter's problems and divisions behind it was to organize its most active members against President Wilson's segregationist policies. In late 1913, therefore, Grimké called for a mass meeting whose stated agenda was "To Protest Against Segregation—the New Slavery." The meeting, held at the African Methodist Episcopal Metropolitan Church, attracted more than four thousand African Americans, half of whom could not even get into the building and instead congregated in the street. Grimké gave a rousing speech condemning Wilson, then sent Villard outside to quiet those who were demanding to be let into the church. At a stroke, with one day's labor, Villard and Grimké, working together, made the NAACP's Washington chapter the national organization's premier and most powerful branch. Grimké repeated the effort in 1914 and agreed to join the NAACP board, where he once again faced his old nemesis W. E. B. Du Bois. Du Bois was now insisting that he needed greater autonomy as editor of the *Crisis*, which, he argued, ought to operate without any interference from the national board—an arrangement that would in effect make it a forum for Du Bois's own ideas. But there was no cause for concern there, he maintained, since he had never disagreed with the NAACP's policies.

Grimké sided with the national board on this question, though it meant siding with the NAACP's white leadership against a man he admired (despite their differences). Grimké tried to explain his position to Du Bois by saying that the NAACP offered African Americans their best hope of winning equal rights, but Du Bois was angry, and he took that anger out on Grimké by refusing to reprint his essay "Modern Industrialism and the Negroes" in the *Crisis*. Grimké was disappointed and frustrated, and he could see that once again, he and Du Bois were headed for a collision, but he said nothing. He was one of the NAACP's most powerful and successful senior officials, and there was nothing Du Bois could do to harm him.

In January 1914, Grimké was elected president of the D.C. chapter, thus dropping the "Interim" from his title. That same month, as if to confirm his new stature, he was asked to testify before the House Committee on Reform in the Civil Service on two bills that would institutionalize segregation among federal employees. He delivered an eloquent defense of integration and equal rights. When he was advised by Southern congressman Martin Dies that "the Southern people are the best friends you have in the world," Grimké angrily demurred and cataloged, in a ten-minute off-the-cuff rebuttal, all the instances he could remember of lynchings and race riots in the South. Dies heard him out but then asserted, as if in defense of such acts, that "one of the races must be the ruling race, and the negro race as rulers is unthinkable." Grimké replied that his very appearance before the committee was testimony to the falsehood of that claim, for, he said, he had "the blood of both races in my veins." The response was so unlike him that for a time he feared he might be roundly criticized by the NAACP's national leaders. But they were ecstatic about his performance, reprinted his words, and sent him a letter of congratulations.

———

In 1914, the world went to war. America, not yet drawn into the conflict, was at peace and had a new president, the scholarly and bespectacled Woodrow Wilson. In Central America, that greatest of all engineering feats, the Panama Canal, opened, and at home, Congress passed a resolution establishing the first national celebration of Mother's Day. In New England, Robert Frost published *North of Boston*, his first collection of poetry. From Mexico, the journalist John Reed, who would later cover the Russian Revolution and write *Ten Days That Shook the World*, was telling Americans about the bloody revolution south of the Rio Grande. And in Washington, D.C., on July 23, 1914—just as the Guns of August were to commence across the Atlantic—Charlotte Forten Grimké died after a long illness. She was seventy-three.

The next morning, before settling in to prepare his sermon and look after the details of his wife's burial, Francis Grimké penned a tribute to her. He wrote of her great compassion and love of life, of his love for her, and then of how much he would miss her. But he was happy to know that she was finally out of pain, after five months spent battling the effects of a stroke. He had ministered to her, nursed her, every single day of those months. He recalled her pain and the wish she had made as a young girl, that she would "meet death calmly." This she had done, slipping off as if wading into sleep. "She was one of the rarest spirits that ever lived," he wrote. One year later, the Grimké family would contract yet again as word came by letter that Archibald and Francis's brother John—who had seldom communicated with them in the last five decades and had lived a mysterious and apparently lonely life in Florida—was dead. That left only the three of them: Archibald, Francis, and Angelina.

Angelina Weld Grimké was a joy to her father, as well as a sometimes troublesome companion. As a District of Columbia schoolteacher, she occasionally quarreled with her superiors, forcing her father to intervene on her behalf. He was always on her side, as she was always at his. She taught during the day, then sat with him and her uncle Francis at home in the evenings. They were a family. With her father now, at long last, satisfied with his new life in Washington, and with his disputes with Trotter and Du Bois finally forgotten, Angelina was free to turn her attention to her writing. In 1915, she completed a play, *Blessed Are the Barren*, eventually to be retitled *Rachel*. Archibald helped her to get it produced.

Staged first in Washington and then in New York, *Rachel* received good reviews. Critics remarked on its depth and the power of its message. But it soon died a silent death. Over the years since, however, *Rachel* has taken on increased importance and is now recognized as one of the premier instances of the African American literary flowering known as the Harlem Renaissance. Distinguished for its treatment of political subjects, the movement was heavily influenced by both the NAACP's *Crisis* and the cultural exploration of the unique and rich African roots of black Americans. Angelina Weld Grimké's *Rachel* was one of the first examples of that political trend, for it bravely confronts the issues of lynching and rape, depicting a young woman who repudiates marriage and motherhood in the belief that her having children would only provide more black people for whites to lynch. The same theme appears in a number of Angelina's stories, including "The Closing Door," "Goldie," "Black Is, as Black Does," and "Blackness." These and *Rachel* are her protest against America, against the restrictions it placed on her as an African American and, though her father would never face this, as a lesbian.

Angelina's fiction soon began to be accepted for publication by a number of periodicals, and her writing was favorably reviewed by such literary bastions as the *Atlantic Monthly*. *Rachel* made Angelina Weld Grimké's reputation as a writer. She was pleased, and her father was overjoyed. Yet in our own day, it is Angelina's poetry that has gained a certain following, and especially her poem "Beware Lest He Awakes." Angelina worked it over in three different forms for two years until it was just the way she wanted it. She left it in her notebooks, then cut out the published version after its appearance in *Pilot* in May 1902. It reads, in part:

> Ah, no! The cruel jeer
> The ready curse and sneer
> Are all that he may have—
> A little less than slave,
> He's spurned by your scorn,
> And bound, both night and morn
> In chains of living death;
> And if with longing breath
> He breathes your air so free,
> You hang him to a tree,
> You hound of deviltry.
> You burn him if he speak,
> Until your freelands reek
> From gory peak to peak,
> With bloody, bloody sod,
> And still there live a God.
> But mark! There may draw near
> A day red-eyed and drear,
> A day of endless fear;
> Beware, lest he awakes!

EPILOGUE

"... the crisis has come ..."

Archibald and Francis Grimké would live on for two decades after the performance of Angelina's *Rachel*. Archibald continued in his role as the NAACP's most effective local leader, fighting tirelessly against segregation, working diligently to build a strong and financially sound NAACP chapter, and regularly sniping—though not nearly as often or as vehemently as before—at both W. E. B. Du Bois and William Monroe Trotter. His brother Francis kept on at the Fifteenth Street Presbyterian Church and persisted in going over and over his planned sermon nearly every morning of each week.

But times had changed. In 1919, as a result of his outspoken opposition to segregation and his leadership position in the NAACP, Archibald was investigated by the federal government on suspicion of disloyalty. He ignored the charges and went on to do battle with Woodrow Wilson over the death sentences given to thirteen black soldiers after a riot in Houston. He wrote a powerful poem about the executions, "Her Thirteen Black Soldiers," then argued with Du Bois, when he refused to publish it in *Crisis*. He watched in horror as white mobs attacked black communities. To his brother Francis's great satisfaction, Archibald was awarded the Spingarn Medal, the highest honor given by the NAACP, for his seven decades of national service to the cause of equal rights. Grimké was overcome with emotion when he was presented with the award. Although he had never become the organization's national president, everyone knew he was its most powerful force and most public voice.

By 1920, each brother had been alive for seven decades, and Francis commented to Archibald that at least according to the Bible, their time was up. So it seemed, too, to the NAACP, as a new generation of leaders took control of the organization and struggled to remake it in their image. The once interracial organization was now becoming a black leadership association, with deep roots in the African American community. Already, in 1920, the NAACP had eclipsed the power of the defunct Tuskegee Machine and the Niagara Movement combined. After a generation of discontent, the memory of the old arguments was fading. Booker T. Washington had died in November 1915, leaving a mixed legacy. The Grimké brothers, Kelly Miller, William Monroe Trotter, and even W. E. B. Du Bois were viewed as part of the "old school" by new leaders such as A. Philip Randolph and Chandler Owen.

In the summer of 1928, Archibald Grimké's health failed. He was seventy-nine years old. He took to his bed and remained there for two years, telling his brother Francis, "I guess the crisis has come." His daughter, Angelina, her own health precarious due to the effects of a train crash fifteen years before, stayed at his bedside. Angelina and Francis argued about Archibald's care and about household finances, trading long-repressed accusations dating from her adolescence. Their arguing was personal and bitter and served each of them poorly. Angelina was a headstrong and frustrated woman, and she worried about her father; Francis was a minister whose flock now took notice of his age. That the two disagreed and always had was obvious—no family can go for so long, through so many years, without such tensions.

Archibald Grimké died on February 25, 1930; his brother Francis would cling tenaciously to life for another seven years. The District of Columbia named a school for him, and he continued to fight racism and segregation well into his final year; he died on October 11, 1937. His church held a memorial service that was attended by nearly every religious luminary on the East Coast. The leadership of the NAACP came to Washington in force to honor the last of the Grimké brothers. Francis's coffin was escorted to its grave by his niece. Angelina Weld Grimké later moved to Brooklyn, where she kept a small house; as far as anyone knows, she had few friends and carried on an indifferent correspondence, though she could occasionally be seen, an elderly black woman, walking to a nearby grocery store. No one knew who she was. She died a recluse in 1958.

The two most passionate opponents of the Grimké brothers, and the two other great voices of their era, William Monroe Trotter and W. E. B. Du Bois, were both unhappy in their last years, though they had achieved much. Trotter, a man of talent and emotion who fell victim to financial troubles and mental instability toward the end, either fell from or jumped off the roof of his apartment building on his sixty-second birthday, April 7, 1934. Du Bois had a far different trajectory. He left and then rejoined the NAACP and became a Communist. In the 1950s, he published a series of novels before emigrating to Africa, where he befriended the president of Ghana, Kwame Nkrumah. He applied for membership in the U.S. Communist party and then renounced his U.S. citizenship. On the same day that Martin Luther King, Jr., led his March on Washington, in 1963, Du Bois died in Accra.

Archibald and Francis Grimké are today not nearly as well known as their aunts, or as well remembered or influential in African American history as Booker T. Washington or W. E. B. Du Bois. In the history of the nation, though, even the names of Angelina and Sarah Grimké have now been relegated to footnotes. Certainly Angelina Weld Grimké is largely forgotten, except perhaps as a "precursor" to the literary movement that she helped establish. Fine biographies have been written of each of them—first the sisters and then, separately, their two nephews and then again, as a part of larger studies of African American writers, Archibald's talented and driven daughter.

It may be an injustice to group them all together as a single whole—the Grimké family—for they were very different individuals: Sarah the seeker of God, Angelina the activist, Archibald the militant, Francis the moralist, and the younger Angelina the woman who loved life, who hated hate, and who remembered in her words the ghost of her white mother. They were different, yes, but all of them were Grimkés, and all of them were Americans. In their struggles we can find ours, and in the arc of their lives can be traced the history of our nation.

AUTHOR'S NOTE

There are two histories of America. First there is the history that we learn in school, the one that has heroes: Washington and Jefferson and Lincoln, Frederick Douglass and Martin Luther King, Jr., Susan B. Anthony and Elizabeth Cady Stanton. It is also a history of villains, such as Robert Barnwell Rhett, Jefferson Davis, and the racist Ben Tillman. This is our political and social history, the record of the Democratic and Republican parties, the Progressives and the Populists. It is, as well, the history of the Ku Klux Klan.

Then there is a second history of America, tracing the progressive ideas that have motivated our country and the reformist impulse that defines and shapes our destiny. From our perspective, the triumph of this ideal seems assured. It seemed so, too, to the Grimké sisters, who believed that their cause would prevail, that black Americans would be freed, and that the nation would work to build a society based on equal opportunity and equal rights. But no such inevitability was evident to the Grimké brothers, who lived in an era of increasingly blind race hatred, when lynch law formed the basis of black-white relations in the South.

Difficult though it may be to acknowledge, deep in the cell structure of this second history is the certainty that the narrative of post–Civil War America was written by Southern historians, most prominent among whom was William A. Dunning. Dunning and his colleagues believed that Reconstruction was less an attempt on the part of the federal government to guarantee the gains of the Civil War for black Americans than a punishment of the South by the North. Reconstruction, they argued, was a Republican conspiracy designed to overthrow accepted Southern institutions. Although later historians would discredit that interpretation, it lives on today in multiple forms.

Frequent conversations with history students have persuaded me that many, many Americans still believe that slavery was not the primary cause of the Civil War, which was instead the result of a combination of economic, social, and cultural factors. This view has the advantage of being elegantly complex ("Slavery as the cause of the war? Ah, if only it were that simple!" one professor said to me), and complexity in scholarship seems irrefutable, a sure sign of deep thinking. But it is pseudoscholarship, an attempt at once to forgive the South the sin of slavery, to absolve the North of its long history of acquiescence, and to provide white America with a comfortable explanation of why such terrible things happened in our country's past. I believe that this interpretation is actually a reflection of a kind of intellectual segregation that has in fact alienated black Americans from their nation's history.

I have seen it myself. I spent the better part of a year promoting my last book, on the lives of two Civil War colonels, before various groups. Invariably, most of the invitations to do book signings came from Civil War clubs. I spoke before hundreds of people at dozens of such gatherings, but in all of that time, I saw only two black Americans in the audience. More than seventy thousand African Americans died in the Civil War; I can attribute the lack of black interest in the history of that struggle and its aftermath only to the intellectual segregation that is still so much a part of our understanding of American history. In the course of my book tour, I was able to speak with a number of history teachers, most of them from the nation's high schools, who told me that their black students seemed almost resentful during sessions devoted to slavery, abolitionism, and Reconstruction. How, they asked me, could they engage their African American students in what one teacher called "a truly *American* history"?

This book is my attempt to find an answer to that question. I have suggested in these pages that slavery was not simply a matter of white people holding black people in bondage (though it clearly was that as well), but also a matter of *Americans* holding *other Americans* in bondage. And even more than that, slavery was not just something that some Americans did to other Americans, but something *we* did to *ourselves*. I have also posited that black culture, far from "emerging" from slavery, was instead fully developed, separately, out of ties that slaves maintained to their lands of origin. It is a fact, though one rarely acknowledged by white America, that black American slaves had a greater claim to being American than many of their masters: their ancestors had arrived earlier, and so they themselves understood more of what it meant to be Americans.

In this sense, the Grimké family was a truly American family, and any history of the Grimkés must provide a more accurate portrayal of what it means to be an American than a history of, say, the Rockefellers or the Carnegies. That Archibald and Francis Grimké could feel the sting of race prejudice when in fact they were arguably of only one quarter African descent (their father was Caucasian, their mother a "mulatto") shows that racial hatred in America, then as now, really has a great deal less to do with cultural and social differences (a point still innocently made by defenders of the "differences" in the races—instead of emphasizing our "common" heritage) than with skin tone. This phenomenon is by now well known, of course, but it is still shocking, and still divisive.

What does the history of the Grimké family tell us about ourselves? I believe it demonstrates that racial prejudice remains the central fact of the American experience. This is true even though the story of the Grimkés, the most prominent interracial family in our history, is the story of a single family, not of two separate families. Moreover, in recounting the Grimkés' history, we recount the history of this nation in its purest form; through the experiences of Sarah, Angelina, Archibald, and Francis, we view the experiences of all Americans over a period of 150 years. I must therefore admit that my supposition at the outset of this book, and again at the beginning of this essay—that there are really two histories of America, progressive and reactionary, black and white—is wrong. There is only *one* history, and we all share in it.

Finally, I hope that the Grimkés teach us that the answers to the three most important questions facing our nation—Who are we? Why are we here? Where are we going?—must be answered by all of us together, lest they not be answered at all.

ACKNOWLEDGMENTS

The vast portion of the research for *Lift Up Thy Voice* consisted in a careful reading of primary texts: the diaries, letters, speeches, testimonials, and sermons of Angelina, Sarah, Archibald, and Francis Grimké, Angelina Weld Grimké and Charlotte Forten Grimké, and Theodore Weld.

Materials on the lives of the Grimkés may be found in four primary collections: the Theodore Dwight Weld Collection of the William L. Clements Library at the University of Michigan in Ann Arbor; the Grimké Family Collection at the Moorland-Spingarn Research Center at Howard University in Washington, D.C.; the Theodore Dwight Weld Papers at the Library of Congress; and the Grimké Personal Papers of the Library of Congress. The most extensive of the collections is that held by the Moorland-Spingarn Research Center of Howard University, whose director and staff have my profound and sincere gratitude for making available to me selected papers from the collection.

While a reading of primary materials provided the foundation of this work, the reader will also detect here an echo of those who have already worked as researchers and writers in this field. I am most especially indebted to those historians who have spent a lifetime uncovering the mysteries of the Grimké family, the abolitionist movement, and the struggles of the African American community in the post–Civil War era.

I owe a great debt to Gerda Lerner, whose biography of the Grimké sisters, *Rebels against Slavery*, first pointed the way for a generation of historians. No less am I indebted, however, to Catherine Birney (for *The Grimké Sisters*, first published in the 1880s), to Dickson Bruce (for *Archibald Grimké: Portrait of a Black Independent*), to Henry Justi Ferry, for his dissertation on Francis James Grimké (the only full-length treatment of Francis Grimké's life), to Robert H. Abzug for *Passionate Liberator* (his biography of Theodore Dwight Weld), to Stephen R. Fox for *The Guardian of Boston*, his account of the life of William Monroe Trotter, and to Henry Mayer for his brilliant biography of William Lloyd Garrison, *All On Fire*.

Historians often find unappreciated nuggets of valuable information in strange places, and this has certainly been my experience with this book. At the end of my researches, I was pleased to discover Mary Bushkovitch's *The Grimkés of Charleston*, a work of fiction based on the author's in-depth research into the Grimké family and its life in Charleston. It is a work of sublime simplicity that nonetheless gives powerful testimony to the critically important historical study done by often overlooked, and surely overworked, local historians.

The most moving essay I have read on the antislavery movement was written by the historians Gilbert Barnes and Dwight Dumond; it appears as the introduction to *The Letters of Theodore Dwight Weld, Angelina Grimké Weld and Sarah Grimké*. I highly recommend it to anyone seeking to understand the abolitionist impulse. Barnes and Dumond propose that that impulse evolved through a series of distinct phases: from the Great Revival of the late 1820s into a national movement and only then into a highly structural attempt to influence the political process. This view in turn suggested to me that the abolitionist movement might well have contained the seeds of modern political organizing, a proposition that I have put forward in these pages. At the Vietnam Veterans of America Foundation, where I have been privileged to work on the global campaign to ban land mines, my colleagues—including most especially Bobby Muller, John Terzano, and Marissa Vitagliano—will undoubtedly recognize, in these pages, traces of our collective musings on how best to influence public opinion and shift national policies. I am indebted to the foundation, one of the leading humanitarian organizations in the world, for allowing me the time to complete this work.

I wish to thank, once again, my agent, Gail Ross, for her continued support, her constant optimism, and her endless patience through what is now five books in ten years. Additionally, my gratitude goes to Caroline White, my editor at Viking, for bringing this manuscript to print. Her acute eye and careful pen reflected a genuine love for this topic and this book.

I have dedicated this book to my two sisters, Anne Balderson and Lois Brown. They cannot begin to know the impact they have had on my life. They were, and are, avid readers—and so pushed me to be a writer. I will always be grateful to them for their inspiration.

Finally, I owe a special debt of gratitude to my wife, Nina Mikhalevsky. A number of years ago, she showed me a paper she had written entitled "Sarah Grimké and the Reclamation of Speech." Both unique and powerful, it has been a constant source of inspiration to me ever since. She has taught this subject for twenty years, to thousands of students, bringing to life for them the Grimkés and their accomplishments. She did the same for me. This book could not have been completed without her tireless devotion, her unstinting and loving support, and her dedication to teaching and scholarship. Nina, as well as my children, Cal and Madeleine, showed amazing patience during the three years it took me to research and write *Lift Up Thy Voice*.

NOTES

PROLOGUE

1 When he caught her with her brother's Latin text: Gerda Lerner, *The Grimké Sisters from South Carolina* (Boston: Houghton Mifflin Company, 1967), 18–19 (hereafter, Lerner). See also Catherine Birney, *The Grimké Sisters: Sarah and Angelina Grimké, The First Women Advocates of Abolition and Woman's Rights* (New York: Lee & Shepard, 1885), 17 (hereafter, Birney). The latter is based on the diaries and manuscripts of the sisters kept in the Weld Papers at the University of Michigan, Ann Arbor.

2 One day when Sarah was barely eleven: Lerner, 20. In Birney, the date for this incident is given as 1803, and the author adds this quote from Sarah's father: "You are a girl, what do you want of Latin and Greek and Philosophy?" (page 18). These were seen as "unwomanly" aspirations.

2 Hetty was harshly reprimanded, shaken, chased from Sarah's room: Sarah Grimké (1827) Diary, in the Weld Papers. There are two separate diaries; the first, Sarah's recounting of her childhood, is dated 1827. All references to this 1827 diary will be indicated herein. Both diaries may be found in the Weld Papers.

2 "I took an almost malicious satisfaction in teaching my little waiting-maid at night": Quoted in Lerner, 23. The quote is taken from the Sarah Grimké (1827) Diary, in the Weld Papers.

3 Having fled France in 1685: Allen Johnson and Dumas Malone, eds., *Dictionary of American Biography* (New York: Charles Scribner's Sons, 1991), 7: 633–34.

4   "On a signal given, such as the beat of a drum": Herb Boyd, ed., *Autobiography of a People* (New York: Doubleday and Co., 2000), 24–25. Excerpt from "The Interesting Narrative of the Life of Olaudah Equiano, or Gustavus Vassa, the African Written by Himself."

5   Slave rebellions were reported in Virginia: Hugh Thomas, *The Slave Trade* (New York: Simon & Schuster, 1997), 510–11. See also David Brion Davis, *The Problem of Slavery in the Age of Revolution* (Ithaca, N.Y.: Cornell University Press, 1975), 308–10, and William W. Freehling, *The Road to Disunion* (New York: Oxford University Press, 1990), 178–79.

6   In 1754, the Quaker yearly meeting issued a public circular opposing slavery: Davis, *The Problem of Slavery*, 213.

7   A short walk down a well-worn path from the Grimké manor at Belmont: Lerner, 15.

CHAPTER 1

11 Its oldest families, who were descended from the original settlers: Walter Edgard, *South Carolina: A History* (Columbia, S.C.: University of South Carolina Press, 1998), 252.

12 A visitor to Charleston in 1800: Ibid., 260–68.

12 One of Charleston's best-known and best-appointed offices: Hugh Thomas, *The Slave Trade* (New York: Simon & Schuster, 1997), 545.

12 In that period, nearly forty thousand Africans landed on Charleston's shores: ibid., 546. See also Edgard, *South Carolina*, 287. The U.S. Census records for South Carolina give precise numbers of slaves for each ten-year period—the result of a desire on the part of Southern politicians, in particular, to maintain an equilibrium (or as near to one as possible) of Southern representation in the U.S. House of Representatives.

13 The Grimké family spent other Sunday evenings calling on close friends: Lerner, 16.

14 Just as they had once been fired to stave off Blackbeard: Edgard, *South Carolina*, 101–3. The role of the Grimkés in helping to save Charleston from Blackbeard was, apparently, somewhat controversial within the family itself, and remains uncertain now. Given the timing of the pirate raids on the South Carolina coast, it is unlikely that any Grimké played a major role.

15 South Carolina's constitution was derived: Ibid., 42–44.

17 Originally from Alsace-Lorraine and German by birth: Register of Saint Philip's Parish, Charlestown or Charleston, S.C., 1754–1810.

17 Ambitious, intelligent, and prudent, John Paul Grimké: "A Charlestonian's Recollections" D. E. H. Smith, (Charleston: Carolina Art Association, 1950). See also Allen Johnson and Dumas Malone, eds., *Dictionary of American Biography* (New York: Charles Scribner's Sons, 1978), 7: 635–36.

17 As a young man he excelled at his studies: Lerner, 41–49.

18 He purchased lots in Charleston: Ibid., 43.

18 In 1779, at the age of thirty: Lerner, 47.

18 John Grimké married well, in 1784: Ibid., 14.

20 "Judge Grimké, his family and connections": Birney, 11.

21 "the children of the strangers that sojourn among you": A discussion of the pamphlet war over the justification of slavery by appeal to Scripture appears in David Brion Davis, *The Problem of Slavery in the Age of Revolution* (Ithaca, N.Y.: Cornell University Press, 1975), 530–38.

22 For those who doubted, good ministers had ready at hand: *Ibid.*, 539.

22 As Polly grew older and her responsibilities increased: Birney, 14.

23 "As children multiplied": Ibid., 14–15.

23 The friendship would be a lifelong one: Lerner, 28–29.

24 "Would you like to stand all day long": "A Southern Churchwoman's View of Slavery," *Church Intelligencer*, November 22, 1860.

25 "Every man who resides on his plantation": Harriet Martineau, *Society in America* (New York: Saunders & Otley, 1837), 2: 112.

25 "Under slavery, we live surrounded by prostitutes": Mary Boykin Chesnut, *A Diary from Dixie*, ed. Ben A. Williams (Boston: Houghton Mifflin, 1961), 21–22.

26 Charleston contained a large population of "free people of color": Edgard, *South Carolina*, 272–73. See also Lerner, 30.

27 On February 20, 1805, Angelina Emily Grimké: Lerner, 24.

27 Immediately after her youngest sister's birth, Sarah begged: Ibid., 26.

27 "I had been taught to believe in the efficacy of prayer": Quoted in Birney, 12–13.

28 Sarah was painfully aware of what was expected of her: Ibid., 14.

28 "a doll, a coquette, a fashionable fool": Ibid., 18.

28 In 1807, Thomas Grimké graduated from Yale: Lerner, 27.

29 Thomas Grimké eventually bowed to his father's wishes: Ibid.

31 She wrote in her diary that her brother Thomas had saved her: The incident is recounted in the Sarah Grimké (1827) Diary, in the Weld Papers. Birney writes of the incident in more detail than any other biographer, undoubtedly because she heard the story from the Grimké family, perhaps even from Sarah herself.

31 "I believe for the short space I was exhibited on this theatre": Sarah Grimké (1827) Diary, in the Weld Papers.

31 Judge Grimké's political enemies began impeachment proceedings: This episode is among the most ambiguous events in John Faucheraud Grimké's history and has never been dealt with in depth by any Grimké biographer. The papers of the South Carolina State Historical Society are nearly silent on the matter; hard though it is to trace, the case against Judge Grimké seems, however, to have been clearly political, and not based on any substantive malfeasance in office.

32 In the spring of 1812, Sarah Grimké attended a lecture: Lerner, 40.

32 In the summer of 1813, at the age of twenty-one: Ibid., 51.

33 She reiterated her pledge to turn away from "sinful indulgence": Sarah Grimké (1827) Diary, in the Weld Papers.

33 "I fed the hungry and clothed the naked": Ibid.

33 "merciful interposition of Providence": Ibid.

34 None of Charleston's leading doctors could adequately diagnose: Lerner, 42.

CHAPTER 2

35 In that year, there were eleven free and eleven slave states: Merrill D. Peterson, *The Great Triumvirate* (New York: Oxford University Press, 1987), 52–53.

35 John Faucheraud Grimké disembarked in Philadelphia: Lerner, 42. Both Lerner and Birney quote extensively from the Sarah Grimké diary, parts of which were transcribed (probably from an earlier, now lost copy) in her hand in 1827. The original appears to have been written in 1821. No other account of the sickness of John Faucheraud Grimké survives, and there are no records of his treatment by Dr. Phillip Synge Physick. The nature of Judge Grimké's illness must thus remain a mystery.

36 Himself a Quaker, like their hosts, Physick was a kind and gentle man: Lerner, 43.

36 In June, his options exhausted, Dr. Physick advised Sarah: Ibid.

36 "His life is in God's hands": Quoted ibid.

37 At the time, Long Branch was not yet the seaside resort: Ibid.

38 Nina, just fourteen years old: Birney, 25.

39 At fourteen, Angelina came to a startling conclusion: Ibid., 39–40. Birney consulted the diaries and letters of the Grimké family to gain insight into Sarah and Angelina's awakening to the problem of slavery. Additionally, she enjoyed an advantage denied to modern historians: she was able to talk to the sisters directly and ask them about their views.

39 One day, while attending classes at the Charleston Seminary: "The Testimony of Angelina Grimké Weld," in Theodore Dwight Weld, *American Slavery as It Is* (New York: American Anti-Slavery Society, 1839).

39 At the age of thirteen: Lerner, 68.

39 "If, with my feelings and views as they now are": Quoted ibid.

40 Polly Grimké was particularly angered and humiliated: Angelina Grimké to Anna Frost, March 18, 1828, in the Weld Papers.

40 . . . Angelina's announcement that she intended to convene an all-female prayer group: Lerner, 68.

41 When Angelina at last agreed to care for a young slave named Kitty: Ibid., 67.

41   "[Angelina] was neither so demonstrative nor so tender": Birney, 39.

42   John Faucheraud Grimké died on August 8, 1819: Lerner, 47. Sarah recorded her father's last moments in her (1827) diary.

42   Thomas was now a prominent lawyer in Charleston, John was a doctor: Angelina Grimké did not get along with her brother John, who disapproved of her religious decisions. Nor, it seems, did she enjoy a good relationship with her older brother Henry, who at one point moved into the Grimké home on Front Street with his new wife, Selina, whom Angelina disliked.

44   It was because of this that Judge John Grimké was: Catherine Birney provides the best description of the Grimké family philosophy; see Birney, 10–13. John Faucheraud Grimké left no personal diary.

44   Jefferson's "extraordinary capacity to sound like an enlightened reformer": Dumas Malone, *Thomas Jefferson and His Time: The Sage of Monticello* (Boston: Little, Brown & Co., 1981), 326. Malone's discussion of Southern elite attitudes toward slavery, particularly among the generation that led the American Revolution, is authoritative (see especially 322–27).

44   "My opinion has ever been that, until more can be done for them": Quoted ibid., 322.

44   "The concerns of each generation are their own care": Quoted ibid., 323.

45   She changed his sheets and his clothes: Lerner, 44–45.

46   A local minister uttered words of kind assurance: Lerner, 47.

47   She was drawn to Morris's powerful personality: Ibid., 58.

48   Thomas and Sarah would talk for hours: Ibid., 57.

49   By 1820 . . . the American Colonization Society: David Brion Davis, *The Problem of Slavery in the Age of Revolution* (Ithaca, N.Y.: Cornell University Press, 1975), 335.

50   She feared she would never be at peace with her religious beliefs: Lerner, 56–60.

50   "Tears never moistened my eyes; to prayer I was a stranger": Sarah Grimké (1827) Diary, in the Weld Papers. Also quoted in Lerner, 53. Being only fourteen at the time, Angelina was unaware of the details of Sarah's religious crisis.

51   "by the sadness of countenance, the heart is made better": Sarah Grimké (1827) Diary, in the Weld Papers.

51   Sarah Grimké arrived at her uncle James Smith's plantation: Lerner, 55–56.

52   Woolman's memoirs tell the story of an exceptional man: John Woolman, *A Journal of the Life, Gospel Labours and Christian Experiences of That Faithful Minister of Jesus Christ, John Woolman, Late of Mt. Holly in the Province of New Jersey, North America* (London: W. Phillips, 1824). See also William Henry Smith, *A Political History of Slavery*, 2 vols. (New York: G. P. Putnam's Sons, 1903), 1: 190–92.

53   "I was brought seriously to consider my ways": Woolman, *A Journal*, 22.

53   "In a while I resolved totally to leave off some of my vanities": Ibid., 31.

54   voice calling to her, distant and indistinct at first: Lerner, 57. See also Sarah
      Grimké (1827) Diary, in the Weld Papers. Sarah mentions the voices promi-
      nently in both of her diaries, but evidently they went silent—or she simply
      stopped writing about them—when she reached her forties.

CHAPTER 3

55   Historians call this religious revolution: Henry Mayer, *All On Fire* (New York:
      St. Martin's Press, 1998), 224–25. See also William Henry Smith, *A Political
      History of Slavery*, 2 vols. (New York, G. P. Putnam's Sons, 1903). A very
      good short treatment of the Second Great Awakening can be found in Robert
      H. Abzug, *Passionate Liberator: Theodore Dwight Weld and the Dilemma of
      Reform* (New York: Oxford University Press, 1980), 39–51.

55   At the heart of the revival: William G. McLoughlin, ed., *Lectures on Revival
      of Religion: The Lectures of Charles Grandison Finney* (Cambridge, Mass.:
      Harvard University Press/Belknap, 1960).

56   "though He will know that you cannot bear the weight of omnipotence:"
      Ibid., 22. See also Abzug, *Passionate Liberator*, 44. For the Edwards sermon,
      see "Sinners in the Hands of an Angry God," in Clarence H. Faust and
      Thomas H. Johnson, eds., *Jonathan Edwards: Representative Selections, with
      Introduction, Bibliography and Notes*, rev. ed. (New York: The American Book
      Company, 1984), 112.

58   "You have prayed enough since I have attended these meetings": Quoted in
      Abzug, *Passionate Liberator*, 42.

58   "Will you accept salvation today?": Quoted ibid., 42.

59   Finney's message held out hope that a life of sin: Ibid., 42–49.

59   "You old, gray headed sinner, you deserved to be in hell long ago": Quoted
      ibid., 47.

60   "While depicting the glories or the terrors of the world to come": Henry B.
      Stanton, *Random Recollections* (New York: Lee & Shepard, 1887), 40–42.

60   In Troy, a minister urged his parishioners: Abzug, *Passionate Liberator*, 49.

61   "roll back the wheels of time to semi-barbarism": Quoted ibid., 45; also
      quoted in William G. McLoughlin, *Modern Revivalism: Charles Grandison
      Finney to Billy Graham* (New York: Dodd, Mead, 1959), 31.

61   "The importance of truth in religion": Quoted in Abzug, *Passionate Libera-
      tor*, 45.

61   "saw and communed with spirits": Quoted in Birney, 30. It is difficult to de-
      termine where Birney got this quote, though it is similar in tone to a comment
      made by Sarah in an entry in her (1827) diary, in the Weld Papers.

62   Sarah arrived in Philadelphia on May 15, 1821: Lerner, 58. Sarah Grimké's
      first seven years in Philadelphia are treated by her in her (1827) diary, in the
      Weld Papers.

63   "On last Fifth Day . . . ," she would write in her diary, "I changed my dress":
      Sarah Grimké (1827) Diary, in the Weld Papers.

64   "Oh, had I received the education I desired": Lerner, 59–60; also in Sarah
      Grimké (1827) Diary, in the Weld Papers. Even into her last years, Birney
      says, Sarah harbored the hope that she might somehow, one day, study for
      the law.

64   Vesey believed that a clash of the races was inevitable: Johnson Ajibade Ade-
      fila, "Slave Religion in the Ante-Bellum South: A Study of the Role of African-
      ism in the Black Response to Christianity" (Ph.D. diss., Brandeis University,
      1975). This is a very convincing account, the best summary I have read of the
      relationship between religion and rebellion among Southern slaves. The reader
      will note that I believe there was, in fact, a planned uprising among Vesey's
      followers, despite Vesey's denials even on the scaffold. I am convinced by his-
      torian William H. Freehling's view that all slave plots were exaggerated by
      white slaveholders, even as the plans for such revolts were regularly dismissed
      by the slaves themselves. Nonetheless, Denmark Vesey, I suspect, did plan a
      major uprising.

65   Such rumors were not uncommon: William H. Freehling, *The Road to Dis-
      union* (New York: Oxford University Press, 1990), 79.

66   South Carolina's John Calhoun believed that the debates of 1820: Merrill D.
      Peterson, *The Great Triumvirate* (New York: Oxford University Press, 1987), 59.

66   On June 17, a special court of five citizens: Freehling, *The Road to Disunion*, 81.

66   William Johnson, a U.S. Supreme Court justice: Ibid.

68   "sit down in meeting in a cold and indifferent state": Sarah Grimké (1827)
      Diary, in the Weld Papers.

68   They were unfailing allies: Lerner, 62. See also Birney, 63, and Sarah
      Grimké (1827) Diary, in the Weld Papers.

68   "I struggle against feelings and temptation I blush to think of": Sarah Grimké
      (1827) Diary, in the Weld Papers.

69   "Conventional marriage [Sarah believed]": Lerner, 65.

70   "I have found it very hard work to give him up": Sarah Grimké (1827) Diary,
      in the Weld Papers.

70   "It is a beautiful theory, but my experience belies it": Ibid.

71   "Landed this morning in Charleston, and was welcomed by my dear mother":
      Ibid.

CHAPTER 4

72   "God has given us Missouri": Quoted in Robert V. Remini, *Henry Clay:
      Statesman for the Union* (New York: W. W. Norton & Co., 1991), 183.

72   "Hell is about to enlarge her borders": Quoted in Merton L. Dillon, *The Abo-
      litionists: The Growth of a Dissenting Minority* (New York: 1974), 23.

72   "grieved my heart": Quoted ibid., 30.

73   While there he met William Lloyd Garrison: Henry Mayer, *All On Fire* (New York: St. Martin's Press, 1998), 51–53.

73   "I shall not hesitate to call things by their proper names": Quoted ibid., 53.

73   "Take right hold! Hold on!": Quoted ibid., 70.

74   On July 4, 1829, Garrison gave the Independence Day address: Ibid., 66–67.

74   David Walker's "Appeal to the Colored Citizens of the World": David Walker, "Walker's Appeal, in Four Articles; Together with a Preamble, to the Colored Citizens of the World, but in Particular and Very Expressly, to Those of the United States of America, Written in Boston, State of Massachusetts, September 28, 1829," in William H. Pease and Jane H. Pease, eds., *The Anti-Slavery Argument* (Indianapolis: Bobbs-Merrill, 1965).

75   "America is more our country than it is the whites' ": Ibid.

75   "O, my dear mother": Angelina Grimké to Sarah Grimké, September 1826, in the Weld Papers. Also see Birney, 43.

76   "The Presbyterians, I think, enjoy so many privileges": Quoted in Birney, 43.

77   "This morning my dear Angelina proposed destroying Scott's novels": Quoted in Birney, 51. See also the Diary of Angelina Grimké, 1838, in the Weld Papers. Sarah noted this incident in her own diary as well.

77   "I have no idea what it is, and I may be mistaken": The Diary of Angelina Grimké, (winter) 1828, in the Weld Papers. Angelina began her diary in 1828 and kept it religiously until the death of Edward Bettles. It contains long philosophical and religious discourses, her views on friends and neighbors, and an account of her bitter exchanges with her mother.

78   "My friends tell me that I render myself ridiculous": Ibid.

79   "My beloved Angelina arrived yesterday": Sarah Grimké (1827) Diary, in the Weld Papers.

79   "The Lord's poor tell me": Ibid.

80   "I spoke to her of how great a trial it was": Quoted in Birney, 70–71. The full dialogue is recounted by Angelina in her diary, in the Weld Papers.

81   "I remarked that true believers had but one leader": Ibid.

81   "I sit in silence with dear mother": Ibid.

82   "for so acute have been my sufferings": Ibid.

82   "Whilst returning from meeting this morning, I saw": Ibid.

83   "Sometimes I think that the children of Israel": Ibid.

84   "I think no criminal under sentence of death": Sarah Grimké (1827) Diary, in the Weld Papers.

85   "I have passed through some trying feelings of late about becoming": The Diary of Angelina Grimké, 1832, in the Weld Papers.

85   "full of rebellion": Ibid.

85   "I am not at all surprised at the account": Angelina Grimké to Sarah Grimké, [undated], in the Weld Papers.

86 Ironically, Nat Turner was much like the Grimkés: William H. Freehling, *The Road to Disunion* (New York: Oxford University Press, 1990), 178–79.

86 Born a slave in 1800, Turner became a valued and talented worker: Ibid., 178.

86 "To a mind like mine, restless, inquisitive, and observant": Quoted in Herb Boyd, ed., *Autobiography of a People* (New York: Doubleday and Co., 2000), 83. Boyd quotes from the extensive notes made by journalist Thomas Gray, within days of Turner's capture. The notes were later circulated in pamphlet form before appearing in *A Documentary History of the Negro People in the United States*, vol. 2 (New York: Carol Publishing Group, 1994).

87 "As I was praying one day at my plough": Ibid., 84.

87 "the knowledge of the elements": Ibid.

87 "And I wondered greatly at these miracles, and prayed": Ibid.

88 "The murder of this [Travis's] family, five in number": Ibid., 85.

89 In its aftermath, the South reacted by imposing new: Freehling, *The Road to Disunion*, 185–87. Nat Turner, it should be noted, recounted his rebellion in detail, while awaiting execution, to a journalist who then wrote a sensational— and since questioned—"Confession," which William Styron would take as the basis for his best-selling *The Confessions of Nat Turner* (1967). The facts of the rebellion, however, are well documented. See also James Brewer Steward, *Holy Warriors: The Abolitionists and American Slavery* (New York: Hill and Wang, 1976), 45.

CHAPTER 5

91 A brilliant speaker and gifted thinker, Weld was descended: Robert H. Abzug, *Passionate Liberator: Theodore Dwight Weld and the Dilemma of Reform* (New York: Oxford University Press, 1980), 6–10. A detailed accounting of the ancestry of the Weld family can be found in the Weld Papers at the University of Michigan in Ann Arbor.

91 Welds had been among the nation's first "revolutionary Puritans": Abzug, *Passionate Liberator*, 7.

92 At Hamilton, Weld was a giant: Ibid., 31.

92 "My father," he said, "was a real minister of the Gospel": Quoted ibid., 47.

92 "We had heard of the revival at Utica": Sissy Weld, quoted ibid., 58.

93 During his Utica sermon, Finney seemed: Ibid., 48–49.

93 "Ah is it not enough? Have you followed a minister": Quoted ibid. Theodore Weld did not himself write of his conversion or, apparently, pass on the details of his confrontation with Finney to Angelina or Sarah Grimké. The conversion story was observed by Finney and told to Lyman Beecher, who wrote about it in his papers. An account of the incident may be found in Barbara M.

Cross, ed., *The Autobiography of Lyman Beecher*, 2 vols. (Cambridge, Mass: Harvard University Press, 1961).

93   Throughout 1827, Theodore Weld traveled the back roads of New York: Ibid., 52.

94   Weld insisted to Beecher: Ibid., 57–58.

95   Staid, conservative, disciplined, and upright Lyman Beecher: Joan D. Hedrick, *Harriet Beecher Stowe: A Life* (New York: Oxford University Press, 1994), 41–42 and 102–4. See also Cross, ed., *Autobiography of Lyman Beecher*, for an account of Beecher's attitudes and religious career. I have relied heavily, too, on Milton Rugoff, *The Beechers: An American Family in the Nineteenth Century* (New York, Harper & Row, 1981). Although the papers of the Beecher family are scattered, many of the most valuable are deposited in the Stowe-Day Library in Hartford, Connecticut.

Beecher had much in common with Weld, at least in terms of personality. Here is how the historian Robert H. Abzug has described Beecher: "Lyman Beecher was the kind of man who felt that the world depended on him for ultimate salvation; his hyperbolic prose spilled over with notions of disaster if his own way [was] blocked" (*Passionate Liberator*, 78).

95   "The state of feeling in Oneida County": Theodore Weld to Charles Grandison Finney, September 1831, in the Weld Papers.

96   Oneida was literally built from the ground up: Abzug, *Passionate Liberator*, 61.

97   The Tappans were known for supporting crusaders: William H. Pease and Jane H. Pease, *Bound with Them in Chains: A Biographical History of the Antislavery Movement* (Westport, Conn.: Greenwood Press, 1972), 39–42. See also Merton L. Dillon: *The Abolitionists: The Growth of a Dissenting Minority* (New York: W. W. Norton & Co., 1974), 129–30.

97   "Satan's seat," he told Finney, could be conquered only: Theodore H. Weld to Charles Grandison Finney, July 1831, in the Weld Papers.

97   "Kindle back fires, back fires, back fires": Theodore H. Weld to Charles Grandison Finney, in the Finney Manuscript Collection, Oberlin College, Ohio.

98   "If we gain the West": Quoted in Abzug, *Passionate Liberator*, 74–75.

98   "bring forth an hundredfold more": Quoted in Joan D. Hedrick, *Harriet Beecher Stowe: A Life* (New York: Oxford University Press, 1994), 98.

99   The students kept their ranks undiluted by skeptical outsiders: Abzug, *Passionate Liberator*, 75–77.

99   "Oneida has lost the spirit which she once possessed": Quoted ibid., 80.

99   In late 1832, Weld traveled to Hudson, Ohio: Ibid., 87.

100   "I hardly know how to contain myself": Theodore Weld to Elizur Wright, January 10, 1833, in Gilbert H. Barnes and Dwight L. Dumond, eds., *Letters of Theodore Dwight Weld, Angelina Grimké Weld and Sarah Grimké, 1822–1844*, 2 vols. (New York: Appleton-Century, Co., 1932; reprint, New York: Da Capo Press, 1970) (hereafter, *Weld-Grimké Letters*), 1:99.

100   "proximity of Cincinnati and the whole eastern line of Ohio": Ibid., 1:100.

101 "We early began to inculcate our views by conversation": Quoted in Cross, ed., *Autobiography of Lyman Beecher*, 2:241–42.

102 "We believe that faith without works is dead": Quoted in Abzug, *Passionate Liberator*, 95.

104 "If you want to teach [in] colored schools": Quoted in Cross, ed., *Autobiography of Lyman Beecher*, 2:244.

104 "Is research to be hoodwinked, and debate struck dumb": Theodore Weld to James Hall, in *Weld-Grimké Letters*, 1:138.

105 "If you, doctor, were a thorough Anti-Slavery man": Tappan quoted in Abzug, *Passionate Liberator*, 116.

105 In October of 1834, Weld and his followers decided to leave Lane: Ibid., 120.

105 "The Providence of God has for some time": Theodore Weld to the Reverend John J. Shipherd, Lane Seminary, June 21, 1834, in *Weld-Grimké Letters*, 1:190.

106 "I give him one year to abolitionize all of Ohio": Entry from 1835, Diary of James G. Birney, in the James G. Birney Papers, Library of Congress.

106 In Nashville, Tennessee, Amos Dresser: Dillon, *The Abolitionists*, 66. Dresser was one of the Lane Rebels.

106 In Canaan, New Hampshire, townsmen: Ibid., 66.

107 In Southern ports, mail sacks were seized: Ibid., 67–68.

107 "patting the greasy little fellows on their cheeks": Quoted in Henry Mayer, *All On Fire* (New York: St. Martin's Press, 1998), 197.

108 "That infamous foreign scoundrel, THOMPSON, will hold forth": Quoted ibid., 197–99.

108 "If you go now, I will protect you": Quoted ibid., 205.

109 Dressed "in a borrowed coat and pantaloons": Ibid.

109 "William Lloyd Garrison was put into this cell . . .": Quoted ibid.

110 In September 1834, Thomas Grimké went to see his sisters: Lerner, 109.

110 He appeared, unarmed, on his front porch: Ibid., 110. The incident is also recounted by the sisters in their remembrance of Thomas's life, entitled "A Sketch of T.G.'s life written by his sisters in Philadelphia and sent to his friends in Charleston, for their approbation," contained in the Weld Papers. Thomas is also discussed extensively in Sarah's diary of 1827, in the Weld Papers.

110 "comforted in believing that my kingdom": A. Grimké to T. Grimké, June 10, 1832, in the Weld Papers.

110 "My fears respecting you are often prevalent": Quoted in Birney, 117.

111 In early October 1834 he traveled west: Lerner, 109.

111 Bettles had been introduced to Angelina shortly after she first arrived: Ibid., 110–11.

112 On March 3, 1835, she attended: Ibid., 119.

113 "What to do? What to do?": The Diary of Angelina Grimké, 1835, in the Weld Papers.

113 "I can hardly express to thee the deep and solemn interest": Angelina Grimké,

"Slavery and the Boston Riot: A Letter to William Lloyd Garrison," broadside, Philadelphia, 1835.

114   "To have the name of Grimké associated": The Diary of Angelina Grimké, September 1835, in the Weld Papers.

115   ". . . It seemed as though the very exercises I was suffering under": Angelina Grimké, "Slavery and the Boston Riot."

CHAPTER 6

119   A Boston clergyman named Amos Phelps was almost killed: Henry Mayer, *All On Fire* (New York: St. Martin's Press, 1998), 189.

119   *"One year ago* there were but three newspapers in the United States": Quoted in Robert H. Abzug, *Passionate Liberator: Theodore Dwight Weld and the Dilemma of Reform* (New York: Oxford University Press, 1980), 125–26.

120   In 1827, Quaker Elias Hicks had founded the Free Produce movement: Lerner, 129. The most comprehensive account of the impact of this movement may be found in Ruth Kettering Nuermberger, *The Free Produce Movement: A Quaker Protest Against Slavery* (Chapel Hill, N.C.: Duke University Press, 1956; reprint, New York: AMS Press, 1970).

121   The leaders of the three wings of the abolitionist movement: Mayer, *All On Fire*, 173–77. See also Merton L. Dillon, *The Abolitionists: The Growth of a Dissenting Minority* (New York: W. W. Norton & Co., 1974), 65–66, and James Brewer Steward, *Holy Warriors: The Abolitionists and American Slavery* (New York: Hill and Wang, 1976), 51–58.

121   The organizing meeting of the American Anti-Slavery Society: Mayer, *All On Fire*, 173–77.

121   "Looking over the assembly, I noticed": John Greenleaf Whittier, "Voices of Freedom," in Louis Ruchames, ed., *The Abolitionists: A Collection of Their Writings* (New York: G. P. Putnam's Sons, 1963), 68.

122   After three days of meetings, the convention adopted: Ibid., 78–83. Whittier wrote the "Declaration of Sentiments" at Garrison's suggestion.

122   Their first act was to bring Elizur Wright: Mayer, *All On Fire*, 177.

122   Mercurial and impossible to control: Abzug, *Passionate Liberator*, 144.

123   "Yes, they said, the AAS wanted immediate emancipation": Mayer, *All On Fire*, 176–77. See also Whittier, "Voices of Freedom," 57. Surprisingly, Garrison was responsible for the compromise slogan; he was hoping to make the movement more palatable to mainstream America. This was one of the few instances in which he ever moderated his views.

124   Women, too, were shut out of AAS leadership: Steward, *Holy Warriors*, 58.

124   She offered several resolutions that were adopted: Mayer, *All On Fire*, 174. See also Lerner, 121.

125   The young Forten women: Mayer, *All On Fire*, 174.

126   It is difficult to gauge the precise influence of Mott: A. Oliver Johnson, *William Lloyd Garrison and His Times* (Boston: B. B. Russell & Co., 1880), 255–56.

126   "so thoroughly imbued with women's rights": Quoted in Otelia Cromwell, *Lucretia Mott* (New York: Russell & Russell, 1971), 125.

127   "The Friend of sinners opened a door of escape": Quoted in Lerner, 134.

128   "I feel no openness among Friends": Quoted in Birney, 137–38.

128   "I cannot think of acceding to it ": Quoted in Lerner, 136.

128   "My beloved sister does indeed need the prayers ": Quoted in Birney, 137.

129   "It has all come to me": Quoted in Lerner, 138. The incident is also recounted in the Diary of Angelina Grimké, in the Weld Papers.

130   "The bare idea that such a thing may be required of me": Quoted in Birney, 140.

130   "endeavor to undeceive the South": Ibid., 141.

131   "Oh that it could be rained down": Quoted ibid., 147. Elizur Wright to Angelina Weld, [undated], in the Weld Papers.

131   "It is because I feel a deep and tender interest": Angelina Grimké, "Appeal to the Christian Women of the Southern States" (New York: American Anti-Slavery Society, 1836). The essay is reprinted in *The Public Years of Sarah and Angelina Grimké*, ed. Larry Ceplair (New York: Columbia University Press, 1989), 36–79.

132   "It has been justly remarked": Ibid.

132   "And who last hung around the cross of Jesus": Ibid.

133   Its reception in the South was predictable: Lerner, 147. Sarah Grimké mentions that her sister's work was burned on the dock in Charleston in her own essay "An Epistle to the Clergy of the Southern States."

133   The mayor paid a courtesy call: Lerner, 147; Birney, 150. Birney gives the most extensive and authoritative account of this incident, which was likely related to her by Sarah.

134   Weld thought of himself as the John the Baptist: Abzug, *Passionate Liberator*, 146.

134   "I have slept since you left us, but not in peace": Sarah Carpenter to Theodore Weld, October 22, 1835, in the Weld Papers.

135   "In discussing the subject of slavery": Theodore Weld to Lewis Tappan, December 22, 1835, in *Weld-Grimké Letters*, 1:247.

135   "a man like Weld thinks": Lewis Tappan to Charles Grandison Finney, March 22, 1832, in *Weld-Grimké Letters*, 1:68n.

136   called the meeting a "sham and show off": Theodore Weld to Lewis Tappan, undated letter written aboard Erie Canal transport boat, in the New-York Historical Society.

136   "I am a Backwoodsman": Theodore Weld to Lewis Tappan, April 5, 1836, in *Weld-Grimké Letters*, 1:287.

136   "Has an agent a right to be more 'egotistical' to one of us": Elizur Wright, Jr., to Theodore Weld, May 26, 1835, in *Weld-Grimké Letters*, 1:221.

137 "The Lord is with us—truth tells. Mob dead, buried, and rotten": Quoted in Abzug, *Passionate Liberator*, 147.

138 "As to my feelings towards the Colored people, suffice it to say": Theodore Weld to Lewis Tappan, April 5, 1836, in *Weld-Grimké Letters*, 1: 287.

139 "Stones, pieces of brick, eggs, cents, sticks": Quoted in Abzug, *Passionate Liberator*, 148.

139 "What is Troy compared to the nation?": William Lloyd Garrison to William C. Chace, [undated], in the Garrison Papers, Boston Public Library.

140 In July 1836, Weld met with the Tappan brothers: Abzug, *Passionate Liberator*, 150.

CHAPTER 7

142 "ambitious, unprincipled time-serving demagogue": Quoted in William E. Cain, ed., *William Lloyd Garrison and the Fight Against Slavery: Selections from* The Liberator (Boston: Bedford Books, 1995), 37. The description appeared in *The Liberator*'s June 14, 1844, issue.

142 "lick spittle of the slaveholding oligarchy": Cain, ed., *William Lloyd Garrison*, 37. The phrase appeared in *The Liberator* on March 16, 1849.

143 Although the society had printed millions of antislavery pamphlets: Merton L. Dillon, *The Abolitionists: The Growth of a Dissenting Minority* (New York: W.W. Norton & Co., 1974), 56–57.

143 "Working with common purpose, these men were": Birney, 72.

144 The training commenced on November 15: Robert H. Abzug, *Passionate Liberator: Theodore Dwight Weld and the Dilemma of Reform* (New York: Oxford University Press, 1980), 151.

145 "Her disapproval, more than anything else": Quoted in Lerner, 163.

145 "I have realized very sensibly of late": Quoted in Birney, 153.

146 "A solemn sense of duty I owe as a southerner": Sarah Moore Grimké, "An Epistle to the Clergy of the Southern States" (New York: American Anti-Slavery Society, 1836).

146 They began with a series of parlor meetings: Lerner, 154–55.

147 "dear sister did her part better than I did": The Diary of Angelina Grimké, September 1836, in the Weld Papers.

147 "I would not give up my abolition feelings": Quoted ibid., 165.

148 "incendiaries," "instigators": James Henry Hammond to M. M. Noah, August 19, 1835, in the Hammond Papers, Library of Congress.

149 James Henry Hammond of South Carolina: William H. Freehling, *The Road to Disunion* (New York: Oxford Univeristy Press, 1990), 154-55.

149 "And I warn the abolitionists, ignorant, infatuated, barbarians": Quoted ibid., 315.

149 "Abolitionists," Hammond thundered: Ibid.

151   The result was that more than one half of all AAS members: Merton L. Dillon, *The Abolitonists: The Growth of a Dissenting Minority* (New York: W.W. Norton & Co., 1974), 102.

151   "are striving to perpetuate slavery": Quoted in Lerner, 156–57.

151   "Northern men go to the South to make their fortunes": Sarah M. and Angelina Grimké, "Letter to Clarkson," *New Haven Intelligencer*, March 1837.

152   if "Northerners were to do all": quoted in Mayer, *All On Fire*, 236.

152   defended the policy of gradualism: Lerner, 184–85.

152   "Men are the proper persons to make appeals": Quoted ibid., 184. Beecher's "Essay on Slavery and Abolitionism with Reference to the Duty of American Females" was published in 1837 by Henry Perkins, Philadelphia.

153   "Who can look without disgust and abhorrence": Quoted in Catherine Beecher, "Letters on the Difficulty of Religion," prologue to "An Essay on Slavery and Abolition with Reference to the Duty of American Females."

154   "Every true friend of the oppressed American": Angelina Grimké, "Letters to Catherine E. [*sic*] Beecher, in reply to 'An Essay on Slavery and Abolitionism,' Addressed to A. E. Grimké" (Boston: Isaac Knapp, 1838).

155   "And so," wrote Angelina, "the colored people": Ibid.

155   "Women ought to feel a peculiar sympathy in the colored man's wrong": Angelina Grimké, "An Appeal to the Women of the Nominally Free States," issued "by an Anti-Slavery Convention of American Women & held by Adjournment from the 9th to the 12th of May, 1937," 1st ed. (New York: W. S. Dorr, 1837).

156   The meeting was a great success: Lerner, 163.

156   "Upon this subject of antislavery my principles": Quoted ibid., 167.

156   By the end of 1837, they had spoken to hundreds of listeners: Ibid., 168–69.

157   "I well remember evening after evening": Quoted in Birney, 180.

157   "She swept the chords of the human heart" Quoted in Lerner, 233.

157   In late 1837, she began to study: Lerner, 174–77.

158   "I have sometimes been astonished and grieved:" Sarah Grimké, "Letters on the Equality of the Sexes and the Condition of Woman," *The Liberator*, 1837.

159   His argument provoked such consternation: Birney, 184–85.

160   "Surely, there is nothing either astonishing or novel": Sarah Grimké, "The Province of Woman," *New England Spectator*, summer 1837.

160   "If the vine, whose strength and beauty": Quoted in Lerner, 139. The "Pastoral Letter" is quoted verbatim in *Weld-Grimké Letters*, 1: 478–79.

161   "So this is all—the utmost reach": John Greenleaf Whittier, "The Pastoral Letter," *The Liberator*, [undated], 1837. Later, Whittier, that wit, compared the Pastoral Letter (issued in Brookfield, Massachusetts) to a papal edict, calling it "that Brookfield bull."

161   In November 1837, an abolitionist editor named Elijah Lovejoy: Dillon, *The Abolitionists*, 93.

161 "My heart sinks within me when I remember": Sarah Grimké, "Letter from Sarah M. Grimké," *The Liberator*, January 1838.

162 "I know it will surprise and even amaze you": Theodore Weld to Angelina Grimké, in *Weld-Grimké Letters*, 2: 532–35, February 8, 1838.

162 "I felt [,] my Theodore": Angelina Grimké to Theodore Weld, ibid., 536, February 11, 1838.

CHAPTER 8

163 Just after noon on February 21, 1838: Lerner, 1.

164 "I never was so near fainting": Angelina Grimké to Theodore Weld, *Weld-Grimké Letters*, 2: 564, February 21, 1838.

164 "I stand before you as a southerner": Quoted in Lerner, 7.

165 "[Her] testimony was not only the testimony": On the Death of Angelina Grimké, Wendell Phillips (undated), in the Weld Papers.

165 "We Abolition Women": Quoted in Lerner, 12.

165 "She exhibited considerable talent for a female": *Boston Gazette*, March 19, 1838.

166 "My heart's desire": Quoted in Lerner, 217.

166 "From your knowledge of my natural impulsiveness": Quoted in Birney, 191–92.

167 Sarah's talks did not go well: Lerner, 231.

168 monotonous and heavy: Theordore Weld to Sarah Grimké, *Weld-Grimké Letters*, 2: 604, March 24, 1838.

168 "the lack of interest in your lectures": Quoted in Lerner, 232.

168 "Now my beloved sister" Quoted ibid., 231.

169 The fame of the Grimké sisters: Merton L. Dillon, *The Abolitionists: The Growth of a Dissenting Minority* (New York: W. W. Norton & Co., 1974), 114–18. A clear discussion of this issue may be found in Birney, 178–82. Birney, writing nearer that time—when women did not yet have the vote—than ours (and so, it would seeming, lacking our perspective), maintains that the Grimkés had no intention of starting a women's rights revolution until they realized, after their New England lectures, that they already had done so.

169 Garrison and his followers: Henry Mayer, *All On Fire* (New York: St. Martin's Press, 1998), 231–34. Garrison was perhaps Sarah and Angelina's most ardent supporter.

170 "Be not afraid to look the monster *Slavery*": Quoted ibid., 233. See also Garrison's nearly monthly charges that abolitionists were being too faint of heart. His "Rights of Woman," published in the January 12, 1838, edition of *The Liberator*, was aimed at giving the Grimké sisters public support, just when they were under the greatest fire: "Free discussion will finally break all fetters," he assured them, "and put down all usurpation."

170 The New York reformers: Dillon, *The Abolitionists*, 114–16.

171 "It is vain to think of succeeding in emancipation": Quoted ibid., 98.

171 "Brethren, 'cease from man,' ": Quoted in Mayer, *All On Fire*, 256–57. Many of Garrison's most public battles were fought not with the Tappans (who preferred to attack him from a distance) but with Henry B. Stanton. At one meeting, Stanton shouted a question at Garrison: "Do you or do you not believe it a sin to go to the polls?" But Garrison would not fall into that trap: "It is a sin for *me*," he said.

171 "Practically I have always been a 'peace man' ": Quoted in Birney, 208.

172 "Sometimes the hope": The Diary of Angelina Grimké, August 1838, in the Weld Papers.

172 "Theodore addressed Angelina in a solemn and tender manner": Sarah Grimké to Catherine Beecher (undated), in the Weld Papers.

172 The greatest lights of the abolitionist movement were in attendance: Lerner, 242. See also Mayer, *All On Fire*, 244.

173 The wedding was unadorned, the ceremony simple: Mayer, *All On Fire*, 244.

173 The hall had been built by subscription: Ibid., 245–46.

173 "A number of individuals of all sects, and those of no sect": Quoted ibid., 247. See also Lerner, 244.

174 A crowd of men endeavored to keep the speakers: Lerner, 244.

174 "What is a mob?": Quoted ibid., 246.

174 "I have seen it! I have seen it!": Quoted ibid.

175 "The crowd around the building increased": Quoted in Birney, 235–36.

176 William Lloyd Garrison did not linger in Philadelphia: Mayer, *All On Fire*, 245.

176 "doctrines repulsive to the moral sense of a large majority": Quoted in Lerner, 250.

176 "identify themselves with these oppressed Americans": Quoted ibid., 251.

177 Together, the couple planned a book on slavery in America: Ibid., 260–63.

178 "It is just such a monument of suffering": Quoted in Birney, 250–51. See also Angelina Grimké Weld to Ann W. Weston, [undated], in the Weston Papers, Boston Public Library.

178 The "Graham diet": Birney, 245–46.

179 "We believe it [the Graham-Alcott regimen]": Quoted ibid., 247.

179 "the testimony of slaveholders in all parts of the slave states": Theodore Dwight Weld, *American Slavery as It Is* (New York: American Anti-Slavery Society, 1839), 9.

180 To aid his study, Weld purchased: Lerner, 262–63.

180 "[That] they are overworked, underfed, wretchedly clad": Weld, *American Slavery as It Is*, 9.

181 "It cost us more *agony of soul*": Angelina Grimké Weld to Anna Frost, August 18, 1839, in the Grimké-Weld Personal Papers, Library of Congress.

182 "I began to think it was with you": Lydia Maria Child to Angelina Grimké Weld and Sarah Grimké, August 14, 1839, in the Weld Papers.

182   "The Grimkés, I think, are extinct": Deborah Weston to Ann W. Weston, April 1, 1839, in the Weston Papers, Boston Public Library.

182   "The great body of Abolitionists": Theodore Weld to Gerrit Smith, September 1839, in the Weld Papers.

183   the "bitter cup": Anna Grimké to Angelina Grimké Weld and Sarah Grimké (undated), in the Weld Papers.

183   Sarah was horrified by the baby's "gluttony": Lerner, 279.

183   "little teacher sent from God": Quoted in Birney, 261.

183   " Oh, the ecstasy and the gratitude!": Quoted ibid., 260.

184   The long-anticipated showdown: Mayer, *All On Fire*, 280–84. See also Lerner, 286–87, and Dwight Lowell Dumond, *Anti-Slavery: The Crusade for Freedom in America* (Ann Arbor, Mich.: University of Michigan Press, 1961), 290–97. The reports of the American Anti-Slavery Society may be seen in the American Anti-Slavery Society Collection at the Boston Public Library.

184   The meeting opened with a raucous call for order: Dumond, *Anti-Slavery*, 292.

186   "In Congress the masters speak": Quoted in Dumond, *Anti-Slavery*, 293.

187   They viewed its proceedings with distaste: Lerner, 284.

187   "The Societies have done a good work in their day": Zebina Eastman, letter to the *Western Citizen*, March 30, 1843.

CHAPTER 9

188   In March 1840, the Welds and Sarah Grimké moved: Lerner, 294. See also Robert H. Abzug, *Passionate Liberator: Theodore Dwight Weld and the Dilemma of Reform* (New York: Oxford University Press, 1980), 206, and Birney, 261.

188   Weld labored to rebuild a long stone wall: Abzug, *Passionate Liberator*, 206

189   "Early in her married life": Quoted in Theodore Dwight Weld, *In Memory, Angelina Grimké Weld* (G. H. Ellis: Boston, 1880), 11.

189   "In correspondence with her friend Harriot Hunt": Lerner, 290.

190   "These men are in a position": Theodore Dwight Weld to Angelina Grimké Weld, December 14, 1841, *Weld-Grimké Letters*, 2: 881.

191   "I know you well sir": Adams (undated) quoted in Lerner, 301.

192   Adams was convinced that sooner or later: William Lee Miller, *Arguing About Slavery* (New York: Random House, 1995), 372.

192   "Wise of Va., Raynor of N.C., W.C. Johnson of Md.": Quoted ibid., 431.

193   But Adams had been doing his own strategizing: Ibid., 429–33.

194   "a vast proportion of the resources": Ibid., 430.

194   "*Mr. Wise:* Is it in order to move to censure": Quoted ibid.,438.

194   The trial of John Quincy Adams: Ibid., 429–54.

195   "If the right of habeas corpus": Quoted in Miller, *Arguing About Slavery*, 431.

195   "If I withdraw the petition": Quoted ibid., 432.

196   "Slave holding, slave trading and slave breeding": Theodore Dwight Weld to Angelina Grimké Weld (undated), in the Weld Papers.

196   In March 1844, Angelina gave birth: Lerner, 307.

196   "He is in the ditch opposite his house": Quoted in Abzug, *Passionate Liberator*, 245.

196   "They have saved me from I knew not what": Sarah Grimké to H. Hunt, December 31, 1854, in the Weld Papers.

197   The "Belleville School" would ultimately enroll: Lerner, 316.

197   Spring had left the Fourierist North American phalanx: Ibid., 317.

198   "branches of agriculture and mechanics whereby": Quoted ibid., 318.

199   The Eagleswood School was a model: Abzug, *Passionate Liberator*, p. 260. See also, "Eagleswood School, Perth Amboy, New-Jersey," a circular for the school, in the Garrison Family Papers, Sophia Smith Collection, Smith College Library.

199   Eagleswood became a meeting ground: Abzug, *Passionate Liberator*, 262.

200   Angelina and Sarah "take it for granted": Quoted ibid., 329.

200   In the early 1840s, the sisters had been attracted to the prophecies: Abzug, *Passionate Liberator*, 249–53.

200   In 1849, she had met the spiritualist Andrew Jackson Davis: Ibid., 249.

201   "A. J. Davis believes and teaches that the time will come": Quoted ibid., 250.

201   News of the rappings: Slater Brown, *The Heyday of Spiritualism* (New York: Hawthorn Books, 1983), 98–104. See also Ann D. Braude, *Radical Spirits: Spiritualism and Women's Rights in Nineteenth-Century America* (Boston: Beacon Press, 1969).

202   an "unbroken chain of communication exists": Quoted in Mayer, *All On Fire*, 465.

202   "We hold these truths to be self-evident": Quoted in Elisabeth Griffith, *In Her Own Right: The Life of Elizabeth Cady Stanton* (New York: Oxford University Press, 1984), 53.

203   "The investigation of the rights of the slave": Angelina Emily Grimké, "Letters to Catherine E. Beecher, in Reply to 'An Essay on Slavery and Abolition,' Addressed to A. E. Grimké" (Boston: Isaac Knapp, 1837), 126.

203   Women got married, Grimké maintained: Sarah Grimké, "Letters on the Equality of the Sexes and the Condition of Woman" (Boston: Isaac Knapp, 1838).

203   "Thousands are thus sacrificed": Ibid.

204   Angelina and Theodore had disagreed: Lerner, 288. See also Abzug, *Passionate Liberator*, 242.

204   "Effectually to soften and subdue those impulses": Theodore Weld to Angelina and Sarah Grimké, February 1842, in *Weld-Grimké Letters*, 2: 892.

205   "Thousands of minds have been dwarfed": Ibid.

205   "I thought nothing else would be effectual": Angelina Grimké to Theodore Weld, in *Weld-Grimké Letters*, 2: 894.

205   "There is plenty of work to be done": Quoted in Lerner, 320.

206   "There are times I feel humbled in the dust": Quoted ibid., 321.

206   "Separation from these darling children": Sarah Grimké to H. Hunt, December 31, 1852, in the Weld Papers.

206   The term was meant to ridicule the style: Lerner, 332.

206   "It is not wise . . . to use up": Quoted ibid., 333.

206   "We put the dress on for greater freedom": Quoted ibid., 335.

207   Sody was sent to Boston for physical conditioning: Ibid., 346.

207   "It is only necessary to lay upon the small of the back": Quoted ibid., 348.

208   "What can I say," she wrote: Sarah Grimké to Theodore Weld (undated), in the Weld Papers.

209   After a two-day siege: Stephen B. Oates, *To Purge This Land with Blood* (New York: Harper & Row, 1970), 290–306.

209   In the aftermath of the Harper's Ferry bloodletting: Mayer, *All On Fire*, 503.

210   Sarah and Angelina, pacifists and "nonresisters," celebrated Brown's raid: Lerner, 338–39.

CHAPTER 10

211   There were torchlight parades: Walter Edgard, *South Carolina: A History* (Columbia, S.C.: University of South Carolina Press, 1998), 354–57.

212   "Sir: By authority of Brigadier-General Beauregard": General Stephen D. Lee, "The First Step in The War," in *Battles and Leaders* (Philadelphia: Century Publishing, 1885), 1: 76.

212   The shelling began: Ibid., 78.

213   "South Carolina is too small to be a Republic": James L. Petigru, quoted in Edgard, *South Carolina*, 355.

213   "For God's sake, and the sake of our beloved state": David L. Wardlaw, quoted ibid., 355.

214   "The South are dissolving the Union": Quoted in Lerner, 341.

214   "I am driven to [teaching]": Quoted in Birney, 266.

215   "We had indulged a delightful hope": Quoted ibid., 274.

215   "If Theodore finds that he can use his voice": Quoted in Sarah Grimké to [unknown], November 16, 1862, in the Weld Papers.

216   "An Appeal to the Women of the Republic": Lerner, 351.

216   "My country is bleeding": Quoted ibid.

216   "This war is not, as the South falsely pretends": Quoted ibid., 354–55.

217   Sarah had a dream one night: Birney, 286.

217   Sarah and Angelina's sisters Eliza and Mary: Lerner, 356.

218   "I am called into service": David Harris, *The Letters of David Harris, a Confederate Soldier of South Carolina* (Columbia, S.C.: South Carolina University Press, 1981), 22.

218 "Against us," he would later write, "the fort presented an armed front": General Quincy A. Gillmore, "The Army before Charleston in 1863," in *Battles and Leaders* (Philadelphia: Century Publishing, 1885), 3: 53.

219 "Although the troops went gallantly forward": Ibid., 59.

219 Among those killed on this day was Colonel Robert Gould Shaw: Ibid., 66–67.

219 "Our noble, beautiful young Colonel is killed": Charlotte Forten Grimké (July 20, 1863), *The Journals of Charlotte Forten Grimké*, ed. Brenda Stevenson, the Schomburg Library of Nineteenth-Century Black Women Writers (New York: Oxford University Press, 1988), 494.

220 "one of the best and noblest types of manhood": Ibid., 496.

221 "one earnest sympathizing soul": Ibid., 504.

221 "I am not satisfied to teach": Angelina Weld to Rebecca, [undated, 1867], in the Weld Papers. The "Rebecca" to whom this letter is addressed remains unidentified, but she may have been a colleague.

222 In Charleston, meanwhile, the situation was deteriorating: Edgard, *South Carolina*, 370–71.

223 "The Nation is its *citizens*": Theodore Dwight Weld, "The Nation, Its Rights and Duties," 1863, manuscript in the Weld Papers.

223 In 1867, at the age of seventy-five: Lerner, 356.

223 In mid-1867, Eliza Grimké: Ibid., 356.

224 "His slaves will feel his loss deeply": Quoted in Birney, 289.

227 On a February evening in 1868: Ibid., 358.

227 "Negroes and Higher Studies": Ibid., 358. The article first appeared in the *National Anti-Slavery Standard*, February 8, 1868.

228 "Dear Madam, I am very happy to hear from Miss Angelina Grimké": Quoted in Dickson D. Bruce, Jr., *Archibald Grimké, Portrait of a Black Independent* (Baton Rouge, La.: Louisiana State University Press, 1993), 23 (hereafter, Bruce).

229 "Her brother had wronged these children": Sarah Weld Hamilton, "Memories of Theodore Dwight Weld, the St. John of the Abolitionists," undated manuscript in the Weld Papers, Box 18. Also see Lerner, 361–62, and Birney, 287.

229 "Dear young friends, I cannot express the mingled emotions": Quoted in Lerner, 361.

229 It was an uncomfortable moment: Bruce, 24–25.

230 "To the boys this was a great occasion": Angelina W. Grimké, "A Biographical Sketch of Archibald H. Grimké," *Opportunity* 3 (February 1925), 47.

CHAPTER 11

234   "He very openly acknowledged": Bruce, 4–5. See also Lerner, 360–63.

234   He set aside his wild habits: Henry Justi Ferry, "Francis James Grimké: Portrait of a Black Puritan" (Ph.D. diss., Yale University, 1970), 8–11 (hereafter, Ferry).

235   He bought a large rice plantation: Ibid., 3.

235   Henry lived at Cane Acre for most of the year: Ibid., 4.

235   But the evidence we do have: Archibald H. Grimké, unpublished memoirs, (hereafter, A.H.G. Memoirs), in the Grimké Papers at the Moorland-Spingarn Research Center, Howard University (hereafter, Grimké Papers).

237   At a time when nearly every other male slave child at Cane Acre: Bruce, 6.

237   She was thin but tough: Ferry, 12–13.

237   One day, she later told her sons: A.H.G. Memoirs, 12.

238   Henry Grimké died on September, 28, 1852: Ferry, 9.

238   The small house was located on Coming Street: Ibid., 10.

239   for they lived in "a part of the city": A. H. Grimké, "A Madonna of the South," *Southern Workman* 29, no. 7 (July 1900): 391.

240   The white minister there was dedicated to black education: Ferry, 21.

241   Frank continued to outwit his captor: Ibid., 26–27.

242   The Coles devised a sophisticated series of signals: A.H.G. Memoirs, 14.

242   He followed the war closely: Ibid., 16.

242   Frank wanted to stay on with Rhett: Ferry, 33.

243   FIFTY DOLLARS REWARD: *Charleston Mercury*, September 12, 1863.

243   "There I remained for several months:" Francis Grimké, *The Collected Works of Francis James Grimké*, ed. Carter G. Woodson, (Washington, D.C.: The Associated Publishers, 1952), 1: viii (hereafter F.J.G., *Works*).

244   In mid-February 1865: Ibid., 1: ix.

244   Woodford chose James Redpath: Ferry, 43.

245   Archie, Frank, and John Grimké were enrolled at: Ibid., 44.

245   At the end of the summer of 1865: Ibid., 45.

246   "During my whole stay with them": F.J.G., *Works*, 1: viii.

247   But Lincoln was a small and struggling school: Ferry, 50.

247   "The late wonderful providences of God": Lincoln University catalog (1866), 11.

248   "I thought," Archie would later write: A.H.G. Memoirs, 109–11.

248   "I never heard him preach a poor sermon,": Quoted in Ferry, 32.

249   The advice came in a torrent of letters: Ferry, 63–66.

249   The summer of 1869 found Frank in Saint Leonard's: Ibid., 66.

250   "It seems a long time since I sent you": Sarah Grimké to A. H. Grimké and F. J. Grimké, October 18, 1869, in the Grimké Papers.

250 Archie lasted only a year: Ferry, 70.

251 In 1875, after much reflection: Ibid., 74. Frank recounts his decision to become a lawyer in F.J.G, *Works*, 2: 317.

251 In the 1870s, Washington was a city: Ferry, 73.

252 Frank acquitted himself adequately before the examining board: Ibid., 76.

253 The training at Princeton: Ibid.

253 Archibald Grimké, meanwhile, had entered the Harvard Law School in 1874: Bruce, 31.

253 Among his classmates was Henry Cabot Lodge: Ibid., 29.

253 He graduated at the head of his class: Ibid., 30.

253 Over the course of his two years of study, Archie met: Ibid., 31.

254 In 1870, when the Massachusetts Woman Suffrage Association: Lerner, 366.

254 In 1871, at the age of seventy-nine: Birney, 297.

CHAPTER 12

255 On most mornings in 1874: Bruce, 33–34.

256 Archie had been taken into Bowditch's firm: Relevant papers from Bowditch's firm are in the Grimké Papers.

256 Archie had fallen in love with Nelly Bradford: Bruce, 34–35.

257 "manners so exactly right": Nelly Bradford Stebbins to Angelina (Weld) Grimké, January 20, 1936, in the Grimké Papers.

257 "I cannot do what I now intend": Archibald H. Grimké to M. C. Stanley, February 9, 1879, in the Grimké Papers.

257 In a separate letter to Sarah, he was more explicit: Bruce, 38.

257 "We look upon it as a sad day": The Reverend Stanley, quoted ibid., 38.

258 conducting prayer meetings: Ferry, 75–76.

258 "a well-deserved reputation": Ibid., 79–82.

258 "he scarcely again glanced at the Testament": Ibid., 88.

259 she petitioned for membership in his church: Ibid., 106.

259 Diminutive, strong-willed, opinionated: Ibid., 106–8. See also Charlotte Forten Grimké, *The Journals of Charlotte Forten Grimké*, ed. Brenda Stevenson, the Schomburg Library of Nineteenth-Century Black Women Writers (New York: Oxford University Press, 1988), 4–8.

259 Francis Grimké married Charlotte Forten: Ferry, 108.

260 the victim of a series of debilitating strokes: Lerner, 367.

260 "I hope that the time is not far distant when": Quoted in Eric Foner, *Reconstruction: America's Unfinished Revolution* (New York, Harper & Row, 1988), 118.

261 The Compromise of 1877: Ibid., 575–81.

262 The debate over black activism: August Meier, *Negro Thought in America, 1880–1915* (Ann Arbor, Mich.: University of Michigan Press, 1963), 26–31.

262 The most persistent and influential champion: Ibid., 95–101.

262 "Oh, for thy voice high-sounding o'er the storm": Paul Laurence Dunbar, "Douglass," in Henry Louis Gates, Jr., and Nellie Y. McKay, eds., *The Norton Anthology of African-American Literature* (New York: W.W. Norton & Co., 1997), 903.

263 He urged them on in their careers: Bruce, 60.

263 "Neither we, nor any other people": Frederick Douglass, untitled article, *Douglass' Monthly*, August 1862.

264 Francis Grimké presided over the marriage: Ibid., 146–48. See also Francis James Grimké, "The Second Marriage of Frederick Douglass," *Journal of Negro History*, July 1934.

264 "Why he decided in his second marriage": Quoted ibid., 149.

265 he had walked to work every day: Bruce, 36–37.

265 "I no longer have a separate being": Sarah Stanley to Archibald H. Grimké, March 1, 1879, in the Grimké Papers.

265 But there was tension in the marriage: Bruce, 38–39.

266 Magnanimously, he suggested: Ibid., 40–41.

266 She would commit suicide: Ibid., 41.

267 In August 1883: Ibid., 43.

267 he wanted to persuade black Bostonians: Ibid., 44–45.

268 "the protector of the Ku Klux Klan": *Boston Hub*, August 18, August 25, and September 1, 1883. Clippings in the Grimké Papers.

268 Trotter, seven years Grimké's senior: Bruce, 46. See also Stephen R. Fox, *The Guardian of Boston: William Monroe Trotter* (New York: Atheneum Publishers, 1970).

269 "Although it cannot be fairly claimed that the colored break ": James M. Trotter to the Editor, *New York Globe*, November 17, 1883.

269 Archibald Grimké, just thirty-five years old, was making a name for himself: Bruce, 47.

270 He quickly backtracked: Ibid., 393.

270 "If the Republican party cannot stand": Quoted ibid., 51.

271 Although the "bolters" included his lifelong friends: Ibid., 52.

271 "eloquent cant and twaddle": Clipping in the Grimké Papers. Also see *The Gentle Reformers: Massachusetts Democrats in the Cleveland Era* (Cambridge, Mass.: Harvard University Press, 1966), 20–24.

272 "base ingratitude, subterfuge and hypocrisy": Clipping in the Grimké Papers.

CHAPTER 13

273 Archibald Grimké officially left: Bruce, 55–57.

273 He felt deceived: Ibid., 58.

274   "Corporate wealth has become the motive force": Archibald Grimké, "Corporate Wealth," *Boston Hub*, November 22, 1884.

274   Higginson publicly argued: Bruce, 59–60. During the campaign, Grimké focused on Higginson's abolitionist past and did not call attention to his defense of segregation.

275   wrote a letter to the *Boston Herald*: Archibald Grimké to the Editor, *Boston Herald*, October 30, 1888.

275   he pleaded with the black community: Archibald Grimké, "A Comment on the Tariff," *Boston Evening Transcript*, October 5, 1888.

276   In Mississippi, in March 1886: August Meier, *Negro Thought in America, 1880–1915* (Ann Arbor, Mich.: University of Michigan Press, 1963), 162–63.

277   In 1888, Grimké still believed: Bruce, 62. A.H.G. Memoirs.

278   T. Thomas Fortune was one of those: Bruce, 56–57. See also Linda O. McMurry, *To Keep the Waters Troubled: The Life of Ida B. Wells* (New York: Oxford University Press, 1998).

278   "get all they can for their own use": Ida B. Wells, untitled article, *Cleveland Gazette*, January 3, 1885.

278   "I am not a Democrat": Ida B. Wells, untitled article, *New York Freeman*, January 15, 1887.

279   "But why speak of our drawing": Ida B. Wells, untitled article, *New York Age*, March 18, 1886.

279   In Washington, Grimké encountered a black community: Ferry, 114–18.

280   "The pulpit, the sacred desk": F.J.G., *Works*, 3: 214.

280   In 1885, Francis was embroiled: Records of the Presbytery of Washington, D.C., 1:303.

281   After a series of board meetings: Ibid., 304–7.

281   On the evening of November 1, 1885: Untitled article, *New York Freeman*, November 7, 1885. An account of the evening also appeared in other newspapers, along with a number of testimonials from Francis Grimké's friends.

281   "We sincerely commend him to those": Quoted in Ferry, 156.

282   "When I think of the sad inheritance": F.J.G., *Works*, 2:488.

283   Grimké had been impressed by Washington: Ferry, 159–60. See also F.J.G., *Works*, 2:477–79.

283   "It is not only training the young men": Francis Grimké to T. Thomas Fortune, [undated], in the Grimké Papers.

284   "It was a piece of bread here and a scrap of meat there": Booker T. Washington, *Up from Slavery* (New York: Penguin Books, 1986), 5. The work was originally published as a serial in *Outlook* magazine in 1900.

284   In 1881, Armstrong had recommended: Stephen R. Fox, *The Guardian of Boston: William Monroe Trotter* (New York: Atheneum Publishers, 1970), 32.

285   "Only a few hours' ride": F.J.G., *Works*, 2:491.

286   Cleveland agreed to the idea: Bruce, 64.

286 "Mr. Grimké is a scholarly gentleman": Clipping (untitled) in the Grimké Papers.

287 Grimké angrily rejected Cope's assertion: Archibald H. Grimké, "The Opening Up of Africa," *New Ideal* 3 (1890).

288 "He watched with stern and vigilant eye": Archibald H. Grimké, *William Lloyd Garrison, the Abolitionist* (New York: Funk and Wagnalls, 1891), 391.

288 In June 1891, Grimké announced: Bruce, 64.

289 Archibald Grimké believed in the political process: Ibid., 64–67.

289 "spiritual nature, a logical mind": Robert H. Abzug, *Passionate Liberator: Theodore Dwight Weld and the Dilemma of Reform* (New York: Oxford University Press, 1980), 301. See also *Hyde Park Times*, February 8, 1895.

289 Stanton was appalled that black males: Elizabeth Griffith, *In Her Own Right: The Life of Elizabeth Cady Stanton* (New York: Oxford University Press, 1984), 133–35.

290 He arrived on November 16, 1895: Bruce, 68–69.

CHAPTER 14

292 Washington opened his remarks: Booker T. Washington, "The Atlanta Exposition Address" (1895), in Deirdre Mullane, ed., *Crossing the Danger Water* (New York: Doubleday, 1993), 364.

292 "It is well to bear in mind": Ibid.

293 "Cast down your bucket where you are": Ibid.

294 "As we have proved our loyalty to you in the past": Washington, "The Atlanta Exposition Address," 366.

295 "That man's speech": Quoted in David Levering Lewis, *W. E. B. Du Bois: Biography of a Race* (New York: Henry Holt, 1993), 175 (hereafter, Lewis).

295 "Here might be the basis of a real settlement": W. E. B. Du Bois to Booker T. Washington, September 24, 1895, in the Correspondence of W. E. B. Du Bois, in the Du Bois Papers, University of Massachusetts.

295 "Here is the key to the future": F.J.G., *Works*, 2:51.

296 "proud fop with his beaver hat": Quoted in Bruce, 107.

296 Archibald Grimké proved to be a surprisingly good diplomat: Ibid., 74–75.

297 "There will appear for the first time": Archibald Grimké to "Dear Ones at Home," February 27, 1895, in the Grimké Papers.

297 "There is not the slightest hint": Ibid.

298 "I had hoped against hope": Archibald Grimké to Angelina Grimké, November 20, 1894, in the Grimké Papers.

298 "You don't want to be like": Archibald Grimké to Angelina Grimké, October 29, 1895, in the Grimké Papers.

299 living with Francis and Charlotte in Washington: Bruce, 78.

299 "devoted to literary, statistical, ethnographical": Ibid., 81.

299 "If thou dost not soon kill the mob": Quoted in "Black Leader in Boston," *Boston Evening Transcript*, May 10, 1899.

300 "They are so·anxious for union": Quoted in Ferry, 254.

300 "Let the right be done": Francis James Grimké, "An Argument Against the Union of the Cumberland Presbyterian Church and the Presbyterian Church of the United States of America," in F.J.G, *Works*, 3:22.

300 "Hundreds of the men of our race": Ibid., 1:238.

301 "I am not counseling violence": Ibid., 1:254.

301 "A race that permits itself to be trampled upon": Ibid., 254.

302 "Let me not be understood": Ibid., 1:258. Francis James Grimké's sermons on lynching and "the crisis" are collected in the Grimké Papers at the Moorland-Spingarn Research Center, Howard University. The most important of these are "The Negro and his Citizenship," "Equality of Rights for All Citizens, Black and White Alike," and "A Phase of the Race Problem, Looked at from Within the Race Itself." Also included in the materials is the mailing list of those to whom the Reverend Grimké circulated his sermons, in an effort to get the widest readership for them; the list includes the most prominent black leaders in the nation at that time. See also Volume 4 of F.J.G., *Works*.

304 "his oppressors were strong": Archibald H. Grimké, "Right on the Scaffold, or the Martyrs of 1822," *Occasional Papers of the American Negro Academy*, no. 7 (1901).

304 "inveterate hostility": Archibald Grimké, "Modern Industrialism and the Negroes of the United States," in the Grimké Papers.

305 "Blood proves thicker than water": Archibald Grimké, "The Negroes' Case Against the Republic," in the Grimké Papers.

305 "On the race question": Ibid.

306 Archibald Grimké and a group of prominent black Bostonians: Bruce, 95.

306 "The plain result of the attitude of mind": W. E. B. Du Bois, *The Souls of Black Folk*, introduction by John Edgar Wideman (New York: Vintage Books/The Library of America, 1990), xiii–xiv. Also see Lewis, 287.

307 Washington's response to this threat: Lewis, 297–99.

308 "It was wonderful to see how completely": Quoted in Stephen R. Fox, *The Guardian of Boston: William Monroe Trotter* (New York: Atheneum Publishers, 1970), 46–47.

308 "agitation is the best means": Quoted ibid., 48.

308 "The Boston gang, at least": Quoted ibid.

308 "These young men who come from Boston": Quoted in Ferry, 204.

309 "positive, constructive action": Quoted in Lewis, 245.

309 "Are you not actually upholding oppressing our race": Quoted in Fox, 49–51.

309 "If there are any geese in the audience": Quoted in *Boston Evening Transcript*, July 31, 1903.

310 It took five policemen several minutes: Fox, *Guardian of Boston*, 51–54.

310 "Throw Trotter out the window ": Ibid., 52.

310 "You will be glad to know that Trotter": Quoted ibid., 54.

310 "If the Boston negro is not capable of understanding": Untitled article, *St. Louis Post-Dispatch*, August 2, 1903.

311 "In no case is the old text": Untitled article, *Boston Evening Transcript*, August 2, 1903.

311 "colored for leadership and revenue only": Quoted in Fox, *Guardian of Boston*, 57.

311 A second trial: Ibid., 58.

312 "represents a noisy, turbulent, and unscrupulous set of men": Quoted ibid., 57.

312 After two years in Minnesota: Bruce, 76–77.

312 "a consummate ass": Quoted ibid., 99.

312 "As bright as is this day": Angelina Weld Grimké, "To My Father Upon His Fifty-fifth Birthday," in *Selected Works of Angelina Weld Grimké*, ed. Carolivia Herron (New York: Oxford University Press, 1991), 61.

313 "I know you are too young now": Quoted in Bruce, 75–76.

313 "All you care about is self": Quoted ibid. See also Archibald Grimké to Angelina Weld Grimké, January 29, 1899, in the Grimké Papers.

314 "Whose voice the last I heard before I close my eyes": Angelina Weld Grimké, "To My Father Upon His Fifty-fifth Birthday," in Herron, *Selected Works of Angelina Weld Grimké*, 61.

315 Although Du Bois was suspicious of Washington's motives: Lewis, 297.

315 "strongly against my own will": Quoted in Bruce, 104. Also see Lewis, 305.

315 "attempts to have the same kind of 'nigger meeting' ": Quoted in Bruce, 105. Also see Lewis, 306.

CHAPTER 15

316 The Carnegie Hall Conference was held: Lewis, 304–9.

317 "The main issue of this meeting is Washington": Quoted ibid., 304.

317 A Washington partisan, he was disturbed: Ibid., 305.

318 What followed over the next three days: Ibid., 303–7. See also Bruce, 107–9.

318 Under Grimké's guidance: Bruce, 108.

318 In his final address, though: Louis R. Harlan, *Booker T. Washington: The Wizard of Tuskegee, 1901–1915* (New York: Harper & Row, 1983), 72.

319 He nearly pleaded for forgiveness: Ibid., 73.

319 "completely overcome": Quoted in Bruce, 108.

319 The most profound achievement of the Carnegie Hall Conference: Bruce, 108–9.

319 Just one month after the Carnegie meeting: Ibid., 111–12.

319 "a body of fearless people": Quoted in Lewis, 314.

319 "a terribly suspicious man": Quoted ibid., 311.

320 "I count it a clear misfortune to the Negro race": "W. E. B. Du Bois to Archibald Grimké and Kelly Miller, March 21, 1905, in the Grimké Papers.

320 On July 10, 1905, twenty-nine black men: Lewis, 316.

320 "organized determination and aggressive action": Quoted ibid., 316.

321 After three days of meetings: Ibid., 316–18.

321 "The Negro race in America, stolen, ravished and degraded": "Declaration of Principles," the Niagara Conference, quoted in Lewis, 322.

322 He located a suitable press, in Memphis: Lewis, 326.

322 the Niagara Movement's second conference: Ibid., 328.

322 "They deprecate the sight of scattered counsels": Ibid.

323 "We are citizens, clothed with citizenship rights": Francis James Grimké, "The Negro and His Citizenship," *The Negro and Effective Franchise: The American Negro Academy* (Washington, D.C.), no. 11 (1905).

324 "Union? Yes!": Quoted in Ferry, 260. See also Francis James Grimké, "The Argument Against Union," in the Grimké Papers.

324 "one of the most insensitive figures ever to direct": Ibid., 266.

325 the "moral deterioration of the masters": Archibald Grimké, "The Heart of the Race Problem," *Arena* 35 (1906), 30–31.

326 "at the heart of the race problem": Ibid., 33.

327 It would be passed from hand to hand through the next decades: Bruce, 115–17.

328 believed that Du Bois's talk of the "black ideal": Ibid., 138–42.

329 The Niagara Movement had prospered since its founding: Lewis, 332–33.

329 The first incident took place in a military backwater of Brownsville, Texas: Bruce, 156–57. See also Linda O. McMurry, *To Keep the Waters Troubled: The Life of Ida B. Wells* (New York: Oxford University Press, 1998), 276, 278.

329 "Once enshrined in our hearts as Moses": Adam Clayton Powell, Sr., quoted in Lewis, 333.

330 "Neither Mr. Washington nor the colored people": Editorial, *New York Age*, November 15, 1986.

330 "There are some qualities, mental and moral": Quoted in Bruce, 143.

330 Just one month after Brownsville: Lewis, 333–37.

331 "Extra! Bold Negro Kisses White Girl's Hand": Quoted in McMurry, *To Keep the Waters Troubled*, 276.

331 "A mob of poor white crackers": Quoted in Lewis, 335–36.

331 "in the shadow of Lincoln's tomb": Quoted in McMurry, *To Keep the Waters Troubled*, 279.

331 "What are you fellas afraid of?": Quoted in "Frenzied Mob Sweeps City, Wreaking Blood Vengeance for Negroes' Heinous Crime," *Illinois State Journal*, August 15, 1908.

332 "Either the spirit of the abolitionists": Quoted in Lewis, 389.

333 "not to be a Washington movement": Quoted ibid., 392. See also Bruce, 174–75.

334 At a New York meeting in 1911: Bruce, 175.

335 In 1913, the D.C. chapter: Ibid., 185.

335 "self-seekers like Dr. Waldron": Quoted in Bruce, 187.

335 Waldron was finally removed as the head of the D.C. branch: Bruce, 189.

336 "To Protest Against Segregation—the New Slavery": Ibid.

337 "The Southern people are the best friends you have": "Hearings Before the House Committee on Reform in the Civil Service: Segregation of Clerks and Employees in the Civil Service," Sixty-third Congress, Second Session, 18–19.

337 Grimké replied that his very appearance: Ibid., 20.

337 Charlotte Forten Grimké died after a long illness: Ferry, 310.

337 "She was one of the rarest spirits that ever lived": Quoted ibid., 311.

338 Angelina Weld Grimké was a joy to her father: Bruce, 231.

338 *Rachel:* Ibid., 212–13.

339 "Ah, no! The cruel jeer": Angelina Weld Grimké, "Beware, Lest He Awakes," in *Selected Works of Angelina Weld Grimké,* ed. Carolivia Herron (New York: Oxford University Press, 1991), 114–15.

EPILOGUE

340 Archibald was investigated: Bruce, 223.

340 "Her Thirteen Black Soldiers": Bruce, 238. The poem appeared in *The Messenger,* vol. 7, ed. A. Philip Randolph, 1925, 209–10. Du Bois, fearful of a white blacklash, refused to publish it when it was originally written (in 1917) in *The Crisis.*

341 In the summer of 1928: Ibid., 257.

341 Archibald Grimké died on February 25, 1930: Ibid., 258

342 She died a recluse in 1958: *Selected Works of Angelina Weld Grimké,* ed. Carolivia Heron (New York: Oxford University Press, 1991), 21.

342 On the same day that Martin Luther King, Jr.: Lewis, 1.

BIBLIOGRAPHY

I. BOOKS

Abbott, Martin. *The Freedmen's Bureau in South Carolina, 1865–1872*. Chapel Hill, N.C.: University of North Carolina Press, 1967.

Abzug, Robert H. *Passionate Liberator: Theodore Dwight Weld and the Dilemma of Reform*. New York: Oxford University Press, 1980.

Alcott, William A. *The Young Woman's Guide to Excellence*. Boston: Dexter S. King, 1842.

Aptheker, Herbert. *American Negro Slave Revolts*. New York: International Publishers, 1963.

———, ed. *A Documentary History of the Negro People of the United States*. New York: The Citadel Press, 1951.

Barnes, Gilbert Hobbs. *The Antislavery Impulse, 1830–1844*. New York: Appleton-Century Co., 1933.

Barnes, Gilbert H., and Dwight L. Dumond, eds. *Letters of Theodore Dwight Weld, Angelina Grimké Weld and Sarah Grimké, 1822–1844*. 2 vols. New York: Appleton-Century Co., 1932. Reprint, New York: Da Capo Press, 1970.

Bartlett, Irving H. *Wendell Phillips: Brahmin Radical*. Boston: Beacon Press, 1961.

Beecher, Catherine H. "Essay on Slavery and Abolitionism, with Reference to the Duty of American Females." Philadelphia: Henry Perkins Publishing, 1837. Reprint, Books for Libraries, 1970.

Beecher, Catherine H., and Harriet Beecher Stowe. *The American Woman's Home; or, Principles of Domestic Science, Being a Guide to the Formation and Maintenance of Economical, Healthful, Beautiful, and Christian Homes.* New York: J. B. Ford & Co., 1869.

Bell, Howard, ed. *Proceedings of the National Negro Conventions, 1830–1864.* New York: Arno Press, 1969.

Bemis, Samuel Flagg. *John Quincy Adams and the Foundations of American Foreign Policy.* New York: W. W. Norton & Company, 1949.

Bennett, John. *The Doctor to the Dead: Grotesque Legends and Folk Tales of Old Charleston.* Columbia, S.C.: University of South Carolina Press, 1943.

Berg, Barbara J. *The Remembered Gate: Origins of American Feminism.* New York: Oxford University Press, 1978.

Berlin, Ira. *Many Thousands Gone: The First Two Centures of Slavery in North America.* Cambridge, Mass.: Harvard/Belknap, 1998.

Berlin, Ira, and Barbara Fields, eds. *Free at Last: A Documentary History of Slavery, Freedom and the Civil War.* New York: The New Press, 1992.

Birney, Catherine. *The Grimké Sisters: Sarah and Angelina Grimké, the First Women Advocates of Abolition and Woman's Rights.* New York: Lee & Shepard, 1885.

Birney, William. *James G. Birney and His Times.* New York: D. Appleton & Co., 1890.

Botkin, B. A., ed. *Lay My Burden Down: A Folk History of Slavery.* New York: Dell Publishing, 1973.

Boyd, Herb, ed. *Autobiography of a People.* New York: Doubleday and Co., 2000.

Braude, Ann D. *Radical Spirits: Spiritualism and Women's Rights in Nineteenth-Century America.* Boston: Beacon Press, 1989.

Bruce, Dickson D., Jr. *Archibald Grimké: Portrait of a Black Independent.* Baton Rouge, La.: Louisiana State University Press, 1993.

Bushkovitch, Mary. *The Grimkés of Charleston.* Greenville, S.C.: Southern Historical Press, 1992.

Cain, William E., ed. *William Lloyd Garrison and the Fight against Slavery: Selections from* The Liberator. Boston: Bedford Books, 1995.

Caskey, Marie. *Chariot of Fire: Religion and the Beecher Family.* New Haven, Conn.: Yale University Press, 1978.

Chesnut, Mary. *Mary Boykin Chesnut: A Diary from Dixie.* Edited by Ben Ames Williams. Boston: Houghton Mifflin Co., 1961.

Child, Lydia Maria. *An Appeal in Favor of That Class of American Called Africans.* New York: Allen and Ticknor, 1833.

———*The Evils of Slavery and the Cure of Slavery: The First Proved by the Opinions of Southerners Themselves, the Last Shown by Historical Evidence.* Newburyport, Mass.: Whipple, 1836.

———. *A Brief History of the Condition of Women, in Various Ages and Nations.* 2 vols. New York: Francis, 1845.

Clark, Clifford E., Jr. *Henry Ward Beecher: Spokesman for a Middle-Class America.* Urbana, Ill.: University of Illinois Press, 1978.

Clinton, Catherine. *The Plantation Mistress: Woman's World in the Old South.* New York: Pantheon Books, 1982.

Cromwell, Otelia. *Lucretia Mott.* Cambridge, Mass.: Harvard University Press, 1958.

Cross, Barbara M., ed. *The Autobiography of Lyman Beecher.* 2 vols. Cambridge, Mass.: Harvard University Press, 1961.

Douglass, Frederick. *Narrative of the Life of Frederick Douglass, American Slave, Written by Himself.* Boston: American Anti-Slavery Office of Boston, 1845.

———. *The Frederick Douglass Papers.* Edited by John W. Blassingame. 2 vols. Vol. 2, *Speeches, Debates, and Interviews.* New Haven, Conn.: Yale University Press, 1982.

Du Bois, Ellen Carol. *Feminism and Suffrage: The Emergence of an Independent Women's Movement in America, 1848–1869.* Ithaca, N.Y.: Cornell University Press, 1978.

Du Bois, W. E. B. *The Souls of Black Folk.* New York: A. C. McClurg, 1903; reprint, New York: Vintage Books/The Library of America, 1990.

Dumond, Dwight L. *Antislavery Origins of the Civil War in the United States.* Ann Arbor, Mich.: University of Michigan Press, 1939.

———. *Antislavery: The Crusade for Freedom in America.* Ann Arbor, Mich.: University of Michigan Press, 1961.

———, ed. *Letters of James Gillespie Birney, 1831–1857.* New York: D. Appleton–Century Co., 1938.

Drake, Thomas E. *Quakers and Slavery in America.* New Haven, Conn.: Yale University Press, 1950.

Egerton, Douglas R. *Gabriel's Rebellion: The Virginia Slave Conspiracies of 1800 and 1802.* Chapel Hill, N.C.: University of North Carolina Press, 1993.

Elkins, Stanley. *Slavery.* Chicago: University of Chicago Press, 1959.

Ferry, Henry Justi. "Francis James Grimké: Portrait of a Black Puritan." Ph.D. diss. Yale University, 1970. UMI Dissertation Services, Ann Arbor.

Filler, Louis. *The Crusade Against Slavery, 1830–1860.* New York: Harper & Bros., 1960.

Flexner, Eleanor. *Century of Struggle: The Woman's Rights Movement in the United States.* Cambridge, Mass.: Harvard University Press, 1959.

Foner, Eric. *Free Soil, Free Labor, Free Men: The Ideology of the Republican Party Before the Civil War.* New York: Macmillan, 1970.

———. *Reconstruction: America's Unfinished Revolution.* New York: Harper & Row, 1988.

———, ed. *The Life and Writings of Frederick Douglass.* 4 vols. New York: International Publishers, 1950.

Fox, Stephen R. *The Guardian of Boston: William Monroe Trotter.* Atheneum Publishers, 1970.

Frazier, E. Franklin. *The Free Negro Family.* Nashville, Tenn.: Fisk University Press, 1932.

———. *Black Bourgeoisie.* New York: Collier Books, 1962.

———. *The Negro Church in America.* New York: Schocken Books, 1963.

Franklin, John Hope. *From Slavery to Freedom*. New York: Alfred A. Knopf, 1967.

Franklin, John Hope, and August Meier, eds. *Black Leaders of the Twentieth Century*. Urbana, Ill.: University of Illinois Press, 1982.

Friedman, Lawrence J. *Gregarious Saints: Self and Community in American Abolitionism, 1830–1870*. Cambridge: Cambridge University Press, 1982.

Frothingham, Octavius Brooks. *Gerrit Smith: A Biography*. New York: G. P. Putnam's Sons, 1879.

Garrison, Wendell P., and Francis J. Garrison. *William Lloyd Garrison, 1805–1879: The Story of His Life Told by His Children*. 4 vols. New York: The Century Co., 1885.

Giddings, Paula. *When and Where I Enter: The Impact of Black Women on Race and Sex in America*. New York: Bantam Books, 1984.

Goldsmith, Barbara. *Other Powers*. New York: Alfred A. Knopf, 1988.

Griffith, Elisabeth. *In Her Own Right: The Life of Elizabeth Cady Stanton*. New York: Oxford University Press, 1984.

Grimké, Angelina Weld. *Rachel: A Play in Three Acts. Competitor* 1 (Boston), January 1920.

————. *Selected Works of Angelina Weld Grimké*. Edited by Carolivia Herron. The Schomburg Library of Nineteenth-Century Black Women Writers. New York: Oxford University Press, 1991.

Grimké, Archibald H. *William Lloyd Garrison, the Abolitionist*. New York: Funk and Wagnalls, 1891.

————. *The Life of Charles Sumner: The Scholar in Politics*. New York: Funk and Wagnalls, 1892.

Grimké, Charlotte Forten. *The Journal of Charlotte Forten, A Free Negro in the Slave Era*. Edited by Ray Allen Billington. New York: W. W. Norton & Co., 1981.

————. *The Journals of Charlotte Forten Grimké*. Edited by Brenda Stevenson. The Schomburg Library of Nineteenth-Century Black Women Writers. New York: Oxford University Press, 1988.

Grimké, Francis James. *The Works of Francis James Grimké*. Edited by Carter G. Woodson. 4 vols. Washington, D.C., The Associated Publishers, 1942.

Grimké, Sarah M., and Angelina E. Grimké. "Sketch of Mr. Grimké's Life." *The Calumet* (New York), January–February 1835.

————. *The Public Years of Sarah and Angelina Grimké: Selected Writings, 1835–1839*. Edited by Larry Ceplair. New York: Columbia University Press, 1989.

Gutman, Herbert. *The Black Family in Slavery and Freedom, 1750–1925*. New York: Pantheon Books, 1976.

Harlan, Louis R. *Booker T. Washington: The Wizard of Tuskegee, 1901–1915*. New York: Harper & Row, 1983.

Hays, Elinor R. *Morningstar: A Biography of Lucy Stone, 1818–1893*. New York: Harcourt, Brace, and World, 1961.

Hedrick, Joan D. *Harriet Beecher Stowe: A Life*. New York: Oxford University Press, 1994.

Hersh, Blanche Glassman. *The Slavery of Sex: Feminist-Abolitionists in America.* Urbana, Ill.: University of Illinois Press, 1978.

Higginson, Thomas Wentworth. *Contemporaries.* Boston: Houghton Mifflin Co., 1898.

Hull, Gloria. *Color, Sex and Poetry: Three Women Writers of the Harlem Renaissance.* Bloomington: Indiana University Press, 1987.

Hurmence, Belinda, ed. *Before Freedom: When I Just Can Remember.* John F. Blair, Publisher. Winston-Salem, N.C.: University of North Carolina Press, 1992.

Johnson, Oliver. *William Lloyd Garrison and His Times; or, Sketches of the Anti-Slavery Movement in America, and of the Man Who Was Its Founder and Moral Leader.* Boston: Houghton Mifflin Co., 1881.

Julian, George W. *The Life of Joshua Giddings.* Chicago: A. C. McClurg, 1892.

Kolchin, Peter. *First Freedom.* Westport, Conn.: Greenwood Press, 1972.

Korngold, Ralph. *Two Friends of Man: The Story of William Lloyd Garrison and Wendell Phillips and Their Relationship with Abraham Lincoln.* Boston: Little, Brown and Co., 1950.

Lumpkin, Katherine DuPre. *The Emancipation of Angelina Grimké.* Chapel Hill, N.C.: University of North Carolina Press, 1984.

Lerner, Gerda. *The Grimké Sisters from South Carolina: Rebels Against Slavery.* Boston: Houghton Mifflin Co., 1967.

———. *The Majority Finds Its Past: Placing Women in American History.* New York: Oxford University Press, 1979.

———. *The Feminist Thought of Sarah Grimké.* New York: Oxford University Press, 1998.

———, ed. *Black Women in White America: A Documentary History.* New York: Pantheon Books, 1972.

Lewis, David Levering. *W. E. B. Du Bois: Biography of a Race.* New York: Henry Holt and Company, 1993.

Litwack, Leon F. *North of Slavery: The Negro in the Free States, 1790–1860.* Chicago: University of Chicago Press, 1961.

———. *Been in the Storm So Long: The Aftermath of Slavery.* New York: Vintage Books, 1979.

Loewenberg, Bert, and Ruth Bogin, eds. *Black Women in Nineteenth-Century Life: Their Thoughts, Their Words, Their Feelings.* University Park, Pa.: Pennsylvania State University Press, 1976.

Lutz, Alma. *Crusade for Freedom: Women of the Antislavery Movement.* Boston: Beacon Press, 1968.

Martineau, Harriet. *Society in America.* 2 vols. New York: Saunders & Otley, 1837.

———. *The Martyr Age of the United States.* Boston: Weeks, Jordan & Co., 1839.

May, Samuel J. *Some Recollections of Our Antislavery Conflict.* Boston: Fields, Osgood, 1869.

Mayer, Henry. *All On Fire.* New York: St. Martin's Press, 1998.

McLoughlin, William G., ed. *Lectures on Revival of Religion: The Lectures of*

Charles Grandison Finney. Cambridge, Mass.: Harvard University Press/ Belknap, 1960.

McMurry, Linda O. *To Keep the Waters Troubled: The Life of Ida B. Wells.* New York: Oxford University Press, 1998.

McPherson, James. *The Struggle for Equality: Abolitionists and the Negro in the Civil War and Reconstruction.* Princeton, N.J.: Princeton University Press, 1964.

Meier, August. *Negro Thought in America, 1880–1915.* Ann Arbor, Mich.: University of Michigan, 1963.

Melder, Keith E. *Beginnings of Sisterhood: The American Women's Rights Movement, 1800–1850,* New York: Schocken Books, 1977.

Merrill, Walter M. *Against Wind and Tide: A Biography of William Lloyd Garrison.* Cambridge, Mass.: Harvard University Press, 1963.

Moss, Alfred A., Jr. The American Negro Academy: *Voice of the Talented Tenth.* Baton Rouge, La.: Louisiana State University, 1981.

Noyes, John Humphrey. *History of American Socialisms.* New York: Hillary House Publishing, 1870.

Nuermberger, Ruth Kettering. *The Free Produce Movement: A Quaker Protest Against Slavery.* Chapel Hill, N.C.: Duke University Press, 1956; reprint, New York: AMS Press, 1970.

Nye, Russell B. *Wm. Lloyd Garrison and the Humanitarian Reformers.* Boston: Little, Brown & Co., 1955.

Pease, William H., and Jane H. Pease. *Bound with Them in Chains: A Biographical History of the Antislavery Movement.* Westport, Conn.: Greenwood Press, 1972.

Perry, Lewis, and Michael Fellman, eds. *Antislavery Reconsidered: New Perspectives on the Abolitionists.* Baton Rouge, La.: Louisiana State University Press, 1979.

Russell, Elbert. *History of Quakerism.* New York: Macmillan Co., 1942.

Scott, Anne Firor. *The Southern Lady: From Pedestal to Politics, 1830–1930.* Chicago: University of Chicago Press, 1970.

Sinclair, Andrew. *The Better Half: The Emancipation of the American Woman.* New York: Harper & Row, 1965.

Smith, William Henry. *A Political History of Slavery.* 2 vols. New York: G. P. Putnam's Sons, 1903.

Stanton, Elizabeth Cady. *Eighty Years and More.* London: T. Fisher Unwin, 1908.

Stanton, Elizabeth Cady, Susan B. Anthony, and Matilda Joslyn Gage, eds. *History of Woman Suffrage.* 2 vols. New York: Fowler and Wells, 1881.

Staudenraus, P. J. *The African Colonization Movement, 1816–1835.* New York: Columbia University Press, 1961.

Sweet, William Ward. *Religion in the Development of American Culture.* New York: Scribner's, 1952.

Tappan, Lewis. *The Life of Arthur Tappan.* New York: Hurd and Houghton, 1870.

Thomas, Hugh. *The Slave Trade.* New York: Simon & Schuster, 1997.

Thomas, John L. *The Liberator: William Lloyd Garrison, A Biography.* Boston: Little, Brown & Co., 1963.

Walker, David. "Walker's Appeal, in Four Articles; Together with a Preamble, to the Colored Citizens of the World, but in Particular and Very Expressly, to Those of the United States of America, Written in Boston, State of Massachusetts, September 28, 1829." In *The Anti-Slavery Argument*, edited by William H. Pease and Jane H. Pease. Indianapolis: Bobbs-Merrill, 1965.

Washington, Booker T., *Up from Slavery*. New York: Doubleday, Page & Co., 1901.

Weisberger, Bernard. *They Gathered at the River: The Story of the Great Revivalists and Their Impact upon Religion in America*. Boston: Little, Brown & Co., 1958.

Wells-Barnett, Ida. *On Lynchings*. New York: Arno Press, 1900.

White, Laura A. *Robert Barnwell Rhett: Father of Secession*. New York: Century Co., 1931.

Wills, Garry. *Lincoln at Gettysburg*. New York: Simon & Schuster, 1992.

Wintz, Carl D., ed. *African American Political Thought, 1890–1930*. Armonk, N.Y.: M. E. Sharpe, 1996.

Woodson, Carter G. *The History of the Negro Church*. Washington, D.C.: The Associated Publishers, 1945.

———, ed. *The Mind of the Negro as Reflected in Letters Written during the Crisis, 1800–1860*. Washington, D.C.: Association for the Study of Negro Life and History, 1926.

Woodward, C. Vann. *Origins of the New South, 1877–1913*. Baton Rouge, La.: Louisiana State University Press, 1951.

———. *Reunion and Reaction*. Boston: Little, Brown & Co., 1951.

———. *The Strange Career of Jim Crow*. New York: Oxford University Press, 1966.

Woolman, John. *A Journal of the Life, Gospel Labours and Christian Experiences of That Faithful Minister of Jesus Christ, John Woolman, Late of Mt. Holly in the Province of New Jersey, North America*. London: W. Phillips, 1824.

Wright, Francis. *Course of Popular Lectures*. New York: Free Enquirer, 1829.

II. ARTICLES AND MONOGRAPHS

Adams, Samuel L. "Ida B. Wells: A Founder Who Knew Her Place." *Crisis* 101 (January 1994).

Blumenthal, Henry. "Woodrow Wilson and the Race Question." *Journal of Negro History* 48 (1968).

Cadbury, Henry J. "Negro Membership in the Society of Friends." *Journal of Negro History* 21 (April 1936).

Dillon, Merton L. "The Failure of American Abolitionists." *Journal of Southern History* 25 (May 1959).

Du Bois, W. E. B. "An Essay Toward a History of the Black Man in the Great War." *Crisis* 18 (1919).

Greene, Maud Honeyman. "Raritan Bay Union, Eagleswood, New Jersey." *Proceedings of the New Jersey Historical Society* 68, no. 1 (January 1950).

Grimké, Angelina W. "A Biographical Sketch of Archibald H. Grimké." *Opportunity* 3 (February 1925).

Grimké, Francis J. "Archibald H. Grimké, Born in Charleston, S.C. . . . A Brief Statement of His Brother . . ." (1930). Francis J. Grimké Papers, Moorland-Spingarn Research Center, Howard University.

Meier, August. "The Beginning of Industrial Eduation in Negro Schools." *Midwest Journal* 7 (spring 1955).

Mikhalevsky, N. V. "Sarah Grimké and the Reclamation of Speech." Washington, D.C.: unpublished manuscript, 1983.

Miller, Robert M. "The Attitudes of American Protestantism Toward the Negro, 1919–1939." *Journal of American Negro History* 41 (July 1956).

National Association for the Advancement of Colored People, District of Columbia branch. "What Will the Negro Get Out of the War?" Statement adopted at meeting of December 11, 1918.

Shanks, Carolina. "The Biblical Anti-Slavery Argument." *Journal of Negro History* 40, no. 3 (July 1955).

Steen, Ivan D. "Charleston in the 1850s, as Described by British Travelers." *South Carolina Historical Magazine* 3 (September 1906).

Wailing, William E. "The Race War in the North." *Independent* 45 (September 1908).

Walker, Lewis Newton, Jr. "The Struggles and Attempts to Establish Branch Autonomy and Hegemony: A History of the District of Columbia Branch National Association for the Advancement of Colored People, 1912–1942." Ph.D. diss., University of Delaware, 1979.

Wilson, Gold Refined. "The Religion of the American Negro Slave: His Attitude Toward Life and Death." *Journal of Negro History* 8 (January 1923).

Zorn, Roman J. "The New England Anti-Slavery Society: Pioneer Abolition Organization." *Journal of Negro History* 43 (July 1957).

III. PUBLISHED SPEECHES AND PAPERS BY ANGELINA AND SARAH GRIMKÉ

Grimké (Weld), Angelina Emily. "Slavery and the Boston Riot: A Letter to Wm. L. Garrison." Broadside, Philadelphia, August 30, 1824.

———. "Appeal to the Christian Women of the Southern States." New York: American Anti-Slavery Society, 1836.

———. "An Appeal to the Women of the Nominally Free States." Issued "by an Anti-Slavery Convention of American Women & Held by Adjournment from the 9th to the 12th of May, 1837." 1st ed. New York: W. S. Dorr, 1837.

———. "Letters to Catherine E. Beecher, in Reply to 'An Essay on Slavery and Abolitionism,' Addressed to A. E. Grimké." Boston: Isaac Knapp, 1838.

———. "Speech Before the Legislative Committee of the Massachusetts Legislature (February 21, 1838)." Reprinted in *The Liberator*, March 2, 1837.

———. "Speech in Pennsylvania Hall (May 16, 1838)." Reprinted in Gerda Lerner, *The Grimké Sisters from South Carolina: Rebels Against Slavery*. Boston: Houghton Mifflin Co., 1967.

———. "Letter from Angelina Grimké Weld to the Woman's Rights Convention, Held at Syracuse." Master's Print, Syracuse, N.Y., 1852.

———. "Speech to the National Convention of the Woman's Loyal National League (May 14, 1863)." Reprinted in Gerda Lerner, *The Grimké Sisters from South Carolina: Rebels Against Slavery*. Boston: Houghton Mifflin Co., 1967.

———. "Address to the Soldiers of Our Second Revolution (May 15, 1863)." Reprinted in Gerda Lerner, *The Grimké Sisters from South Carolina: Rebels Against Slavery*. Boston: Houghton Mifflin Co., 1967.

Grimké, Sarah Moore. "Letters on the Equality of the Sexes and the Condition of Woman, Addressed to Mary Parker, President of the Boston Female Anti-Slavery Society." Boston: Isaac Knapp, 1838.

———. *Joan of Arc: A Biography*. Boston: Adams and Co., 1867.

Grimké, Sarah Moore, and Angelina Emily Grimké. "A Sketch of Thomas Grimké's Life, Written by His Sisters in Philadelphia and Sent to His Friends in Charleston for Their Approbation." *The Calumet* (magazine of the American Peace Society) 2, no. 1 (January 1835).

IV. SELECTED PUBLISHED WORKS BY ANGELINA WELD GRIMKÉ

"Beware Lest He Awakes." *Pilot*, May 10, 1892.

"The Grave in the Corner." *Norfolk County Gazette*, May 27, 1893.

"To Theodore D. Weld—On His Ninetieth Birthday." *Norfolk County Gazette*, November 25, 1893.

"Street Echoes." *Boston Sunday Globe*, July 22, 1894.

"Black Is as Black Does." *Colored American Magazine* 1 (August 1900).

"Longing." *Boston Transcript*, April 16, 1901.

"May." *Boston Transcript*, May 7, 1901.

"El Beso." *Boston Transcript*, October 27, 1909.

"To Keep the Memory of Charlotte Forten Grimké." *Crisis* 9 (1915).

"To the Dunbar High School." *Crisis* 13 (1917).

"The Closing Door." *Birth Control Review*, September 1919.

"*Rachel*, the Play of the Month: The Reason and Synopsis by the Author." *Competitor* 1 (January 1920).

"The Black Finger." *Opportunity* 1 (November 1923).

"I Weep." *Opportunity* 2 (July 1924).

"Little Grey Dreams." *Opportunity* 2 (July 1924).

"Death." *Opportunity* 3 (March 1925).

"For the Candle-Light." *Opportunity* 3 (September 1925).

V. SELECTED MAJOR ARTICLES BY ARCHIBALD HENRY GRIMKÉ

"Anti-Slavery in Boston." *New England Magazine*, December 1890.

"The Opening Up of Africa." *New Ideal* 3 (1890).

"Lessons of the Hour"(1895). In Archibald Grimké Papers, Moorland-Spingarn Research Center, Howard University.

"Protest by Citizens of Boston in Mass Meeting Assembled in Faneuil Hall, Friday, November 16, 1894 . . ." (1895). In Archibald Grimké Papers, Moorland-Spingarn Research Center, Howard University.

"William Lloyd Garrison." *Christian Register*, December 3, 1895.

"A Madonna of the South." *Southern Workman* 29 (July 1900).

"The Negroes' Case Against the Republic" (1901). In Archibald Grimké Papers, Moorland-Spingarn Research Center, Howard University.

"Right on the Scafford, or the Martyrs of 1822." *Occasional Papers of the American Negro Academy*, no. 7 (1901).

"Modern Industrialism and the Negroes of the United States" (1902). In Archibald Grimké Papers, Moorland-Spingarn Research Center, Howard University.

"An Education and Property Basis." *Voice of the Negro* 1 (1904).

"Why Disenfranchisement Is Bad." *Atlantic Monthly* 94 (1904).

"Biographical Oration." *Alexander's Magazine* 1 (January 1906).

"The Heart of the Race Problem." *Arena* 35 (1906).

"Charles Sumner" (1911). In Archibald Grimké Papers, Moorland-Spingarn Research Center, Howard University.

VI. PUBLISHED ARTICLES BY FRANCIS JAMES GRIMKÉ

"Colored Men as Professors in Colored Institutions." *AME Church Review* 4 (July 1885).

"The Negro and His Citizenship." In *The Negro and Effective Franchise: The American Negro Academy* (Washington, D.C.), no. 11 (1905).

"Segregation." *Crisis* 41 (June 1934).

"The Second Marriage of Frederick Douglass." *Journal of Negro History* 19 (July 1934).

"The Battle Must Go On." *Crisis* 41 (August 1934).

"Valiant Men and Free." *Opportunity* 12 (September 1934).

"The Negro's Attitude Toward Religion. *Southern Workman* 43 (December 1934).

VII. SELECTED MAJOR SERMONS OF
FRANCIS JAMES GRIMKÉ

"God and the Race Problem." Washington, D.C., 1903.

"Highest Values." Washington, D.C., 1903.

"The Inheritance Which All Parents May and Ought to Leave to Their Children." Washington, D.C., 1903.

"The Atlanta Riot." Washington, D.C., 1906.

"Equality of Rights for All Citizens, Black and White Alike." Washington, D.C., 1909.

"Character: The True Standard by Which to Estimate Individuals and Races and by Which They Should Estimate Themselves and Others." Washington, D.C., 1911.

"Fifty Years of Freedom." Washington, D.C., 1913.

"Effective Christianity in the Present World Crisis." Washington, D.C., 1918.

"Scotsboro." Washington, D.C., 1918.

"Spiritual Life." Washington, D.C., 1918.

"A Look Backward Over a Pastorate of More Than Forty-Two Years Over the Fifteenth Street Presbyterian Church." Washington, D.C., 1923.

"What Is the Trouble with the Christianity of Today?" Washington, D.C., 1923.

"The Paramount Importance of Right Living." Washington, D.C., 1926.

"My Farewell Quadrennial Message to the Race." Washington, D.C., 1933.

"Christianity Is Not Dependent Upon the Endorsement of Men Great in Worldly Wisdom." Washington, D.C., 1934.

"Christ's Program for the Saving of the World." Washington, D.C., 1934.

"Jim Crow Christianity and the Negro." Washington, D.C., 1934.

"What Is to Be the Real Future of the Black Man in this Country?" Washington, D.C., 1934.

"Conditions Necessary to Permanent World Peace." Washington, D.C., 1935.

"Quadrennial Message to the Race." Washington, D.C., 1937.

VIII. MANUSCRIPT COLLECTIONS

John Faucheraud Grimké and Mary S. Grimké: Materials on the parents of Angelina and Sarah Grimké can be found in the Charleston Free Library of Charleston, South Carolina.

Angelina and Sarah Grimké: The Grimké Family Papers are held in the Theodore

Dwight Weld Collection of the William L. Clements Library at the University of Michigan, Ann Arbor. Other manuscripts, personal papers, unpublished articles, letters, and speeches can be found in the Moorland-Spingarn Research Center at Howard University in Washington, D.C. Other materials on the Grimké family are contained in the William Lloyd Garrison Papers collection at the Boston Public Library and in the Theodore Dwight Weld Papers at the Library of Congress in Washington, D.C. Special collections include the Grimké Papers of the New-York Historical Society and the Grimké Personal Papers of the Library of Congress. Finally, a small but valuable collection of Grimké papers can be found in the Sophia Smith Collection at Smith College.

Angelina Weld Grimké: The papers and manuscripts of Angelina Weld Grimké, including a number of powerful unpublished manuscripts, can be found in the Moorland-Spingarn Research Center of Howard University in Washington, D.C.

Archibald and Francis Grimké: The major papers of the two Grimké brothers are held at the Moorland-Spingarn Research Center at Howard University in Washington, D.C. Occasional papers by and extensive references to them are held in the Antislavery Papers of the Library of Congress in Washington, D.C. The Howard University Library has the most complete collection of papers relating to Archibald and Francis Grimké: the Archibald Henry Grimké Papers (1866–1930) and the Francis James Grimké Papers (1866–1937). Related materials on the Grimké brothers can be found in the Booker T. Washington Papers and the Carter G. Woodson Papers, both in the Manuscript Division of the Library of Congress.

Charlotte Forten Grimké: The Schomburg Center for Research in Black Culture, the New York Public Library, and Oxford University Press provide the most extensive resources on black women writers and together have published a comprehensive volume of Charlotte Forten Grimké's work. The original manuscript of her exhaustive journal is kept at the Moorland-Spingarn Research Center at Howard University in Washington, D.C.

The American Anti-Slavery Society: The holdings of the American Anti-Slavery Society, including copies of the minutes of AAS meetings, records of committees and committee members, and executive committee reports, as well as rolls of officers, members, and chapters, may be found in the Weston Papers of the Boston Public Library.

IX. ANTISLAVERY AND AFRICAN AMERICAN NEWSPAPERS OF THE GRIMKÉ ERA

Afro-American
American Anti-Slavery Almanac
American Anti-Slavery Standard

Anti-Slavery Examiner
Anti-Slavery Record
The Calumet: The Magazine of the American Peace Society
Charleston Courier
Charleston Mercury
Daily Advertiser
The Emancipator
Evening Star
Evening Transcript
The Friend
The Liberator
The Liberty Bell
The Lily
National Anti-Slavery Standard
National Enquirer
National Era
National Intelligencer
New York Age
New York Freeman
The Olive Branch
Philadelphia Evening Bulletin
Washington Bee
Washington People's Advocate

INDEX

398   INDEX